The Israeli Economy

THE ISRAELI ECONOMY

Maturing through Crises

EDITED BY

Yoram Ben-Porath

HARVARD UNIVERSITY PRESS
Cambridge, Massachusetts
and London, England
1986

Printed in the United States of America
10 9 8 7 6 5 4 3 2 1

This book is printed on acid-free paper, and its binding materials have been chosen for strength and durability.

Library of Congress Cataloging-in-Publication Data
Main entry under title:

The Israeli economy.

Bibliography: p.
Includes index.
1. Israel—Economic conditions—Addresses, essays, lectures. I. Ben-Porath, Yoram.
HC415.25.I85 1986 330.95694'054 85-17609
ISBN 0-674-46878-3 (alk. paper)

To the memory of Simon Kuznets—
scholar, teacher, friend

Preface

This volume is the result of several years of collective effort at the Maurice Falk Institute for Economic Research in Israel to provide a comprehensive analysis of the Israeli economy and the processes that led to its recent crises. In this, the Institute resumes a task that began with Don Patinkin's survey of Israel's first decade (1960) and Halevi and Klinov's account of the period until the mid-1960s (1968). The individual contributions, each focusing on some particular facet of the Israeli economy, were conceived as parts of a general research plan. The major theme was the interpretation of Israel's recent economic crises as a consequence both of shocks that occurred in the 1970s and of a phasing out of a long period of rapid growth based on immigration. The drama of the Israeli economy is partly idiosyncratic, but it also brings out in high relief some phenomena of general interest that cannot easily be discerned and analyzed in a more conventional setting. In hindsight it is not difficult to identify remaining lacunae; future work will have to be even more attentive than the present study to the peculiarities of the institutional system and the relationship among economy, society, and politics.

This has indeed been a collective effort. Most of the contributors are members of the Hebrew University of Jerusalem's Economics Department. Adding to their individual skills and diverse specialities are colleagues from other institutions. The research for two chapters (6 and 16) was carried out at the Research Department of the Bank of Israel. Michael Bruno and Nadav Halevi participated in the coordination of the project and in the editorial work. Zvi Griliches and Moshe Sicron (both members of the Falk Institute's Board of Trustees) and Yaakov Kop made many useful comments and suggestions on drafts of each chapter. We thank the many friends who commented on earlier drafts of individual chapters and regret that space does not allow us to thank them all.

The book owes much for its existence to the unique skills and devotion of Maggie Eisenstaedt, who acted as managing editor, producer, draftsperson, and computer specialist, assisted by Benjamin Feder, Mimi Feigelson, Ziva Litvak, and Susan Tamari. The staffs of the Central Bureau of Statistics and the Bank of Israel helped with data, advice, and comments. The tables were typeset by CTS in Jerusalem.

An able group of graduate students provided both research assistance and independent work: Yarom Ariav, Carlos Bachrach, Jonathan Isaacs, Ruben Lamdany, Yaron Lotan, Danny Rosenman, David Semana, Yardena Slovik, Daliah Steiner, Nachum Zicherman, Avi Temkin, and Danny Tsiddon.

Research was conducted under the auspices of a program on the economy of Israel commemorating David Horowitz, the first Governor of the Bank of Israel. The program was financed by the Bank of Israel, the Israel Council for Research and Development, and the National Insurance Institute; it was also supported by Bank Leumi Le-Israel B.M., Bank Ha-Poalim, and the Israel Discount Bank.

Michael Aronson of Harvard University Press provided encouragement and enthusiasm from an early stage. Ann Hawthorne of the Press provided painstaking editing. Having said all this, we remain responsible for errors.

This book is dedicated to the memory of Simon Kuznets of Harvard University, Nobel Laureate in Economics, who set the standards for the empirical study of economies and their growth patterns. He stood behind the establishment of the Falk Institute, guided it for many years, and encouraged Don Patinkin to write the first overview of the Israeli economy. Simon Kuznets inspired the project that led to this volume and provided wise counsel ranging from comments on the original design to detailed responses to individual papers. He possessed a singular capacity to grasp an economy in its totality and had a broad view of his discipline as a true social science. He had intended to write the preface to this volume. When the volume was ready he, as always, stepped back and sought the roots of the uniqueness of the Israeli case. Against the broad perspective of modern economic growth, and given his particular interest in the economics of the Jewish people, he intended to focus his preface on the role of ideology in explaining the impressive Israeli growth record and some of its structural peculiarities. His recent passing was indeed a loss of a scholar, a teacher, and a friend.

Yoram Ben-Porath

Jerusalem
July 1985

Contents

The Israeli Economy

Introduction

Yoram Ben-Porath

For twenty-five years after its establishment in 1948, Israel was considered an economic miracle, with one of the highest rates of growth in the world. For the twenty-five years before 1948, the same was true for the Jewish economy of Palestine. Throughout these years there was a remarkable rapid increase in population through immigration, increase in per capita income, and increase in total product. During the 1970s, however, immigration slowed down, the economy almost stagnated, and Israel has become synonymous with running inflation and balance-of-payments crises.

The immediate sources of the turnabout were the energy crises and the escalation of defense expenditures following the 1973 war. These coincided with a long-term shift from growth based on immigration and a need to develop an alternative growth strategy. For the most part the government's economic policies failed to cope with these challenges: the standard of living continued to improve despite the cessation of growth, the public sector increased its claim over resources, investment declined, and economic dependence on the United States became greater. Inflation can be interpreted as the manifestation of the conflict between attempts to solve the real economic problems and the social and political constraints that weakened the government. These constraints may reflect in part the ideologies and institutions forged during the earlier period of growth based on immigration but ill suited to cope with the crises facing a maturing economy. It appears that if Israel is to heal its economy, it will have to undergo a basic structural change.

Distinguishing Characteristics

Israel, with per capita income of $5,090 in 1982, headed a 1984 World Bank list of "upper middle income countries." It is a major exporter of manufactured goods, together with the industrializing countries of Asia, some southern European countries, Argentina, and Brazil. Among the 118 countries surveyed in that year's *World Table* (which does not include the nonmarket Eastern European economies), Israel ranked thirtieth in per capita income, surpassed only by the rich oil exporters, the "industrialized market economies" (the developed countries of North America and Western Europe plus Japan), and Italy, Spain, and Ireland.

With population of 4.1 million, Israel is a small open economy, smaller than most individual states of the United States. It is not well endowed with natural resources, but it has an exceptionally highly educated population and labor force. The major distinguishing characteristics of Israel's economy, however, are tied to its existence as a Jewish state in a hostile environment.

The Jewish population of Palestine was built up by successive waves of immigration, starting in the last quarter of the nineteenth century. As the Jewish community grew, conflict with the Arab population escalated. In 1948, when independence was declared, the new state was already engaged in the first of a series of wars (1956, 1967, 1970, 1973, and 1982) with neighboring Arab countries. The war of independence established the borders of the new state and caused the departure of a significant part of the Arab population. However, the proportion of Jews in Israel's population declined from 89 percent in the early 1950s to 83 percent in 1984 as a result of higher Arab fertility and the incorporation of East Jerusalem into Israel in 1967. Most of the non-Jews in Israel are Muslim Arabs, with smaller communities of Christian Arabs and of Druze.

The Jewish sector in Palestine developed as a separate economic entity in terms of institutional structure and patterns of trade with the non-Jewish community. From 1948 on, the economy of Israel coincided to a large extent with the economy of the Jewish population. The 1967 occupation of the remaining areas of British Mandatory Palestine, with a population of over a million Arabs, brought the proportion of Jews in the whole of Palestine (including the occupied territories) down to 65 percent. These territories are not treated as an integral part of the economy of Israel.

Israel's position as a Jewish state has four main manifestations.

A country of immigrants. Israel is a country established for and run by immigrants from diverse countries and backgrounds. Its *raison d'être* is to gather, retain, and forge these immigrants into one nation. Preventing social and economic splits along lines of origin has been a major objective in Israel's development as a welfare state, and the discouragement of emigration is an important constraint on economic policy. The early immigrants' ideologies and aspirations and the institutions created to achieve them have had a lasting effect on the country's social and economic structure. In particular, they shaped the role assumed by Israeli governments.

Strong ties with world Jewry. Immigration is one aspect of a broader affinity with Jews worldwide. This strong and lasting relationship has concrete implications for the country's resources and its balance of payments. As a haven for survivors of the Holocaust, Israel received German reparations at a crucial stage in its economic development. Transfers from world Jewry have been Israel's most consistent source of external financing. This aid, which is especially responsive to emergencies (as in the 1967 war), provides a unique economic safety net. These ties were of course instrumental in forming the close economic links between Israel and the United States, which have affected economic life in Israel in many ways.

The hostile environment. To ensure its survival Israel has had to devote an increasingly large share of its resources to defense and to conducting economic and social activities in a context of constant preparedness for overt or covert hostilities. With certain historical variations, existence in a hostile environment isolates Israel from adjacent economies and obstructs economic relations with countries in the Eastern bloc and the Third World.

Dualism: The Jewish state and the Arab minority. The tension between the national aspirations of indigenous Arabs and the objective of forming and maintaining a Jewish state based on principles of equality and democracy has introduced elements of dualism into Israel's economic structure, both in its 1948 borders and much more so in the larger territory controlled by Israel since 1967. This dualism is apparent in the standard of living, education levels, occupational structure, government services, and institutional structure.

Immigration and Product

Immigration and the Growth of Product

Immigration drove the growth of the Jewish economy sector of Mandatory Palestine and of Israel for the fifty years or so ending in the early 1970s. From 1922 to 1948 the Jewish population increased eightfold, and total product increased twenty-fivefold, allowing a 4.8 percent annual increase in per capita income. In the years of mass immigration, 1948-1951, the population doubled again and per capita income continued to grow. Over the next two decades GNP rose 9 percent annually, while the population increased by 4 percent and 3 percent respectively; per capita income thus grew more than 5 percent each year. In the 1970s population growth slowed to an annual rate of 2 percent, the annual growth of total product to 3.2 percent, and that of per capita product to less than 1 percent (see Chapter 1).

Population and product growth underwent three long swings, with peaks in the mid-1920s, mid-1930s, and early 1950s. Though largely caused by noneconomic forces, immigration also responded to economic fluctuations in Israel. It stimulated economic growth both by pushing demand and by increasing productive capacity through the provision of labor; through capital imports, which financed the increase in the stock of productive capital; and through productivity change. Productivity depended both on the quality of labor and on the institutional structure. The high education level of the pre-1948 population—one of the highest in the world—and the institutional structure formed during the Mandate period enabled Israel to absorb the mass immigration of 1948–1951, largely composed of Jews from less developed countries in Asia and Africa and from war-ravaged Europe. Their entry initially reduced the population's average level of schooling and skills; their economic absorption and the improvement in their skills were significant elements in the productivity increase that lasted until the mid-1960s or early 1970s.

Labor, Capital, and the Decline in Growth of Productivity

More than half of the 6 percent decline in the business sector's growth of product after 1973 from that of the preceding decade was caused by a sharp drop in the improvement of productivity. The other half was caused by a slower rate of growth for both labor and capital. Although the stock of capital continued to grow faster than both labor and output, the energy crises and other price changes probably rendered a significant fraction of the pre-1973 stock obsolete. Increased government subsidization of investment in the 1970s may also have bred misallocations of investment. For this reason, or because of changes in demand, capital stock utilization has declined appreciably, rendering the effective growth of capital services inputs in the 1970s negligible (see Chapter 3).

The composition of the Israeli labor force also underwent several changes. The share of men decreased (from 76 percent in 1965 to 63 percent in 1982) and that of women increased (from 29 to 36 percent); women now make up two-fifths of the Israeli labor force. The share of highly educated workers increased significantly—faster than population, output, and the stock of capital (see Chapter 5). Educated men entered the business sector in large numbers with no decline in their relative wage, but educated women experienced a wage decline (see Chapters 6 and 7). Since 1967 significant numbers of manual laborers from the occupied territories have entered the Israeli labor force, slightly offsetting the effect of reduced participation by Israeli men.

Changes in labor utilization, as reflected in unemployment rates, were relatively small. Unemployment fluctuated between 4 and 5 percent. The significance of full employment and its relation to the industrial structure of employment are discussed in later sections.

External Shocks

The Energy Crises

Besides a slowdown in immigration—a long-term phenomenon—Israel underwent external shocks: the energy crises of 1973–74 and 1979, with associated changes in world prices and world trade. These developments made the 1970s a period of worldwide slow growth and stagflation (see, for example, Matthews 1982). As an open economy with a large import surplus, Israel was particularly hard hit. Rising defense expenditures after the 1973 war (discussed below) and the return of the Sinai oil fields to Egypt as part of the Camp David accord exacerbated the problem.

Israel's commodity terms of trade declined 17 percent between 1972 and 1975, improved briefly, and then declined again from 1978 to 1982. A loss on the current account was partly offset by a capital gain on the outstanding foreign debt, which was unindexed and still bore relatively low interest rates (see Chapter 12). Israel's energy bill grew from less than 1 percent of GNP in the 1960s to 7.3 percent after the first oil shock and to 11 percent after the second shock (see Chapter 13). At least 30 percent of the increase in the balance-of-payments deficit in the 1970s can be attributed to these prices changes. Chapter 14 traces the consequences of the shocks in Israel and compares them with the effects in the OECD countries.

Defense Expenditures: Escalation of a Persistent Problem

What distinguishes resource use in Israel is the growing share of its defense expenditures. From 8 to 10 percent of GNP before the 1967 war, it rose to approximately 22 percent in 1968–1972 and to 28–29 percent in 1974–1980. Berglas suggests in Chapter 8 that a more complete accounting of the defense burden would have added approximately another 8 percent of GNP to these figures.

The defense burden is directly, though not exclusively, responsible for many of the oddities in the rest of Israel's national accounts. Between the late 1950s and the 1970s expenditures rose from less than 50 percent of government consumption to more than 70 percent, accounting for almost the entire increase in the share of government consumption in GNP, from less than one fifth to two-fifths. In the late 1950s half of the net taxes collected by the government financed defense; in the 1970s total taxes could not finance even the domestic component of defense expenditure.

Another dimension of the defense burden is reflected in the balance of payments. About half of all defense outlays in the 1970s went for imports, even though substantial foreign aid financed a rising share of those imports. Post-1973 military imports account for much of Israel's current debt. Military preparedness also has some favorable effects: the development of a sophisticated domestic military industry contributed to exports, and possibly to technological development as well.

The size of the defense expenditure interacts both with actual and expected military buildups in the confrontation states surrounding Israel and with the short- and long-term availability of resources. Since 1973, increased oil revenues have improved the Arab countries' ability to sustain an expensive arms race, while the oil crises and the economic slowdown have hindered Israel's ability to do so. The competition for resources between defense and investment, together with the danger that the economy may someday not be large enough to support higher levels of defense expenditures, has been a persistent dilemma. These conditions have also made U.S. aid of crucial importance.

Defense expenditures increased in stages associated with the wars. Berglas (see Chapter 8) explores the relationship between the change in defense expenditures and in consumption, investment, and the import surplus. The steep rise associated with the 1967 war was absorbed by a sharp reduction in the share of consumption and a decline in domestic investment. Relative to GNP, public consumption did not decline and the import surplus hardly rose from that of the full-employment years 1963 and 1964. When the postwar period is compared with the depressed years 1965 and 1966, the increase in the defense share is associated with an increase in the import surplus and the investment share and a decline in both civilian public and private consumption. In contrast, the post-1973 increase in defense expenditures was accompanied by a significant increase in the share of private consumption and by some increase in public civilian consumption, at the expense of a sharp rise in the average import surplus and a decline in investment. The wars, of course, were not the only factors in these trends: the 1967 war followed a recession and was followed by a boom; the 1973 war came after a boom and was followed by a long recession.

The Uses and Misuses of Resources: Preferring the Present to the Future

After 1973 Israel experienced structural problems both in the use of resources and in production. The increasing defense burden was not the only cause: higher standards of living, added to government expenditures on public services, squeezed out investment and forced dependence on a growing foreign debt. Correspondingly, the key prices in the economy—the real wage, the real interest rate, and the exchange rate—were maintained at levels that supported this undesirable allocation of resources.

Private Consumption

Private consumption as a share of GNP went through a long swing. From absorbing approximately three-quarters of GNP in the 1950s, it declined to 57 percent of GNP in 1972, increasing again to 66 percent in 1982. Over successive decades starting in 1952 the annual growth rates of per capita GNP were 5.7, 5.5, and 0.8 respectively, while the growth rates of per capita consumption were 5.3, 3.8, and 3.2.

The resilience of private consumption to deceleration in growth is not merely a delayed adjustment of consumption to short-term variations in income: the figures cited above are decadal averages. Moreover, annual data show that consumption could sometimes adjust downward fairly rapidly (in the 1965–1967 recession, in 1975, and in 1980).

The Civilian Public Sector

Israel has a relatively high level of civilian public consumption—that is, education, health, and administration services provided by the government. Like private consumption, civilian public consumption went through a long swing with some cycles—a decline from approximately 12 percent of GNP in the mid-1950s to 10–11 percent in 1961–1975 (interrupted by an upswing in 1965–1968, associated with the recession). Then public consumption rose to an all-time peak of approximately 13 percent in the late 1970s, sliding back in the early 1980s. If the services provided by nonprofit institutions, which are largely and increasingly financed by the government, are included, then public civilian consumption increased from approximately 17 percent of GNP in the early 1960s to 20 percent in the early 1980s (see Chapter 9).

The contraction from the 1950s to the 1960s probably reflects the public sector's gradual shedding of functions associated with large-scale immigration waves and with the costs of establishing Israel's infrastructure. There was also a change in the way the government intervened in and managed the economy—from direct administrative allocation of goods to taxes, subsidies, and control of the capital market (see, for example, Chapter 12). The share of economic and general services in government expenditures declined, perhaps reflecting part of this change, but there was also an increase in the share of government expenditure on education and health. The latter items, which serve the public as consumption or as investment in human capital, are responsible for the increase in the share of public services in the 1970s. Not only did the public sector increase production of these services, but also the public was paying less and less for them.

The puzzling upswing in both private and public civilian consumption in a period of external shocks and stagflation is discussed below, in the first subsection of "Economic Policy."

Domestic Investment

The share of investment in GNP declined from close to 30 percent until 1977 to around 25 percent in 1978–1982 (see Chapter 4). This change, when viewed in relation to trends in other countries, represents a convergence to a normal ratio after a long period of exceptional growth (see Chapters 2 and 4). What is striking is the composition of investment. Israel devotes one-tenth of its GNP to investment in housing. There seems to have been a swing here too—the share of residential investment was lower in the 1960s than in the preceding and following decades. The high demand for housing since the late 1960s is less a consequence of population growth than of a higher standard of living. Another factor is the high and rising share of capital in services. Thus, there is a tendency to mobilize an increasing share of resources to the immediate, direct and indirect, improvement of living standards (see Chapter 4).

In sharp contrast, the entire share of gross business investment in fixed investment was only one-third of total investment, and that of manufacturing only 14 percent, or approximately 4 percent of GNP. Even this level was achieved only through massive government intervention and subsidization, which in the late 1970s mostly took the form of inflation-induced gains to firms and households on their unindexed debt to the government (and to the extent that some of the acceleration of inflation was unexpected this was an ex-post transfer). The gross capital-output ratio seems quite high, but the degree of government intervention may have rendered much of the investment inefficient. Thus, in evaluating the position at the end of the period, Chapter 4 considers not only the level of productive, or tradable-oriented, investment, but also the extent of government intermediation.

The Import Surplus

An import surplus, defined as the excess of imports over exports of goods and services, represents an addition to a country's resources. To the extent that it is financed by loans or unilateral transfers from abroad that make the country dependent on another (in Israel's case, on the United States), it raises both economic and political questions. The import surplus has been a central economic issue since Israel was established.

In absolute terms Israel's import surplus was \$4.7 billion in 1982. In terms of 1982 U.S. producer prices, the import surplus was less than \$1.5 billion in 1960, \$2.5 billion in 1970, and \$4.1 billion in 1975. The size of the import surplus relative to GNP fluctuated around 20 percent. The worst years were 1973–1975, when it exceeded 36 percent. This long-term stability of the import surplus level combines two trends: a rapidly growing ratio of imports to GNP (from less than 30 percent in the early 1950s to approximately 70 percent in recent years) and a growth in the ratio of exports to imports, from 22 percent in 1952 to 68 percent in 1982 (see Chapter 12).

Long-term financing, including both borrowing and unilateral transfers, covered the deficit in the period 1958–1973. Long-term loans accounted for between one-third and one-half of the deficit. Unilateral transfers consist mainly of transfers from Jewish communities abroad; German reparations; and U.S. government aid, which was important in the 1950s and became important again in the 1970s. The accumulation of debt has become a serious problem. The net national external debt increased from $0.5 billion in 1964 to over $15 billion in 1982. A serious consequence in recent years was Israel's need to resort to short-term financing, with a corresponding deterioration in its short-term net asset position (see Chapter 12).

In earlier decades the import surplus reflected mainly the availability of long-term financing, and foreign borrowing could be viewed as a means of financing domestic capital formation. In the past decade, the import surplus has grown in response to aggregate demand and the constraints on GNP. Chapter 5 interprets the growth of the nontradable (mostly public) sector in response to factor supplies and attributes the import surplus to the structure of production.

Another way of saying that the import surplus is too large is to say that the real rate of exchange is too low. Much of the debate over the inflationary process is linked to the feasibility of effecting changes in this rate through nominal devaluations. Under full-employment conditions, which have prevailed in Israel for most of the period since 1968, the resilience of domestic demand makes nominal devaluations ineffective.

Implications for the Structure of Production

Although many specific features of Israel's structure of production merit elaboration, the focus here is how the structure of production reflected the major macroeconomic problems: the conflict between the need to improve the balance of payments and countervailing pressures on the structure of production, caused either by the structure of demand or by problems associated with factor supplies.

In its early years Israel pursued a strategy of import substitution (see Chapter 2). In the late 1960s it accomplished a major shift, spectacularly expanding exports and retreating somewhat from import substitution. But because imports grew from 38 to 65 percent of GNP, the growth of exports was far from sufficient. In the 1970s the rise in exports accounted for most of the growth of the business sector.

Much of this growth was based on sophisticated industries' greater use of the growing supply of educated manpower in the manufacture of electrical and electronic products, metal products, and chemicals. In the same period skill content of locally marketed output declined (see Chapter 12). The demand generated by defense needs also helped promote the development of sophisticated manufacturing (see Chapter 8). Trade relationships with the European community and intangible learning gains in marketing and innovation seem to have played an important role in the process. Export expansion, based on an ample supply of educated manpower and backed by Israel's research and science infrastructure, seems a likely alternative basis for economic growth.

But other developments have thwarted this transformation. The entire business sector has been squeezed by the growth of the public sector. The share of manufacturing failed to grow over several decades because Israel prematurely deindustrialized along with the developed countries (see Chapter 2). The growth rate of worker hours in the public sector accelerated from 4.3 percent in 1961–1972 to 4.6 percent in 1973–1981, in sharp contrast to the deceleration (to 1 percent) in the business sector (see Chapter 3). Inputs were diverted to public services and to nontradable sectors: the share of the public sector in civilian employment rose from 18 percent in 1951 to a relatively stable 22 percent in the 1960s and to 28 percent in 1981 (see Chapter 5). Over the same period the share of financial and business services increased from 6 to 10.8 percent.

Several related hypotheses link the adverse structural problem to the labor market: both Klinov (Chapter 5) and Amir (Chapter 6) note a remarkable increase in the education level of the labor force in the 1970s, coupled with a large increase in the share of (educated) women. Klinov maintains that the deviant growth of the public sector served as a solution to the excess supply of educated labor in general. The excess supply may have been more an issue of educated women (see Chapter 7). The growth of the public sector may have been part of a general attempt to prevent unemployment.

The Decline of National Savings

With private and public consumption increasing and GNP almost stationary, national savings, which by definition are equal to domestic investment *minus* the import surplus, had to decline. The national saving rate, which was 6.1 percent in 1953–1962 and 7.1 percent in 1963–1972, averaged −1.1 percent in 1973–1982 (see Chapter 4). This calculation regards the entire import surplus as negative investment abroad. If unilateral transfers are deducted from the import surplus, national savings do not turn negative, but the decline remains very steep.

National savings are generated in both the private sector (households and firms) and the public sector. By international standards the rate of private savings as a share of disposable income remains very high—around 30 percent in 1978–1982. This share grew from approximately 20 percent in the late 1950s to a high of 40 percent in 1972, fell to 35 percent in 1973–1977, and declined further to a still respectable 26 percent in 1982. The sharp decline in national savings in the 1970s was a result of the decline in private savings and the steep rise in the government's negative savings. Budget deficits ran at roughly 4 percent of GNP before the 1967 war, jumped to 15 percent in 1967–1972, declined to 30 percent in 1973–1975, and have remained at around 25 percent since then (see Chapter 4). By an alternative definition of the deficit that deducts foreign unilateral transfers, the numbers are smaller but the trend is similar: no deficit in the early 1960s, a peak deficit of close to 18 percent of GNP after the 1973 war, and a deficit of approximately 15 percent in recent years (see Chapters 16 and 17).

Economic Policy

Policy Dimensions of High Consumption

The increase in the standard of living of the population, both directly and through improved government services, rested on the following factors.[1]

Maintenance of full employment. Unemployment did not exceed 5.1 percent in 1968–1983. This low rate was achieved not only through measures affecting aggregate demand but also through the government's direct role as an employer.

Increase in real wages. In 1968–1973 real wages increased 18.7 percent, per capita GNP 35 percent, and per capita consumption 22.4 percent. In 1973–1976 real wages declined 2.8 percent, per capita GNP increased only 3.3 percent, and per capita consumption increased 5 percent. Most striking are the figures for 1976–1983, when real wages increased 24.1 percent, per capita GNP 5.6 percent, and per capita consumption 30 percent.[2] In only four years since 1968 did the real wage actually decline (the sharpest decline was in 1980—6.9 percent; in the same year per capita consumption declined 5 percent, and per capita GNP hardly changed). Thus there was no *short-term* rigidity of real wages. This fact disproves the widespread belief that wage indexation prevents declines in real wages. Chapter 15 demonstrates that the indexation of wages to the cost of living would not have been an effective barrier to declines in real wages. Hence the observed increase in real wages must have been caused by real forces.

Decline in net taxation. A decline in net taxation was associated with a large increase in gross taxation and an even larger increase in transfers. Gross taxation rose from 28 percent of GNP in 1960–1965 to nearly 50 percent in the early 1980s. Net taxes, which were 19 percent of GNP in the 1960s, certainly did not rise, and according to some definitions even declined (see Chapters 9 and 11).

The growth of gross taxation and of subsidies was associated with increased inefficiencies. In fact the sum of the two rather than their difference is a better indication of the excess burden of the tax system. The high rate of personal income tax bred various tax exemptions and distortions in the wage system. Also, the tax administration found it increasingly difficult to collect taxes from nonwage income. A tax reform in 1975 eliminated many of the tax exemptions, expanded the tax base, and reduced the formal rates, but it failed to solve the problem of tax evasion. In the early 1980s, tax collection from corporations also eroded steeply.

An important component in the rise of both taxes and transfers was the expansion of the National Insurance Institute, which levied heavy payroll taxes as well as taxes on the self-employed. These taxes, which have become known as "Income Tax B," widened the gap between the cost of labor to employers and the net reward to labor, with associated inefficiencies. The expansion of transfers to households started in the late 1960s and, despite the 1973 crisis, was not reversed until 1976. The expansion occurred first in child allowances, then in old-age assistance, and later in disability insurance (see Chapter 10). Owing to the low rate of unemployment, the rise in transfers was not a result of growth in unemployment insurance, as in many European countries. Households also benefited from intensive subsidization of basic foods.

As inflation accelerated, a new source of transfers emerged—capital gains by the private sector on its unindexed debt to the government. As the domestic (indexed) government debt to the public increased, the real interest it bore became an increasingly important component in the public's income and in the government's deficit. Domestic debt finance grew from nil in the mid-1960s to approximately 5 percent of GNP in the mid-1970s and to over 7 percent of GNP in 1978–1983 (see Chapter 17).

Sharp increase in financial assets of the private sector. The net financial assets of the public sector grew from 60 percent of disposable income in 1973 to 150 percent of disposable income in 1982 (a blow to the stock exchange in 1982 reduced the share to 130 percent). This growth reflects the increase in the domestic debt, which has become larger than GNP and is largely indexed. The government and the Central Bank had to stabilize the real rate of interest in order to sell more bonds to the public. They also avoided short-term rises in interest rates to prevent the value of existing stocks from falling. Government financing and monetary policy were thus constrained by both the level and the variability of the interest rate. The combination of inflation and the complex form of government intervention in the capital market produced odd, sometimes exotic, phenomena. For no good reason as far as the real performance of the economy was concerned, the Tel Aviv stock exchange was booming, providing in 1982 an average real return of 73 percent on stocks and 29 percent on what were then considered to be blue chips, the stocks of the banks. This bubble, based on a chain effect, eventually burst in 1983.

Maintenance of too low an exchange rate and growth of the public foreign debt. Israel's low exchange rate is made possible by and supports the import surplus and external aid and borrowing. Until recently the population did not take full account of the collectively assumed liability and therefore overestimated its true wealth.

Exchange policies may have affected private consumption more directly through relative prices. The purchase of durables contributed one-third of the growth of consumption in 1980–1982 (compared with one-quarter in the preceding five years). This higher share may have been the result of exchange-rate policies and reduced taxation on durables, pursued in the early 1980s, and may have caused part of the decline in private savings (as conventionally measured).

Budget cuts proved unfeasible both because some budgeted expenditures (public employment, debt servicing, and, to some extent, transfers to households) were inflexible and because some budgeted items (notably subsidies) were designed to counteract the detrimental effects of other policy measures (such as subsidies to investment and to exports). But the crucial constraints on the budget were political.

All these policies disconnected the economic incentives facing the individual from the realities confronting the national economy. This separation was probably made possible to a large extent by the safety net provided by external support. Direct responsibility lies with the government; but the government itself operates in a social and political context. The next section describes some of the constraints on government policies and examines the post-1973 macroeconomic policies and acceleration of inflation in this perspective.

The Constraints: The Institutional Heritage

Older, richer countries have developed rigidities that prevent rapid growth and adjustment to change. Olson (1982) attributes them to the emergence and cumulative impact of special-interest groups. The "sclerosis" of the developed countries became apparent from their slow response to the energy crises and the resultant sharp fluctuations in their terms of trade and was reflected in rigidities in the real wage, prolonged periods of unemployment, and oversized public sectors. This pattern contrasts with that in some of the successful developing countries of Asia—Taiwan, Korea, Hong Kong, Singapore. Israel, which until recently seemed to belong to the latter group, displays symptoms of premature aging, combining the structural problems of some of the richer and older European countries with the inflation, balance-of-payments crises, and foreign indebtedness observed in some Latin American countries.

Some of the difficulties confronting Israel in the 1970s originated in the period of rapid inflation and in the institutional structure that evolved in earlier decades to foster growth based on immigration. Recently political and social constraints have curtailed the country's ability to cope with crises and to shift to a new mode of economic growth. The major relevant elements in this context are as follows:

The prominence of collective activity. Israel's organizational infrastructure was established in the Mandate period, when the leadership of the Jewish community was voluntarily recognized as the quasi-government of the state-to-be. The Jewish Agency was a government in the making. The Hagana was its military arm. The Histadrut (the national federation of labor) developed in a unique form alongside the Jewish Agency, combining the role of trade union with the establishment of a developed system of social and health insurance. It fostered entrepreneurship in economic development by creating a large labor-owned economic sector consisting of communal rural settlements *(kibbutzim, moshavim),* large transportation cooperatives, and huge enterprises in construction and industry.

The preference for collective action rested on the Zionist version of socialism that evolved in Palestine from eastern and central European ideologies of the late nineteenth and early twentieth centuries.Throughout the Mandate period and its first twenty-nine years of statehood, Israel was led by the labor movement, which laid down the norms and the organizational modes for running the economy and society. Collective action was a natural and probably necessary way to achieve specific national goals of organizing and absorbing immigration and securing a foothold in a disputed land. The socialist ideology included a distrust of the market, a view of profits as mere rewards to parasitism, and (paradoxically) a view of services as unproductive.

With the establishment of Israel the government's dominant role in economic affairs reflected both the étatist bias of the socialist ideology and the new needs and opportunities: only the state could cope with the combined (and differently weighted) challenges of defense, immigration, and economic development. Foreign aid, which was necessary to achieve those goals, flowed to the government. As the recipient of these funds and arbiter of their distribution, it gained enormous power. Secure in the knowledge that aid was forthcoming, it could embark on economic ventures without having to bear the political consequences of making the taxpaying public foot the bill. Government intervention has changed form, shifting from quantity allocations, administrative controls, and ad hoc decisions to greater reliance on general taxes, transfers, and subsidies. Compared with the U.S. government, Israel's government seems to have less regulation of and fewer legal confrontations with business. It is the control of the capital market and of subsidization that provides it with so much power.

Over the years there has been a major change in the government's attitude toward the private sector. From socialist ideals and strong preferential treatment of the Histadrut sector in the 1950s, it moved in the 1960s to a development drive that relied on private entrepreneurs, or would-be entrepreneurs, who used mostly government money. Thus the labor-led government created a new "quasi-private," government-dependent class. In the 1970s this quasi-private sector reorganized around large corporations associated with the banks and cooperating with the Histadrut sector. These large enterprises not only depended on the government but also exerted considerable influence on it.

The government's prominent role has several important effects. First, excessive economic activity takes place in budgeted organizations motivated by complex objective functions, uncontrolled by market pressures, facing budget constraints that in the long run tend to be cost accommodating. Second, vested-interest groups apply for government aid instead of relying on efficiency and market forces to ensure their survival. These groups include labor unions in the public and semipublic sectors and their employers, as well as labor and management in the private sector. Although these phenomena are fairly common in many developed countries, the size of the public sector in Israel makes this trend a particularly severe problem there.

Strong commitment to full employment and to job security. Israel's policy regarding unemployment and job security is related to its status as a country of immigrants. Both immigration and emigration are responsive to the level of unemployment (see Chapter 1 and Lamdany, 1982). One of the traumatic lessons of the 1965–1967 recession was the ensuing wave of emigration. The threat of emigration also influenced economic policy in the 1970s, thwarting the adoption of sustained deflationary policies.

At the microeconomic level, the commitment to job security makes mobility expensive and dismissal difficult. It also makes the level of employment remarkably resilient to demand conditions. Whereas in the period of rapid immigration additions to the labor force provided flexibility, the costs of immobility to the economy increased when the growth of the labor force slowed down (see Klinov, 1976).

Preservation of wages and financial assets. A norm of economic security that became entrenched in the labor market is the preservation of both the level of real wages and of the relative earnings of different groups. Although relative wages did in fact fluctuate during collective bargaining, this norm did have an independent effect in pushing up real wages, particularly in the budgeted sector.

It is interesting to note that more recently the norm of income security previously applied to labor has also been extended to private wealth and in particular to the financial assets of households (see below).

The ethnic gap, the welfare state, and the growth of consumption. The wide social differences between immigrants of European origin and immigrants from Arab countries helped shape the Israeli welfare state. Government efforts in the 1950s concentrated on providing shelter and employment. The rapid rise in the standard of living made social and economic gaps easier to tolerate. But in the late 1960s the tensions created by the ethnic gaps became acute political and social issues. The growth of the social security system, particularly the expansion of child allowances (building on wide differences in fertility by continent of origin), was a response to that concern.

During the 1970s ethnic gaps became more a middle-class issue than a poverty-line one. The earning gap between Jews from Asia and Africa and Jews from Europe and America has narrowed, owing to the elimination of differentials that could not be explained by schooling or age. Some of the pressure on real wages may have been a result of competition between these groups. Gaps in consumption, in housing density, and in ownership of durable goods were narrowing too. Among the more basic variables, fertility differentials narrowed considerably, promising a possible long-term convergence. Despite the expansion of the education system, gaps in education and in other indicators of social status persisted into the second generation. Jews of Western origin dominated the white-collar occupations, Jews from Arab countries the blue-collar ones (see Chapter 7).

The rapid growth of per capita consumption helped Israel cope with the social tensions associated with its ethnic divisions in the early period. Such growth was then both inevitable and feasible. But in the 1970s the price to the economy became too high. The translation of ethnic cleavages into political life became overt. Deflationary policies or increased unemployment would have widened the ethnic gap. The Labor party, which led the Jewish community before 1948 and ruled the country, in coalition with other parties, from then until 1977, had such a wide margin of strength that elections did not threaten its primacy. The strong connection between economics and politics was structural. The government could afford to maintain a reasonable balance among long-term needs, available resources, and pressures for higher standards of living. After 1973, political competition intensified as a change of government became feasible. The immigrants of the 1950s had become more assertive; many had moved into the middle class and were striving for the standards of living and the durable consumption goods enjoyed by the more affluent. The political competition had a strong—though not exclusive—ethnic dimension, expressed in affiliation with one of the two major political parties. The populist line pursued during most of the period 1977–1983, reflecting consumers' aspirations and the government's sensitivity to them, determined the nature of Israel's crisis in the early 1980s.

Stop-Go Macro Policies and Failure to Resolve Conflicting Constraints

Israel has a long history of inflationary experiences. But the period 1968–1972, marking the recovery from the 1965–1967 recession, began with no inflation. With the first supply shock, the rate of inflation accelerated from 14 percent in

1970–1973 to 36 percent in 1973–1977. In 1974–1976 deflationary fiscal and monetary policies achieved some success at the cost of a small increase in unemployment. As noted earlier, this period was also marked by cessation of growth in real wages and private consumption (Chapters 14 and 17).

In 1977 the Likud party gained control of the government. Although many factors contributed to this change, the preceding years of contractionary policy must have been part of the reason. The new government liberalized the exchange rate, allowed the possession of foreign exchange and dollar-indexed money, and pursued expansionary policies. In 1977–1979 the rate of inflation increased to 71 percent. Bruno and Fischer in Chapter 17 attribute this increase to the decline in the demand for money associated with this innovation, as well as to the monetary and fiscal expansion. During this period subsidies for basic food items were increased, and a package deal with the Histadrut went into effect as part of an effort to deal with inflation from the cost-push side.

From the end of 1979 to 1983 the average rate of inflation was 123 percent. In a sharp policy reversal at the beginning of this period, a new minister of finance, Yigael Hurwitz, made the balance of payments a priority. Both policy and rhetoric emphasized the need to reduce the government budget deficit and private standards of living. Real wages and consumption declined, and the balance-of-payments deficit was kept in check despite the second oil crisis and the loss of the Sinai oil fields following the Camp David accord. The new level of inflation was precipitated by the sharp cut in subsidies. This time, however, the deflationary policies lasted less than a year. Mindful of the approaching elections and the dire predictions of the polls, the finance minister was replaced again.

In the pre-election period Yoram Aridor, the new minister of finance, restored and increased subsidies, reduced taxes on household durables, and reversed some of the erosion in transfers. The Likud was returned to power.

The declared shift in economic policy gave first priority to fighting inflation. Inflation was viewed as a bubble, a consequence of a cost-push-expectations mechanism. Starting in the autumn of 1982 the government raised the prices it controlled, including the exchange rate, at a constant rate of 5 percent a month, in the hope that expectations and other prices would converge down to this rate. This policy was initiated during the war in Lebanon, when domestic defense expenditure increased. At the same time other large projects were continued (such as the massive settlement effort in the West Bank; the planning of Israel's new military airplane, the Lavie; and Project Renewal, the rehabilitation of low-income neighborhoods) and new ones planned (such as the Mediterranean–Dead Sea canal). Despite increased taxation, private consumption kept rising. The "5 percent policy" was a grand failure. Actual prices rose by more than 5 percent, requiring increased expenditures on subsidies and causing progressive overvaluation of the currency. Anticipating the imminent collapse of the policy, people accumulated dollars, sold their free stocks, and then tried to sell government bonds and bank stocks. To prevent a total collapse, the banks borrowed abroad and reportedly asked the government to pump money into the stock exchange. This glaring paradox demonstrates the conflict between policy objectives.

In October 1983 a crash of the banks' stocks brought a collapse of the policy, a sharp devaluation, and a new minister of finance, Yigal Cohen-Orgad. The balance-of-payments deficit again became the priority. The acceleration of inflation to an annual rate of 400 percent produced a real wage cut, and subsidies were reduced. But within a few months a call for early elections reversed policies again. During the election campaign a new two-year wage agreement was signed, restoring the earlier cut in real wages, and a law was passed guaranteeing the value of the public's financial assets, thus further restricting the government's ability to pursue economic policy.

Yet 1984 was different. The civilian import surplus and public and private consumption declined because of a cut in real wages induced by the price shocks of late 1983 and a decline in the real financial wealth of the public. In the fall of 1984 a Unity government, composed of the two major blocs, was established with the express purpose of reforming the economy. Early in 1985 a package deal sharply reduced the monthly rate of inflation, subsidies were increased again, and foreign exchange reserves rapidly declined. Political considerations (including elections for the Histadrut, held in mid-1985) again constrained economic policy. In the summer of 1985 a new economic policy was announced. It was based on a sharp cut in real wages, a cut in subsidies, a price freeze, and a cut in government expenditure and manpower. It was accompanied by a special emergency grant by the United States.

All of the various explanations of the acceleration of inflation and the growing balance-of-payments deficit reflect the conflict, indeed the schizophrenia, affecting the government as it wavered between its obligation to deal with pressing economic problems and what it perceived as the constraints imposed by the public and the political process. These tensions led to short-term policy reversals, with shorter and shorter intervals of restraint.

Inflation accelerated in steps, with a rapid increase followed by a period of quasi-stability. Typically, the upward step was associated with an innovation in government policy, reflecting worry about the budget, the balance of payments, or foreign reserves. The initial effect of devaluation or subsidy cuts is higher prices. With partial indexation of wages, there was an immediate decline in real wages. Built-in asymmetry prevented the translation of the deflationary spell into quick price deceleration. Only at the end of a sustained period of restraint (1974–1976) did inflation show signs of yielding. Since then, the periods of restraint have been shorter. After the short-term setbacks real wages tended to rise through formal and informal bargaining rather than automatic mechanisms; subsidies were restored and devaluations started lagging behind prices.

Monetary policy has played an important part in Israel's inflation. It became increasingly accommodating, adjusting to the higher rate of inflation. As the real stock of domestic money held by the public shrank because of increased inflation, the monetary injections became more potent. Also, as the growth in product slowed, less of the growth in the money base could be absorbed in a noninflationary way. With most of the public's financial assets linked to the price index or to the dollar, there was an automatic increase in an important component of the money supply, as well as automatic protection of households' wealth. Thus the system was deprived of any self-correcting mechanism with which to combat inflation by relying on the real balance or real wealth of effects (see Chapter 17).

When the consequences of these policies were felt in the balance of payments, the public, aware of the inevitable need for correction, accumulated dollars. Increasingly in recent times, such waves of speculation have prompted devaluations. It became clear that the stop-go policies fueled rather than quenched the inflationary process.

Interpretations of the role of the government deficit differ. Bruno and Fischer (Chapter 17) emphasize the roles of the large deficit (15 percent of GNP) and the accumulation of an intolerably large national debt in contributing to inflexibility in the budget and in money creation. Liviatan and Piterman (Chapter 16) emphasize the lack of any short- or even medium-term correspondence between the size of the deficit and the rate of inflation. They attach importance to the link between expenditures and the import surplus, which induced inflationary measures.

The issue of Israel's inflation tax is particularly interesting because of the asymmetry in indexation between the government's assets and obligations. In the late 1970s and early 1980s, when the public sector still had a sizable outstanding unindexed debt to the government, it was not even clear whether the inflation tax was positive. It was, at any rate, fairly small. Does this mean, as Liviatan and Piterman suggest, that such a small tax could not have been responsible for inflation of such magnitude, or could it be that it takes a great deal of inflation fueling in Israel to obtain even a modest tax?

This is only one aspect of indexation. In a sustained inflationary environment, institutional adjustments become ingrained (and some of the indexation arrangements date back to World War II). Every advance in inflation creates a short-term shock, because the old formulas are not tight enough to handle it; then the public views inflation as intolerable, and real wages fluctuate violently. Eventually, however, institutions and habits adjust: indexation formulas are revised, prices are adjusted often, and prices and contracts come to be quoted in dollars, resulting in a daily price adjustment. In fact, by the early 1980s the dollar had become a unit of account as well as a partial means of payment, and certainly an important store of value. Inflation has increasingly become a function of itself.

Obviously the indexation system is not perfect. It may be argued that it is close enough to perfection, so that in fact it makes the price level indeterminate, and

TABLE I-1. The economy of Israel, 1950–1983

	1950	1960	1965	1967	1970	1973	1974
Population (1000s)	1,370	2,150	2,598	2,776	3,022	3,338	3,422
% annual increase		4.6	3.8	3.3	2.9	3.4	2.5
Labor force participation rate							
Men		78.1	76.1	72.1	69.2	68.3	65.8
Women		27.3	29.4	28.6	29.3	31.3	31.3
Unemployment rate (men)		4.5	3.4	10.0	3.4	2.4	2.4
% annual change[a]							
GNP		10.8	9.7	1.5	12.0	9.2	5.5
Per capita GNP		5.1	5.5	−1.4	8.6	5.7	2.4
Per capita consumption		4.4	5.4	−0.9	5.5	4.5	4.5
Real wages						−2.7	−2.5
Ratios to GNP							
Private consumption	74.1	70.4	68.1	68.0	61.2	58.9	61.8
Government consumption	18.6	18.7	20.7	30.2	36.3	43.4	41.4
Gross domestic capital formation	31.0	27.5	30.0	17.4	29.0	34.3	32.8
Import surplus	23.9	16.7	19.2	15.7	26.6	36.7	36.1
Imports ($ mill.)	330	682	1,234	1,447	2,664	5,376	6,754
Exports ($ mill.)	45	336	711	911	1,402	2,812	3,559
Transfers ($ mill.)	114	311	321	521	650	2,190	1,718
Net foreign debt ($ mill.)		676	979	1,144	2,621	3,029	4,892
Consumer price index (1973 = 1.0)	0.1	0.4	0.5	0.6	0.7	1.0	1.4
Inflation rate[a]		12.7	7.1	4.8	3.6	14.9	39.7
Money supply/GNP		0.26	0.26	0.29	0.28	0.28	0.23

Source: CBS, *Statistical Abstracts*, various years.

a. Calculated relative to preceding column.

1975	1976	1977	1978	1979	1980	1981	1982	1983
3,493	3,575	3,653	3,738	3,836	3,922	3,978	4,064	4,149
2.1	2.3	2.2	2.3	2.6	2.2	1.4	1.8	2.1
64.9	64.6	64.9	65.0	63.9	63.7	63.8	63.4	63.5
31.9	31.9	32.7	34.3	34.9	35.7	36.1	36.1	36.6
2.5	3.1	3.3	2.9	2.4	4.1	4.1	4.4	4.0
3.5	1.9	2.6	3.4	4.2	2.8	4.0	–0.4	1.3
1.2	–0.3	3.0	1.2	1.6	0.4	2.2	-2.3	–0.5
–2.0	2.5	2.5	5.8	5.4	–5.2	8.9	5.1	5.1
–0.5	0.6	8.7	1.2	7.7	–6.9	10.1	–1.0	3.2
60.3	62.8	60.8	63.6	64.6	61.5	63.1	65.7	67.5
44.2	40.7	35.0	37.7	33.9	36.1	37.8	35.5	33.1
32.1	27.4	24.5	27.1	28.0	23.6	21.5	24.4	23.9
36.7	31.1	20.4	28.6	26.5	21.3	22.5	25.7	24.7
7,536	7,469	7,861	9,743	11,687	13,567	14,800	14,936	14,985
3,687	4,400	5,479	6,624	8,030	9,792	10,445	10,112	9,946
1,770	2,210	2,071	2,227	2,793	2,966	2,930	2,616	2,862
6,315	7,491	8,499	9,076	10,990	12,010	13,437	15,473	17,740
1.9	2.5	3.4	5.2	9.2	21.3	46.3	101.9	250.4
39.2	31.3	34.6	50.5	78.2	131.0	116.8	120.3	145.7
0.21	0.18	0.18	0.15	0.10	0.08	0.06	0.05	0.04

thus allows an unbounded acceleration of inflation. Certainly the automatic indexation of financial assets and the existence of "indexed money" is an important element. On the other hand, Chapter 15 demonstrates that the formal indexation agreements for wages would have allowed significant erosion in the real wage. In fact these imperfections may have created short-term fluctuations in real wages that sought compensation in other components of the wage structure and thus may have had an inflationary bias.

It is clear that the indexation system, interpreted in a broad sense to include many informal practices, allowed people to survive inflation and thereby made it impossible to muster the political coalition to combat it, and to bear the costs and the risks of doing so. Inflation, like the balance-of-payments deficit, has become an externality. This fact raises the questions whether inflation entails real costs and whether it is necessary to fight it.

With imperfect indexation the price system is subject to "noise" and uncertainties. The indicators for the cost of inflation, though fragmentary, are very telling: an excessive share of the financial sector in employment, the collapse of the tax system, perhaps the high share of dwelling in investment, plus much anecdotal evidence that people spend their time looking after their assets, pursuing "bubbly" profits or searching for the lowest price. It is hard to believe that both the public and private sectors operate efficiently in such an environment. It is not established at what rate inflation in Israel can be defined as hyperinflation. It may well be that a balance-of-payments crisis, with associated mass unemployment, is a more acute threat. In either case a collapse of the economic system also has frightening implications for the political democratic system.

Epilogue: Problem and Promise

Many of Israel's economic problems are related to its heavy defense burden. Several of the structural features that have handicapped Israel's transition to a new growth path and its ability to cope with external shocks resemble the rigidities that have plagued other economies during the past decade. Other features—such as the strong aversion to unemployment, the overprotection of individual welfare, and the role of government in the economy—derive from the period of large-scale immigration and rapid economic growth. In Israel's case they may have been necessary to meet the economic and social challenges of that phase. Thus there may be a dialectic connection between the height of past achievements and the depth of the recent fall.

If Israel's present economic straits do involve not only the fortuitous conjunction of bad luck and erroneous policies but also basic structural problems, the required remedies may necessitate an operation as drastic as the problems. The country as a whole must achieve self-reliance and change its economic and social structure, bringing about a convergence of standards of living, effort, and productivity. This task involves reassessing the role of the public sector and abandoning many of the modes of behavior that characterize both a private sector that has grown under the protective canopy of government and an entire economy that has grown under the protective shield of another country. There is no simple formula for such a change, because some of the circumstances that produced the current situation still exist. The concern that many elements of such a change, though desirable in the long run, would have an immediate adverse effect on inflation, unemployment, and equity, is a legitimate one. However, the longer the delay, the higher the price paid. Whether the political system will muster the strength to effect a change before some major catastrophe occurs, and whether it can design an equitable way to do so, remain to be seen.

The title of this section is borrowed from a pioneering study, *Palestine: Problem and Promise,* by Nathan, Gass, and Creamer (1946), written before the establishment of the state of Israel in the face of what seemed to be insurmountable economic problems and vaulting hopes. In the midst of today's crisis, too, it is hard to discern the promise. But the potential is there. Israel has a reservoir of human capital and a scientific infrastructure that can be used to increase productivity and expand exports. Its national determination, used to achieve political independence and self-defense, could also be harnessed to achieve economic independence.Thus, economic maturity may still prove to be a starting point for a new phase of sustained growth.

I

Maturing: Growth and Structural Change

1

The Entwined Growth of Population and Product, 1922–1982

Yoram Ben-Porath

Israel's Jewish population and economy are based on a hundred years of immigration. Immigration has shaped the rate of growth of the Jewish population and its demographic composition; it also created much of the socioeconomic diversity within the Jewish population. This chapter discusses aggregate-level interactions between Jewish immigration and economic growth both in the Jewish sector of Mandatory Palestine and in Israel.

Under the British mandate a Jewish economy existed alongside an Arab one. The Jewish population in 1919 was so small that it hardly constituted an economic entity. But the rapid growth of that population (485,000 immigrants) in 1919–1948 and a concurrent huge growth of product with its own institutional structure created a distinct Jewish economy, separate but not completely isolated from the Arab sector (Metzer, 1982). Since 1948 the Jewish economy and the economy of Israel have been synonymous, with only a small Arab sector remaining integrated into the general economy. After the 1967 war, however, the West Bank and the Gaza Strip became part of the Israeli market, and the labor pool there both benefited from the higher wages in the Israeli market and acted as a buffer to domestic fluctuations. Both Szereszewski's (1968) estimates of product and capital for the years 1922–1948 and the estimates for the first years of statehood are necessarily rough, so that comparisons with the more recent period are difficult. The estimates for 1948–1950 are particularly rough and are not considered here. These are some of the factors that prevent treatment of the entire period 1919–1982 as a single block. However, because the Mandate period provides a useful perspective on the relationship between population and economic growth in the period of statehood, most of the discussion here will refer to both periods.[1]

Nahum Gross (1981) divided the Mandate period into two major subperiods: 1918–1932 and 1933–1947. Each began with a very large wave of immigration. In 1919 the Jewish population of Palestine was 57,000; 95,600 immigrants arrived in 1920–1926, adding 9–15 percent to the population each year (28.3 percent in 1926 alone). In 1932 the Jewish population was 175,000; 147,000 immigrants arrived in 1933–1935, adding 17–20 percent annually, and another 30,000 came in 1936 (Sicron, 1957). In the quarter-century before 1948 the Jewish population increased eightfold, with the population more than doubling on average each decade, and reached approximately 650,000 by the end of the period. The total product of the Jewish economy in Palestine in the same years increased twenty-fivefold at an average annual rate of 13.7 percent. The total stock of capital increased fifteenfold (Szereszewski, 1968).

From mid-1948 to the end of 1951 687,000 immigrants arrived, averaging 19 percent of the general population annually (24 and 27 percent in 1948 and 1949 respectively); by the end of 1951 the Jewish population had more than doubled, to 1.4 million. In the next two decades it redoubled, growing 47 and 35 percent respectively. The 1970s marked the end of an exceptionally high and sustained period of population growth, with an increase of 26 percent for the decade. Over the period 1948–1982 the Jewish population grew from 650,000 to 3.4 million. Immigration contributed 1,385,000 and natural increase 1,337,000.

From 1950 to 1982 total product increased elevenfold and capital stock sixteenfold. Product tripled in the first decade, doubled in the second. But from 1972 to 1982 total product increased only 37 percent. Most remarkable is the high growth rate of per capita income that tended to accompany the rapid increase of population—4.8 percent annually in the Mandate period, a similarly high rate in

TABLE 1-1. Rates of growth of Jewish population, product, and capital, 1922–1982 (percentages)

	Annual rates of increase							Share of immigrants in population[b]
				Capital stock				
Interval	Population	GNP[a]	Per capita GNP[a]	Total	Dwelling	Non-dwelling	Consumption per capita	
1922–32	8.0	17.6	7.8	13.7	—	—	—	8.2
1932–47	8.4	11.2	3.0	9.8	—	—	—	6.4
1947–50	21.9	—	—	—	—	—	—	19.8
1950–51	20.0	29.7	10.0	—	—	—	—	13.2
1951–64	4.0	9.1	4.9	12.3	11.6	12.8	5.1	2.2
1964–72	3.0	8.9	5.5	8.4	7.7	8.7	3.6	1.3
1972–82	2.1	3.2	0.8	6.7	7.7	6.1	3.2	0.9

Sources: CBS, *Statistical Abstract,* various years; Szereszewki (1968); Halevi (1983).
a. Refers to the Jewish economy in Palestine until 1947 and in Israel since 1950.
b. Means do not include the first year except for 1922–1932.

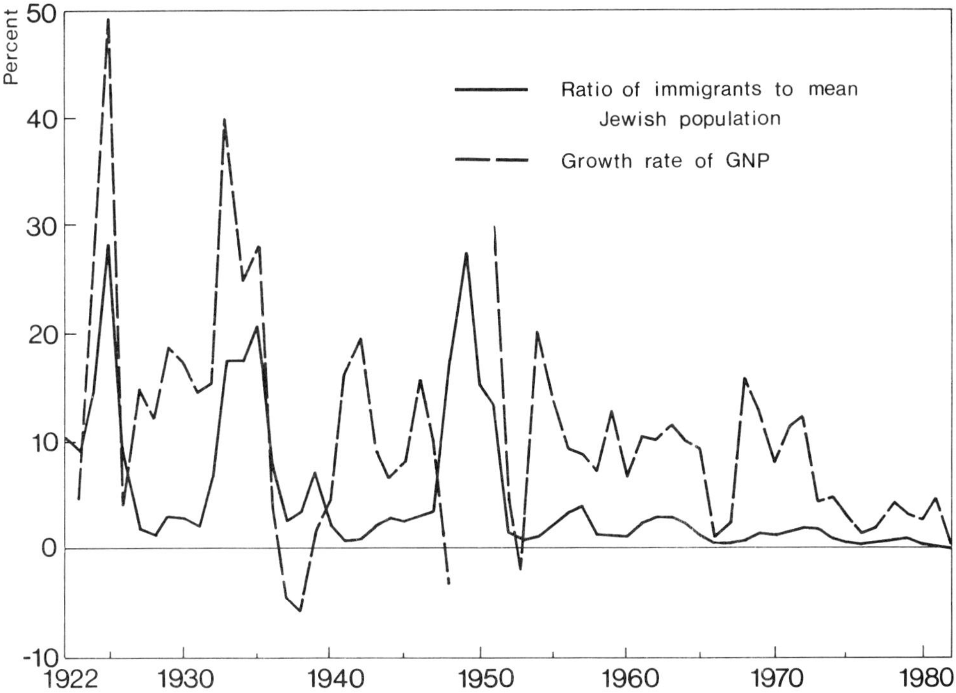

Figure 1-1
Immigration and gross national product, 1922–1982.

1948–1951, and 5.2 percent in 1951–1972, in contrast to 0.8 percent in 1972–1982 (Table 1-1).

Figure 1-1 shows the correspondence between the ratio of immigrants to mean Jewish population and the growth rates of GNP. The correlation is 0.72 in both the Mandate and state periods; the correlation between immigration and per capita GNP is much lower. It is hard to detect consistent leads or lags in the earlier period. After 1948, however, cycles in immigration tend to follow cycles in GNP.

Figure 1-2 shows a remarkable correspondence between fluctuations in immigration and in the growth rate of capital stock before 1948 and after 1951; in the latter period the correspondence holds for both dwelling and nondwelling capital (not shown). In addition to three large swings in immigration and economic growth in the mid-1920s, the mid-1930s, and 1950, there are short-term cyclical comovements (a glaring exception is the period of the Arab boycott and disruptions in 1936–1939, followed by World War II, when growth picked up while immigration declined). The short-term movements are more clearly discernible in the years after the last big swing.

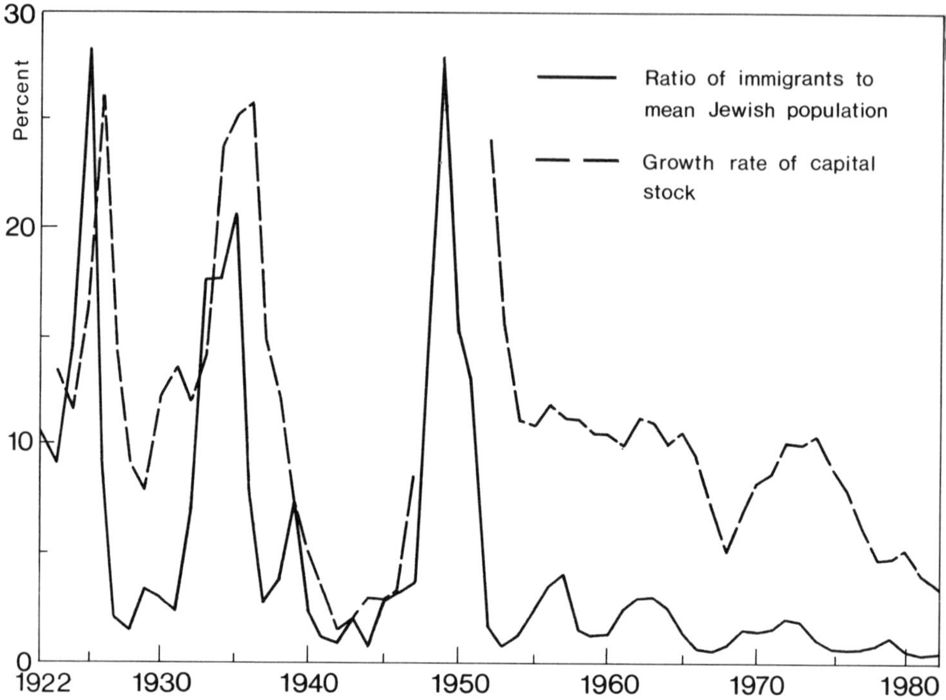

Figure 1-2
Immigration and capital growth, 1922–1982.

Such aggregate relationships between immigration and economic growth have been studied for the United States. Jerome (1926) observed the responsiveness of migration to employment conditions. Kuznets and Rubin (1954) and Kuznets (1958) observed the relationships between long swings in the growth of product and immigration. For the period before World War I they found that "the long swings in net immigration tended to follow those in gross national product per worker and to precede those in the constant dollar volume of residential construction" (1954, p. 32). Abramowitz (1961) explored what he dubbed "Kuznets cycles" and emphasized the roles of demand and intensity of factor utilization in bringing about an increase in population through migration and an increase in capital stock. Several studies discussed the response of immigration to inverse swings in economic growth in the United States and the European countries of origin. Easterlin (1968) has shown that the cessation of large immigration shifted the demographic response to fertility.

Population as an Engine of Growth

The record of long-term growth in total product and Jewish population in Palestine and Israel is truly exceptional by world standards (see Chapter 2). Also remarkable is the fact that in Israel such high rates of population increase were accompanied by a long-term increase in per capita income. In fifty-nine years of recorded growth, per capita income is reported to have declined in only twelve. The United States also experienced growth in per capita income during the periods of rapid population increase before World War I. There is no proof, however, that the growth in per capita income was caused by population growth, and the debate surrounding the favorable effects of population growth continues (see Simon, 1977).

Steady-state growth theory does not provide much useful guidance for understanding and interpreting the effect of population growth through immigration on the economy. Immigration affects the economy through the supply side, by expanding the supply of labor (and often of capital); it generates surges in demand that directly affect the level of activity and may induce further changes in factor supplies.

Obviously the rate of immigration—which dictated the rate of population increase—was a dominant factor in changing Israel's working-age population and the labor supply. However, as the composition of immigrants by country of origin and age has changed, so too has the translation of immigration into working-age population. Most of the pre-1948 immigrants were of or near working age (20–64) and in this respect resembled European migrants to other countries. The surge of immigrants in 1948–1951 included a high proportion of families with many children. Consequently, between 1950 and 1965 the working-age population grew at significantly lower rates than the total population (Table 1-2). During that period net immigration directly contributed between one-half and two-thirds to the growth of the adult population. Immigrant children growing to adulthood also made a significant net contribution to the adult population: over two-thirds, in contrast to less than one-third by the Israeli-born. From 1965 on, however, the Israeli-born contributed a rapidly growing share to the growth of the adult population; even though direct immigration in the early 1970s was still significant, the foreign-born made a net negative contribution to the adult population in that decade. In the growth of the labor force the foreign-born contributed three-quarters in 1955–1961, about half in 1961–1970 and only 14 percent in 1970–1980 (Ben-Porath, 1983).

There have also been sharp differences in the skill levels of immigrants. The pre-1948, 84 percent European, immigrants were among the most highly educated population in the world (Easterlin, 1961a). The immigrants arriving in

TABLE 1-2. Growth of the Jewish male population, age 20–64, 1950–1980 (percentages)

	1950–1955	1955–1960	1960–1965	1965–1970	1970–1975	1975–1980
Total change						
All ages	39.2	20.8	20.1	10.9	15.2	10.6
Age 20–64	28.5	15.9	16.0	13.0	16.4	9.6
Israeli-born age 20–64	13.3	31.6	32.0	59.2	87.0	130.4
Foreign born maturing in[a]	35.0	52.8	51.9	96.9	37.0	43.7
Foreign born maturing out[b]	12.6	29.6	38.0	56.6	51.6	82.9
Net maturing	22.4	23.2	13.9	40.3	–14.6	–39.1
Net migration and mortality[c]	64.3	45.2	54.0	0.5	27.5	8.7

a. Age 15–19 at beginning of each period.
b. Age 60–64 at end of each period.
c. 100.0 *minus* Israeli-born, age 20–64, *minus* net maturing.

1948 - 1960 had a much lower level of schooling: according to one estimate the per capita human capital of immigrants (age 30+) in those years was 57.1 percent that of the pre-1948 population (76 percent for the European-born and 32 percent for immigrants from Asia and Africa; see Baruh, 1965). This situation changed after the first decade: the immigrants of the 1960s had slightly more schooling than the 1960 host population; those of the 1970s had a significantly higher level of schooling than the host population[2] (83 percent of those arriving in 1969 - 1982 came from Europe and America, mostly from the USSR, compared with 43 percent in 1948 - 1968 and 84 percent in 1919 - 1948; see CBS, 1982).

Immigration initially entails the obsolescence of skills acquired in the country of origin. The process of economic absorption involves learning the host country's language, other specific skills of living, and on-the-job acquisition of skills. Mass immigration was associated with a decline not only in level of education but also in the level of country-specific skills. In Israel this phenomenon is expressed in dramatic occupational changes and upward occupational mobility (Ben-Porath, 1973a). It is reflected also in the cross-section differentials in earnings associated with length of residençe (Hanoch, 1961; Levy, 1968; Amir, 1981, 1984). The average length of stay in Israel increased following mass immigration. Kuznets (1973a) estimated that this factor contributed approximately 1.5 percent to growth in the 1950s and 1960s. Because the effect of length of stay in Israel on earnings diminishes over time as the proportion of new immigrants declines, this factor lost its relevance in the 1970s.

The response of capital depends on the supply of resources available for capital formation (that is, capital imports and domestic savings) and on the demand for investment. Immigration creates direct demand for housing and exerts an indirect effect through consumption-derived demand for producer capital. In addition, the increased supply of labor raises the demand for capital. In the Mandate period, private capital imports were substantial and were directly related to immigration —the correlation between private capital imports and immigration for 1924–1939 is 0.95. There is also some evidence that institutional capital imports were related to population growth (Gross and Metzer, 1977). The post-1948 immigration brought insignificant private capital imports. Capital imports were mostly in the hands of the public sector, driven by a demand created by immigration and other factors. No analysis is available on the effect of immigrants on domestic savings. Obviously, part (probably a substantial one) of the negative public-sector savings can be attributed to the gap between the demand for services created by immigrants and their initially low contribution to the tax base.

An important element in the effect of population on economic growth is based on increasing returns to scale. Despite rapid growth in the Mandate period, the Jewish population was still small in 1948. The Mandate authorites restricted immigration on the grounds of "limited absorptive capacity," that is, strongly decreasing returns to scale in the short run. In the long run, however, there were increasing returns to scale. The establishment of Israel in the midst of a war dramatized the issue of minimum viable population size, not only in terms of physical survival but also in economic terms. Empirically, this phenomenon raises a related question: is the rate of technical change independent of the rate and nature of population growth? As shown by Metzer (1982), the period of rapid growth in per capita income is associated not only with an increase in capital per capita but also with an increase in total factor productivity. (He points to a correlation of 0.5 between total hours of work and total factor productivity.)

How did immigration affect public and private consumption? The public sector played an inordinately large role in the economy, in part because of the need to provide immigrants with employment, shelter, and services, followed by a more gradual social and economic absorption effort. The public sector's continued involvement in improving housing and providing employment, health services, and education had a lasting effect on its size and function, extending well beyond the period of mass immigration.[3]

On the aggregate level there is no systematic statistical relationship between civilian public consumption and population growth for the post-1948 period. In the Mandate period cyclical movements were transmitted from population to product, unmitigated by active government macroeconomic policy. Indeed, because the role of government has been much more dominant since 1948 than in the Mandate period, macroeconomic fluctuations have been affected by a variety of other considerations. The creation of a large public sector was partly induced by immigration in a variety of ways: through the need to provide the services and means of absorption, the desire to control the process (such as the control of initial geographic allocation), and the desire to provide employment directly in hard times to groups experiencing labor-market difficulties. But immigration cannot explain the significant growth in public-sector employment in the 1970s (see Chapter 5).

In the period 1951–1964 private per capita consumption doubled. This rapid rise in the standard of living occurred while a large fraction of resources was devoted to capital formation and a rising share was devoted to defense—obviously at the expense of the foreign account. Although economists (such as Patinkin, 1960) protested at the time, the government's strategy may have been considered necessary to promote social cohesion, discourage emigration, and attract further immigration; otherwise growth itself might have been jeopardized. The growth in per capita consumption continued in the period of slower population growth, 1964–1972. What requires an explanation is the fact that during the stagnant years, 1972–1982, per capita consumption continued to increase (more than one-third over the decade) while product per capita rose no more than 8 percent.

The natural short-term effect of immigration on total product is quite different: it is reasonable to expect immigration to push up aggregate demand initially and then to raise labor supply, creating cycles (see Merhav, 1963).

It is no simple matter to find statistical support for the effects of population growth and to differentiate them from short-term relationships. As mentioned earlier, there were three long swings in immigration. A major event such as mass immigration must have left a lasting impression on economic life. Yet for this very reason it cannot be captured by a regression. Similarly, it is hard to isolate the effect of immigration on the extensive role of government in the public sector. The series are too short and the number of "major events" too small for statistical verification of the long-term hypotheses, and the statistical relationships are probably dominated by short-term relationships.

I first examine a series of regressions in which the economic variables are assumed to depend on the population variables, ignoring the possibility of reverse causality (Table 1-3). The first strong relationship emerges from an examination of capital accumulation: the growth rate of capital stock responds positively to the following alternative population variables: the ratio of immigrants to the population, the ratio of net migration to population, and the rate of population increase. The coefficients of the population variables are higher in the statehood period

TABLE 1-3. Rate of growth of the capital stock: regressions, 1924–1982

Independent variable	RCAP 1924–47 (1)	RCAP 1953–82 (2)	RCAP 1924–47 (3)	RCAP 1953–82 (4)	RCAPD[a] 1953–82 (5)	RCAPND 1953–82 (6)
Constant	1.240	0.499	−0.651	0.169	−2.529	−0.250
	1.3	1.0	0.6	6.2	1.3	0.4
Lagged dependent variable	0.645	0.575	0.568	0.571	0.681	0.622
	9.9	13.7	6.4	13.6	9.4	12.3
RGNP $(t-1)$	0.206	0.132	0.200	0.142	0.225[b]	0.093
	3.9	3.3	3.3	3.8	5.2	2.0
RPOP	0.255	0.682	—	—	—	0.903
	2.9	3.6				3.9
IMMIG	—	—	0.131	0.261	0.690	—
			1.6	1.1	2.9	
IMMIG $(t-1)$	—	—	0.233	0.547	—	—
			1.7	2.4		
EMIG	—	—	—	−0.579	—	—
				1.3		
$\bar{R}^2$	0.90	0.92	0.91	0.92	0.84	0.91

Note: R = annual rate of growth; POP = population; CAP = capital stock; CAPD = capital stock in dwelling; CAPND = CAP in nondwelling; IMMIG = ratio of immigrants to mean Jewish population; EMIG = difference between IMMIG and net migration balance. Small numerals are *t*-values.

a. Ratio of gross investment to the capital stock.

b. The independent variable is the rate of growth of per capita GNP.

than in the Mandate period. I have also included lagged growth of GNP in these equations in order to capture an accelerator mechanism. It is interesting to see whether this last relationship is solely a reflection of "population-related capital," mostly residential building. In the study of long swings in the United States, Kuznets (1958) found that investment in dwellings and railroads swung in conformity with population while other investment had an inverted swing. A function estimated for investment in dwellings showed a reaction to the growth of population, to per capita income, and to the share of population age 20–29. But in Israel also the growth of nondwelling capital stock responds to the population variables (Table 1-3).

The growth rate of total GNP depends positively on the current rate of immigration (immigrants divided by population) and inversely on the lagged rate of immigration (Table 1-4). The same is true when the growth rate of population replaces immigration in the regressions. The positive current coefficient is much

TABLE 1-4. Variables affecting growth rates of product and immigration, 1923–1982

Independent variable	GNP 1923–47	GNP 1951–82	Per capita GNP 1923–47	Per capita GNP 1951–82
Constant	7.388	4.172	8.243	2.875
	2.1	3.9	2.4	2.1
IMMIG	1.779	2.484	0.802	1.554
	7.2	4.6	2.9	2.9
IMMIG ($t-1$)	−0.828	−0.417	−1.191	−0.776
	3.3	1.1	4.3	2.1
$\bar{R}^2$	0.68[a]	0.50	0.44[a]	0.18
D.W.	1.7	1.8	1.9	1.8

(Dependent variable and period)

Note: IMMIG = ratio of immigrants to mean Jewish population. Small numerals are *t*-values.

a. Corrected for first-order serial correlation.

higher than the lagged negative effect, and higher for 1951–1982 than for the Mandate period. Correspondingly, population growth reduced current unemployment but raised it with a lag in 1924–1947.[4]

Per capita income also responds positively to the current rate of immigration and adversely to the lagged rate (Table 1-4, columns 3 and 4). The sum of coefficients is negative for 1923–1947, indicating a net depressive effect, while for 1951–1982 the sum is positive, indicating a growth-enhancing effect of immigration.

Was the Size of the Population Dependent on the Economy?

This direction of causality also has both long- and short-term aspects. Immigration, emigration, and the rate of natural increase are responsive to income and employment opportunities. Short-term fluctuations in these variables also reflect the adjustment of the timing of migration or fertility to economic fluctuations. As already mentioned, there is a long tradition of studies on the cyclical responsiveness of immigration (such as Jerome, 1926). In studies of long swings in immigration (and fertility) Kuznets (1958), Abramowitz (1961), and Easterlin (1961b) all emphasize the dominant role of demand conditions in the United States in initiating waves of immigration. This is probably not the case in Israel. The immigration waves before 1948 were not "caused" by economic fluctuations in Palestine.

Apparently exogenous shocks in the countries of origin, including economic fluctuations there, constituted dominant "push" factors. This does not, however, rule out the possibility that rising unemployment, following an initial boom, checked further immigration and diverted it elsewhere. There is also evidence that the immigration policy of the Zionist movement was sensitive to the conditions of employment.

The mass immigration of 1948–1951 was certainly independent of the domestic economic scene in Israel. For most of these displaced Jews from Europe and Jewish communities from Arab countries, Israel was the only option. Economic conditions in Israel affected immigration in the early years of statehood largely through the immigration policies of the government and the Jewish Agency. Thus the lull in immigration after 1951 reflected a reaction to the economic hardships associated with immigration. In later years immigration of entire communities diminished and became dependent on political turning points in various Eastern European and Latin American countries. The last and most significant was the partial relaxation of Soviet emigration restrictions in 1970. And it is quite possible that the declining share of those arriving in Israel out of those leaving the Soviet Union reflects a response to economic conditions in Israel. As immigration declined in volume, it grew more and more dependent on individual choice and, as such, on economic conditions. Another implication of the decline in immigration is that the relative weight of emigration in the fluctuations of net migration (which is the difference between immigration and emigration) increased. Lamdany (1982) has shown that emigration from Israel responds to economic fluctuations, and in this respect the experience of the 1965–1967 recession influences current policy.

Table 1-5 shows that in 1954–1982 the rates of immigration, net migration, and population growth respond weakly to current, and significantly to (three-year) lagged, rates of increase in per capita consumption. A similar relationship holds for per capita GNP. For 1923–1947 the relation is strong with current and one-period lagged variables (similar results are reported by Ablin, 1979a). There is also evidence that the birth rate is responsive to economic fluctuations (Ben-Porath, 1973b). Data for the longer period, 1951–1982, seem to suggest that after 1973 the simple associations no longer hold (Figure 1-3).

Causality Tests

Causality between population and product runs both ways. The only empirical grip available is the sequence in which the variations occur. According to the procedure suggested by Granger (1969), x "causes" y if, in a regression of y on both x lagged and y lagged, there is a significant reduction in residual variance compared with a regression of y on lagged y alone; that is, x is said to "cause" y if lagged x has an independent effect on current y after y is purged of all its autocorrelation.

TABLE 1-5. Dependence of immigration on economic variables, 1926–1982

Independent variable	IMMIG 1926–47	IMMIG 1951–82	IMMIG 1926–47	IMMIG 1951–82		IMMIG 1926–47	IMMIG 1951–82		NET MIG 1954–82
Constant	−1.864	−0.318	3.947	0.217		0.273	−0.957	Constant	0.959
	1.5	0.9	1.3	0.2		0.1	2.4		1.6
IMMIG ($t-1$)	0.509	0.371	—	—		—	—		
	4.9	5.1							
RGNP	0.362	0.169	—	—		—	—		
	6.3	4.6							
RGNPPC	—	—	0.058	0.209	RGNP	0.284	0.135	RCONS	0.064
			0.5	3.7		3.3	5.8		1.6
RGNPPC ($t-1$)	—	—	0.116	0.085	RGNP ($t-1$)	0.132	0.078	RCONS ($t-1$)	0.159
			1.1	1.5		2.1	3.4		3.8
RGNPPC ($t-2$)	—	—	0.149	0.215	RGNP ($t-2$)	0.026	0.109	RCONS ($t-2$)	0.121
			1.6	3.7		0.4	9.4		2.9
RGNPPC ($t-3$)	—	—	−0.028	−0.039	RGNP ($t-3$)	−0.032	0.050	RCONS ($t-3$)	0.159
			0.3	0.9		0.6	0.5		3.7
$\bar{R}^2$	0.75	0.73	0.05[a]	0.58[a]		0.40[a]	0.90[a]		0.34

Note: IMMIG = ratio of immigrants to mean Jewish population; NET MIG = ratio of migration balance to the mean Jewish population; RGNP, RGNPPC, RCONS = ratios of growth of GNP, per capita GNP, and private per capita consumption. Small numerals are t-values.

a. Corrected for first-order serial correlation.

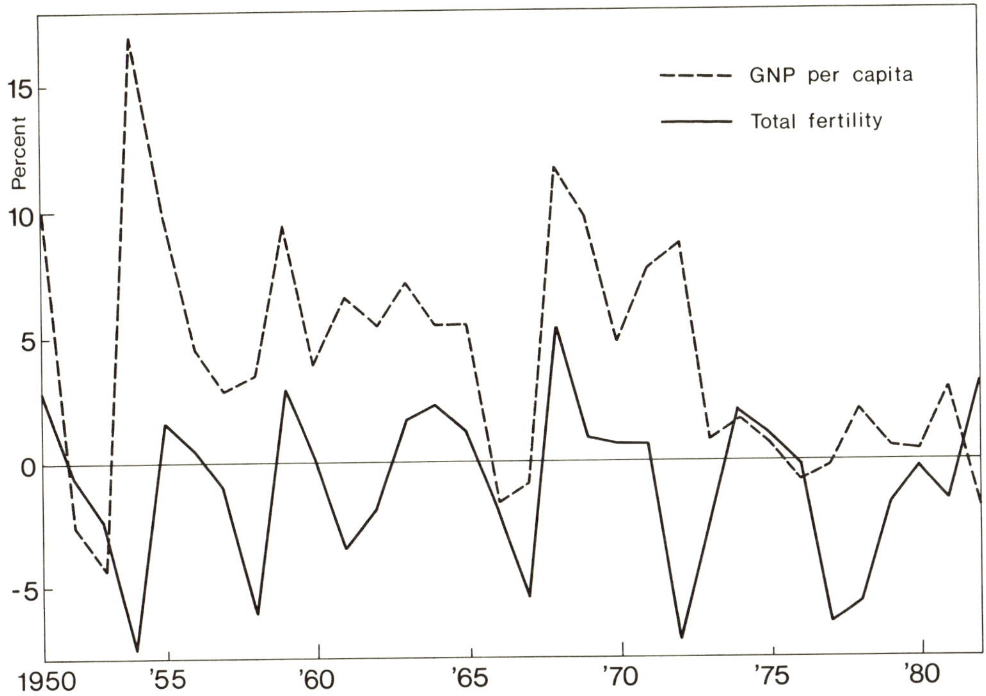

Figure 1-3
Growth rates of per capita GNP and total fertility, 1951–1982.

The causality tests were run with lags for each variable. The period 1948–1950 is generally excluded from the analysis where GNP figures are concerned because the linkage among the different series of estimates for the period is dubious. Table 1-6 shows the main results of the causality tests. There is strong evidence in support of the hypothesis that in the Mandate period immigration "caused" economic growth. On the other hand, most of the evidence on causality from the economic indicators to population is for the post-1951 period: the growth rates of per capita GNP or of total GNP, and of per capita or total private consumption,"cause" the rate of population growth, the ratio between immigrants and population, and the net immigration ratio. There is two-way causality between the unemployment rate and the growth rate of population in 1926–1948; that is, unemployment is the only economic variable that also affects immigration in this period. A marginally significant relationship in both directions is also observed between the growth rate of per capita income and the ratio of immigrants to population in 1954–1982, but vanishes for 1951–1982. One-way causality is indicated from population or immigration to the growth in capital stock—it is very clear in the Mandate period, and marginally significant in the statehood

TABLE 1-6. Results of causality tests (annual rates of growth)

Period	Variable	Direction of causality and *F*-statistic	Variable
1926–1947	GNPPC	← 6.5	IMMIG
1926–1947	GNPPC	← 6.0	POP
1926–1939	GNPPC	← 7.1	POP
1926–1948	UNEMPR	← 5.1	POP
1926–1948	UNEMPR	4.2 →	POP
1926–1939	UNEMPR	5.2 →	POP
1926–1947	CAP	← 15.1	POP
1926–1947	CAP	← 20.8	IMMIG
1954–1982	GNPPC	← 2.8	IMMIG
1954–1982	GNPPC	2.7 →	IMMIG
1951–1982	GNP	9.0 →	IMMIG
1954–1982	CAP	← 2.8	IMMIG
1954–1982	GNP	4.8 →	POP
1954–1982	GNPPC	4.8 →	POP
1954–1982	PCPC	4.2 →	POP
1954–1982	PC	4.8 →	POP
1954–1982	GNPPC	5.0 →	NET IMMIG
1954–1982	PC	7.5 →	NET IMMIG
1954–1982	PCPC	4.6 →	NET IMMIG

Note: GNPPC = per capita GNP; UNEMPR = rate of unemployment; CAP = capital; PC = private consumption; PCPC = per capita PC; POP = population; IMMIG = ratio of immigrants to population; NET IMMIG = ratio of the immigration balance to population.

period. The test certainly confirms the visual impression gained from Figure 1-2, that immigration leads capital.

Conclusion

This brief study of the two-way relationship between population and growth found stronger evidence for causality from immigration to economic growth in the Mandate period. For the whole period 1922–1982, it is very clear that immigration pushed the rate of increase of capital stock. For the period from 1954 on, immigration responded to the growth rate of per capita income or consumption. The graphs show both strong correspondence with and exceptions to the comovements of population and product (such as the large growth in product and the downturn in immigration during World War II). There were swings associated with three large waves of immigration (two in the Mandate period and the mass immigration in the early years of statehood). Each provided a push to economic growth that affected the economy for many years. The drive provided by these waves of immigrants seems to have lost momentum sometime in the mid-1960s. Further exogenous waves of equal magnitude failed to emerge. In addition to the swings, there were short-term variations. It is quite possible that the two types of fluctuations are responsible for the difference in the dominant direction of causality between the periods: the swings largely represent the effect of population on the economy and they dominate the Mandate period and the early state period. The response of immigration to per capita income was more closely related to short-term variations. Whereas in the early period this relationship was swamped and dominated by the (largely exogenous) long swings, the latter period allowed this dependence of immigration on the economy to emerge. But there may be another substantive reason for the difference between the periods: the Israeli government's large role in the economy may have eliminated or suppressed the short-term effects of population movements on the economy.

The evidence strongly supports the notion that the economic stagnation of the past decade had a demographic component. After half a century of extraordinarily rapid growth in population, total product, and per capita product, the slowdown in population growth and the stagnation in productivity growth (despite continued growth in the capital stock) must have reinforced one another. Although there are important autonomous reasons for both—the depletion of sources of immigration, the energy crises, and decade-long worldwide economic stagflation—the response of population to the economic loss of momentum may have aggravated the situation.

2

Economic Growth and Structural Change: An International Perspective

Moshe Syrquin

Israel's per capita income in 1980 was one of the highest among middle-income countries, and not far below that of some Western European countries. This relatively high level of income was attained by rapid growth from a much lower level around 1950. This chapter compares the pattern of growth and structural changes in the Israeli economy over the past three decades, with some reference to the Jewish economy of Palestine before 1948.[1] Drawing on comparative studies of the patterns of growth and structural change in the process of development,[2] it focuses on the transitional or semi-industrialized countries that have been catching up with the industrial leaders since World War II. When relevant, Israel is also compared with advanced countries. The first section examines long-term growth in total and per capita output; the second, total factor productivity growth in Israel and other countries. The third section presents a disaggregated analysis of structural changes in the patterns of demand, trade, and production, followed by a section on the sources of industrial growth and resource use.

The Level and Growth of Output

The period 1950–1973 was one of very rapid and sustained increase in both total and per capita output. All regions and most countries took part in this acceleration of growth, especially during the 1960s. The transitional or semi-industrialized countries led the trend, with higher growth rates than either the industrial or the less developed economies; among these transitional countries, Israel was one of the best performers.[3] This period may prove to have been unique, and the subsequent worldwide slowdown of economic growth may signal a return to a more sustainable long-term pattern.

The remarkable performance of the economy in Israel's first quarter-century was in many respects a continuation of the no less remarkable performance of the

Jewish economy in Mandatory Palestine in the quarter-century before 1948. Tables 2-1 through 2-3 compare Israel with two groups of countries; one consists of twelve semi-industrialized and three less developed countries, the other of Western European developed countries plus Australia, Canada, the United States, and Japan. The variety of experiences summarized in the tables is more relevant than simple group averages for an assessment of Israel's performance.

Relative Income Levels around 1950

Table 2-1 compares relative levels of development in 1939 and 1950 as measured by per capita income in U.S. dollars. Because international data are difficult to compare, the table presents estimates and ranks only by orders of magnitude. The estimates in column 1 are based on official exchange rates; those in column 2 compare real income, using a common set of prices. The "Point Four" estimates for 1939 for Palestine and other countries appear in column 3. In all cases per capita income is expressed relative to the U.S. level.

All the estimates indicate that around 1950 Israel's per capita income was about one-fourth the U.S. level. In terms of converted exchange rates its position was similar to that of Italy and the richer Latin American countries (Argentina and Venezuela), well above that of Japan and most developing countries, but only about half the level of Western Europe. Income figures converted at exchange rates tend to exaggerate the real gap between poorer and richer countries, as the real-income comparisons (column 2) confirm. The latter show higher incomes for most countries, especially for lower-income countries, relative to the United States. Israel in 1950 was a notable exception: the available estimates show no significant difference between real income and converted income for that year. As a result Israel occupies a lower position on the first scale, but its relative position is not affected much: Argentina and Venezuela appear wealthier, and other Latin American countries (and Spain) draw closer, but the main picture does not change.[4]

Per Capita Income Growth since 1922

Israel's relatively high income level in 1950 was the result of rapid growth in the preceding decades. Income data for the British Mandate period are fragmentary; the main source, covering the period since 1922, is Szereszewski (1968), who relied on Gruenbaum's (1941) work on the Jewish economy of Palestine in 1936. Per capita income in the Jewish economy of Palestine grew almost 5 percent annually in 1922–1947. Such a rate would have been considered remarkable even in the years after 1950, and was more so in the interwar period, as Table 2-2 shows. These figures are for 1913–1950, and since 1913–1922 in general were years of

TABLE 2-1. Relative per capita national income in 1939 and 1950 ($U.S. = 100)

	According to —		
Country	Morawetz 1950 (1)	ICP 1950 (2)	"Point Four" 1939 (3)
Israel/Palestine	28	28	15[a]
Poorer countries			
Argentina	23	44	39
Brazil	9	18	8
Chile	15	38	31
Egypt	5	11	15
Greece	14	19	25
India	2	7	6
Korea	4	8	—
Mexico	14	21	11
Peru	10	20	13
Philippines	4	10	6
Spain	18	22	—
Taiwan	6	10	—
Turkey	8	13	—
Venezuela	25	42	17
Yugoslavia	11	19	17
Richer countries			
Australia	76	77	73
Belgium	61	55	47
Canada	85	75	70
France	52	49	51
Italy	24	28	25
Japan	17	18	17
Norway	68	53	50
Sweden	87	67	79
United Kingdom	52	60	84

Sources: Column 1: Morawetz (1977); Column 2: Summers, Kravis and Heston (1980); Taiwan and Yugoslavia – Marris (1981); Column 3: U.S. Department of State (1950).

a. Palestine: Jews = 30, non-Jews = 8; see calculation in Syrquin (1984), appendix.

TABLE 2-2. Average annual growth of per capita income, 1913–1980 (percentages)

Country	1913–1950 (1)	1950–1970 (2)	1970–1980 (3)
Palestine/Israel	4.9[a]	5.2	2.1
Poorer countries			
Argentina	0.7	2.0	0.6
Brazil	2.4[b]	2.7	6.2
Chile	0.6	1.5	0.7
Egypt	0.2	1.3	5.3
Greece	–0.1	5.8	4.8
India	0.2	1.9	1.5
Korea	—	4.5	7.8
Mexico	1.2[c]	3.1	2.1
Peru	1.5	2.3	0.4
Philippines	0.1	2.7	3.6
Spain	–0.3	5.2	3.0
Taiwan	0.7	5.4	6.0[d]
Turkey	—	3.5	3.5
Venezuela	—	3.0	1.7
Yugoslavia	0.9[e]	4.4	4.9
Richer countries			
Australia	0.5	2.5	1.6
Belgium	0.7	3.4	2.8
Canada	1.3	2.6	2.8
France	1.0	4.0	3.0
Italy	0.7	4.9	2.4
Japan	0.5	8.6	3.9
Norway	2.1	3.3	4.3
Sweden	2.2	3.3	1.4
United Kingdom	0.9	2.3	1.8
United States	1.6	2.0	2.0

Sources: Israel 1922–1947: Szereszewski (1968); 1950–1980: Metzer (1983). Column 1: Maddison (1970, 1980b); Column 2: Morawetz (1977); Column 3: World Bank, *World Development Report* (1982).

a. 1922–1947.
b. 1920–1950.
c. 1910–1950.
d. 1970–1977.
e. 1909/12–1950.

slower growth, they underestimate growth after 1922—though not by much. In only three countries (Brazil, Norway, and Sweden) did annual per capita income growth exceed 2 percent; in most countries it was less than 1 percent. Even allowing for a large margin of error in the data it is safe to conclude that per capita income in Jewish Palestine expanded at at least twice the rate found in most developing or developed countries in the interwar period.[5] The relative contributions of input expansion and productivity growth to the growth of output are discussed below in the section on the growth of factor productivity.

The difference in income growth between Jewish Palestine and other countries has interesting implications for the relative position of the countries at the beginning of this period. If real incomes in Jewish Palestine and in the United States are extrapolated backward to 1922, and the U.S. growth rate is set at 2 percent (to account for the slower growth before 1922), per capita income in Jewish Palestine in 1922 was no more than 15 percent that of the United States. Since the United States performed better during this period than most other countries, *their* relative position in 1922 was above the 1950 levels of Table 2-1; hence Jewish Palestine's catching up with Europe was even faster, and the gap with less developed countries (LDCs) must have widened. Combining the growth figures in Table 2-2 with the income relatives of Table 2-1 yields the income of other regions and countries relative to that of the United States. The results suggest that in the early 1920s per capita income in Jewish Palestine was about one-quarter of the average level in Western Europe. This was lower than the level in Japan and did not differ significantly from the income level in Brazil (or even Egypt). These are measures of production but do not necessarily reflect the standard of living. In Jewish Palestine, large capital imports permitted levels of consumption that at times exceeded total income.

The growth performance of Jewish Palestine was qualitatively different from that of Israel after 1950. In the 1920s immigration led to rapid population growth, but from a very low base within a larger total population. The low starting point together with the high quality of the immigrant labor force and the large inflow of capital—mostly immigrant transfers—facilitated the rapid growth of output and productivity. Throughout the Mandate period the pace of economic activity followed external stimuli—primarily immigration.[6]

As the absolute and relative weight of the Jewish economy increased, so did the importance of internal processes. In the mid-1930s, when the separation of the Jewish and Arab economies became almost total,[7] Jewish Palestine entered the stage of what Kuznets (1966a) labeled "modern economic growth" that was to continue after independence.

From 1950 to 1970 per capita income grew more than 5 percent annually, but in this period Israel was no longer alone. Similar rates were recorded in Europe (France, Greece, Italy, and Spain) and East Asia (Korea and Taiwan), and an even higher rate prevailed in Japan. In most of these cases, the high postwar rates of growth involved an element of recovery from a previous drop in output. Seen in this light, Israel's performance is even more noteworthy: not only was it a continuation of previous rapid growth, but it was accomplished concurrently with the absorption and integration of mass immigration.

In the 1970s growth slowed considerably, to about 2 percent—a lower rate than in Western Europe and far below the rates in the rapidly growing semi-industrialized countries, particularly in the more export-oriented economies (Brazil, Korea, Taiwan). (For analyses of the slowdown see Chapters 3 and 14.) The full impact of the 1979 oil shock is not reflected in Table 2-2.

The rapid growth after 1950 led to an increase in Israel's relative real income to over half that of the United States by 1980, and to about 75 percent of the average level in Western Europe around 1980. By 1970 Israel's income level was closer to Western Europe's than to that of the wealthier semi-industrialized countries.

The Growth of Population and Total Output since 1922

The rapid growth of per capita income since 1922 was accompanied by an even faster increase in population. Total output increased at an extremely high rate for about half a century, as shown in Table 2-3. By 1922 the Jewish population of Palestine had reached about 82,000. Immigration then accelerated, boosting the population to over 600,000 by 1947, and to more than 1.4 million by the end of 1951. Table 2-4 shows the average annual growth rates of population for the periods summarized in Table 2-3.[8]

Domestic output expanded quite rapidly in Jewish Palestine, both in relation to other countries and in absolute terms. Even starting from a very low base in 1922, maintenance of growth rates half as high as those in Table 2-3 for the same length of time would still be impressive. During the 1920s, when growth of 4–5 percent in total output was not uncommon, the *annual* growth rate in Jewish Palestine reached 18.5 percent. In the 1930s, while growth slowed or was negative in most countries (except in Japan), in Jewish Palestine it remained quite high.This came about during the worst years of world depression, despite an inability to pursue an independent monetary policy and the narrow application of Article 18 by the Mandate authorities, which prevented implementation of retaliatory tariff policies at a time when they were in widespread use (see Halevi, 1979).

Israel's success story after 1950 is better known. From 1950 to 1970 Israel's performance was matched only by that of Japan, although by the late 1960s several other countries (the "gang of four"—Hong Kong, Korea, Singapore, and Taiwan—and several oil exporters) performed as well or better. From 1970 on, growth in Israel was no higher than the average, and more recently it appears to have come to a complete halt.

TABLE 2-3. Average annual growth of GDP, 1920–1980 (percentages)

Country	1920–1929 (1)	1929–1938 (2)	1938–1950 (3)	1950–1970 (4)	1970–1980 (5)
Jewish Palestine/Israel	18.5[a]	13.9	9.9[b]	9.7	4.9
Poorer countries					
Argentina	5.6	0.7	3.4	3.6	2.2
Brazil	4.5	3.1	5.9	6.1	8.4
Chile	4.8	0.2	2.9	4.2	2.4
Egypt	—	1.8	2.6	4.2	8.1
Greece	3.4[d]	1.4	−2.1	6.7	4.9[e]
India	1.9	1.0	0.8	3.6	3.6
Korea	—	—	—	6.8	9.5
Mexico	1.7[c]	1.7	5.6	6.4	5.2
Peru	3.2[d]	⟵ 3.1 ⟶		5.1	3.0
Philippines	2.4[d]	⟵ 2.0 ⟶		5.8	6.3
Spain	2.2[d]	⟵ -0.7 ⟶		6.7	4.0
Taiwan	4.4[f]	3.6[f]	−0.3	8.4	8.0[g]
Turkey	—	—	1.8	6.1	5.9
Venezuela	—	—	7.4	6.9	5.0
Yugoslavia	4.5	1.3	1.2	5.7	5.8
Richer countries					
Australia	2.3	1.8	3.2	5.1	3.0
Belgium	3.4	−0.0	1.3	3.9	3.5
Canada	4.0	−0.2	6.0	4.8	3.9
France	4.9	−0.4	−1.6	5.1	3.5
Italy	3.0	1.4	1.1	5.4	3.0
Japan	3.4	4.7	−2.7	8.6	5.0[e]
Norway	3.2	3.1	−5.9	4.3	4.8
Sweden	4.8	2.3	3.1	3.9	1.7
United Kingdom	1.9	1.9	−2.3	2.8	1.9
United States	4.0	−0.6	5.0	3.8	3.0

Sources: Israel 1922–1947: Szereszewski (1968); 1950–1980: Metzer (1983). Columns 1–3: Maddison (1970, 1980b); Column 4: Morawetz (1977); Column 5: World Bank, *World Development Report* (1982).

a. 1922–1929.
b. 1938–1947.
c. 1921–1929.
d. 1913–1929.
e. 1970–1979.
f. 1913–1928, 1928–1938.
g. 1970–1978.

TABLE 2-4. Average annual growth of population, 1922–1980

Years	Jewish population	Total population
1922–1929	9.7	—
1929–1938	11.1	—
1938–1947	4.7	—
Total, 1922–1947	8.3	3.8
1948–1950	25.9	—
1950–1970	4.3	4.4
1970–1980	2.5	2.7

Sources: Jews, 1922–1947: Halevi (1979); total, 1922–1947 and 1948–1950: Halevi and Klinov-Malul (1968); 1950–1980: CBS (1982).

The Growth of Factor Productivity

Economic growth results from the growth of productive resources and from increased efficiency in their use. This section summarizes the information on total factor productivity growth (TFPG) in Israel since 1950 and compares it with that of other countries. To provide a better appreciation of longer-term trends it also presents the meager data for Jewish Palestine.

Table 2-5 shows the result of calculating the elements of the growth-accounting equation:

$$g_Y = \alpha_L g_L + \alpha_K g_K + g_A$$

where g_Y, g_L, g_K, and g_A are the annual growth rates of output, labor, capital,and total factor productivity, and α_L and α_K are the elasticities of output with respect to labor and capital, usually assumed to equal their distributive shares. Also shown is total factor input growth ($\alpha_L g_L + \alpha_K g_K$).

The resultant pattern for 1922–1972 is one of high growth in output, inputs, and productivity.[9] The average growth rate of total factor productivity is close to 4 percent throughout most of these years—again, a very respectable rate. Japan is the only other country to have matched this experience after World War II. High as it was, TFPG accounts for less than one-third of output growth during the Mandate period, and for about 40 percent after 1950. The rapid expansion of inputs is the chief factor in the high rates of output growth.[10]

The relatively low contribution of increases in efficiency to output growth conceals the magnitude of the achievement of having incorporated into the productive process the vast increase in inputs while improving their efficiency.

TABLE 2-5. Average annual growth of outputs, inputs, and total factor productivity, 1922–1981

	Output (1)	Labor (2)	Capital (3)	Total input (4)	TFP (1 – 4)	TFP/ output (5)
Jewish Palestine						
1922–1936	19.3	14.8	16.2	15.5	3.8	0.20
1936–1947	7.0	4.5	5.6	5.0	2.0	0.29
Israel						
1950–1960	11.2	4.3	13.5	6.5	4.7	0.42
1961–1972	9.7	3.9	8.9	5.5	4.2	0.43
1973–1981	3.4	1.0	6.0	2.8	0.6	0.18

Sources: Jewish Palestine 1922–1947: Total economy, Szereszewski (1968) and Halevi (1979). Israel 1950–1960: Private nondwelling economy: Gaathon (1971). TFPG computed as difference between growth of output and of total input. Israel 1961–1981, business sector: Metzer (1983).

How does Israel's performance compare with that of other countries? In a recent study, Chenery (1983) assembled sources of growth estimates for a large number of developing and developed countries in several periods between 1950 and 1973. His summary of the results facilitates international comparisons by plotting the relation between factor inputs and productivity growth in each country (as in Figure 2-1). The chart plots the tradeoff between factor inputs and productivity growth along lines of constant growth and also relates these elements to the rate of growth. The thirty countries studied fall into three distinct groups. Figure 2-1 shows only the boundaries of the clusters. The nine developed European countries form group *a*, characterized by low input growth (g_L no more than 1 percent) offset by relatively high TFPG, which accounts, on average, for over one-half of output growth. The LDCs fall into two distinct groups: in group *b* are the typical middle-income developing countries, with higher rates of labor and total input growth but somewhat lower TFPG, amounting to less than 30 percent of output growth;[11] group *c* consists of Japan and five semi-industrial economies (Hong Kong, Israel, Korea, Spain, and Taiwan) with average growth rates of over 10 percent, achieved both by higher factor inputs and by higher factor productivity than the countries of group *a* or *b*. Since the 1960s the group *c* countries have had a strong outward orientation, with an emphasis on the export of manufactures. Most of them have relied for at least part of the period on high inflows of foreign capital.

The Jewish economy of Palestine until 1936 (JP1 in Figure 2-1) experienced

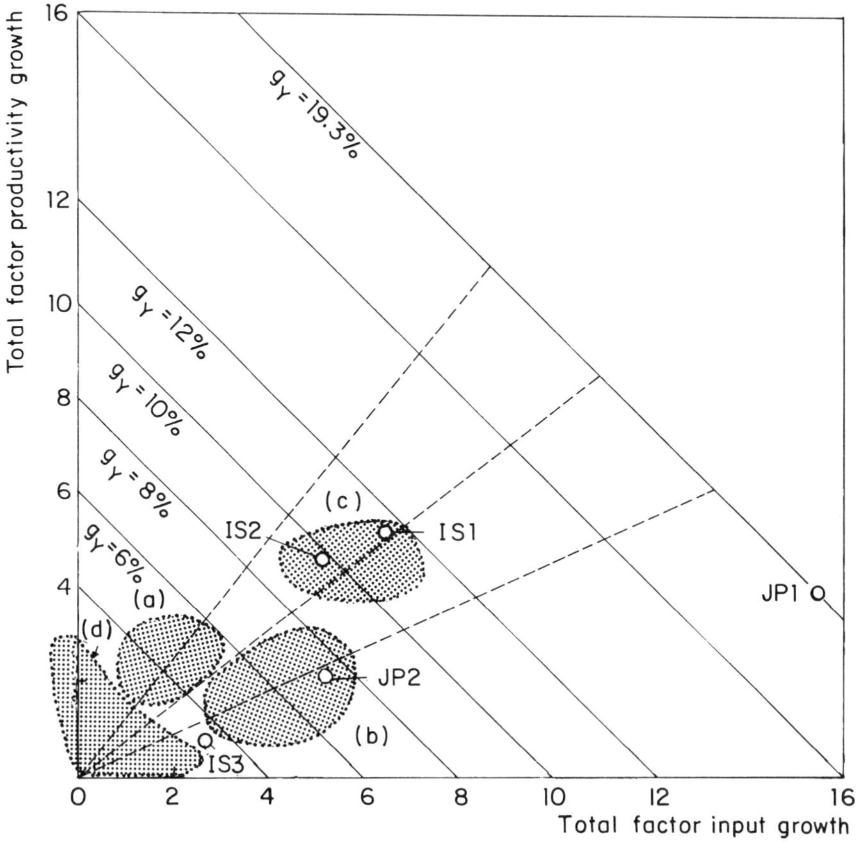

Figure 2-1
Total factor productivity and total input growth.

a = Belgium, Canada, Denmark, France, Italy, West Germany, Netherlands, Norway, Sweden, United Kingdom, United States (1960–1973).
b = Argentina, Brazil, Chile, Colombia, Mexico, Venezuela (1960–1974); Ecuador, Honduras (1950–1962); Greece (1951–1965); Peru (1960–1970); Philippines (1947–1965); Turkey (1963–1975).
c = Hong Kong (1960–1970); Japan, Korea (1960–1973); Spain (1959–1965); Taiwan (1955–1960).
d = Belgium, Italy, Sweden, United Kingdom, United States, West Germany (1973–1979).
JP1 = Jewish Palestine (1922–1936); *JP2* = Jewish Palestine (1936–1947).
IS1 = Israel (1950–1960); *IS2* = Israel (1961–1972); *IS3* = Israel (1973–1981).

very high growth of output and inputs, with TFPG contributing only 20 percent to aggregate growth. After 1936 (JP2), growth of output and inputs slowed down and TFPG increased to a level typical of the LDCs in group *b*. The average results for this second period hide the severe contraction in the Jewish economy in 1936–1940. Output growth and TFPG were virtually nil in these years but rose markedly afterward. Severe disruption of maritime transportation during World War II made it almost impossible to continue importing capital equipment. Capital accumulation dropped to even lower levels than in 1936–1940, but utilization of existing capacity increased sharply. Growing demand by the British forces and neighboring countries led to a stretching of capacity and to numerous adaptations and innovations, reflected in the growth of TFPG. This wartime experience was very similar to Latin America's (see Bruton, 1967).

In the 1950s output and productivity growth returned to high levels. Israel's experience during the high-growth years 1950–1972 is typical of group *c* countries'.

Group *d* represents six advanced countries whose productivity slowed in 1973–1979. In the same period output and productivity growth declined significantly in Israel (IS3), yet capital accumulation remained at a high level throughout the period (see Chapter 4 for an analysis). The decline in economic activity but not in capital accumulation led to reduced utilization of capacity. This reduction is a major reason for the decline in productivity growth. For 1950–1980 the simple correlation between annual TFPG and changes in an index of capacity utilization is 0.69.[12]

Table 2-6 shows TFPG rates in agriculture and manufacturing for Israel and three countries with long-term records. The United States, the United Kingdom, and Japan experienced significant acceleration in TFPG in the production of commodities, especially in agriculture. In Israel, the high priority accorded to agriculture in the allocation of investment and in research and extension services appears in its very high TFPG rate. The rapid growth in productivity was an important factor in the economy's successful performance during the period.

For each country and period in the table there is a significant disparity in the rates of factor productivity growth between manufacturing and agriculture. In the United States and Japan a large gap in favor of manufacturing appears for most of the periods reported. In Japan the gap widens sharply over time. In the United Kingdom the gap narrows for most of the twentieth century through a combination of substantial productivity growth in agriculture and unimpressive TFPG in industry. The gap in Israel has more to do with the performance of agriculture than with a lag in industry, particularly in 1960–1972 (see Chapter 3).

Growth in Israel, both before and after 1948, was propelled much more than in other countries by the growth of inputs originating outside the country. Immigration was a major source of labor growth and was related to the large inflows of

TABLE 2-6. Long-term estimates of total factor productivity growth in agriculture and manufacturing in four countries (percentages)

	Years	Annual TFPG	
		Agriculture	Manufacturing
Israel	1950–1981	5.4	1.9[a]
United States	1839–1859 } 1869–1929 }	0.3	1.9
	1929–1973	1.6	2.0
United Kingdom	1856–1913	0.6	0.7
	1924–1973	2.6	1.8
Japan	1887–1938	1.0	2.1
	1954–1976	2.4	6.1

Sources: Israel 1950–1960: Gaathon (1971); Israel 1961–1981: Metzer (1983); United States: Williamson and Lindert (1980); United Kingdom: Matthews, Feinstein and Odling-Smee (1982); Japan: Ohkawa and Takamatsu (1983).

a. Includes mining.

foreign capital. These transfers permitted the high accumulation rates necessary to absorb the expanding labor force without painful adjustments in living standards, and permitted continued improvement in the latter.

The absorption of immigrants adds an extra dimension to the increase in labor productivity. Massive immigration has contradictory effects on the labor force: it depresses the average *level* of productivity, but over time the *growth* of labor productivity increases as the immigrants are assimilated into the labor force. The productivity increase will be faster if the immigrants have a relatively high skill level. When immigration slows down, or when its weight in the additions to the labor force becomes minimal, this potential source of growth in productivity vanishes.

The rapid growth of factor inputs and the increase in trade ratios (discussed in the next section) expand markets and impart a general dynamism to the economy. An expanding economy with high investment rates can benefit from faster adoption of new technology, accommodate the reallocation of resources necessary for continued growth, and exploit the opportunities associated with increased size and faster growth.

Structural Changes

The transformation of the structure of production lies at the heart of the economic and social changes that characterize economic development. Associated with a rise in income are changes in the composition of demand, international trade, and factor use. These interact with the pattern of productivity growth, the availability of natural resources, and government policies to determine the pace and nature of industrial growth.

This section summarizes the stylized facts of structural transformation in a developing economy, based on a series of comparative studies of industrialization and development.[13] It thus helps explain the main changes in the structure of the Israeli economy.

Final Demand

The most uniform of the demand factors affecting industrialization are the decline in the share of food in consumption and the rise in the share of resources allocated to investment. Together they imply a shift in demand from agricultural goods to industrial commodities and nontradables. Figure 2-2 shows the average pattern of change in the composition of final demand derived from international comparisons for 1950–1970; the shorter lines show the actual experience in Israel.[14] In the international pattern, the share of food consumption in total final demand declines from about 40 percent at low levels of income to less than 20 percent at the upper end of the transition range. The rise in nonfood demand is typically divided in similar proportions between nonfood consumption and investment.

Table 2-7 shows rough averages for the distribution of national product by final use (in current prices). For the period before 1948 the figures are approximations indicative only of trends.[15] The high levels of capital inflow for the entire half-century are especially noteworthy. Imports of capital during the Mandate period were much larger than those after 1948. Often they even exceeded total output, thus allowing standards of living substantially higher than the low values for per capita income (discussed in the first section) would indicate. They also financed high levels of investment.[16]

The nature of these large inflows of external capital changed considerably over time. Before 1948, immigrants' private capital accounted for most of the capital imports. In the 1950s unilateral transfers were the main component, and after 1973 public and private borrowing became an additional important element (see Chapter 12).

Investment remained high after 1950 but did not rise further with income; thus by the 1970s it was no higher than the average level for countries with similar levels of income and capital inflow (see Figure 2-2). In contrast, the initial overexpansion of public consumption—accounted for by the myriad tasks devolving on the public sector after 1948 and by the availability of external capital—skyrocketed after 1973 in the wake of the Yom Kippur War, absorbing close to 40 percent of GDP.

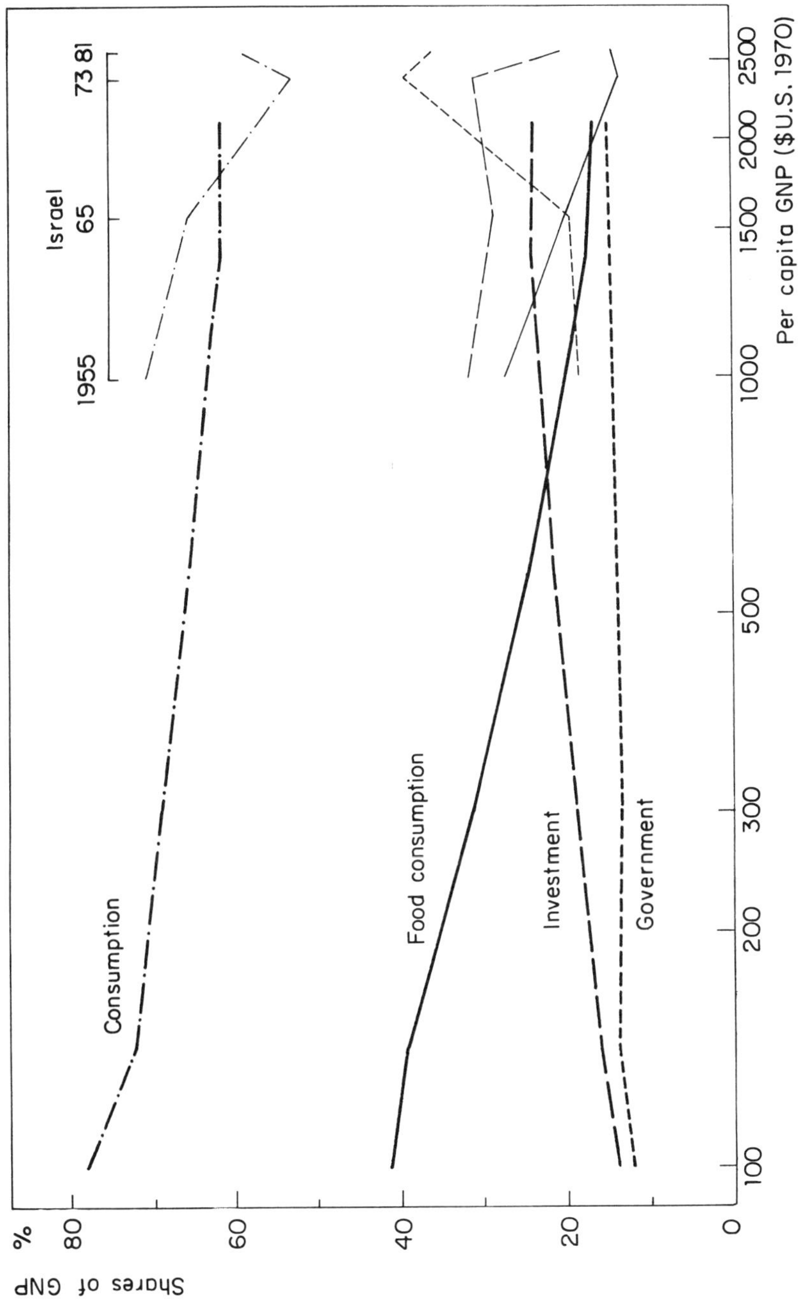

Figure 2-2
Major components of demand.

TABLE 2-7. Distribution of national product by final use, Jewish Palestine and Israel

	1922–1930	1931–1939	1940–1945	1955	1965	1973	1981
Percent of GNP							
Private consumption } (Private and public consumption combined, 1922–1945)	160	115	110	70.7	65.2	53.1	58.7
Public consumption }				19.0	19.7	39.4	36.3
Gross investment	40	45	10	31.7	28.6	31.0	20.2
Exports (E)	30	25	15	11.5	18.7	26.9	43.2
Imports (M)	—	—	—	32.9	32.2	50.4	58.4
$M - E$	100	60	20	21.4	13.5	23.5	15.2
E/M	—	—	—	35	58	53	74
Food consumption							
Percentage of private consumption	64	51	—	38.7	30.6	25.7	24.4
Percentage of GDP	—	—	—	27.4	20.0	13.6	14.3
GNP per capita ($U.S. 1970)	—	—	—	960	1,590	2,410	2,550

Sources: Percentage of GDP: 1922–1945: Approximated from data in Szereszewski (1968) and Jewish Agency, *Statistical Handbook of Jewish Palestine* 1947. 1955–1981: *World Tables* (1980 and 1983). Food consumption: 1922–1945: Jewish Agency (1947), p. 315 (data for 1926 and 1939 refer to urban workers); 1955–1981: CBS, *Statistical Abstracts 1966* and *1982*.

The share of food consumption in demand shows an expected decline. In the early 1950s there was a slight increase, attributable to mass immigration. The newcomers had lower income levels and different initial consumption patterns. The increase in the newcomers' numbers and in food demand per household led to large increases in total food demand at a time when neighboring sources of supply were shut off. This demand posed a serious challenge to the production system.

Intermediate Demand

Even at low income levels a substantial proportion of all goods produced serve as intermediate inputs. Industrialization usually increases the share of intermediates in total gross output while varying their composition from primary to manufacturing output. The increase in the share of intermediate demand for manufactured goods in total gross output is the result of transformation of the production process from a comparatively simple to a more diversified, roundabout system with a higher degree of fabrication and specialization. It also reflects the shift from small-scale handicrafts to large-scale factory production.

In Israel the share of intermediates in total output increased from about 30 percent in the early 1950s to over 50 percent in the late 1970s, about as high as that in advanced countries. A similar deepening in the production structure was also observed in rapidly industrializing countries from the 1960s on. The weight of manufactured intermediates also rose, from about 18 percent in 1958 to almost 30 percent in 1977 (see Syrquin, 1984, table A-2).

The Level and Composition of Trade

The most variable element influencing a country's structure of production is the extent of its participation in the international economy. In small countries the shares of trade and of capital inflows in GDP are relatively high and domestic markets relatively small, and the production structure is therefore much more specialized than in larger countries. The composition of trade and the type of specialization in small countries are largely determined by the availability of natural resources and the development policies adopted. In practice, the accumulation of human and other capital, the evolution of comparative advantage, and the commercial policies pursued have combined to create an export pattern that reinforces the shift from primary goods to industry, implicit in the pattern of domestic demand. The strength and timing of the reorientation of exports have varied: small countries, lacking a broad base of natural resources, have had to develop manufactured exports at an earlier stage than resource-rich countries. Figure 2-3 shows the trade pattern for small (SM) countries, poor in resources and therefore oriented toward manufactured exports, together with Israel's experience since 1955.[17]

Israel's level of exports was abnormally low in 1950. Since then it has steadily increased, accounting for over 40 percent of GDP in the mid-1970s. The share of exports relative to imports climbed from 15 percent in 1950 to over 70 percent in 1978.

The composition of merchandise exports has also changed significantly. In Jewish Palestine citrus products accounted for most of merchandise exports until World War II. When the British market was cut off, citrus exports declined sharply and the sale of manufactures to the British forces and to neighboring countries increased. In 1950 agricultural products (mostly citrus) and polished diamonds (Israel has no diamond deposits) accounted for almost three-quarters of merchandise exports (see Table 2-8). Over time primary exports were replaced by

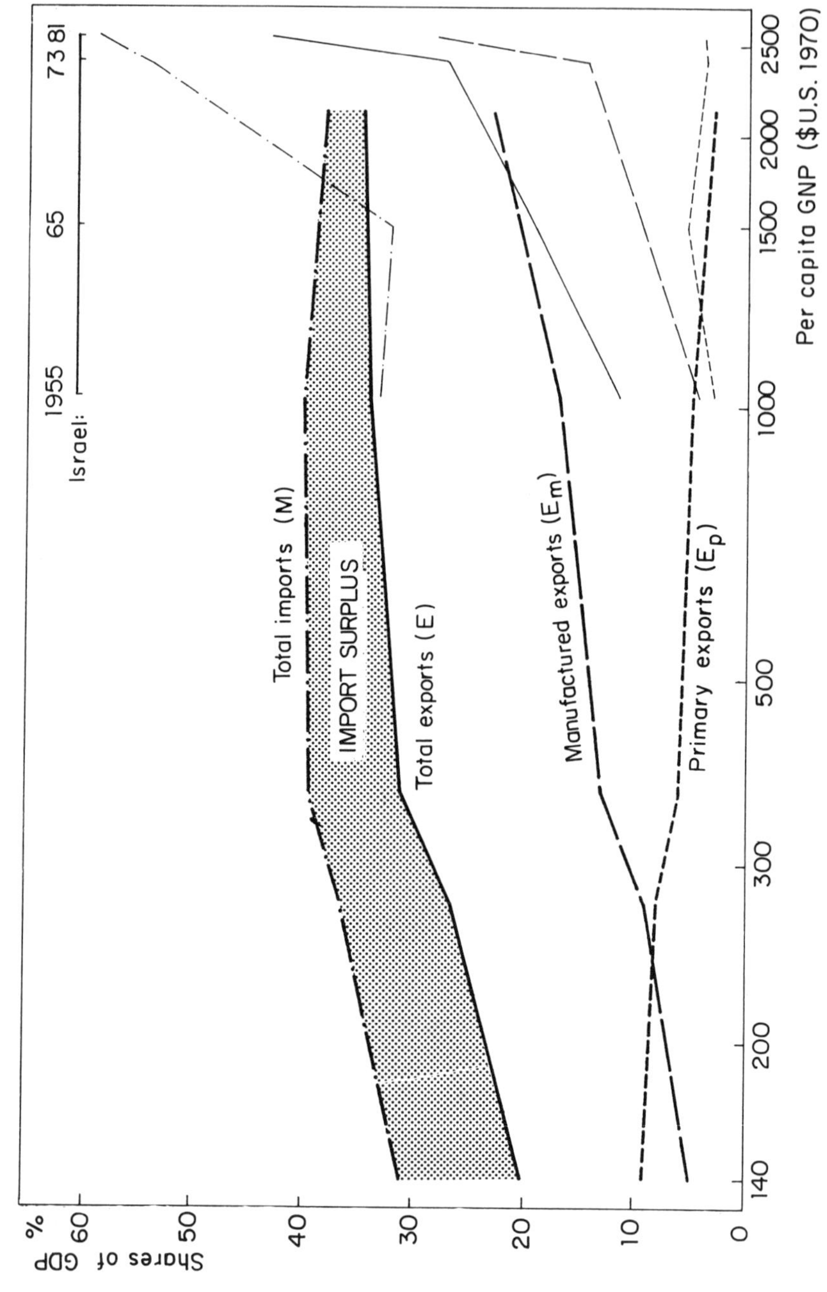

Figure 2-3
Structure of trade: SM countries and Israel.

TABLE 2-8. Structure of merchandise exports, selected years, 1925–1977 (percentages)

	1950	1958	1965	1972	1977
			Merchandise exports		
Primary exports (agriculture and mining)	48.7	32.6	23.8	17.2	14.9
Manufactured exports	51.3	67.4	76.2	82.8	85.1
Food and light industry	21.5	23.1	26.3	39.5	22.9
Diamonds	25.1	28.1	31.7	19.2	29.5
Heavy industry	4.5	13.3	16.4	17.2	21.0
Machinery	0.2	2.8	1.8	6.9	11.7

Export and import ratios

Sector	Share of exports in sectoral gross output			Share of imports in total supply[a]		
	1950	1965	1977	1950	1965	1972
Diamonds	78.5	98.6	86.5	—	—	—
Food products	—	5.6	18.6	—	16.8	20.5
Light industry	2.0	14.4	25.8	14.8	13.5	23.3
Heavy industry	1.6	11.7	25.1	43.3	28.2	52.9
Machinery	0.2	2.6	33.4	65.9	51.4	57.0
Manufacturing	4.1	15.7	33.4	32.9	26.4	40.8

Sources: 1950: Computed from Lubell (1958) and Michaely (1975); 1958–1977: input-output data in Chenery, Robinson, and Syrquin (1986).

Note: Food processing = food, beverages and tobacco; light industry = textiles, clothing, leather, wood products, paper and printing, diamonds, miscellaneous; heavy industry = rubber, chemicals, petroleum, nonmetallic minerals, metal products; machinery = machinery, transport equipment.

a. Imports for 1965–1972 include nominal tariffs to make them compatible with domestic production. Adding tariffs to the 1950 figures would raise the import ratios at least 30 percent, strenthening the impression of import substitution after 1950.

manufactures—initially light industry goods and then increasingly products from heavy industry (chemicals and metal products) and machinery (electronics and transport equipment).[18]

Table 2-8 shows an increase in the ratio of exports to (gross) output in all the broad manufacturing sectors, particularly in the 1950s and 1970s. The change in import ratios by sector gives a rough indication of significant import substitution up to the mid-1960s and of equally significant import liberalization (or import penetration) afterward (see note to Table 2-8 and Pack, 1971). The next subsection provides a quantitative assessment of the contributions of export expansion and import substitution to output growth.

In sum, since 1950 (and even before that) the weight of agricultural products in domestic demand and exports has declined steadily. Rising incomes, the change in comparative advantage, and the high capital inflow ratio led to the expected shift in total demand from primary to industrial production and, in the case of Israel, to public and other services as well. The main departure from the average pattern is that the reduction in the share of private consumption is made up by rising public consumption and not by an increase in investment—which was unusually high to begin with. This difference shows up in the production structure, discussed next.

The Structure of Production

Changes in internal demand and in trade combine to determine the transformation in the structure of output. To provide a convenient frame of reference for long-term comparisons, implied changes in output structure have been derived for "prototype" countries in which demand and trade vary with income in accordance with international estimates for the period after World War II. Figure 2-4 shows the results for a typical small industry-oriented country for the transition range together with comparable information for Jewish Palestine and Israel.

Since changes in domestic demand and trade reinforce each other, the total change in the productive structure is more pronounced. The share of nontradables in GDP seems to increase along with income,[19] but the main feature of the transformation is the change in the composition of tradable output. Value added in primary production falls more than 25 percentage points during the transition. The decline in the share of the labor force engaged in primary activities is even sharper, with important implications for the pattern of relative labor productivity across sectors (discussed below).

It is useful to examine the effects of size and capital inflow on the small, resource-poor country of Figure 2-4 by allowing these parameters to vary in two simulations. Since the main expected change occurs in trading patterns, final demand and interindustry relations are not altered. The first simulation assumes the average patterns of exports, imports, and capital inflows for a country of average size. The second reverts to the small, industry-oriented group and superimposes on the industrial specialization a higher level of capital inflow—twice as large as the average in the group of small industry-oriented countries. These alternative simulations of trade and production patterns are calculated at two

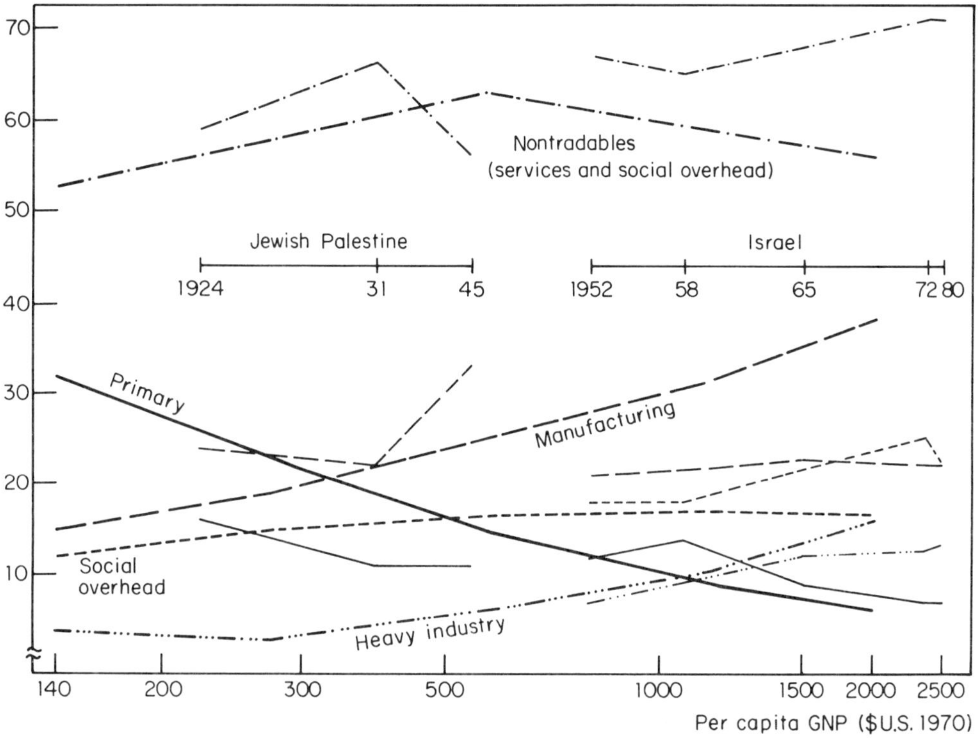

Figure 2-4
Structure of production: SM countries, Jewish Palestine, and Israel.

income levels: $560 and $2,100 ($U.S. 1970), close to actual levels in Israel around 1955 and 1972. Table 2-9 summarizes the results.

The typical small industry-oriented country in Figure 2-4 (SM1 in Table 2-9) starts engaging in manufactured exports much earlier than average. It substitutes foreign capital for primary exports while developing the capacity to export manufactures, often aided by an adequate supply of skilled labor. These patterns of trade and capital inflow increase the share of nontradables at the expense of primary output. Within manufacturing, light industry increases substantially while heavy industry and machinery lag behind. In the high-capital-inflow case (SM2), the effects are intensified; however, once the manufacured exports do not have to expand as quickly as in the SM1 case, light industry expands less rapidly. At higher income levels there is a reduction in the capital inflow share, which results in rapid growth of the heavy industry and machinery sectors.

Israel shares many characteristics with typical SM countries: limited natural resources, adequate skilled labor, and access to foreign capital. The comparison in Table 2-9 highlights some factors peculiar to Israel. The elimination of trade with neighboring markets from 1948 on and the high priority given to internal issues (absorption and settlement of immigrants, defense) are reflected in the low export ratio (3.6 percent in 1950), although they are amply compensated for by high capital inflows. Exports of light industry, primarily textiles and clothing, were never as prominent as in some Asian SMs, for example. The low exports of light industries were more than offset by exports of diamonds and heavy industry and machinery products, which had developed behind protective barriers in the early import-substitution phase. Capital inflows remained high throughout the period 1950–1980.

The share of manufacturing in GDP, which was relatively high in the early 1950s, shows little change over time, mostly because of the continued lag in light industry. In the 1970s these sectors shrank further as Israel seemed to depart from the SM pattern, joining the advanced countries in the shift from light industry to services (known as deindustrialization).

The GNP share, in current prices, originating in the manufacturing sector was not significantly different in 1981 from the level attained half a century earlier in the Jewish economy of Palestine (Figure 2-4). This surprising stability is deceptive, for it seems to suggest an absence of change in the industrial sector. Three points must be made in this connection. First, the figure is based on current price shares. In constant prices the manufacturing share shows a significant increase since the late 1950s, when the relative price of industrial goods starts a continuous decline. Second, any stability at the aggregate level hides considerable changes in composition and in the very nature of the activities covered: the small handicrafts of the 1930s are a far cry from today's enterprises. The share of heavy industry and machinery in GDP almost doubled from 1952 to 1979 while the share of light

TABLE 2-9. Simulated effect of size, trade orientation, and capital inflow as percentage of GNP ($U.S. 1970)

	Income = $560			Israel	Income = $2,100			Israel
	Average pattern	SM1[a]	SM2[b]	1955 ($960)	Average pattern	SM1[a]	SM2[b]	1972 ($2,400)
Capital inflow	1.2	8.6	17.2	26.2	0.6	3.1	6.2	19.1
Trade:								
Primary exports	12.8	6.9	2.8	2.8	9.1	4.5	3.0	2.4
Manufactured exports	5.3	12.3	9.1	4.5	11.6	19.2	18.1	14.7
Total exports	24.1	31.1	29.4	12.1	27.6	34.7	34.0	32.5
Total imports	25.3	39.7	46.6	38.3	28.2	37.8	40.2	51.6
Value added:								
Primary	20.6	15.0	11.0	13.0	9.5	6.2	5.0	7.7
Light industry	15.8	18.9	17.5	12.8	18.9	21.7	21.5	10.5
Heavy industry	8.6	5.8	4.1	8.3	17.2	16.0	15.3	12.6
Manufacturing	(24.4)	(24.7)	(21.6)	(21.1)	(36.1)	(37.8)	(36.8)	(23.1)
Nontradables	54.9	60.2	67.4	65.9	54.4	56.0	58.2	69.2

Sources: Chenery (1979) and unpublished simulations. Israel: trade: Klinov (1984); value added: Gaathon (1971) and Metzer (1983); breakdown for manufacturing from Chenery, Robinson, and Syrquin (1986) and from Bank of Israel information kindly provided by Arie Bregman.

a. SM1 = small, industry-oriented country with average inflow of capital.

b. SM2 = small, high-capital-inflow country.

industry steadily declined. Finally, a certain relation of the economic system may remain stable while the functioning of the system is drastically altered; structural change, when defined as changes in the parameters of the structural model of the economy, has been commonplace in the industrialization process in Israel.

It is customary to regard the production structure of an economy as being determined endogenously by the interplay of changes in demand and trade and by differential productivity growth. In Israel, it was often the economic structure that was determined exogenously, with foreign capital inflows responsible for the adjustment between demand and supply.[20] The stability of agriculture's share in Jewish Palestine and its increase in Israel's early years were the result of ideology and of security considerations. The absence of change in these periods is therefore an indication of the success of policies in averting the transformation that would otherwise have taken place.

The production structure in Israel in the early 1950s, shown in Figure 2-4, resembles that of an advanced country. Since it was not much different in 1950 from what it had been thirty years earlier, it follows that the economic structure had by then reached a stage of maturation beyond the economy's income level (paraphrasing Kaldor's 1966 assessment of the British economy in the 1960s). The limited subsequent change in Israel implies that its income level has been catching up with its economic structure.

The structures of output and employment reflect the preferences of immigrants and continuing efforts to provide them with a minimal standard of living. Most of the immigrants were employed in nonagricultural activities in their home countries, and those who chose (or were directed to) agriculture in Israel entered a relatively high-productivity sector. The difference in labor productivity between sectors never approached that observed in less developed countries (see below).

The shares of construction and services are quite high for 1950–1980. The level of construction activity is highly correlated with immigration and population growth in general. Various explanations have been offered for the overexpansion of services, among them the high capital inflow, which by its nature is commodity intensive, thus substituting for the domestic product of tradables (see, for example, Ofer, 1967).

Beginning in World War II, production in agriculture and manufacturing expanded rapidly, fueled by demand from the British forces and surrounding countries. After 1948 the main challenge was to absorb mass immigration without depressing the standard of living. Highest priority was given to agriculture, which increased its share in output during the first decade.

Manufacturing started at a slower pace. The high level of the war years could not be maintained in the first years of statehood, both because of other priorities and because of the early shortage of foreign exchange, which limited imports of raw materials and created excess capacity in industry. Both factors changed during the 1950s, giving way to a more active industrialization policy based initially on import substitution and then increasingly on export expansion.

Sources of Industrial Growth and Change

It is possible to break down industrial growth and change into its sources on the demand side—similar to the supply-side growth accounting described in "The Growth of Factor Productivity," above—by relating the change in the structure of production to variations in the structures of demand and trade and to changes in the interindustry relations of production (summarized by an input-output table). This section presents one approach to demand-side growth accounting, compares factor use by sector in Israel and other countries, and concludes with a discussion of resource reallocation and productivity growth.

Based on a simple linear model of production, the changes in output in sector i can be expressed as the sum of four factors:[21]

Expansion in final demand in all sectors with constant structures of import and production

Export expansion in all sectors with a constant production structure

Import substitution, or the total effect on sector i of reducing the proportion of total demand supplied from imports

Technological change, or the total effect on sector i of changes in input-output coefficients throughout the economy

Chenery, Robinson, and Syrquin (1986) calculated the sources of growth for a group of semi-industrialized countries in various periods, depending on the availability of input-output data, and for Israel in 1958–1972.[22] Their output figures differ from the shares in Figure 2-4 in two ways: they refer to *real* values in constant prices, and they are gross measures, not value added. In 1958–1972 the relative price of manufacturing declined more than 20 percent.[23] Although the share of manufacturing in value added at current prices remained almost constant, the constant-price share increased in the same period from 16 to 22 percent.

Table 2-10 shows the sources of output growth in Israel as a whole in 1951–1972 and in manufacturing growth in six other countries in approximately the same period. For Japan it was possible to make calculations for the prewar period. In the first period (1951–1958) there was extensive import substitution in manufacturing, which allowed a rapid increase in consumption with a stable level of imports. The increase in exports from the very low levels of 1951 appears as sizable contributions to output growth in primary production (citrus) and manufacturing (primarily diamonds).

TABLE 2-10. Sources of output growth in Israel and in manufacturing in six other countries, various years (percentages)

		Percent average annual growth	Percent of total				Share in output growth
			Domestic demand expansion	Export expansion	Import substitution	Change in I/O coefficients	
Israel							
1951–1958	Agriculture	15.8	72	23	–9	14	18
	Industry	14.6	48	14	24	14	43
	Services	7.5	60	20	–31	51	39
1958–1965	Primary	7.3	63	38	11	–12	7
	Manufacturing	13.6	57	26	12	5	39
	Services	9.9	93	23	–4	–12	54
1965–1972	Primary	5.6	32	90	–18	–4	5
	Manufacturing	11.3	76	50	–37	11	46
	Services	7.9	66	30	–2	6	49
Manufacturing							
Korea	1955–1963	10.4	57	12	42	–11	55
	1963–1973	20.4	53	48	–2	1	58
Taiwan	1956–1961	11.2	35	27	26	12	46
	1966–1971	21.1	35	57	4	4	68
Mexico	1950–1975	7.7	81	8	3	8	42
Turkey	1953–1973	8.0	77	7	4	12	44
Japan	1914–1955	4.2	70	13	10	7	51
	1955–1970	13.3	76	18	–2	8	59
Norway	1953–1969	5.2	56	50	–18	12	44

Sources: Israel (1951–1958): adapted from Pack (1971) (see appendix to Syrquin, 1984); all others Chenery, Robinson, and Syrquin (1986).

From 1958 on, manufactured exports begin increasing very rapidly, accounting for over one-quarter of total growth in manufacturing output in 1958–1965 and for one-half of output growth in 1965–1972. Import substitution remains quite significant in the early 1960s, but after 1965 it becomes negative and large, especially in heavy industry, where it more than offsets the export contribution, making sectoral growth depend on the expansion of domestic demand. Negative import substitution (or import liberalization) may be the result of more efficient intraindustry specialization, especially when it coincides with high export growth (as in Korea and Taiwan), or of a loss of comparative advantage in manufacturing and a shift in domestic demand to services, including the rapidly growing government sector (as in the case of light industry in Norway and Japan). The large domestic demand contribution in 1965–1972 probably reflects the investment boom after the Six Day War and the increase in private consumption of durables, accompanied by the ever-high capital inflow.

The variety of national experiences summarized in Table 2-10 provides a useful perspective on the magnitudes presented for Israel. In all countries except Norway (for the years shown) there is an initial period of import substitution in manufacturing. In large countries whose development strategy was based on prolonged import substitution (represented by Turkey and Mexico), the contribution of export expansion is rather modest. At the other extreme, Korea and Taiwan shift from import substitution to a very strong export expansion, which leads to a rapid acceleration in industrial growth. Between these two groups are Israel and Norway, with sizable contributions by exports, though largely offset by import liberalization.

The last column of Table 2-10 shows the contribution of manufacturing to total (gross) output growth. The incremental share in Israel is similar to that of the large inward-oriented countries or the Asian countries during the import substitution phase. The counterpart of this relatively low contribution of manufacturing to output growth is a high share of services, which rises with income (Norway) and with capital inflow (Israel).

After 1972 the growth of manufacturing and total output slowed considerably in Israel. The real share of manufacturing in value added remained almost constant from 1972 to 1981 (see Chapter 3). Input-output data for 1977 suggest that in 1972–1977 the share of manufacturing in gross output may have declined slightly. The contribution of manufacturing to output growth after 1972 was therefore not higher than 40 percent, a level comparable to that reported for the early 1960s in Table 2-10.

Total exports, particularly industrial exports, continued to expand rapidly after 1972 (see Table 2-7). This expansion probably mitigated the extent of the slowdown in growth. In terms of the decomposition of growth shown in Table 2-10, exports after 1972 undoubtedly account for an even larger fraction of growth than in earlier periods.

Factor Use and Resource Allocation

The foregoing analysis regards economic growth as one aspect of the transformation of the productive structure led by changes in demand and comparative advantage. The analyses of separate sources of growth do not directly consider the accumulation of primary inputs and their productivity. This section considers factor accumulation in a disaggregated framework as a first step toward integration of productivity growth at the sectoral level with the reallocation effects of changes in demand and trade that occur as income levels rise. Given intersectoral differences in factor returns, structural change emerges as an essential component in the rate and pattern of aggregate growth. It can retard growth if its pace is too slow or its direction inefficient, but it can become an additional source of growth if it improves the allocation of resources.

Tables 2-11 and 2-12 present the structures of employment and capital utilization for the simulated average pattern and various countries and for Israel, respectively. A comparison of the changes in the output structure (Figure 2-4) and in the composition of factor utilization reveals a similar expected shift in resources from primary production to manufacturing (and then to services), but the timing and magnitude of these shifts differ significantly.

The difference between the pattern of variation in the composition of employment and the one in output reflects the variation in labor productivity across sectors (relative labor productivities and relative factor proportions are given in Tables 2-11 and 2-13).

The productivity gap between primary production and industry is greatest in the middle-income range ($700–$1500). At high income levels relative wages increase, capital intensity in agriculture rises faster than in other sectors, and the gap in labor productivity narrows. In the advanced nations during the period 1950–1976 there was a marked reduction in the spread of productivity between sectors (see Maddison, 1980a). In most countries productivity in agriculture in 1950 was well below average productivity for the economy, and although the gap has narrowed significantly, differentials in productivity persist.[24] Since the agricultural sector in these countries does not exceed 10 percent of output or of the labor force, the importance of the productivity gap has of course diminished.

In Israel the productivity differential among sectors has always been relatively small. The gap widened in 1948–1951 but narrowed afterward. Agriculture was never a backward, low-productivity sector, partly because of its very intensive use of capital (see Table 2-13). As in other developed and less-developed countries, product per worker in services went from above to below the economywide average. The relatively low increase in productivity in services, coupled with its increasing share in employment, played a role in productivity slowdown in the 1970s.

TABLE 2-11. Factor use and relative productivity in selected countries (percentages)

Factors	Average pattern, per capita income in $U.S. 1970		Mexico	Japan		Korea	Taiwan	Belgium	France
	$560	$2,100	1975	1955	1970	1973	1971	1973	1973
Employment									
Primary	48	21	40	43	20	38	37	5	13
Light industry	10	15	11	10	12	13	14	34	28
Heavy industry	3.5	6	11	8	15	6	10		
Capital stock									
Primary	17	13	15	22	13	10	13	5	6
Light industry	10	12	9	11	11	8	11	33	25
Heavy industry	7	14	11	13	26	9	12		
Capital intensity									
Agriculture	34	52	25	48	62	27	36	91	41
Manufacturing	124	126	89	132	139	93	93	98	87
Social overhead	408	289	200	286	175	262	370	159	104
Services	97	57	163	91	58	136	95	81	124
Labor productivity									
Agriculture	39	34	26	46	27	57	41	89	45
Manufacturing	182	175	115	138	152	175	138	107	115
Social overhead	161	131	107	118	110	123	123	108	102
Services	138	84	177	148	96	96	132	94	105

Sources: Belgium and France: Stein and Lee (1977); all others: Chenery, Robinson, and Syrquin (1986).

TABLE 2-12. Industrial distribution of employment and capital, selected years

	Jews			Total population				
	1931	1945	1951	1931	1958	1965	1972	1979
Per capita income ($U.S. 1970)	390	540	800[a]	—	1,067	1,590	2,370	2,490
Employment (percent)								
Agriculture[b]	22.1	13.4	13.8	55.3	17.8	12.3	8.6	6.9
(Non-Jewish agriculture)		(50)		(65)	(49)	(37)	(19)	(12)
Industry	23.8	31.1	23.6	12.1	22.8	24.5	24.0	24.0
Light	17.7	18.2	16.3[c]	—	12.7	13.1	12.6	11.6
Heavy	4.1	12.9	7.3[c]	—	10.1	11.4	11.4	12.4
Social overhead	14.2	55.5 (Social overhead and Services combined)	16.5	10.2	17.1	19.0	19.7	16.9
Services	39.9		46.1	22.4	42.3	44.2	47.7	52.2
Capital (nondwelling) stock (percent)								
Primary	—	—	—	—	24.1	21.4	16.5	14.3
Irrigation	—	—	—	—	11	9	6	4
Manufacturing	—	—	—	—	25.0	21.5	21.5	23.3
Light industry	—	—	—	—	11.8	10.2	10.3	9.9
Heavy industry	—	—	—	—	13.2	11.3	11.2	13.4
Social overhead	—	—	—	—	34.9	38.7	41.2	39.5
Services	—	—	—	—	16.0	18.4	20.8	22.9

Sources: Employment 1931–1951: Ofer (1967); 1958–1979: Chenery, Robinson and Syrquin (1986). Non-Jewish employment 1931 and 1945: Ben-Porath (1966); other years: CBS, *Statistical Abstract*, various issues. Capital (excluding irrigation): Chenery, Robinson and Syrquin (1986). Irrigation: Gaathon (1971), Buch (1982).

a. Total population.

b. Includes mining from 1958 (less than 0.5 percent).

c. The internal distribution refers to 1952 (source: Kuznets, 1960).

The industrial sector accounted for a high share of employment and capital use in Israel's early years and before. Despite very high investment, however, the relative capital-labor ratio in manufacturing did not increase, and even declined. The reasons are to be found in the composition of investment, which has always included a very high level of construction (see Chapter 4). The high level of construction activity shows up in the high share of employment in "social overhead."

TABLE 2-13. Capital intensity and labor productivity: sectoral relatives (total = 100)

	1922	1931	1945	1951	1958	1965	1972	1979
Relative capital intensity								
Agriculture	—	—	—	—	132	154	164	183
Manufacturing	—	—	—	—	109	88	90	97
Social overhead	—	—	—	—	204	203	209	233
Services	—	—	—	—	38	41	43	44
Relative labor productivity								
Agriculture	61	51	79	44	59	67	75	114
Manufacturing	101	94	130	106	81	90	108	101
Light industry	—	—	—	—	88	85	97	85
Heavy industry	—	—	—	—	72	96	119	116
Social overhead	116	122	88	113 {	100	102	115	131
Services					127	112	93	87

Sources: 1922–1931: Szereszewski (1968); 1945–1951: (Jews) Ofer (1967); 1958–1979: Chenery, Robinson, and Syrquin (1986).

The agricultural share of factor utilization has declined over time as expected, but the resources released have gone into services rather than into manufacturing. In all the advanced nations the share of employment in manufacturing has been falling since the late 1960s (see, for example, OECD, 1979). After 1973 the same trend began in Israel.

The structure of employment of Israel's non-Jewish labor force differs significantly from the average, resembling that of a typical LDC.[25] The proportion engaged in agriculture is two to three times higher than for the total labor force and has declined rapidly with the increase in income (Table 2-12). Part of the increase in the measured share of agriculture during the early 1950s merely reflects this difference.

Resource Shifts and Productivity Growth

Structural change in the productive structure has not been important in the growth of total factor productivity in Israel. For broad sectors the change has been minor and the productivity gap limited. Other types of resource reallocation have been more important. Differences in productivity were not large *across* broad sectors, but at a more disaggregated level they were present and widened during the period of mass immigration. As a matter of social policy the newcomers were accorded a standard of living higher than their initial productivity. As Kuznets aptly described it (1960a, p. 1657):

> Given the intent and desire to develop an economy that would yield a relatively high product per capita, a fairly high standard of consumption had to be established. Recent immigrants would, by and large, probably not reach a level of productivity that would yield income sufficient to provide for savings until *after* some years in the country—a period varying from group to group, and even person to person, depending upon previous training and other factors. Hence, at any given time, the Jews in Palestine and Israel comprised settled groups whose product was above, and recent groups whose product was below, their consumption. The former just about offset the latter, and this in itself was quite an accomplishment when the proportional weight of the recent settlers was strikingly raised by large immigration.

Over time the productivity differential was reduced, partly through capital formation. Bruno (1968) calculated that from 1953 to 1965 the reduction of disequilibrium in factor markets accounted for about one-quarter of aggregate productivity growth (1.4 percent). A more recent reallocation has been the increased weight of the public sector, particularly of well-educated labor, in output and employment (see Chapter 5). The most significant shift in the past twenty years has, of course, been the increase in trade. A more outward orientation has been credited with such beneficial effects as greater capacity utilization, exploitation of economies of scale, and more efficient management exposed to competition from abroad. In an econometric study of growth in semi-industrialized countries (including Israel) in 1964–1973, Feder (1983) found that reallocation from the less efficient nonexport sector to the higher-productivity export sector had a significant effect on growth. This shift into exports fully accounted for the superior performance of the Asian countries and was clearly also an important element in Israel's high growth.

Conclusion

A distinctive feature of the Jewish economy of Palestine was its ability to cope with abrupt changes in the environment. During the Mandate, economic advances were interrupted by recessions related to immigration cycles and by political disturbances. The creation of both a separate economy and an autonomous "government" was a response to hostile neighbors and to less than friendly Mandate authorities. In 1948 the economy was severely disrupted by war and by the departure of hundreds of thousands of Arabs, and its relative isolation became total. Until 1979, when a peace treaty was signed with Egypt, Israel had no possibilities for regional specialization. In 1948–1951 a massive influx of immigrants doubled the population, and the economy expanded on a broad front; no sector was allowed to become a crippling bottleneck. The government made large investments in the development and modernization of agriculture and infrastructure, and their effect was magnified by the rapid growth of factor productivity in these sectors. Industry, consisting of a set of discrete layers fostered by the capitalist immigration of the 1930s and the stimulus of World War II, lagged at first. Though heavily protected, it was hindered by material shortages and low capacity utilization, reflected in the initial poor showing of factor productivity. Thereafter it became a leading sector until it had to contend with the growing role of public and other services.

In 1950 Israel differed in many respects from countries with the same level of income. Over time it experienced a regression toward the mean, population growth slowed, and the initial high shares of services and investment stayed constant while income trebled, the distribution of income became less equitable, and the impressive growth performance became average or less.

The prolonged slump since the mid-1970s and the accompanying spiraling inflation and mounting debt are not nearly as surprising as the economy's maintenance of such a high growth level for so long. Much of the explanation lies in Israel's unique circumstances. Unlike other LDCs, Israel had few or no internal institutional barriers to overcome such as an inefficient semifeudal agrarian system. And unlike the older developed countries of Europe, in the earlier stages of development it had no entrenched interest groups to contend with.[26] Decades of rapid growth, of heavy reliance on unilateral transfers and other external capital, and of an ever-growing public sector provided the proper environment for vested interests to emerge and mature. In the early 1970s Israel experienced a confluence of shocks, some transitory and some more lasting. The Yom Kippur War, the energy crises, recession in the advanced countries, and the slowing of population growth combined to cast doubts on Israel's capacity to accommodate divergent interests. A zero-sum view of the economy and society seems to have eroded the long-standing national consensus on objectives. The next decade will tell whether the proper reference group in a future international comparison will be Scandinavia, as long-term trends indicate, or South America, as the recent past suggests.

3

The Slowdown of Economic Growth: A Passing Phase or the End of the Big Spurt?

Jacob Metzer

In 1973, after over twenty years of rapid economic growth in which gross national product rose about 10 percent annually, Israel's growth rate slowed to an average of 3 percent a year. This change dominates the growth story of Israel (as well as that of many other countries) in the 1970s and is the focal point of the present chapter, which documents, analyzes, and interprets Israel's growth over the period 1961–1981. The chapter is divided into four major sections. The first presents an overview of the economy's growth performance and characteristics and describes the leading role of the nondwelling business sector in determining its growth patterns. The second section discusses the aggregate growth record of the business sector in a growth-accounting framework and concentrates on the differences between the pre- and post-1973 patterns of product, inputs, and productivity changes. The third section disaggregates the business sector's growth slowdown, analyzing factors such as inter- versus intraindustry changes and the growth performance of key industries. The final section summarizes and interprets the growth-affecting changes in aggregate supply and demand, focusing on the basic question posed by the 1973 turnabout: is the Israeli economy at present in a transitory (though protracted) lull or in a new, secular phase of slow growth?

Overview

A convenient starting point for observing Israel's economic growth performance is 1952. This year marked the end of the country's period of infancy—the war of independence, the redrawing of borders, the formation of institutions, and a massive influx of immigrants (see Kuznets, 1973a). In the next two decades (1952–1961 and 1962–1971) there were relatively few changes in the average annual growth rates of population (3.9 and 3.4 percent respectively), total product (9.2 and 9.0 percent), and product per capita (5.2 and 5.4 percent). In the third decade (1972–1981) a sharp downward trend set in: population grew at an average annual rate of 2.5 percent, GDP at 4.2 percent, and per capita GDP at 1.6 percent.

This slowdown of growth is evident not only in the decadal averages but also in the annual data. As Figure 3-1 clearly shows, the annual rate of change in GDP at factor cost started falling in 1973 and never regained the aggregate growth rates of any of the years 1954–1972 (except for the three recession years, 1965–1967). The annual data also reveal the relative stability of the growth rates until 1973, especially from 1955 to 1972. The coefficients of variation of the GDP growth rates (0.38 for 1955–1972) rose to 0.65 for 1973–1981. Moreover, when the sharp recession and equally rapid recovery of 1965–1969 are excluded, the coefficient of variation for the years before 1973 declines to no more than 0.15.

The fact that economic growth since 1973 has been not only considerably slower but also less stable means (in retrospect, of course) that the growth prospects of the past thirteen years have also been far less certain. This relative unpredictability may have had an adverse effect on both investments and productivity and, through them, on growth itself.

Total GDP at factor cost can be divided into three basic components. One is the product of the nondwelling business sector, which includes both the final goods and services produced by the private sector and the paid-for goods and services produced by the public sector. In Israel this component generated about 74 percent of total GDP at factor cost in 1973–1982. The second component is the flow of dwelling services, which accounted for about 9 percent of GDP; and the third is the product of the unpaid-for public services such as defense, internal security, and education, which made for the remaining 17 percent of total GDP (see Metzer, 1983, table A-2).

Since the mid-1950s (as shown in Figure 3-1) the growth pattern of total GDP has been most closely related to that of the nondwelling business sector, with public services and ownership of dwellings diverging quite substantially from the overall growth path. The correlations between GDP growth and the growth of public and dwelling services were only 0.24 and 0.26 respectively.

The relatively milder changes in the growth rate of dwellings throughout the period had a smoothing effect on overall growth. Public services play a similar role because of their somewhat anticyclical pattern, a major component of which was the increased defense expenditure in 1967 and an even greater one in 1973. Hence the changes in the business sector's product growth rates were usually much sharper than those in total GDP. In other words, the nondwelling business sector shaped the economy's growth path: thus it seems appropriate, in documenting and analyzing the economy's growth performance, to concentrate on this sector's growth record.

This emphasis, however, should not be taken to mean that the government played only a minor role in determining the economy's growth rate, or that it is

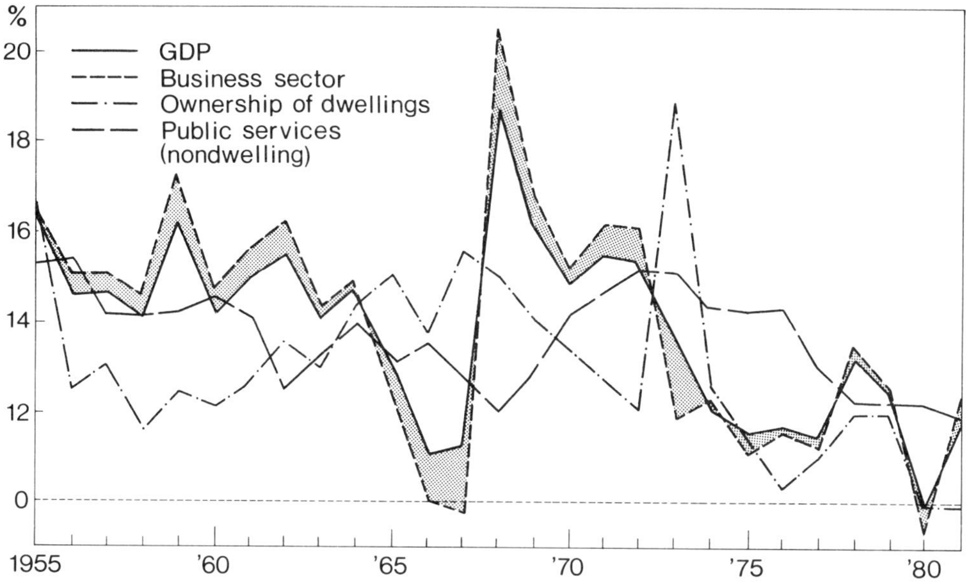

Figure 3-1
Growth rates of gross domestic product and sectoral aggregates, 1955–1981. (Metzer, 1983, table A-2, columns 1, 2, 3, 8.)

excluded from the analysis. Apart from its allocation policies, the government affects production in the business sector through purchases of locally produced goods and services (about 25 percent of the business sector's gross product in 1977–1981) and through direct production of goods and services, which is part of the business sector's product—including goods and services produced for the government's own use, such as defense hardware. It therefore follows that the level of and changes in economic activity in the nondwelling business sector reflect both the private economy and the government's economic activity and policies.

The following discussion is based on a comparative analysis of growth attributes in 1961–1972 and 1973–1981. The year 1961 was chosen as the starting date because it marks the beginning of the continuous Bank of Israel series of real product growth rates by industry, which serve as a basis for the following estimated growth rates of the business sector's product. (See also Manzly, 1970, 1980, for pioneering growth accounting of the Israeli business sector.)

The Slowdown of Growth: An Aggregate View

Table 3-1 summarizes the growth profile of the business sector's product for 1961–1981, including average annual growth rates of GDP, worker hours, gross

TABLE 3-1. Growth attributes in the business sector (average annual rate of change, 1961–1981

	1961–1972		1973–1981	
	Percentage points	Percentage distribution	Percentage points	Percentage distribution
Gross domestic product (GDP) at factor cost	9.7		3.4	
Labor				
Employed persons	3.6		1.5	
Total hours of work	3.9		1.0	
Gross capital stock	8.9		6.0	
Total factor productivity (TFP)	4.2		0.6	
Capital				
Per employed person	5.1		4.5	
Per hour of work	5.0		5.0	
GDP				
Per employed person	6.1		1.9	
Per hour of work	5.8		2.4	
Per unit of capital	0.8		−2.6	
Contribution of growth —				
Total product				
Hours of work	2.5	25.8	0.6	17.6
Capital	3.0	30.9	2.2	64.7
TFP	4.2	43.3	0.6	17.6
Total	9.7	100.0	3.4	100.0
Product per hour of work				
Capital	1.6	27.6	1.8	75.0
TFP	4.2	72.4	0.6	25.0
Total	5.8	100.0	2.4	100.0

Source: Metzer (1983), table A-4.

capital stock, and residual productivity. The picture is one of overall slowdown of all growth attributes for 1961–1972 and 1973–1981. Particularly noticeable is the modest decline in the growth rate of capital in comparison with GDP, labor input, and productivity, which leads to the peculiar result of a slowdown in the annual growth of GDP per worker hour (from 5.8 to 2.4 percent) but no change in the growth of capital per worker hour (it increased at an annual rate of 5 percent in both periods). The picture changes only slightly when labor input is measured by employed persons instead of by worker hours: the annual growth of product per employed person declined from 6.1 percent in 1961–1972 to 1.9 percent in 1973–1981, while that of capital per employed person declined moderately, from 5.1 to 4.5 percent.

Another reflection of the modest decline in the growth of capital relative to GDP is the absolute decline in GDP per unit of capital by 2.6 percent a year in 1973–1981, after a slight increase (0.8 percent a year) before 1973.

These trends raise questions about the connection between capital stock as used in the growth accounting calculations here and the flow of capital services actually used in production. These questions are related to changes in capital utilization on the one hand, and to the accuracy of the capital stock estimates on the other (see Manzly, 1980; Gross and Meron, 1981).

The different intensities of change in capital, labor, and total factor productivity are also reflected in the changes observed in their relative contributions to product growth in the two periods, as shown in the lower part of Table 3-1. Until 1973, the rise in total factor productivity was the major growth-generating factor, accounting for about 43 percent of total product growth and for 72 percent of the increase in product per worker hour. Labor and capital contributed respectively only 26 and 31 percent of total product growth. In the latter period, however, capital dominated the scene, owing to the relatively mild slowdown in its growth, and thus accounted for about 65 percent of total growth, while the contribution of total factor productivity declined to 18 percent of the rise in total product and to 25 percent of the increase in product per worker hour. Thus in the two periods the relative contributions of capital per unit of labor and of total factor productivity to the rise of labor productivity were reversed.

These trends, however, should not be taken to mean that total factor productivity played only a minor role in shaping the post-1973 growth profile. It is precisely because of the sharp decline in its contribution to the growth of product that the change in the rate of productivity accounted for 57.1 percent of the reduction in GDP growth between the two periods. Table 3-2 shows this fact clearly by breaking down the change in aggregate growth rates into its basic components. Following changes in productivity come changes in the growth rates of labor, which account for 28.6 percent of the overall growth slowdown, with capital adding another 15.9 percent.

An interesting comparison can be drawn between the components of the 1973–1981 slowdown and those of the mid-1960s recession. The major difference lies in the role of labor vis-à-vis those of capital and productivity. Unlike in 1973–1981, the dominant growth-reducing factor during the recession was the drop in labor input, which accounted for 68 percent of the overall decline between 1961–1964

TABLE 3-2. Components of the decline in the growth rate of the business sector's GDP between 1961–1972 and 1973–1981

Contributing factors	Percentage points	Percentage distribution
Growth rate of labor	−1.8	−28.6
Growth rate of capital	−1.0	−15.9
Factor shares	0.1	1.6
Growth rate of total factor productivity	3.6	−57.1
Total (growth rate of GDP)	−6.3	−100.0

Source: Metzer (1983), table A-4.

and 1965–1967. The difference stems from the fact that in the mid-1960s employment adjusted by contracting sharply, as one would expect in a classic demand-generated recession. In contrast, the more recent slowdown was more of a full-employment recession that poses substantial problems of characterization. These issues will be addressed in greater detail in the final section.

Another interesting implication of the differences in the various growth attributes' patterns of change has to do with the nature of the statistical association between them. For the two decades as a whole, the change in growth of GDP was highly and positively correlated with changes in labor input and in total factor productivity (with correlation coefficients of 0.873 and 0.862 respectively); the latter was also positively associated (with a coefficient of 0.787) with the percentage change in product per unit of labor. Changes in capital stock, on the other hand, were not positively correlated with any of the other growth attributes; nor were the growth rates of capital and product per unit of labor associated with one another.

These observations suggest that the link between changes in capital stock and the growth of productivity and product has been relatively weak in the Israeli economy. These and related issues are dealt with in the following subsections, which examine in detail the patterns of change of labor, capital, and productivity.

Labor and Employment

The two quantitative components of the change in labor input are the number of employed persons and the number of worker hours per year per employed person. The latter may be viewed as at least a partial indicator of the intensity of labor utilization in production. Table 3-3 summarizes these components and some of their underlying factors in annual averages for 1961–1972 and 1973–1981.

Growth of employment in the business sector slowed substantially, from 3.6

TABLE 3-3. Annual average rates of change in population, labor force, employment, and worker hours, 1961–1981 (percentages)

	1961–1972	1973–1981
Israeli residents age 14+	3.8	2.5
Civilian labor force in population age 14+:		
Total	51.6	49.0
Men	73.6	64.9
Women	29.2	33.4
Civilian labor force	3.2	2.5
Employed persons		
Total economy	3.5	2.3
Business sector	3.2	1.4
Public services	4.3	4.6
Total employment (Israelis and residents of the administered territories)		
Employed persons		
Total economy	3.8	2.4
Business sector	3.6	1.5
Public services	4.3	4.6
Weekly hours per employed person		
Total economy	0.1	–0.9
Business sector	0.1	–0.8
Public services	0	–1.3

Sources: 1961–1977: CBS, *Statistical Abstracts* and *Labor Force Surveys*, various years; 1978–1981: Bank of Israel, *Annual Report 1979*, chap. XI; *1980, 1981,* chap. IV.

percent annually in the earlier period to 1.5 percent annually in the later one. As shown in Table 3-3, four factors caused this decline.

1. Annual growth of population age 14+ slowed primarily because of a decline in net immigration from 3.8 percent in 1961–1972 to 2.5 percent in 1973–1981.

2. The average rate of labor force participation declined in the two periods from 51.6 percent to 49.0 percent. A reduction in the participation rate of men from 73.6 to 64.9 percent outweighed the increase in women's rates of participation from 29.2 to 33.4 percent. Part of the reduced participation by men age 35–55 (from about 95 percent to 90 percent) may stem from a lower incidence of income reporting. The incentive for underreporting has increased with the broadening of the tax base since the 1975 income tax reform and the later introduction of the value-added tax. The possible increase in the time devoted to financial and speculative activities associated with the inflationary spiral of the 1970s may have had a similar effect in reducing the recorded labor force participation rate and the

number of hours worked. Among those age 21 – 34 the decline in participation was due to extension of both military service and higher education.

3. The relative share of employment in the business sector dropped from 77.2 percent of total employment in 1961 – 1972 to only 73.6 percent in 1973 – 1981. However, employment in public services increased 4.6 percent annually in the latter period, compared with only 4.3 percent earlier.

4. The influx of employees from the administered territories slowed down in 1973 – 1981. Employment of Arab workers from the territories in the business sector increased very rapidly in 1968 – 1972 — 80 percent annually — and its share of total employed persons in the business sector rose from a mere 0.7 percent in 1968 to 7.1 percent in 1973 (see sources for Table 3-3). This rapid increase explains the difference between the 3.6 percent annual growth in the business sector's overall employment and the annual rise of only 3.2 percent in the number of Israelis employed in this sector in 1961 – 1972. From 1973 on, growth of employment from the territories slowed considerably, to 4.9 percent a year, and its share in the business sector's employment increased only slightly, converging with the annual growth rates of total and Israeli employment in the sector (1.5 and 1.4 percent respectively).

The pattern of change in worker hours per employee was much the same as that of population and labor force participation, declining from a fairly constant level of about 40 hours of work per week in the earlier period to around 37.5 hours thereafter. Part of this decline stemmed from the rise in temporary absenteeism, from an average of 5.8 percent of employees in 1961 – 1972 to 9.3 percent in 1973 – 1981 (CBS, *Labor Force Surveys*). The exclusion of temporarily absent workers from these calculations results in a lower rate of decline (2.5 percent instead of 6.0 percent) in the average number of weekly hours per employed person.

Another factor contributing to the decline in the number of worker hours is the increase in part-time employment, from 17 percent of all Israeli employed persons in 1961 – 1972 to 21.8 percent in 1973 – 1981. This rise reflects primarily the monotonic rise in the proportion of women in overall employment since 1967 — the part-time employment rate of women is about three times that of men. Gender-based differences in part-time employment also account for the sharper decline in the number of weekly hours in public services than in the business sector; the proportion of women in the former sector grew faster than in the latter during the 1970s.

The overall decline in the number of worker hours per employed person was certainly both a response and a contributing factor to the slowdown of the 1970s. The response effect of this reduction in the utilization of labor seems particularly plausible in view of the very high level of employment in the economy as a whole in 1973 – 1981. Except in 1980 and 1981, when unemployment reached 4.8 and 5.1 percent of the Israeli labor force, it never exceeded 4 percent after 1970.

Moreover, the average unemployment rate of 3.2 percent in 1973–1979 was lower than the 3.4 percent average for the boom years (1970–1972), and the 1973–1981 average was only slightly higher—3.6 percent (CBS, *Statistical Abstracts*).

The low level of unemployment despite a recession in growth may, to some extent, have reflected the rising uncertainty associated with both the high variability of product growth during the 1970s and the unexpected changes in relative product prices due to inflation, which were found to be substantial as early as 1973–1975 (Kleiman, 1977a). This uncertainty, together with various institutional constraints on dismissing employees, could have increased employers' tendency to hoard labor, thereby shifting a larger portion of the adjustment in labor inputs to the hours-of-work component.[1] Another adjustment mechanism may have been the declining influx of employees from the administered territories. However, the extent to which the downward adjustment of labor input was incomplete obviously contributed to the slowdown in the growth of measured productivity.

Another factor that helped prevent an increase in recorded unemployment in 1973–1981 was the offsetting role played by the public sector, which increased its employment share (Table 3-3). If the actual business-sector employment share is taken as given and the share of the business sector in total employment is assumed to have remained constant at 76 percent (as in the early 1970s), the counterfactual unemployment rate of Israeli workers, net of the public services "safety valve" effect for 1973–1981, is 8.5 percent, in contrast to the actual rate of 3.6 percent for the same period. This is obviously an upper limit, because it implicitly assumes that the entire relative increment to employment in public services after 1973 was generated by the growth slowdown and that there was no substitution between Israelis and employees from the territories. Nevertheless, it does indicate that the public sector's accelerated absorption of employment may have played a significant role in keeping down the level of recorded unemployment in the economy as a whole, probably by converting some of it into disguised unemployment.

The most prominent qualitative changes in the labor force in 1961–1981 were the increase in the number of school years completed by Israeli employed persons (the percentage of those who had completed nine or more years increased from about 46 percent in the mid-1960s to 70 percent in the late 1970s; see CBS, *Statistical Abstracts*) and the already mentioned rise in the shares of both women and (from 1968 on) workers from the administered territories in overall employment.

Other things being equal, one would expect the quality of productive labor to rise with an increase in the number of school years per worker, and to decline with the rising employment share of women. The gender effect stems from the self- and socially imposed constraints of family and parenthood, which tend to reduce the number of hours worked, job duration, investment in human capital, and mobility of women, all of which have an adverse effect on the quality of their measured labor input. The rising share of employees from the territories,who tend to have fewer skills and (possibly) less motivation than Israeli workers, would also be expected to affect labor quality negatively. However, the rate of change of worker hours quality-corrected for sex, schooling, and employment from the territories was essentially equal to the growth rate of uncorrected labor input in the economy as a whole in 1973–1980 (1.07 and 1.11 percent a year respectively).[2]

These findings, as well as separate comparisons between current and constant wage differential figures for each quality attribute, show that what caused the trivial order of magnitude of the quality adjustment were not only the offsetting effects of the various attributes but also the declining differentials between the wages of employees from the territories and those of Israeli employed persons (CBS, *Income Surveys;* Meron, 1982, pp. 52–53). Over time the latter substantially reduced the negative effects of employment from the territories.[3]

Another element affecting quality change, and one that has been of particular importance in Israel, is the economic absorption of immigrants. Part of this process is no doubt reflected in the increase in the education level of the labor force, but several other factors—such as learning a new language, adapting to new working conditions and requirements, making adjustments of skill and occupation, and accumulating general and specific job experience—also played a role. Although it is difficult, if not impossible, to obtain direct measurable data on such parameters, some relevant inferences can be drawn from the pattern of wage differentials by continent of origin, corrected for age and education. In an article on the economic development of Israel based on observed wage patterns, Kuznets (1973a) suggested that it may have taken about twenty years for a new immigrant to be fully absorbed and completely integrated in Israel, regardless of country of origin. Lamdany's (1982) calculations show that starting in 1951—the peak year of immigration—the average length of residence of the foreign-born increased monotonically, reaching the twenty-year mark in 1973. Assuming that the length-of-residence profile of employed persons was similar to that of the entire immigrating population, one may infer that the economic absorption of immigrants lasted from 1951–1952 to about 1973–1974. During this period immigrants' quality of labor probably did increase along with their average length of residence. After 1973, however, no appreciable improvement in the quality of labor can be ascribed to this factor. Thus the overall quality of the labor force probably remained relatively constant in 1973–1981.

Capital Stock and Services

The differential growth patterns of capital, GDP, labor, and total factor productivity raise several questions about the accuracy of the existing capital stock data and the link between capital stock and services in the business sector.

The relevant question in the case of the capital stock figures is whether or not their annual rates of change were upward biased in the last ten to fifteen years, as Gross and Meron (1981) have suggested. They argue that the retirement rates used to derive the official Bank of Israel figures for industrial equipment (Buch, 1982) are too low because the life expectancy of industrial equipment is assumed to remain constant, whereas a declining trend has been observed in the major Western countries throughout the past twenty years. Whatever the cause, the shortened life-time of capital before 1973 could only have been reinforced afterward by rising energy prices and the consequent shift to more energy-efficient industrial branches and equipment (see Baily, 1981; Bank of Israel, *Annual Report 1982*, chap. IV). All these factors may have increased the rate of capital obsolescence not captured by the constant-life-expectancy assumption.

To get some idea of the effect that a possible decline in the life expectancy of equipment may have had on the growth rates of capital in the business sector, I recalculated these rates on the basis of Gross and Meron's corrections for manufacturing equipment, by applying their 1968–1981 annual ratios of uncorrected to corrected stock of equipment in manufacturing to the entire stock of equipment in the business sector (see Metzer, 1983, table A-5). Column 2 of Table 3-4 shows the results in terms of average annual growth rates. These figures are *purely illustrative;* they indicate possible orders of magnitude under very strong (and not

TABLE 3-4. Effects of correcting for the age of capital and for capital utilization, various business-sector growth rates: annual averages, 1961–1981 (percentages)

			Adjusted for changes in utilization	
	Uncorrected capital stock (1)	Age-corrected capital stock (2)	Uncorrected capital stock (3)	Age-corrected capital stock (4)
Capital				
1961–1972	8.9	8.8	9.1	9.0
1973–1981	6.0	4.9	1.5	0.6
Capital per hour of work				
1961–1972	5.0	4.9	5.2	5.1
1973–1981	5.0	3.9	0.5	–0.4
GDP per unit of capital				
1961–1972	0.8	0.9	0.6	0.7
1973–1981	–2.6	–1.5	1.9	2.8

Sources: Column 1: Table 3-1; columns 2–4: Metzer (1983), table A-5 and text.

necessarily very realistic) assumptions regarding the accuracy of Gross and Meron's corrections and their application to the entire business sector. They do reveal, however, that within the range of plausible revision of the capital stock data—and assuming that the revision for manufacturing also holds for other industries—the corrected growth rate of capital in 1973–1981 could have been reduced by about one percentage point, from 6.0 to 4.9 percent on average. This change would in turn have reduced the annual growth rate of capital per worker hour from 5.0 to 3.9 percent in 1973–1981, thus lowering its growth between the two subperiods, in contrast to the constancy of the uncorrected figures. Not even such a revision, however, could alter the declining trend of capital productivity since 1973; at most, it could moderate the decline from 2.6 percent a year of GDP per unit of uncorrected capital stock to 1.5 percent per unit of corrected capital stock.

This exercise seems to imply that, within reasonable limits, corrections in capital growth rates could help explain the growth of capital relative to labor, product, and productivity in the 1970s. But they do not explain the link between capital stock and capital services or the changes in the relative utilization of capital.

Although capital utilization is a separate issue from that of measuring capital stock, the two are connected. In the behavioral sense, a decline in the rate of capital utilization (apart from being a common response to a slack in demand) may, at least in the short run, substitute for the scrapping of obsolete equipment. Thus a decline in utilization could reflect frictional (or structural) unemployment of capital associated with alterations in input or output mix due to changes in relative input prices, technology, or composition of demand (Baily, 1981). Viewed thus, and provided that the rate of utilization is calculated independently of the stock figures, the decline in utilization should be added to the stock adjustment to provide a complete account of the changes in capital services.

Manzly (1980) was the first to construct a stock-independent capital utilization index for Israel's manufacturing, based on the ratio of electricity consumption to installed electric motor capacity in five benchmark years. Kondor (1981) calculated an improved index for 1964–1980, based on a similar approach but utilizing annual data on total electricity-using capacity in manufacturing up to 1976. Kondor also applied his index to the entire business sector by adjusting it to relationships between the patterns of change of GDP in manufacturing and in the business sector. Because Kondor's utilization index is closely associated with the variations in GDP over time, it is used in the last two columns of Table 3-4 to correct the rates of change of capital, capital per worker hour, and GDP per capita for utilization.[4]

Obviously, the correction for changes in utilization (as in the case of the stock adjustment dealt with above) serves only to point out possible quantitative effects on the various growth rates in the business sector. Moreover, since Kondor's utilization index declines more sharply after 1973 than any of the alternative indexes (see Bank of Israel, *Annual Report 1982,* table VI-12), the corrections in Table 3-4 may be viewed as an upper-limit estimate of the possible effect of changes in utilization on the growth of capital services in 1973–1981.

The table shows clearly that when changes in utilization are taken into account, the growth rate of capital services relative to that of capital stock declines substantially in 1973–1981, significantly reducing the growth rate of capital per worker hour and raising that of GDP per unit of capital.

The widening gap between capital stock and services in this period indicates that, at least in the short run, some disequilibriums existed in the system. These may have reflected frictions and lags in the adjustment mechanism of productive capacity (versus that of current production) to changes in relative prices of inputs and final goods, and to shifting comparative advantages. Capacity adjustment may also have lagged in its response to slacks in aggregate demand, and there were probably some erroneous expectations of a renewed upswing in growth. The relative instability of growth during the 1970s may have affected these expectations in a fashion similar to the presumed labor-hoarding effect.

Apart from that, however, the buildup of excess capacity was no doubt partly a rational response to the rapidly increasing subsidy embodied in the fixed-interest government investment credit during the inflationary 1970s (Bank of Israel, *Annual Report 1981* and *1982,* chap. VI; Bregman, 1983). Litvin and Meridor (1982) estimated the extent of this subsidy, suggesting that it increased from 25 percent of investments in the business sector in 1973 to more than 70 percent in 1977. As a result of partial adjustment to inflation, the subsidy declined after 1977 to a modest 30 percent in 1979. Given these figures, it is highly probable that the subsidy embodied in investment credit contributed significantly to the mild decline in the rate of capital accumulation relative to the growth slowdown of labor, productivity, and domestic product in the 1970s.

Whatever the causes of the short-term excess capacity and the underutilization of capital in the business sector, using utilization-corrected stock figures in conventional growth accounting clearly has a productivity-increasing effect for 1973–1981.

The Growth of Productivity and of Product

The issue of productivity and the link between productivity changes and product growth can be approached in two different, though related, ways. In the production-function approach, productivity expresses the relationship between *actually* produced output and *actually* employed factors of production. Changes in productivity are viewed as changes in the flow of output per combined unit of utilized inputs. This is the conceptual framework for the residual-type, total factor productivity estimates of various growth-accounting procedures.

A more generalized approach views productivity as society's capacity to utilize its *total* productive potential (that is, all available factors of production rather than only those actually employed) efficiently. A reduction in the gap between potential and actually utilized services of labor and capital would thus reflect an increase, and an increase in the gap a decline in total productivity. In other words, changes in overall productivity consist of two additive components: changes in the residual-type total factor productivity, and changes in the gap between potential and actual product.

The empirical implication of the latter approach is that changes in total factor productivity should be derived from the rates of change of the following actual quantities: product, number of employed persons, number of worker hours per employee, and utilized capital. The growth of potential product, on the other hand, depends on how labor supply, capital stock, and total factor productivity would have grown had potential product been realized. Therefore, with other factors remaining constant, corrections for a decline in the relative utilization of capital in growth-accounting calculations would result in an increase in residual-type total factor productivity, but certainly not in overall productivity, because the increase in the former should be offset by the widening gap between potential and actual product caused by reduced utilization. The distinction is particularly relevant to Israel's growth record in 1973–1981, when the rate of capital utilization declined substantially, as shown above.

To illustrate this point, Table 3-5 substitutes the average growth rate of utilization-corrected capital stock for the uncorrected stock. The effect on the growth of total factor productivity is substantial; its annual rate of change increases from 0.6 to 2.2 percent in 1973–1981, its share in the growth of GDP rises from 17.6 to 64.7 percent, and the share of capital declines in complementary fashion from 64.7 to 17.6 percent of product growth. Correcting for utilization has no appreciable effect in 1961–1972; at most it reduces the average growth rate of total factor productivity by 0.1 percentage points, reflecting the slight increase in capital utilization in those years.

If the downward-revised capital stock figures (following the adjustment of Gross and Meron—see Table 3-3) had been corrected for utilization, instead of the ordinary stock figures, total factor productivity in the 1970s would show an annual increase of 2.6 percent, further reducing the difference in productivity growth between 1961–1972 and 1973–1981. The outcome changes completely, however, when the loss of potential product is considered part of the change in overall productivity. Table 3-6 gives suggestive estimates of the difference between the growth rates of potential and actual GDP in the business sector and the implied changes in conventional total factor productivity relative to overall productivity. The rate of change of potential GDP is the sum of the rates of change of potential labor and capital, weighted by their respective shares in actual gross product (lines 1 and 2), and the growth rate of the residual-type total factor

TABLE 3-5. Effects of correcting for capital utilization on growth accounting in the business sector: average annual rates of change, 1961–1981 (percentages)

	Percentage points				Percentage distribution			
	1961–1972		1973–1981		1961–1972		1973–1981	
	Uncor-rected capital	Corrected for utilization changes	Uncor-rected capital	Corrected for utilization changes	Uncor-rected capital	Corrected for utilization changes	Uncor-rected capital	Corrected for utilization changes
Labor	2.5	2.5	0.6	0.6	25.8	25.8	17.6	17.6
Capital[a]	3.0	3.1	2.2	0.6 (0.2)	30.9	32.0	64.7	17.6 (5.9)
Total factor productivity[a]	4.2	4.1	0.6	2.2 (2.6)	43.3	42.3	17.6	64.7 (76.5)
Total	9.7	9.7	3.4	3.4	100.0	100.0	100.0	100.0

Sources: Tables 3-1, 3-4, and Metzer (1983), table A-4.
a. Figures in parentheses are for age-corrected capital stock.

TABLE 3-6. Growth of potential product and overall productivity in the business sector, 1961–1981 (percentages)

	Average annual growth rates (percent)		Change in growth rate of potential product	
	1961–1972	1973–1981	Percentage points (2 – 1)	Percentage distribution
	(1)	(2)	(3)	(4)
1. Potential labor[a]	2.4	1.1	–1.3	–32.5
2. Capital stock[b]	3.0	2.2	–0.8	–20.0
3. Total factor productivity (net of changes in capital utilization)	4.1	2.2	–1.9	–47.5
4. Potential GDP (line 1 *plus* line 2 *plus* line 3)	9.5	5.5	–4.0	–100.0
5. Actual GDP	9.7	3.4	—	—
6. Product loss (line 5 *minus* line 4)	0.2	–2.1	—	—
7. Overall productivity (line 3 *plus* line 6)	4.3	0.1	—	—

Sources: Line 1: text, and table 3-3; lines 2, 5: table 3-1; line 3: table 3-5.
a. Weighted by share of labor in GDP.
b. Weighted by share of capital in GDP.

productivity, net of changes in factor utilization (line 3). The rate of change of overall productivity is the sum of the percentage change of total factor productivity (line 3) and the growth rate of actual GDP *minus* that of potential GDP (line 6).

The rate of change in the potential labor supply was derived from the actual labor force participation rate, the actual employment share of the business sector, and actual employment from the territories.The governing assumptions are that the entire labor force was employed and that employed persons worked the same maximum number of hours at all times (see also Kuznets, 1973a). Under these assumptions actual labor services grew faster than potential labor in 1961–1972, when the share of employment in the labor force and the average number of worker hours per employee actually increased by 0.6 and 0.2 percent a year respectively.

A similar procedure was applied to the estimate of potential capital, whose growth rate was taken to equal that of actual gross capital stock. This approach assumes that at any given moment the entire existing stock could be, and was, fully utilized, and that the change in utilization was zero over the entire period.

Here, too, as in the case of labor, the actual increase in utilization during the 1960s caused the growth rate of potential capital to be slightly lower than that of actually employed capital services in 1961–1972. The opposite, of course, was true in 1973–1981, by which time the rate of capital utilization had declined substantially. However, since the decline in utilization seems to have been partly a reflection of the buildup of beyond-optimal capacity at the time, the marginal productivity of capital, had it been fully utilized, would probably have been lower than that of the actually utilized stock. If so, including the growth rate of the entire capital stock in the production function with unchanged weights may impart an upward bias to the estimated growth rates of potential product.

On the other hand, there may be downward biases in the potential product growth rate figures, since potential labor and capital growth rates are not corrected for possible adverse effects of the growth slowdown.[5] The same applies to actual total factor productivity (corrected for changes in capital utilization), which probably would have grown faster had it not been for the slowdown of the 1970s. If there was in fact disguised unemployment in the business sector, induced by the growth slowdown, it would have reduced measured productivity. Other possible effects of product on productivity growth may be the realization of economies to scale and various production incentives generated in a fast-growth environment.

Given all these offsetting factors, the 5.5 percent annual growth rate of potential GDP in 1973–1981, as reported in Table 3-6, is entirely plausible. It may be on the lower end of the scale, but it is probably close to the "exact" potential growth, since if the assumption had been that capital grew after 1973 at the same rate as in 1961–1972, potential product would have grown no more than 6.3 percent annually in 1973–1981.

It follows that the failure of the system to utilize fully its productive potential caused actual annual growth to be about 2 percentage points less than it could have been after 1973. In other words, actual growth in the business sector in 1973–1981 was no more than 62 percent of its potential growth rate. Thus overall productivity has stagnated, rising only 0.1 percent a year in 1973–1981. The 2.1 percent annual decline in productivity due to underutilization of product potential roughly offset the slow (2.2 percent) increase in the residual-type total factor productivity. In contrast, in 1961–1972 overall productivity and actual product grew even faster (because of the average increase in factor utilization during the 1960s) than either total factor productivity or potential product.

Figure 3-2 shows the difference between the two decades in the growth of actual and potential product, in terms of indexes of product levels. The 1972 level was taken to be 100 for both actual and potential product, and the 1960 and 1981 levels were linearly extrapolated from the annual average growth rates in Table 3-6. The rationale for fixing 1972 as 100 for both types of product rests on the fact that the indexes of changes in factor utilization used in the calculation for Table

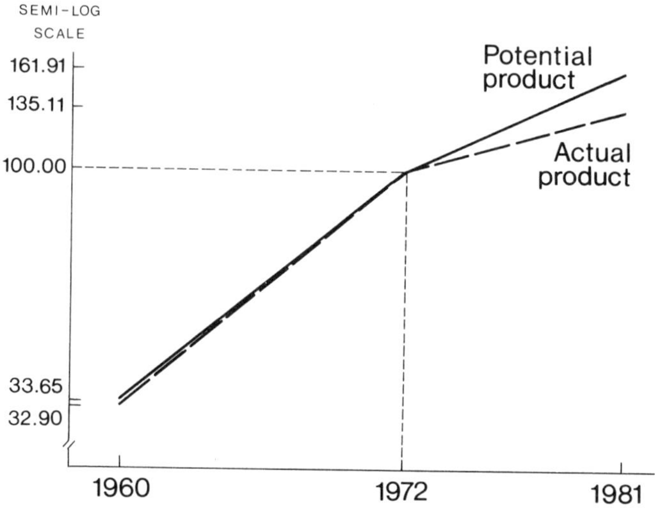

Figure 3-2
Growth of actual and potential product, 1960–1981.

3-6 were assumed to be 100 in 1972; that is, the potential product of 1972 was taken to equal the actual product of that year.

The figure shows that during the 1960s actual product converged upward toward the productive potential of the business sector (by increasing utilization) and diverged downward in the 1970s (because of the decline in utilization), whereas the annual growth of potential product itself deteriorated substantially, from 9.5 percent in 1961–1972 to no more than 5.5 percent in 1973–1981. The major cause of the decline in the growth rate of potential product was the slower increase in total factor productivity (net of utilization changes), which accounted for 47.5 percent of the growth slowdown in the business sector's productive potential, with the decline in labor and capital growth making for 32.5 and 20 percent respectively. Although these figures are at best only suggestive, they do indicate that economic growth in 1973–1981 would have remained substantially slower than in the preceding period even if factor utilization had not declined during the 1970s.

Two related issues concern the slowdown of overall productivity. One is the decline in factor utilization, already addressed in the discussion of labor and capital (and further elaborated on in the concluding section), which widened the gap between actual and potential product after 1973. The other is the decline in the growth of total factor productivity, within the confines of the aggregate production function, which was a key factor in the slowdown of both potential and actual product in 1972–1981.

Although a satisfactory comprehensive explanation of Israel's post-1973 slowdown in total factor productivity net of factor utilization changes has yet to be found (and this is equally true for most industrial economies), some contributing factors come to mind. In an international context, for example, Bruno (1982) has suggested that the post-1973 decline of productivity growth in the OECD economies can largely be explained by the interaction between intraindustry productivity-reducing supply shocks and the derived aggregate demand slack (caused by the adverse real income effects of the supply shocks themselves and by the contractionary response of the OECD governments). This interaction slowed aggregate productivity growth by inhibiting the interindustry resource reallocation called for by the changes in relative input prices.

Bruno's argument has a strong appeal because it can explain the 1973 discontinuity in productivity and product growth in the industrialized nations; thus it could probably also explain some of the analogous discontinuity in Israel, as the breakdown of productivity growth into inter- and intraindustry components indicates (see the next section).[6]

A major factor specific to Israel's diminished productivity is certainly the country's exceptionally high (two- and three-digit) inflation rate since the mid-1970s. This inflationary spiral seems to have introduced a great deal of uncertainty into the system with respect to expected changes in relative prices and in the overall price level (see Jaffee and Kleiman, 1977, for the general argument, and Kleiman, 1977a, for its application to Israel). The need for frequent repricing, contract adjustments, and diversion of an increasing amount of resources to various financial activities as a hedge against inflation probably raised firms' transaction costs. When such incremental costs are not fully reflected in an upward adjustment of product prices, they obviously have a productivity-reducing effect (Kondor, 1981).

Another inflation-related factor reducing firms' motivation to increase production efficiency may have been the adverse effect on productivity of alternative gainful activities in the financial field. Particularly relevant in this context is the increasing speculation in the financial capital market.[7]

Yet another development specific to Israel that may have contributed significantly to the productivity slowdown of the 1970s has to do with the economic integration of immigrants who arrived in the early 1950s. This process, as mentioned earlier, seems to have reached completion in the early 1970s. The suggestion made there, that no appreciable increase in the quality of labor was possible in the past decade on account of immigrants' economic absoprtion and adaptation, applies equally to the growth of total factor productivity. Viewed thus, part of the productivity growth slowdown of the past decade may simply have been a sort of "back-to-normal" movement after the intense growth in Israel's first two decades.

Finally, part of the decline in the growth rate of total factor productivity could be a statistical artifact, reflecting a downward bias in the recorded product figures since 1973. A substantial discrepancy between true and official income data because of tax evasion has been argued to exist in many Western economies, and Israel's exceptionally high income tax rates and newly imposed value-added tax make it particularly susceptible to the development of such gaps. In an interesting attempt to estimate the product gap, Unger and Zilberfarb (1982) derived "true" income figures from an estimated volume of currency held by the private sector as a function of several parameters, including income tax rate. They concluded that "true" GNP may have grown by 4.4 percent annually, compared with the officially reported 3 percent annual growth in 1973–1977, whereas the gap in 1961–1972 did not exceed 0.6 percentage points.

To get some idea of how such an adjustment might affect the business-sector findings, I corrected the figures for 1961–1972 and 1973–1981 according to the Unger and Zilberfarb growth-rate differentials for 1961–1972 and 1973–1977 respectively. The resultant annual growth rates of the business sector's product are 10.3 percent in 1961–1972 and 5.1 percent in 1973–1981; thus the difference between the two periods' product growth rates would narrow from 6.3 to 5.2 percent. This correction does not alter the overall picture of slowed growth for 1973–1981, but it causes a substantial convergence of the pre- and post-1973 growth of net-of-capital-utilization total factor productivity (from a 1.9 to a 0.9 percentage-point gap).

The validity of these findings obviously depends on the soundness of the estimated unrecorded economic activity and on the plausibility of the assumption that the *entire* difference between recorded and unrecorded economic activity is reflected in the product and not in input figures. Even if one chooses not to rely too heavily on these corrected figures, this exercise is useful in pointing out that some part of the post-1973 decline in the growth rate of total factor productivity may reflect a statistical artifact rather than a slowdown in the economy's ability to raise its productive capacity.

The Slowdown of Growth: A Disaggregated View

The final issues to be considered are inter- and intraindustry attributes of the growth slowdown, its industrial composition, and the characteristics of decline in key industries.

Table 3-7 distinguishes between (1) the contribution of changes in total labor, capital, and intraindustry productivity to aggregate growth, and (2) changes in productivity and product growth attributed to interindustry resource allocation, using the breakdown procedure devised by Massell (1961). The data reveal that interindustry resource reallocation (of labor and capital combined) accounted for 9.3 percent of the growth in aggregate product in 1961–1972, but for only 2.9

TABLE 3-7. Components of average annual total productivity and product growth, 1961–1981 (percentages)

	1961–1972			1973–1981			Changes in growth rates between 1961–72 and 1973–81		
	Percentage points	Percentage distribution		Percentage points	Percentage distribution		Percentage points	Percentage distribution	
		TFP	GDP		TFP	GDP		TFP	GDP
1. Intraindustry productivity growth	3.3	78.6	34.0	0.5	83.3	14.7	–2.8	–77.8	–44.4
2. Interindustry reallocation Labor	0.6	14.3	6.2	0.0	0.0	0.0	–0.6	–16.7	–9.5
3. Capital	0.3	7.1	3.1	0.1	16.7	2.9	–0.2	–5.6	–3.2
4. Total (growth rate of TFP)	4.2	100.0	43.3	0.6	100.0	17.6	–3.6	100.0	–57.1
5. Contribution of labor and capital to GDP growth	5.5	—	56.7	2.8	—	82.4	–2.7	—	–42.9
6. Growth rate of GDP	9.7	—	100.0	3.4	—	100.0	–6.3	—	–100.0

Sources: Lines 1–4: Metzer (1983), tables A-6 to A-10 and text; lines 5, 6: table 3-1.

percent in 1973–1981. This drop, though less noticeable when given in terms of percentages of total factor productivity (21.4 percent in1961–1972 versus 16.7 percent in 1973–1981), was obviously one of the factors that arrested total factor productivity growth after 1973.

Part of the decline in productivity-enhancing allocative effects probably reflects the difficulties in implementing the interindustry resource reallocations necessary for adjusting to exogenous supply shocks and the slowdown in aggregate demand. Partly, it may indicate a greater need for resource reallocation in the 1960s because of structural and institutional changes (such as the intensification of industrialization and removal of import barriers) than in the 1970s.

However, most of the decline in the business sector's growth was due to intraindustry shifts in labor, capital, and productivity rates of change. The major contributors were manufacturing and construction. Manufacturing accounted for 39.7 percent of the decline in the GDP growth rate, and construction for another 22.2 percent, although their respective shares in the business sector's product (in current prices) averaged only about 32 and 12 percent (see Metzer, 1983, table 13). Even more impressive are the facts that manufacturing contributed 68 percent of the decline in the growth of the intraindustry component of aggregate total factor productivity between the two periods; and that manufacturing and construction together accounted for 86 percent of this decline (see Metzer, 1983, table 13; Bank of Israel, *Annual Report 1980,* chap. VI). Similarly, construction accounted for 34.8 percent of the deteriorating growth of labor inputs to the business sector (the employment share of construction was only about 13 percent of total business employment), and manufacturing for another 26.1 percent.

Only in the declining growth rate of capital did these two industries combined not play a major role. In fact the growth of capital per worker hour in manufacturing and construction accelerated after 1973, whereas in the other major industries it slowed down. Despite the accelerated growth of capital per unit of labor, the decline in measured total factor productivity was sharpest in manufacturing and construction; these were the only industries for which an absolute total factor productivity slowdown was recorded after 1973 (0.2 and 2.2 percent a year respectively). This decline created a gap of 6.2 percentage points between the 1961–1972 and 1973–1981 average growth rates of productivity in manufacturing,with construction—the runner-up—experiencing a milder deterioration of only 4.9 percentage points (Metzer, 1983, table 14).

As a result of the far steeper decline in manufacturing productivity than in either labor or capital, productivity alone accounted for no less than 78.5 percent of the decline in the manufacturing industry's gross product growth in 1973–1981, compared with only 41 and 57 percent respectively for construction and for the business sector as a whole. Consequently, in the case of manufacturing, the issue of the slowdown in product growth becomes essentially a question of the deterioration in total factor productivity.[8]

Bregman (1983) has demonstrated the major role of declining capital utilization in the productivity slowdown in manufacturing. According to his regression analysis, that decline accounts for 73 percent of the difference between 1965–1972 and 1972–1979 in productivity growth in manufacturing. Possible factors in the decline of utilization have already been mentioned, namely, capital subsidization's major role in the (short-term) buildup of excess capacity, the uncertainty generated by inflation, and the adjustment of capital stock and services to rising raw material prices. Bar-Nathan (1983b), for example, has tentatively suggested that about 45 percent of the decline in total factor productivity growth between 1965–1974 and 1974–1980 can be explained by the rise in the relative prices of raw materials.

In the construction industry, on the other hand, the dominant contributing factor in product slowdown was the decline in labor inputs, which accounted for about half (48.3 percent) of the difference between the 1961–1972 and 1973–1981 product growth rates. The deterioration in productivity was a close second, making for another 45 percent; the remaining 6.7 percent resulted from the moderate decline in the growth rate of capital stock (see Metzer, 1983, table 14).

The drop in the annual growth rate of labor (8.2 percentage points between the two periods) and its large role in the construction industry's overall decline suggest that a weakened demand may have been instrumental in the extended recession in construction. This slackening of demand seems to have reflected both short-term effects (such as the government-induced slowdown of aggregate economic activity in the mid-1970s) and long-term structural changes, a major feature of which has been the decline in net immigration and in overall population growth. Note that by reducing the ratio of (the relatively capital-intensive) construction starts to (the relatively labor-intensive) completions, the slack in demand by itself did contribute to the decline in measured productivity (see Bank of Israel, *Annual Report 1980* and *1981*, chap. VI).

On the supply side, the Bar-Nathan (1983a) study tentatively suggests that rising prices of raw materials may have contributed significantly to the decline in construction productivity in a fashion and order of magnitude similar to their effect on productivity in manufacturing. Another element in the decline in measured construction productivity could have been the rise in the share of the under-recorded maintenance and renovation activity associated with the aging of structures and with the demand-led recession in new construction.

Summary and Interpretation

The factors discussed in the preceding sections may not be a complete list of the causes of the post-1973 slowdown, nor is their relative importance in producing this slowdown analyzed. But they do provide a basis for answering the principal question: is Israel's growth recession since 1973 a temporary phenomenon, or is it a permanent, secular one?

The recent slowdown in growth involved both a divergence of actual from potential product and a decline in the growth of potential product itself. If actual product loss is assumed to be a passing phase, the basic issue becomes the extent to which the decline in the growth of potential product may indicate the beginning of a long-term slow-growth pattern.

One development that could have reduced the long-term growth rate is the structural change embodied in the declining growth rate of net immigration and population, together with the related increase in the average length of residence of the foreign-born. The slowdown in population increase may have negatively affected prospects for long-term economic growth both by reducing the growth rate of labor and by inducing a possible downward phase in a long swing of economic activity (see Kuznets, 1965, pp. 328–354). Whereas the former is a typical supply-side effect, the latter may be viewed as a demand effect transmitted to the entire economy primarily through the weakening of demand for the output (housing and other structures) of the construction industry—traditionally Israel's growth-leading industry. Obviously this long-term demand effect should be distinguished from short-term changes in aggregate demand, which are usually associated with fluctuations in the level and growth rates of actual product.

The rising average length of residence of the foreign-born, to about twenty years by the early 1970s, seems to have marked the completion of the economic absorption of the mass immigration of the 1950s. Exhaustion of this process, along with its inherent potential for increasing overall productivity, acted as yet another supply-type growth-reducing factor.

The population-induced structural changes were obviously gradual, and therefore should have caused a gradual slowdown in the growth of product. But this was not the case. Two explanations can be proposed for this apparent inconsistency. The first has to do with the timing of the growth slowdown: although none of the major economic aggregates showed signs of decline before 1973, quite a few of them started slowing down in the first nine months of that year, that is, before the Yom Kippur War. For example, the annual growth rate of product in the non-dwelling business sector from January to September 1973 was 9.1 percent, compared with 12 percent in 1971 and 1972. Similarly, the per annum growth of domestic investment (net of ships and aircraft) was 20 percent in 1972 but only 10 percent for the first nine months of 1973 (Bank of Israel, *Annual Report 1973,* table II-3).

It should also be recalled that there was by no means consistent growth from the mid-1960s until the downturn of 1973. These years were dominated by recovery from the 1965–1967 recession and by the economic boom and expansion that followed the Six Day War. The growth rate of the business sector's product declined from about 10 percent in 1964 to 5 percent in 1965, to zero in 1966, and to

−0.4 percent in 1967, then bounced back to 21 percent in 1968 and to 14 percent in 1969. In view of these fluctuations, the possibility cannot be ruled out that the short boom after the Six Day War offset (and thereby delayed) the beginning of a secular growth transformation.

The second explanation for the apparent inconsistency described above is that once the catching-up process lost impetus, the chain of post-1973 growth-reducing developments reinforced the gradual slowdown initially caused by population-driven structural changes, and thus made for the sharp 1973 turnabout to a new slow-growth path that is still very much in evidence.

The growth-reducing components discussed in this chapter—namely, the supply shocks embodied in the raw material price increases and the inflationary spiral in the second half of the 1970s—tended to arrest the growth of productivity and *potential* product. This effect may, however, be transitory, depending on the future course of inflation, relative prices of raw materials, and the economy's ability to adjust to these changes.

In addition to their contribution to the slowed growth of production potential, these developments may also have contributed, at least in the short run, to the decline in factor utilization rates and thus to the divergence of actual from potential product. Part of this divergence, however, must have stemmed from weakening aggregate demand. Private consumption, public consumption, and domestic investment combined grew only 1.6 percent a year in 1974–1981, compared with over 10 percent annually in 1961–1972. This overall slowdown was generated by two spans of demand-depressing policies, one in the mid-1970s and one in 1980, which aimed at reducing the large and growing import surplus.[9]

The demand- and resource-originated growth-reducing factors were certainly not independent of one another. As Bruno (1982) has suggested in a different context, the slowdown of demand was in part a reflection of the negative real income effect embodied in the rise of raw material prices and in the implied worsening terms of trade, and in part the result of a deliberate policy response to an increase in the balance-of-payments deficits caused by these supply shocks.

On the other hand, the contribution of demand-depressing policies to the slowdown of actual product growth may also have restrained the growth of aggregate supply factors, thereby contributing to the decline in the economy's productive capacity as well. Two trends mentioned earlier that have special relevance in this context are the chain of causality from a decline in product growth to a drop in productivity and Israel's weakening "pull" effect due to the slowdown in economic growth, which may have contributed to the decline in net immigration and thus to a slower rate of population increase. According to Kuznets (1965, pp. 328–354), such interrelationships between economy and population may explain the synchronization of economic and demographic long swings in the United States. In the Israeli context, Ablin (1979b) went so far as to claim that most of the decline in net immigration during the 1970s was endogenous, the result of contractionary government policies.

Another obvious association between supply and demand factors is that between capital and investment. Among the aggregate demand components the sharpest decline was in gross domestic investment, which was also the only one to suffer an absolute decline (of 3 percent annually) in 1974–1981. Part of this decline may be attributed to direct and indirect demand-depressing macroeconomic policies; but apart from that it reflected the downward-adjusted growth rate of capital stock,necessitated by the slowdown of product growth and the expectations it generated. Moreover, in view of the observed decline in the rate of capital utilization, one could argue that investment would have dropped even further if inflation had not fed an increase in capital subsidization in the second half of the 1970s. The business sector may, in the short run, have partly adjusted its rate of investment to the slowdown of growth, but the resultant decline in the rate of gross capital formation (with net investment falling at an even faster rate) certainly added to the diminishing growth of the economy's productive potential, if not to its actual production (Sussman, 1982).

At this time it is impossible to provide a definitive answer to the question posed in the title of this chapter. For now, it is plausible only to say that a combination of Israel-specific and worldwide exogenous, transitory and long-term, supply factors brought an end to Israel's growth spurt. The large influx of people and capital that induced such extended rapid growth of output and productivity had much in common with the immigration-determined growth upswings recorded during the Mandate period. By this analogy, growth might be expected to recover if high rates of net immigration and population increase could be renewed and sustained. But the major sources of potential large-scale immigration seem to have run dry. A return to the rapid economic growth rates of the 1950s and 1960s, if at all possible, will probably depend more on the economy's ability to substitute alternative sources of sustained growth for substantial immigration and its related industries. This effort will require large investments in new fields such as high-technology and science-intensive industries that can be expected to generate high productivity-related growth. However, the readiness to invest, particularly in new ventures, is largely a function of expectations regarding future prospects, which in turn are associated with current economic indicators such as the recent growth record, and this record has been rather poor.

This interplay between the various growth-arresting factors, some of which are quite transitory, made for the extended growth recession of the 1970s and render the recovery of past high-growth rate a difficult (perhaps impossible) task in the near future. Whether all this means that the economy has embarked on a new, secular, slow-growth path or is merely going through a prolonged slump—in other words, whether the past decade brought an end to *the* big spurt or to *a* big spurt—remains to be seen.

4

Investment Patterns

Joram Mayshar

Patinkin (1960) concluded his economic survey of Israel's first decade by expressing concern over the failure of economic policy to generate sufficient domestic savings and over the resultant slow progress toward economic independence. Only a few years later, a comprehensive survey by Halevi and Klinov-Malul (1968) reflected current optimism about the same issue: "the simplest answer to the question of why Israel failed to generate much domestic saving is that it was not necessary! . . . The import surplus permitted Israel to invest without tightening its belt" (p. 97); "the problem in recent years has been what to do with the [foreign] money, rather than how to get it" (p. 174). Contributing to this confident attitude were the recognition that Israel's rate of product growth in 1950–1965 was among the highest in the world and the belief that the accumulation of tangible capital was the most important single contributing factor to this spectacular growth.[1] Israeli policymakers' belief that long-term growth would ultimately resolve Israel's trade imbalance, their view of growth promotion as synonymous with the promotion of capital formation, and their complacent attitude towards the allocation of investment resources all played a major role in shaping Israel's economic policy throughout the 1960s and 1970s.

This chapter examines the patterns of Israel's physical capital formation from a long-term perspective and poses the following general questions: Is Israel's level of investment adequate? Is the level of domestic savings reasonable? Are investment resources allocated efficiently? The tentative answers, which I attempt to substantiate in the following pages, are that it seems hard to fault private savings, that Israel's overall rate of investment (particularly in the early to mid-1970s) may have been excessive, and, above all, that there is ample evidence that investment resources have been consistently misallocated.

Investment and Savings at the Aggregate Level

Investment

Since investment is a means for promoting growth by increasing the capital stock, the first task is to examine the behavior of the aggregate gross capital stock. In 1960–1972 the capital stock grew at an annual rate of 9.2 percent, almost identical to the rapid growth rate of GNP. As a result, the capital-output ratio was practically constant at 2.9 throughout this period. As Table 4-1 shows, the sharp drop in the product growth rate in 1973–1977 was not matched by a drop in the growth rate of the capital stock. Thus by the end of 1977 the capital-output ratio had increased to 3.6; in 1978–1982 it increased further, though only moderately, to 3.9.

Table 4-1 also shows that since 1973, although the import surplus grew at a faster rate than product, so too did consumption (private and government combined). The squeeze on resources, resulting from increased defense needs and deteriorating terms of trade on the one hand and from the slow growth of product on the other, seems to have been borne largely by a reduction in the share of resources devoted to capital formation. However, the surge in investment until 1973 had created such a high absolute level of investment (exceeding 34 percent of GNP) that even when it was subsequently reduced it was sufficient to increase the capital stock at a higher rate than that of product growth.

This description suggests two complementary reasons for the diminished investment activity in the past decade: a squeeze on resources on the supply side and a rising capital-output ratio on the demand side. It is instructive to compare this reduced growth pattern with the pattern during the brief recession of 1966–1967, when investment activity was sharply reduced and the capital-output ratio increased. The time pattern of the changes suggests that the 1966–1967 slowdown can be considered as depicting a typical Keynesian causal relation from reduced investment, through reduced aggregate demand, to a fall in economic activity. In contrast, the 1973–1982 pattern suggests a reverse causal relation, recognized in the acceleration principle, whereby income (and particularly lagged income) affects investment positively and the capital stock affects it negatively.[2]

A closer look at alternative investment indicators reveals different aspects of the recent decline in investment activity. The most commonly used index, the share of gross investment in gross product, is shown in Figure 4-1 and summarized in Table 4-1. Other than the dip during the 1966–1967 recession, this investment index remained at an average level exceeding 30 percent until 1975—a very high rate by international standards. The decrease in relative investment activity to an average 23 percent of GNP in 1980–1982 brought Israel into line with the inter-

TABLE 4-1. Resource use and investment indicators, 1953–1982

	1953–62	1963–72	1973–77	1978–82
Average annual growth rates[a]				
Gross capital stock (K)	11.2[b]	8.7	7.7	4.4
GNP (Y)	9.5	9.0	3.4	3.0
Import surplus (M^+)	6.5	7.1	3.7	6.8
Gross investment (I)	7.5	9.1	−3.0	0.7
Private consumption (C)	9.1	7.3	5.1	6.3
Public consumption (G)	9.8	11.8	5.2	1.4
Average shares[c]				
K/Y[d]	2.9[b]	2.9	3.6	3.9
I/Y	30.1	27.9	30.1	24.7
$(I - M^+)/Y$	8.6	7.0	−2.2	−0.4
$(I - D - M^*)/(Y - D)$[e]	16.4[f]	10.3	6.1	−1.3
S_P/Y_D[g]	21.9[f]	28.8	35.3	30.6

Sources: K: Buch (1982); *TR* (unilateral foreign transfers) and *YD* (disposable income from all sources): Bank of Israel data; all other data: CBS, *Statistical Abstract 1983*, tables VI-1 and VI-2.

a. Geometric averages (constant prices).
b. 1960–1963.
c. Arithmetic averages (current prices).
d. End-of-period ratio. Product is the average of adjacent two years in constant 1975 prices.
e. D = depreciation; $M^* = M^+ - TR$.
f. 1955–1962.
g. S_P (private saving) = $Y_D - C$.

national average of comparable economies.[3] A surprising feature revealed by this index is the unperturbed high investment activity in 1973–1975 despite the slowdown in product growth and the sharp increase in demand for resources.

The size of Israel's import surplus suggests that this index may not be an adequate measure of Israel's investment effort. The index $(I - M^+)/Y$ takes into account only the part of investment that can be attributed to domestic saving.[4] Until 1972, gross domestic investment exceeded the import surplus by a significant margin, but after that year domestic investment was less than the import surplus. This alarming indicator may, however, reveal more about the retreat from the goal of economic independence than about the long-term growth potential of the economy.

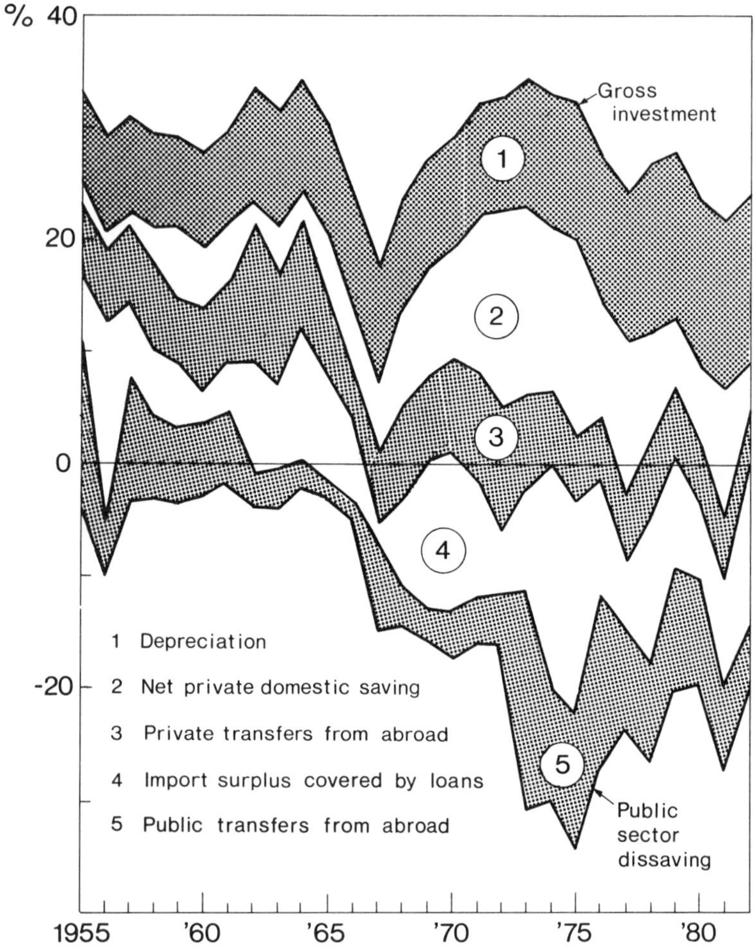

Figure 4-1
Sources of capital formation as a percentage of GNP, in current prices, 1955–1982.

The third investment indicator in Table 4-1 attempts to adjust the two preceding ones, first by taking into account the depreciation of capital stock, and second by recognizing that only part of the import surplus is financed by loans. If one assumes that at the margin the interest on foreign loans equals the yield on domestic net investment, only that part of net investment in excess of loans should be considered as contributing to the ultimate expansion of the economy's income.[5] In 1953–1962 the level of net investment according to this third indicator exceeded the comparable international average (10–15 percent.)[6] Since 1966, however (but excluding 1971 – 1973), this measure has been consistently below 7 percent. Owing to the increased capital-output ratio, estimated depreciation allowances have increased significantly (from less than 9 percent of GNP in 1953 – 1967 to 15 percent of GNP in 1978 – 1982). This increase, coupled with growing dependence on foreign loans and a stagnant absolute level of gross investment, reduced this adjusted measure of Israel's net capital formation to a negative 1.3 percent of net national product in 1978 – 1982.[7]

Domestic Saving and the Sources of Capital Formation

Figure 4-1 presents the sources and uses of saved resources.[8] Gross domestic investment (above the zero line) and public sector dissaving (below the line) are shown as financed by domestic private savings and by the import surplus. The latter is subdivided into three components: transfers to the public sector, transfers to the private sector, and loans.[9] There is a reason to identify at least one source — unilateral transfers to the government — with military imports, especially after 1973 (see Chapter 8). Beyond this fact, however, one should not attach too much significance to the sequencing of the finance sources in Figure 4-1. Although it is true that the government has been the dominant borrower from abroad (and for long-term loans virtually the only such borrower), the government has also dominated the domestic credit market.

The most striking feature of Figure 4-1 is the extent of government dissaving. Whereas until 1966 the government deficit averaged less than 4 percent of GNP, after the 1967 war through 1972 it jumped to an average over 15 percent, and after the 1973 war it jumped again, to over 30 percent in 1973 – 1975 and to 20 – 27 percent since then. Even when savings sources from abroad are taken into account, Figure 4-1 shows that whereas in the 1950s savings generated by the public sector (including its foreign transfers and loans) contributed about half of gross domestic capital formation, in the period since 1966 the government has had to draw on private savings as well. The almost constant share of investment in GNP until 1975, and its limited decline since then, appear surprising in view of the magnitude of public-sector dissaving.

The second striking feature shown in Figure 4-1 is the steady rise in private saving. The average gross private saving rate out of disposable income from all sources (including foreign transfers) increased dramatically, from less than 20 percent in the 1950s to well over 35 percent in the early 1970s (Table 4-1, last line). This increase enabled the economy to maintain a high investment level and still channel resources to increased public expenditures.

What caused the tremendous increase in the private propensity to save?[10] In the absence of reliable data, I can offer no more than a tentative answer.[11] Halevi and Klinov-Malul (1968), writing before private savings started soaring, attribute its growth primarily to government policy, which encouraged private-ownership dwellings (while restricting mortgages) and devised "inflation-proof" and tax exempt long-term savings schemes. The main reason for the increase in savings, however, is probably the rapid rise in per capita real disposable income, notably the two-thirds increase in 1967–1972. In most countries a higher level of per capita income has been found to be associated with a higher saving rate (the United States and United Kingdom in the last century are exceptions; see Kuznets, 1966). Moreover, a rapid increase in income, if not perceived as permanent, is likely to increase consumption only with a lag. Indeed, consumption in 1967–1972 increased only 30 percent.[12] The leveling off and subsequent decline in the (gross) saving rate since 1973 may be attributed at least partly to a catching up of consumption expenditure. It may also be attributed to the substantial capital gains that boosted the perceived wealth of the public, in particular in recent years (see Bank of Israel, *Annual Report 1983,* chap. 8.4).

Not much is known about business savings. According to Tamari (1980, table 3.19), industrial firms nearly doubled their gross savings, from about half their level of investment in 1957 to equal that level in 1964–1972.

The lower profitability of investment in the past decade and the effect of inflation cum tax law in discouraging the internal financing of investment may all have operated to decrease gross business savings to levels well below those of estimated business depreciation.

The Composition of Investment

Figure 4-2 shows the distribution of gross fixed investment among the three principal sectors of the economy—households, business, and government. These three sectors accounted for roughly equal shares in gross fixed investment, with no apparent trend except a possible relative decline in residential investment until the mid-1960s.

Residential investment is divided into two components: private and public. Public-sector investment is in turn divided into investment in public services (including private nonprofit institutions) and investment in infrastructure. The latter includes public utilities (water and electricity) as well as the entire investment in transportation and communications, excluding vehicles. Within the business sector (which still includes a fair share of government enterprises), the figure shows investment in manufacturing, which constitutes a stable 13 percent of total fixed investment. The remainder of business-sector fixed investment includes agriculture, construction, private services, and vehicles. Investment in inventories, presented in Figure 4-2 as a fraction of gross fixed investment above the 100 percent line, may also be considered to be a trendless component of business investment.

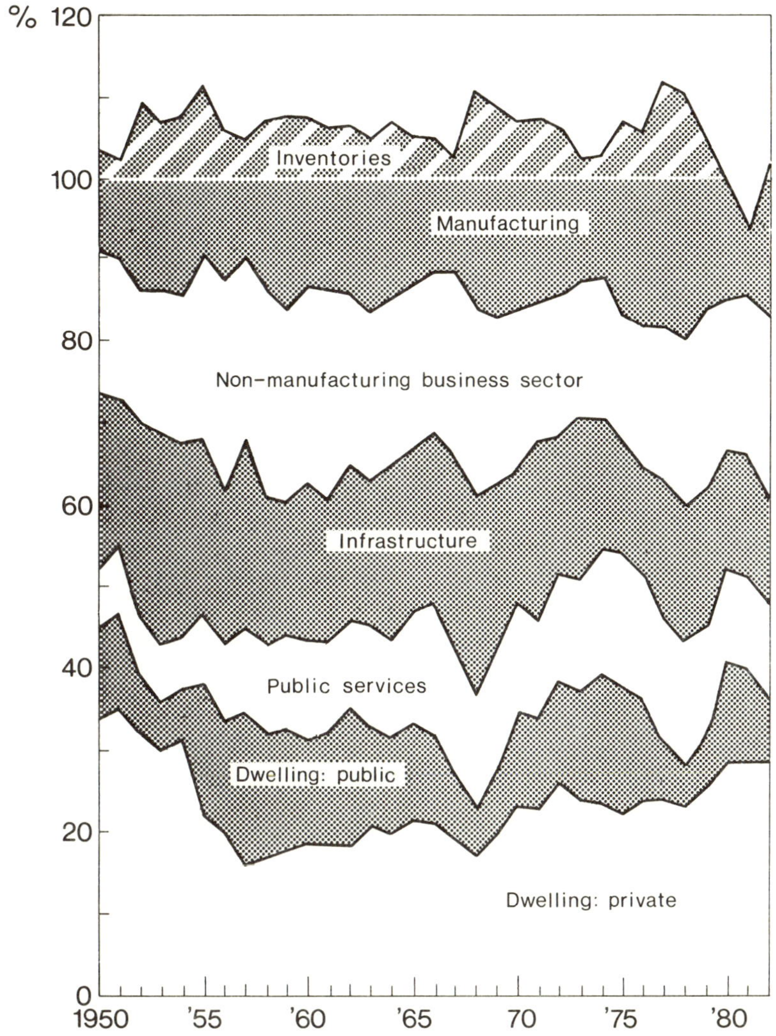

Figure 4-2

Pattern of gross investment as a percentage of gross fixed investment, in current prices, 1950–1982.

Although the stability in the composition of gross investment despite the instability of aggregate investment is quite remarkable, it does not imply a stable composition of the capital stock.[13] The share of public services increased significantly from 5.6 percent of total gross capital stock in 1955 to 13.7 percent in 1982. This shift partly offset a decline in the capital stock share of infrastructure (from

17.2 percent in 1955 to 12.5 percent in 1982). Another significant shift was the decline in the share of agriculture, from 14.3 percent of the capital stock in 1955 to 6.1 in 1982. Manufacturing remained relatively stable, at 13 to 14 percent. The share of dwellings fell from 41 percent of the gross capital stock in 1955 to 36 percent in the late 1960s and then rose to 40 percent by 1982.

One clear trend in the composition of investment that is not reflected in Figure 4-2 is the share of equipment in gross nondwelling investment. This share increased steadily, from less than 40 percent (in current prices) in the early 1950s to over 60 percent in the early 1970s and to 70 percent in 1982. This upward trend appears in all components of nondwelling investment and has important implications for the impact of investment on aggregate domestic demand, since about 75 percent of investment in equipment (vehicles included) consists of direct imports.

Interestingly, the share of equipment in the gross capital stock in constant prices increased only moderately, from 25 to 28 percent, in 1960–1982. (In current prices this share in fact declined in recent years.) These results can be ascribed in part to the shift in the overall composition of the capital stock, toward construction-intensive public services and (in the 1970s) housing. Furthermore, the very rapid rate of capital formation and the much shorter life span of equipment relative to that of structures imply that in the transition period, until structures built in the 1950s would start to be replaced, equipment would account for a growing share of gross investment.

The growing share of equipment; and its relatively shorter life span explain why, even though the sectoral composition of gross investment was stable, the composition of net investment was not. In fact the share of residential construction (in constant prices) in total investment-net-of-discards increased from an average 35 percent in 1960–1965 to 41.5 percent in 1972–1979, and to more than 50 percent in 1980–1982. The combined share in investment-net-of-discards of the construction-intensive and "nonproductive" (in the sense that their product is mostly nontradable) dwellings and public services increased to an unusual (and undoubtedly temporary) two-thirds of the total in 1980–1981. If current prices are used and investment-net-of-depreciation is taken into account, the 1980–1981 figure rises to a baffling 82 percent (52 percent for 1960–1965).[14]

Residential Investment

Because of its magnitude and its vicissitude, residential construction assumes a dominant role in the investment aggregate. The high (45 percent) share of gross residential investment in total investment in 1950–1951 reflected the urgent need to provide housing for the wave of new immigrants. This extensive building activity ebbed by the 1960s (Figure 4-2). The major riddle is the resurgence of residential construction since then.

Israel has had a persistent and exceptionally high rate of housing investment.

Except in the brief recessions of 1966 – 1968 and 1977 – 1978, residential construction constituted no less than 7 percent of GNP, averaging 10.1 percent of GNP for 1948 – 1982. I know of no other country in which this share exceeded 7.5 percent of GNP for more than few years. A share of 4 – 5 percent is fairly typical for comparable countries.[15] In the key 1973 – 1975 subperiod, when aggregate investment reached an all-time high while the growth rate was sagging and the squeeze on resources peaked, residential investment reached an average of 12.4 percent of GNP. In 1980 – 1982 its share in GNP still exceeded 9 percent.

The apparent upward shift in demand for dwellings in the 1960s, especially in the boom years 1969 – 1973, is manifested in the market price of dwellings. As Figure 4-3 shows, the market price of dwellings more than doubled in 1960 – 1973, both relative to the consumer price index and relative to the residential construction input price index.

How does one explain this demand shift and the ensuing price dislocation and persistently high rate of residential investment?[16] The extent of immigration and the overall population growth do not seem to explain much.[17] While the number of households increased in 1960 – 1980 3.2 percent a year (and overall population by 3.0 percent), the residential capital stock increased 8.2 percent annually. Consequently, the residential gross capital stock per household (at replacement factor cost, excluding land) increased by a factor of 2.6.

It seems that the rapid rise in income, the inflationary environment, deficiencies in the capital markets, and accommodating government policies are the main factors in explaining the demand shift. The ratio of gross residential capital stock to disposable personal income from all sources (at constant 1975 prices) rose from 1.3 in 1960 to only 1.6 in 1982, indicating that the overall increase in the standard of living might have played a major part in boosting the investment in residences. And indeed, all housing-quality indicators show significant improvement over time. In 1960, for example, only 6 percent of building starts were dwellings with four or more rooms (and 40 percent had only two rooms); in 1979 – 1980, by contrast, 60 percent of dwellings starts were dwellings with four or more rooms (and only 6 percent had two rooms). Other indicators such as larger areas or fewer apartments per building show a similar trend.

Inflation, too, may explain the pattern of residential construction in Israel. The experience of many countries shows that the real price of housing (and land) increases in the early phase of inflation. During the mild (6.7 percent) inflation of 1960 – 1972, the market price of housing in Israel increased by an average of 14.5 percent annually (Figure 4-3). This price rise reinforced public belief in housing investment as a hedge against inflation, and to date no obvious downward trend in this relative price has occurred to shake this belief. Moreover, until the revival of the stock market in 1979, there was practically no other widely available outlet for personal savings not directly under government control.

The government's role in promoting the apparently excessive construction of

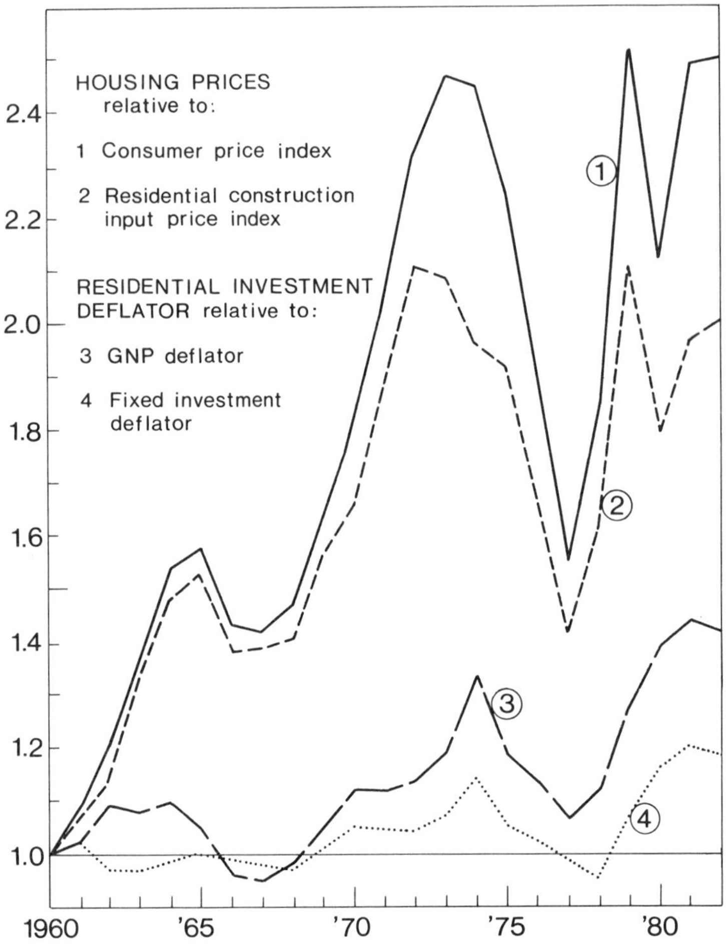

Figure 4-3
Residential investment price indexes, 1960–1982.

dwellings is multifaceted. As Figure 4-2 indicates, a sizable proportion of residential construction was directly initiated by the government: 45 percent in 1955–1962, about one-third in 1963–1976, and about one-quarter since 1977. This reduction in the government's direct involvement was due in part to a gradual shift to indirect financing of housing.

Most of the public housing construction in the 1950s was for rental. In the late 1950s, in a drive to encourage savings, the government began to promote owner-occupied housing. At the same time, however, it prevented the development of a free mortgage market; virtually all mortgages provided by Israeli banks are still funded by the government and provided to preferred individuals (such as new immigrants or poor young couples) on terms stipulated by the government. Yet the total value of mortgages in 1969–1982 was on average only 22 percent of the value of gross residential investment.[18] The capital gains accruing to owners of dwellings as a result of the sharp rise in the real price of housing until 1972 were further increased because after 1967 the mortgages were not linked to the cost-of-living (COL) index; hence the real value of mortgage payments shrank as inflation rose.

Expectations of such double-barreled capital gains encouraged the persistent high demand for housing throughout the 1970s and created public pressure on the government to extend its subsidized mortgage programs and its direct involvement in housing construction.[19] Only in 1979 did the government partly index its subsidized mortgages and allow the banks some freedom in providing "nondirected" mortgages at market-determined rates. The high and increasing marginal income tax rates (see Yitzhaki, 1983), from which the implicit income from owned housing is exempt, and the low rates of the property tax (which was abolished in 1982) are two more government-related reasons for the high demand for owner-occupied housing.

The government's policy of providing housing and subsidizing mortgages, the lack of nongovernment outlets for financial savings, and a widespread belief in housing as a hedge against the erosion of savings by inflation or their appropriation by decree thus reinforced the effect of rising income to promote an extremely high rate of residential investment.

Public-Sector Investment

What was here classified as public-sector investment (see Figure 4-2) does not presume to reflect the full extent of the government's investment activities. Investment in infrastructure (including electricity, water, communications, ports, roads, and ships and aircraft) and public services (including private nonprofit institutions) is indeed determined to a large extent by public officials and is often not motivated by profit. The same can also be said, however, for a significant segment of investment that is here classified as "private," although it is owned either fully or partly by the government (for example, the aircraft and armament industries).[20]

As mentioned above, the rise in the share of gross capital stock in public services more than offset the decline in the share of infrastructure. Even though the public-sector share in gross investment remained constant, its share in net investment increased. This phenomenon stands in contrast to cross-section findings that the government's share in capital formation (unlike its share in consumption) tends to decline as a country's level of development rises (Kuznets, 1960). The declining share of infrastructure investment is understandable given the priority that such investment had to have in the early stages of Israel's rapid economic development, and given the longevity of such investments.

One might also have expected that the extent of public services investment (55 percent of which is in education and health services) would match the growth of the population. Yet in 1960–1982 the capital stock in public services increased an average of 11 percent annually while the population increase was only 3 percent and the number of pupils in educational institutions rose less than 4 percent a year. Thus the stock of capital in public services per beneficiary increased more than fourfold. Part of this increase should be ascribed (as in the case of dwellings) to the improvement in the standard of living. But it may also be due to the fact that so much of Israel's savings (domestic and foreign) is diverted into investment via public channels.

Finally, one feature of direct public investment (including publicly initiated housing) that deserves notice is its nonuse for stabilization purposes. Figure 4-2 shows clearly that the share of public gross investment in total investment has not moved countercyclically. In 1973–1975, when the pressure on resources was greatest, direct government investment activity continued at peak level (and its share in residential construction even increased). This state of affairs can be attributed in part to the long lag between the decision to appropriate funds and the actual construction and completion of public buildings. This lag makes it almost impossible to use direct public investment as a short-term policy tool, other than in the form of crude, temporary, across-the-board public construction freezes such as the one attempted in 1975–1976.

Business-Sector Investment

In discussing the need to boost capital formation as a means to stimulate growth, one tends to think of investment in the business sector, and specifically investment in manufacturing. Figure 4-2 reveals, however, that gross fixed business investment has accounted for only one-third of total fixed investment, and manufacturing for only 14 percent. The expected trend in the composition of capital formation, away from housing, public services, and infrastructure and into branches producing tradable commodities, is conspicuously absent. In fact, as noted above, in terms of *net* investment, in recent years there has even been a clear trend away from the business sector.

The two main business branches that produce tradable commodities are manufacturing and agriculture. Manufacturing retained a stable 23 percent share in domestic product as well as a stable 13–14 percent share in the gross capital stock. Mirroring the development in the economy as a whole, the annual growth rate of manufacturing capital stock declined only mildly after 1973 (from 8.3 percent in

1960–1972 to 7.4 percent in 1973–1981), while the product growth rate dropped sharply (from 11.8 to 3.9 percent), resulting in a sharp increase in the capital-output ratio. On the other hand, the share of agriculture in net product declined from 12 percent in 1952–1961 to a stable 6 percent since 1970. Nevertheless, in 1960–1981 its product continued to grow faster than its capital stock, implying a steadily declining capital-ratio (see Chapter 3).

Manufacturing maintained a rather stable investment share of 4.2 percent of GNP. This share should be considered as somewhat low by international standards (comparable to that of the United States, lower than Italy's 5–6 percent, and significantly lower than Japan's 5–8 percent). This modest share is striking. Supply-side considerations would lead one to expect a relatively high rate of manufacturing investment, given Israel's high overall rate of investment (at least until 1975) and the extensive government subsidization of industrial investment. On the demand side, Israel's growing foreign indebtedness should have been expected to result in a relatively larger manufacturing branch (and investment) as the main potential source for expanding future exports to repay the debt.

In the 1950s, however, it was agriculture that received most of the government support. At its height, in 1955–1956, when gross investment in agriculture constituted 4.5 percent of GNP and 15.5 percent of total fixed investment, the government directly financed 70 percent of that investment. Ben-Shahar (1975) estimated that the average real interest rate charged at the time for loans to agriculture was 1.2 percent (compared with 4.6 percent to manufacturing), while the real cost of foreign funds to the economy was 9–11 percent.

In the 1960s, when the absolute level of investment in agriculture diminished,the share financed by long-term government credit (Table 4-2) increased steadily, exceeding 100 percent in 1969. This share declined somewhat in the 1970s but in 1979–1982 again exceeded 100 percent.

Government support of capital formation in manufacturing has been much less extensive. In the mid-1950s only 40 percent of manufacturing investment was financed by the government, and this share declined steadily to only 10 percent in the mid-1960s. An indication of subsequent greater government involvement was its policy to promote industrial investment in new development townships as a means of creating employment. Under the direction of Pinhas Sapir, then minister of trade and industry and later minister of finance, the government promoted private industrial enterprises in these development towns, primarily in low-skill, labor-intensive textiles. Much of the promotion effort was conducted secretly to avoid public scrutiny. Toren (1979) estimated that in 1958–1965 the cumulative differential grant to these textile plants (over and above grants provided elsewhere) equaled 5 percent of the 1962-level GNP. The primary policy used to promote employment was thus the distortion of factor prices in favor of capital. Furthermore, although many of the grants were provided ex-ante, even more were

TABLE 4-2. Indicators of public finance and business investment (percentages)

Years	Share of gross investment financed by public loans		Share of explicit grant to gross in-investment in manu-facturing	Real interest rate on average industrial development loans[a]
	Agriculture (1)	Manufacturing (2)	(3)	(4)
1956–1960	73	39	—	4.6
1961–1965	85	20	—	3.5
1966–1969	93	40	4	3.8
1970–1972	—	35	7	−2.5
1973–1975	71	39	5	−16.6
1976–1978	72	49	10	−16.6
1979–1982	130	71	13	—

Sources: Columns 1 and 2, 1965–1966: Halevi and Klinov-Malul (1968), table 71; Bank of Israel, *Annual Report 1969*, table V-13. Column 3, 1967–1969, columns 1 and 3, 1970–1978: Ministry of Trade, Industry and Tourism (1969, 1980). Column 2, 1973–1982 and columns 1, 3, 1979–1982: Bank of Israel, *Annual Reports, 1974*, table XVII; *1978*, table XVIII-9; *1982*, tables II-7, II-8. Column 4, 1965–1969: Ben-Shahar, Bronfeld, and Cukierman (1971); 1970–1978: interest rates from Controller of Banks, *Report*, 1974–1978, p. 268.

a. $[(1+r)/(1-\pi)-1]$, where r is the nominal interest rate on development loans in Zone B and π is the rate of increase in GNP deflator.

granted ex-post, as companies on the brink of collapse were bailed out by the government (a practice that could hardly foster entrepreneurial motivation).

In the 1960s the government gradually abandoned the use of allocations from the development budget as its main avenue of promoting capital formation; instead, it resorted more and more to exploiting its control over the financial system. This shift enabled the Treasury to direct subsidized loans without having to obtain parliamentary appropriation. "Approved projects" became entitled, under the Law for the Encouragement of Capital Investments, to an array of privileges. Eligibility for the approved status, which depends primarily on the project's being located in a development zone and on its export orientation, still left the Treasury considerable discretionary control.[21]

Another important change in the mid-1960s was the abandonment, under public pressure, of the linkage (either to the index or to the dollar) on all government loans. The Treasury assumed responsibility for compensating financial intermediaries for any discrepancy between the (linked) rates at which they mobilized funds from the public and the (unlinked) rates at which they granted directed credit. In 1967 the Treasury set a ceiling rate of 9 percent on all loans. Given the 2 percent inflation of 1967–68, the financial system seemed firmly under its control.[22]

In the boom years 1968–1972 manufacturing enjoyed rapid growth in profitability and investment. Increased investment was encouraged by favorable tax cuts in the 1967 amendment to the Law for the Encouragement of Capital Investments and facilitated by a growing share of government long-term finance. Moreover, a rapid expansion of the domestic arms and aircraft industries had major spillovers to private industry. In 1973, however, with the turnabout in the economy, investment in manufacturing had leveled off.

Despite pressure on domestic resources following the 1973 crises, the high level of investment in manufacturing persisted until 1975. The major reason for this, and for the still rather high investment level in manufacturing in the second half of the 1970s (to judge by the growing capital-output ratio), seems to have been the breakdown of the credit-dispensing system as a result of rising inflation. In 1974–1975 subsidized, unlinked, long-term loans at less than 10 percent interest were still widely available while the inflation rate reached 40 percent. In addition to these long-term development loans industry was also offered generous "supplementary" medium-term loans and short-term export credit, all at substantially negative real interest rates. Even when partial linkage was restored to the development loans in 1979, the tax-deductible status of the entire linkage premium of the loan principal and the 50–70 percent inflation rate kept the effective real interest on these linked loans negative.[23]

The rather innocuous abandonment of the linkage system in the mid-1960s and the move toward a less accountable system for dispensing public credit resulted thus in an allocation mechanism that was out of control. Litvin and Meridor (1982), estimating the ex-ante grant element in the government financing of business investment (in manufacturing, agriculture, and hotels), concluded that in 1974–1979 private investors perceived roughly half of every dollar invested as a free grant. Ex-post, with inflation much higher than anticipated, the grant element was even more substantial.[24]

There is little doubt that private business investment has been higher as a result of this massive subsidization than it would have been otherwise.[25] As noted before, however, the level of manufacturing investment in the 1970s, as a share of GNP, can hardly be considered excessive. If the subsidization of private investment did have adverse consequences, they are most likely to be found not in the overall level of investment, but in the microallocation of investment resources between firms (for example, a possible upward bias favoring large firms) and in the capital composition of projects (for example, a possible upward bias for short-lived machinery).

It is often maintained that one proof of excessive investment subsidies to industry is a low rate of capital utilization. A 1971–1972 plant survey by Morawetz (1975) revealed that in these peak years of industrial activity (and before the inflation-induced massive subsidization of the mid-1970s), capital utilization was significantly lower in Israel than in other countries. Very few industrial plants operated multiple shifts, and only one of every five plants operated more than 50 percent of the time. There is reason to believe that capital utilization has diminished further since then (see Chapter 3), and it is tempting to blame this low utilization rate on the subsidization of investment. One should note, however, that with other things (especially wages) unchanged, a larger industrial capital stock should lead to a higher, not a lower, utilization rate (measured by the number of shifts or hours plants are in operation).[26]

The low utilization rate in industry may be related more to excessive labor costs than to subsidized capital costs. The Israeli labor market in the 1970s has been characterized by government policy to guarantee full employment, by increasing employment and relatively high wages in the public and financial sectors, and by a steadily widening gap between labor costs to employers and net wages to employees. Throughout the 1970s, and particularly since 1977, labor costs have increased substantially despite reduced productivity (Chapter 15). It is quite possible that high and rising labor costs have been responsible for a large share of the low industrial capital utilization and, indeed, for the diminished growth in industrial production with the resultant increase in the capital-output ratio.[27]

With a distorted labor market, high distortionary taxes on both wages and corporate profits, and the tremendous uncertainties engendered by inflation and by wars, it may be wrong to apply static first-best notions of optimality to argue that the level of business investment has been excessive. On the other hand, if it is deemed desirable to stimulate industrial activity, it would be imperative to tackle these distortions rather than to resort once again to massive subsidization of industrial investment.

Conclusion

Gross investment in Israel has dropped from exceptionally high levels in 1948–1975 (30 percent of GNP) to what seems to be an average level by international standards (22 percent of GNP in 1980–1982). Gross private saving (relative to disposable income) also declined somewhat in 1973–1982, but its level was nonetheless still surprisingly high, and significantly higher than in the 1960s. On these grounds investment and private savings cannot be considered grossly inadequate.

Given the other major developments of 1973–1982—the vast increase in government dissaving and the growing foreign debt—private savings may still be regarded as not high enough. Nevertheless, the major problem in this context seems to be the extent of public-sector dissaving. The increase in the capital-output ratio in the mid-1970s and the acute problems facing the economy at the same time indicate that the overall level of investment may then have been excessive. For 1978–1982, however, the drop in the level of investment and the increase in depreciation allowances and in the dependency on foreign loans all indicate that investment should not be further curtailed.

The most important lesson to be learned from the preceding discussion is that the major concern should be not the overall *level* of investment but its *composition.* Israel's experience in the past decade has shown that its investment resources are seriously misallocated and that the fault lies mainly with the deficient, inflation-ridden and government-controlled capital market. Economic observers often accuse the government of excessive subsidization of industrial investment. However, the level of investment in manufacturing, only 4.2 percent of GNP, cannot be regarded as excessive. The critical misallocation clearly lies with the 13 percent of GNP devoted largely to residential construction and to investment in public services.

In considering "the basic questions about future investment policy in Israel" in 1960, Patinkin wondered "how soon the backlog of demand for housing . . . will be met, with a corresponding release of resources for investment in other sectors" (p. 82). It is indeed rather incredible that long after the genuine backlog of the 1950s was met, the economy continued after 1973 to devote an internationally unparalleled 9.5 percent of GNP annually to the expansion and upgrading of its stock of housing. It is possible that the uncertainties created by inflation and the government control of capital markets are responsible both for the excessive demand for housing and for the anemic demand (only partly offset by subsidies) for private business investment. Furthermore, the 3.5 percent of GNP devoted to expanding the capital stock in public services, at a rate that far exceeded the growth of the population, is also clearly incongruent with the state of the Israeli economy in the past decade, and is likely to have been the result of a public policy that was oblivious to resource constraints.

These observations point to a deficiency in the mechanism that channels investment resources. An apparently basic test of the appropriate functioning of this mechanism would be whether, during a period of extremely strong pressures on resources (such as wartime), it generated increased savings and curtailed investments (especially long-term, only indirectly productive investments). Events in Israel, especially in 1973–1975, show that the country's capital allocation mechanism failed this test. Savings did not increase and investment continued unabated, reaching peak levels. Furthermore, when investment did fall after 1975, it seems to have done so despite, rather than because of, the terms that the capital market offered private investors.

In 1960 Patinkin observed that "the large degree to which government was responsible for the financing of the investment program was the inevitable consequence of the nature [that is, foreign sources] of funds that could be attained for this purpose." He concluded that "government's share of financing could have been drastically reduced only by a corresponding reduction of the investment program as a whole" (pp. 91–92). There is little reason to believe that either the premise or the conclusion is relevant to Israel's situation in the 1970s or 1980s. Private savings are now large enough to finance the entire investment program (Figure 4-1). In addition, there is little doubt that existing financial institutions can handle the intermediation job.

The government, however, still dominates the intermediation between private savers and investors. This dominance is facilitated by its coercive control over the financial system and its ability (and willingness) to render its securities inflation-proof through index linkage.This dominant role also stems from a deep-rooted (socialist) mistrust of the market mechanism and a bureaucratic impatience with delays, combined with a desire for political control. In the 1960s there were some indications (see Table 4-2) that the government was prepared to abandon its tight grip on domestic financial intermediation; however, the pattern since 1967—partly resulting from inflation—suggests a clear movement toward ever-increasing public involvement in the channeling of investment resources.

In a 1970 essay Ben-Shahar, Bronfeld, and Cukierman concluded that "the loss of resources caused in the past by the inefficiency of the capital market is small in comparison to likely future damage" (p. 415). It is with some irony that one now reads their projected continued high rates of economic growth and their claim that "in view of these high rates of growth, the question of efficiency of the capital market assumes greater importance than it enjoyed in the past." With the benefit of hindsight one may note the ever more pressing need to allocate investment resources efficiently in a period of reduced growth and increased pressure on resources. So far, the Israeli economy does not seem to have met this challenge successfully:

5

Changes in the Industrial Structure

Ruth Klinov

This chapter analyzes changes in Israel's industrial structure of employment and product from 1955 to 1981, with special emphasis on its connection with Israel's balance-of-payments difficulties. Unlike many countries, whose development was marked by an initially high ratio of import surplus to GNP and a subsequent decline, Israel's import surplus-GNP ratio shows no sign of declining: it was 25 percent on average in 1955-1981, dropping mildly in 1955-1965 and rising moderately thereafter. Although unilateral transfers finance 60 to 75 percent of the import surplus, the cumulative debt resulting from the residual, loan-financed part has become increasingly burdensome, and the prospect of a future decline in unilateral transfers is a further source of worry.

Under such conditions, market forces would normally be expected to induce structural changes in inputs, outputs, and final uses through an increase in the real exchange rate, which should raise the profitability of tradable products relative to nontradables (defined below). This increased profitability should in turn generate a mobility of capital and labor into tradable industries, bringing about a relative rise in their product and a rise in the share of exports and import substitutes within final uses, as well as a reduction in imports' share in total resources.

In fact no rising trend is discernible in the real exchange rate since 1955 (Halevi, 1979), and the only expected process that occurred was a rise in the share of exports in the final uses of tradables and semitradables (Table 5-2). The other developments were contrary to expectations: a rise in the share of nontradables in employment, capital, and product.

Definitions

Tradables and nontradables are defined by the share of exports in final uses in each sector's output (see Table 5-2 and Klinov, 1984, tables A-1 and A-2). Hence I define three categories: tradables—agriculture, manufacturing, and transportation; nontradables—public services, and construction; and semitradables—business and financial services, commerce (which includes tourism), and personal services.

Public services are characterized by the nature of the service, not by ownership. They include the administrative services of the government, national institutions, and local authorities; educational, research, and scientific services; and health, religious, political, and trade-union services and defense. The defense sector is included only in part: in GDP accounts, the value added by the defense ministry is included in public services and in military expenditures on local purchases under the appropriate business-sector industries. The omissions are discussed at the end of the section on main trends. The labor force accounts do not include the regular army; reservists are included in their respective civilian industries.

All production other than public services is included in the *business sector.* This sector should not be confused with the subcategory *financial and business services,* which includes financial institutions, insurance, real estate, and business and legal services. *"Education-intensive" manufacturing* includes electrical and electronic equipment, transportation equipment, printing and publishing, and machinery. *"Other" manufacturing* consists of all the rest of manufacturing. In 1979 the proportion out of all employees of those with 13+ years of schooling was 28 percent in education-intensive manufacturing and 10 percent in "other" manufacturing.

Summary of Findings

Table 5-1 summarizes the main facts. The share of public services (regarded as entirely nontradable) in civilian employment rose moderately from 21 to 23 percent in 1955–1972 and then steeply to 28 percent in 1981; there was a further rise in military employment (see Klinov, 1984, table A-4) and a rise in the public services' share in capital. (The share of product fluctuated without a long-term trend.) In an international survey Ofer (1976) found both product and employment shares in public services to be excessively high as early as 1961 and again in 1974, and employment increases in the public sector since then have further increased this gap. In the same study Ofer also found construction, the other nontradable industry, to have an excessively high share by international standards and to have steadily increased its share in GDP. Together, construction and public services increased the share of nontradables from 31 to 35 percent of GDP and from 32 to 38 percent of civilian employment in 1955–1981. On the other hand, the combined share in GDP of agriculture, manufacturing, and transportation, all of which are defined as tradables, declined from 43 to 40 percent of GDP and from 45 to 40 percent of employment.

Two questions arise regarding the share of nontradables in both GDP and

TABLE 5-1. Share of tradables, nontradables, and semitradables in GDP, employment, and capital[a] (percentages)

	Tradables	Total nontradables	Total public services	Semitradables
GDP				
1955	43	31	22	26
1964	45	31	18	24
1972	42	33	18	25
1981	40	35	21	25
Civilian employment				
1955	45	32	21	23
1964	45	34	22	21
1972	42	35	23	25
1981	40	38	28	22
Non-residential capital				
1960	72	21	10	7
1964	69	24	15	7
1972	66	25	19	9
1981	61	30	23	9

Source: Klinov (1984), tables A-6, A-7; Buch (1982).
a. For definitions see the text.

inputs: why was their initial level so high, and why did this level increase further? Ofer (1976) explained the initial high share of nontradables as resulting from the predominance of unilateral transfers in financing the import surplus. Such transfers have both an income and a substitution effect. The income effect is created because gratis transfers can be added to GNP to arrive at the country's "disposable resources" and can influence demand via "resource elasticity," equivalent to "GNP elasticity" in other countries. To evaluate the effect of this elasticity empirically, Ofer compared the Israeli structure with that of other countries whose level of per capita *GNP* is similar to Israel's per capita *resources.* His tests confirm that the share of nontradables in the employment of such comparable countries is roughly similar to Israel's. In addition, the relatively high demand for public services and construction in Israel stems from Israel's special defense and immigration needs.

The substitution effect of unilateral transfers works via a reduction in the real exchange rate and can be analyzed as follows: total *domestic* resources (net of exports) are "produced" by two "production factors": GDP and the import surplus. Since much of the latter is a gift, its price is zero; by definition, it consists of tradable goods and services; hence efficiency considerations lead to specialization in nontradables within GDP.

These ingenuous arguments, though very plausible as explanations of the *level,* do not explain the *growth* in the nontradable sector: because the ratio of unilateral transfers to GNP did not increase, no further resource elasticity effect can be expected. Also, there was no change in the real exchange rate, and hence no further substitution effect. The constancy of the real exchange rate, particularly in 1972–1982, can be understood only as the result of government policy aimed at artificially isolating the structure of employment and production from external pressures. Under such isolation it should be possible to explain changes in the industrial structure by observing ordinary supply and demand forces operating in the economy *as if it did not face an external debt.*

The present analysis uses this framework. It assumes that the import surplus is a residual result rather than a cause of changes in GDP structure. These changes are explained in a general-equilibrium setting that includes supply and demand considerations in both the factor and the product markets. The demand forces are price and income elasticities of domestic demand and of exports; the supply forces (assumed to be exogenous) include increases in employment (divided into two categories by level of education), in capital, and in residual productivity (that is, productivity increases unaccounted for by additions to capital or labor).

Data analysis (not reported here) shows that by dividing the period it is possible to reduce, in each subperiod, the large number of potential supply and demand factors to three: for the subperiod 1955–1972 these are income elasticities favoring nontradables, the increase in capital per worker, and residual productivity—the latter two favoring tradables. The net outcome for this period is an increase in the *real* product of tradables relative to nontradables and a decline in the relative prices of tradables, which shows up as a mild decline in their share in GDP in current prices.

After 1972 the importance of changes in physical capital per worker declined and its place was taken by changes in human capital. In particular, there was a disproportionate increase in the share of employees with postsecondary education, most of which was absorbed in public services and financial and business services. At the same time there was a decline in residual productivity, which arrested the growth of manufacturing. This, in addition to demand forces favoring nontradables, worked to increase the real product of non- and semitradables. The overall outcome was a further decline in the share of tradables in both employment and product (with the notable exception of education-intensive manufacturing, which profited from the increase in the supply of educated labor as well as from an increase in foreign demand).

With regard to the interaction of supply-side forces, it is important to note that the rising trend in the share of public, financial, and business services in employment had already started in 1965. The impact on the structure of product was delayed by the offsetting effect of productivity increases in tradables. As long as these increases were sizable, it was possible to expand capital and employment in nontradables, and at the same time to expand real product in the tradable sector. The decline in productivity makes such a divergence less possible, and increasing the product of tradables requires a simultaneous increase in their share in employment. The repercussions on the educational system may be sizable (see the last section for a brief discussion).

Main Trends

This section describes and analyzes changes in inputs and product structure in greater detail. Since the industrial structure is only one element in the linkage between GDP and the import surplus, the other two elements—import and export components within industries—will also be briefly summarized.

Exports, Imports, and Product

Although the share of tradables in Israel's GDP has shrunk, an increasing share of output is being exported (see Table 5-2). The share of exports in business-sector final uses rose from 13 to 34 percent in 1955–1981. Agriculture, transportation, and several manufacturing branches exported more than half of their output in 1980 (either directly, or indirectly—through their contribution to the exports of other industries). The increase in exports accounted for 40 percent of the growth of the business sector's product between 1958–1972 and for more than 80 percent in 1972–1977 (Klinov, 1984, table A-1).

Total import coefficients in the business sector also rose, though moderately, from 25 percent in 1958 to 30 percent in 1976—mainly through increased imports in "other" manufacturing. There was a sharp rise in the public sector's direct defense imports, from 2 percent of GDP in 1960 to 10 percent in 1980 (see Chapter 8). It does not necessarily follow, however, that the constant import surplus–GDP ratio should be attributed to rising military expenditures. Defense-oriented activities are also responsible for much of the rise in exports and for considerable import substitution. The rapid growth in exports of electrical and electronic equipment, metal products, and machines reflects, to a considerable extent, military product. The constancy of the import surplus–GDP ratio is thus a combination of three forces: rising imports in both public services and the business sector, rising exports of semitradables and tradables, and a decline in the share of tradables in GDP.

TABLE 5-2. Export and import components of output, 1958–1980 (percentages)

	Share of exports in final uses[a]		Total import coefficients[a]	
Component	1958	1980	1958	1976
Agriculture	16	57	20	21
Manufacturing				
"Other"	14	36	31	51
"Education-intensive"	14	48	40	42
Transportation	26	70	30	30
Construction	—	—	15	22
Services, excluding trade	11	30	11	9
Trade	4	16	6	7
Total business sector	13	34	25	30

Sources: Bruno (1962); CBS, Special Publications Series, No. 625; Bank of Israel, *Annual Report, 1981.*

a. Direct and indirect.

Supply and Demand Shifts

Table 5-3 describes the main supply-and-demand shifts in the factor and product markets. For the purpose of the present discussion, production factors are: capital (K), "educated" labor (L_{ED}), "other" labor (L_{OTH}), and productivity.[1]

Table 5-3 shows that until 1973 the fastest-growing factor was capital. Its annual average rate of growth, however, slowed from 17 percent in 1950–1955 to 5 percent in 1973–1981 (when corrected for utilization the latter rate declines to 1.4 percent). From 1965 on, its place was taken by a rise in L_{ED}. In 1973–1981 there was an annual increase of 8 percent in employed persons with 13+ years of schooling, compared with a rise of only 1 percent for those with less than 12 years of schooling. (The data on labor since 1970 include workers from the administered territories, all of whom are included in the L_{OTH} category.) By 1980 the share of those with postsecondary schooling in the population age 25+ was the third highest in the world, surpassed only by the United States and Canada.[2] Last, data presented elsewhere (Klinov, 1984, table A-5) show that until 1972 residual productivity grew at an average annual rate of 5 percent in the tradable sector and by less than 1 percent in nontradables. After 1973 a decline in the productivity of all industries (except agriculture) leveled off the interindustry differences. These changing factor endowments would be expected to have produced an expansion of capital- and productivity- intensive industries (agriculture, "other" manufacturing and transportation, which are tradables, and construction) until the mid-1960s, followed in the 1970s by an expansion of L_{ED}-intensive sectors (public services and financial and business services, which are non- and semitradables, and education-intensive manufacturing).[3]

Two alternative variables were chosen to represent increases in domestic demand: real GDP per capita and real private consumption (Table 5-3). They behaved similarly until 1965, after which private consumption grew first more slowly (1965–1972) and then more rapidly (1973–1981) than income. These divergent growth paths indicate that observed incomes may misrepresent the "true" budget constraint on demand. One reason for this is the changing ratio of disposable to national income; another may be the inertia of consumption growth inherited from previous periods. Other possible reasons are changes in the market value of financial assets relative to current income, and underreporting of incomes. In any case, the sustained increase in domestic demand would be expected to bias the production structure toward industries in which income elasticity exceeds unity—public services, construction, financial and business services, and

TABLE 5-3. Average annual growth rates – selected variables, 1950–1981 (percentages)

Variables	1950–55	1955–64	1965–72	1973–81
Population	6.7	3.7	2.7	2.4
"Educated" labor[a]	6.5	4.0	4.6	5.1
"Educated" labor[b]	—	—	7.8	8.0
"Other" labor[a]	6.5	3.3	2.0	1.0
"Other" labor[b]	—	—	2.3	1.2
Education index	−1.0	0.2	2.9	3.0
Nonresidential capital	17.4	11.0	7.1	5.4[c]
Productivity (business sector)	4.6	3.6	4.4	0.6
Per capita GDP	4.6	5.8	5.6	1.1
Per capita private consumption	4.2	5.2	3.6	3.0

Sources: Population: Metzer (1983), appendix; labor force: CBS, *Statistical Abstracts 1951, 1966, 1982;* Special Publications Series, nos. 56, 68, 243, 452; education index, 1950–1960: Baruh (1965); 1961–1972: Hercowitz (1975); 1970–1979: Amir (1985); Capital and productivity: Gaathon (1971) and Metzer (1983); GDP and consumption: CBS, *Statistical Abstract 1983.*

a. "Educated" = Professions *plus* administrative; "other" = all others.

b. "Educated" = 13+ years of schooling; "other" = 0–12 years of schooling.

c. When corrected for 75 percent utilization, the rate is 1.4 percent.

education-intensive manufacturing.[4] An additional source of increased demand for financial and business services was the accelerating inflation rate.

The expansion of exports is a source of increase in the tradable sector's product, but it may be interpreted either as an autonomous demand shift or as the result of changing relative factor endowments. Tentative tests (described in the next section) suggest that factor endowments explain the increase in exports better than do autonomous shifts, but the evidence is far from conclusive, and both factors probably contributed to the export increase.

Table 5-4 presents the annual real growth rates of product by industry at constant prices, and the change in relative prices. As expected, in 1955–1972 agriculture, transportation, and manufacturing (both M_{OTH} and M_{ED})—that is, the tradable sector—grew faster than nontradables, and their prices (relative to the average price deflator) declined. Among non- and semitradables, only construction grew at a faster-than-average GDP rate.

Table 5-4 shows that since 1973 changes in factor endowments and in income elasticities of domestic demand for product worked in the same direction—expanding the public sector, financial and business services, and education-intensive manufacturing. In the case of housing, demand and supply moved in opposite directions: whereas demand grew, the supply of L_{OTH} and K shrank, raising the relative price of construction (last column of Table 5-4).

Tables 5-4 and 5-5 together reveal that the tradable industries—with the exception of M_{ED}—either diminished (agriculture) or did not expand their labor force shares in 1955–1972, while the proportion of the labor force in the non- and semitradable industries grew: in public services from 21 to 23 percent; in the business sector, financial and business services increased at least from 2 to 4 percent (see note b in Table 5-5). The share of nontradables in nonresidential capital also increased (Table 5-1). The faster-than-average increase in the real product of the tradable sector was almost entirely (again, with the exception of education-intensive manufacturing) a result of differential residual productivity (that is, the increase in product unaccounted for by measured increases in inputs), which grew at a faster rate for tradables than for nontradables, and more than offset the increasing concentration of production factors in nontradables. Hence, despite the lead of tradables in real product growth, the very increase in their residual productivity decreased the labor and capital required, diverting the excess to the low-productivity industries.

After 1973 the growth rate in the productivity of all sectors except agriculture declined sharply; as a result, real product growth rates are accompanied by similar changes in factor allocation: education-intensive manufacturing, public services, and business and financial services grew fastest in terms of both employment and product. Consequently, whereas before 1973 tradables grew in real terms without resort to a larger share of labor and capital, their expansion (agriculture excepted)

TABLE 5-4. Annual rates of change of product and relative prices, by industry, 1955–1981 (percentages)

<table>
<tr><th rowspan="2"></th><th colspan="3">Real annual growth rates of product</th><th colspan="3">Annual rates of change in relative prices[a]</th></tr>
<tr><th>1955–64</th><th>1965–72</th><th>1973–81</th><th>1955–64</th><th>1965–72</th><th>1973–81</th></tr>
<tr><td>Agriculture</td><td>12.2</td><td>5.0</td><td>6.1</td><td>–5.5</td><td>–2.0</td><td>–4.6</td></tr>
<tr><td>"Other" manufacturing</td><td>12.7</td><td>10.0</td><td>2.3</td><td>–2.7</td><td>–1.8</td><td>0.1</td></tr>
<tr><td>"Education-intensive" manufacturing</td><td>13.0</td><td>10.5</td><td>6.4</td><td>–4.5</td><td>–1.7</td><td>–1.4</td></tr>
<tr><td>Construction</td><td>11.8</td><td>8.2</td><td>–1.9</td><td>2.0</td><td>1.2</td><td>3.5</td></tr>
<tr><td>Transportation</td><td>12.2</td><td>10.4</td><td>3.4</td><td>–1.3</td><td>–1.6</td><td>–3.5</td></tr>
<tr><td>Business and financial services</td><td rowspan="2">6.3</td><td rowspan="2">8.0</td><td>4.4</td><td rowspan="2">9.1</td><td rowspan="2">7.2</td><td rowspan="2">0.4</td></tr>
<tr><td>Trade and personal services</td><td>3.2</td></tr>
<tr><td>Public services</td><td>6.4</td><td>7.9</td><td>4.4</td><td>5.7</td><td>4.3</td><td>3.2</td></tr>
<tr><td>Total GDP</td><td>8.5</td><td>8.8</td><td>3.3</td><td>—</td><td>—</td><td>—</td></tr>
</table>

Source: Product: based on Gaathon (1971), CBS, *Statistical Abstract 1983*, and Metzer (1983).

a. Relative prices computed by dividing nominal by real growth in each sector, at factor cost.

since 1973 required larger quantities of production factors, particularly labor (since there there was excess capacity in capital), in order to continue growing. Education-intensive manufacturing was the only tradable industry to benefit from the changing factor endowments, and its growth has been impressive: in 1973–1981 it increased by 6.4 percent annually in real terms. Although the relative price of its product declined, there was still a net increase in its GNP share in current prices, from 8.2 percent in 1968 to 10.1 percent in 1981. Almost the entire increase in its product accrued to exports (see Klinov, 1984, table A-1), and its share in exports grew (see Chapter 12). But despite its growth, education-intensive manufacturing still failed to offset the lead gained by nontradables in GDP, both in real growth rates and in current-price shares.

In sum, the drift of GDP toward nontradables since 1973 appears to be largely

TABLE 5-5. Industrial composition of civilian employed persons, selected years, 1951–1981[a]

Sector	1951	1955	1961	1964	1968[b]	1972	1977	1981
Public sector	18.2	21.0	22.8	21.9	22.5	22.9	24.6	28.2
Business sector	81.8	79.0	77.2	78.1	77.5	77.1	75.4	71.8
Agriculture	16.9	22.1	22.2	16.5	13.4	11.3	9.2	8.9
"Other" manufacturing	28.8	20.0	21.3	22.4	23.4	21.5	22.1	20.9
"Education-intensive" manufacturing	—	7.0	9.5	10.1	7.5	8.8	10.5	11.1
Financial services	—	2.2	2.7	3.7	3.6	3.6	4.8	6.3
Business services[b]	—	—	—	—	2.4	3.5	3.7	4.5
Transportation	8.5	8.5	8.2	9.2	9.7	9.0	8.9	8.7
Other	45.8	40.2	36.1	38.1	40.0	42.3	40.8	39.6

Source: Klinov (1984), table A-7.

a. From 1970 on, includes persons from the administered territories working in Israel.

b. New classification. Business (but not financial) services included in public services until 1968.

the result of the decline in residual productivity growth in tradables and of the increased supply of L_{ED}. The next section attempts to test this conclusion more systematically and to compare it with demand-side explanations; but before that, it is necessary to note the presence of three statistical biases that cause an underestimate of growth in nontradables.

1. Real product in public services (Table 5-4) is estimated as the increase in physical labor inputs. Since the measured product of the public sector in current prices consists almost entirely of wages, the result is roughly equivalent to deflating current product by the nominal-wage index. This procedure ignores increases in labor productivity and biases the growth rate of public services downward, as well as exaggerating the size of productivity differences between it and other industries. In addition, no account is taken in the national accounting procedures of capital services in this sector; this omission, too, biases growth rates of public services downward. Such corrections are attempted elsewhere (Klinov, 1984, table A-3).

2. Another source of a downward bias in the public sector's product is the absence of any account of the value added by the regular army. In addition, payments for reserve military service are recorded as transfers by the National Insurance Institute rather than as value added by the defense sector. Since local military consumption grew steeply (see Chapter 8), the result is an underestimate of the true increase in the public-sector product.

3. Since 1973 the CBS has deducted a net negative interest from banking services, in an attempt to correct for intermediary services of the banking system to other firms. This deduction is responsible for the moderate rate of increase of these services in GDP (Table 5-4), in contrast to their steeply rising share in employment (Table 5-5).

Supply Versus Demand Effects

The preceding section ascribed the changing shares in GDP of different industries to the joint effects of changes in factor endowments, in residual productivity, and in demand elasticities. This section attempts (in spite of the great difficulties involved, including many arbitrary assumptions) to ascertain the relative importance of the various supply and demand factors mentioned, using a general-equilibrium model suggested by Williamson (1976, 1980).[5] The model consists of three simultaneous equations, in which the endogenous variables are: the annual rate of increase in real product in sector i (Q_i), the rate of change in the price of sector i relative to the total GDP price (P_i), and the rate of change in the real return to each production factor (w for "simple" labor, L_{OTH}; q for educated labor, L_{ED}; r for capital, K). The exogenous variables and parameters are: internal demand elasticities of income (μ_i) and prices (ϵi), the latter corrected for external price elasticities; rates of change in population (POP) and factor endowments (L_{OTH}, L_{ED}, K); changes in the residual productivity of sector i (T_i) (assumed to differ between sectors, but not between production factors within each sector); and the elasticity of substitution in production among the different factors of production (σ, assumed to be the same for each pair of factors). Because the number of variables does not permit an ordinary regression procedure, I used a simulation; the data for the exogenous variables were derived from various statistical sources. The equations are:

(5.1) $$P_i = \theta_{iK}r + \theta_{iL_{OTH}}w + \theta_{iL_{ED}}q - T_i.$$

(5.2) $$L_{ED} = \sum_i \lambda_i[Q_i - T_i + \theta_{iL_{OTH}}\sigma(w-q) + \theta_{iK}\sigma(r-q)].$$

(5.3) $$Q_i = \frac{1}{\mu_i\phi_i}\left[\mu \sum_{i \neq n} Q_n\phi_n + POP(1-\mu_i) - \epsilon_i P_i\right].$$

The first equation states that the change in each sector's price P_i is equal to the changes in factor prices (r, w, q) weighted by their (changing) shares in the cost of production (θ_{ij}) *minus* "residual" productivity increases (T_i). The second equation states that the absorption of each production factor, such as L_{ED}, into a particular industry, i, is determined by its product expansion (Q_i) *minus* productivity increases (T_i) and by a rather complicated expression for the elasticity of substitution (σ). The effect of the elasticity of substitution on the factor's absorption depends on changes in relative factor prices ($w - q$, and so on) and on the share of each factor in the cost of production in that industry (θ_{ij}). The final result is a summation over all industries, weighted by the proportion (λ_i) of that factor (for example, L_{ED}) employed in each industry.

The third equation states that the increase in internal demand for each industry's product (Q_i) is inversely related to changes in its own price through price elasticity (ϵ_i) and directly related to the increase in GDP through income elasticity (μ_i). The effect of population increase on demand depends on the elasticity of demand: it is positive for $\mu_i > 1$ and negative otherwise. To avoid double counting, the model corrects the effect of income elasticity for the industry's share (θ_i) in total GDP.

The general purpose of this model is to weigh the relative importance of the various factors affecting the structure of production. The discussion here concentrates on three main questions: (1) How important is differential residual factor productivity (T_i) in explaining the changing structure of production and prices in the post- versus the pre-1973 period? (2) How much does the increasing availability of highly educated manpower (L_{ED}) contribute to explaining the changes in quantities and prices? (3) How important was the increase in domestic demand generated by the rise in per capita income?

To test the reliability of the rather cumbersome model in answering these questions, I first used the simulation to predict changes in product, prices, and factor returns and then compared them with actual changes. I used a preliminary test to see whether increased exports could be better explained by a reduction in the relative prices of the tradable sector or by the introduction of autonomous demand shifts in the demand equation (no. 5.3). Because the correspondence of predictions to actual developments (measured by their weighted standard deviation) was better under the first assumption, I adopted it as part of the basic model.

The findings, presented in Table 5-6, suggest that despite its complicated form, the model predicts product growth reasonably well in the first five industrial categories but underpredicts growth in private and public services. At least part of the underprediction for public services can be attributed to the excessively low income elasticity used in the simulations (see note 4), which was "adopted" from international cross-sections. For many reasons (discussed in Ofer, 1976, and Chapter 11 in this volume) this elasticity may underestimate the Israeli figure.

TABLE 5-6. Actual and predicted growth rates, product (Q_i), and relative prices (P_i)

Industry	1973–1981				1955–1981			
	Q_i		P_i		Q_i		P_i	
	Actual	Predicted	Actual	Predicted	Actual	Predicted	Actual	Predicted
Agriculture	6.1	6.2	–4.6	–3.4	8.0	8.5	–4.1	–4.3
"Other" manufacturing	2.3	1.2	0.1	0.5	8.3	8.0	–1.7	–2.1
"Education-intensive" manufacturing	6.4	4.9	–4.1	–1.7	10.0	12.3	–2.5	–2.3
Transportation	3.4	2.9	–3.5	–0.4	6.1	6.2	–2.1	–0.7
Construction	–1.9	–1.8	3.5	2.7	8.7	8.0	2.2	1.2
Financial and business services	4.4	0.4	0.4	–0.2	5.7	2.4	5.5	2.3
Other services	3.2	–0.6	0.4	0.4	6.2			
Public services	4.4	3.2	3.2	–0.9	6.0	2.7	4.0	2.5

Sources: Actual: Table 5-4; predicted: Klinov (1984), tables A-10, A-11.

Growth of the financial and business services sector (as well as trade and personal services) is also underpredicted, partly because of inflation. However, some additional basic forces affecting the growth of services have admittedly not been captured, and the remaining gap probably reflects Ofer's explanation (see the beginning of this chapter). An additional part of the gap after 1973 may be explained by the divergence between the increases in consumption and income.

Table 5-6 also correctly predicts the decline in the relative prices of tradables (versus nontradables). As mentioned, this decline is probably responsible for a large part of the increase in the share of exports in final demand.

The second step was to rerun the basic model using "counterfactuals." This technique allots hypothetical values to the variables used so as to test their effect on real growth rates and on relative prices. Of the many possible "games" of this sort, the following three were chosen to provide tentative answers to the questions outlined above:

1. To test for the effects of differential productivity growth, I set all T_i to equal T; that is, residual factor productivity was artificially assumed to be the same in all industries, and equal to the overall average growth of productivity.
2. To investigate the effect of L_{ED}, I set L_{ED} to equal L_{OTH}; that is, both "educated" and "other" labor were assumed to grow at the same average rate as the labor force.
3. To study the effect of demand elasticities I set all income elasticities (μ_i) to equal unity.

To quantify the degree of importance of the three effects, I calculated the standard deviation of the counterfactuals from actual growth rates of outputs (weighted by each industry's share in GDP). The larger the standard deviation, the more important the factor.

The main results (reported in Klinov, 1984, tables A-10 through A-12) are as follows. For the period 1955–1981 as a whole, differential residual productivity (T_i) had the strongest influence: if productivity had grown at a uniform rate in all industries, the real product of nontradables would have increased faster than that of tradables. Income elasticities come second: as expected, the higher elasticities for nontradables tilt production in their direction. Last, for 1973–1981 the higher growth rate of L_{ED} had a strong influence: had it increased at the same rate as "other" labor, both private and public services would hardly have grown.

To see whether the results of the simulations depend on the artificial assumption of zero productivity in the public sector, I carried out an additional set of simulations in which the productivity of services, both private and public, was assumed to equal that of the total business sector. The results show a higher predicted rise in services, but the gap relative to actual growth persists because such a redefinition of product raises not only the predictions but also the measure-

	Capital per worker	Workers with 13+ years of schooling / total workers (percent)
Agriculture	6.0	4
"Other" manufacturing	3.4	5
"Education-intensive" manufacturing	2.9	16
Transportation	11.7	7
Construction	5.4	5
Trade	—	8
Financial and business services	1.2	35
Other services		9
Public and community services	2.9	40

Source: Amir (1983), tables 6, 7.

ment of the actual quantity of services. Otherwise, the results are similar in direction (though not in magnitude) to those obtained with the zero-productivity assumption, in that T_i and μ_i are the most important factors in the period as a whole, and L_{ED} is most important in 1973–1981.

The model did not include inflation as another possible source of demand shifts. The expected effects are an increase in demand for employment in and the product of financial and business services, and possibly for housing (as a hedge against capital losses).

It is tempting to attribute the abnormally large size of these two sectors to inflation, but proving such a claim is quite difficult. On the one hand, construction is adequately predicted by the model even without inflation; what is more, construction actually declined after 1973, just as inflation entered a new upswing. On the other hand, the growth of employment in the financial and business sector was extremely rapid, but its share in GDP did not increase as rapidly.

To test the effect of inflation and its acceleration on the employment share of the financial and business services, I ran a set of regressions based on an international cross-section. The explanatory variables were, in addition to the 1979 rate of inflation, its acceleration in 1971–1979, per capita GDP in 1979, and its rate of increase in 1971–1979. Surprisingly, the regressions produced only one significant coefficient, that of per capita GDP.

There may be several reasons why no significant effects of inflation were found in the international cross-section. One is that the special *form* of Israeli inflation caused the exceptionally high rate of employment in the financial and business sector. I refer primarily to the far-reaching indexation of financial assets, which enables individuals to hedge against inflation by reallocation of their financial portfolios—that is, *within* the financial and business sector. It is possible that in other countries, where financial assets are not so thoroughly indexed, the main impact of inflation is felt in other sectors, such as construction. Another possible explanation of the absence of statistical significance is that the market's reaction to accelerated inflation is discontinuous at very high rates of inflation, and because very few countries have Israel's rate of inflation, case studies rather than statistical procedures are required.

The Rise in the Level of Education: Cause or Effect?

Throughout this chapter it is assumed that the educational composition of the labor force affects the industrial structure. This is a rather one-sided assumption. No doubt the growth of L_{ED} (whether defined by education or by occupation) is at least partly a reaction to (rather than a cause of) changing industrial structure. Various attempts have been made to test the direction of causality. The simplest test of the contention that the industrial structure determines L_{ED}, and not vice versa, is the "fixed coefficient" test, which predicts that changes in L_{ED} will be proportional to changes in the composition of product, if each industry needs a certain fixed proportion of labor of various types. This contention has been refuted elsewhere for the period 1961–1976 (Klinov, 1976), and Amir (in Chapter 6 of this volume) has refuted it for the period 1971–1979. Hershkowitz and Sussman (1971) added the effect of differential productivity growth to the factors explaining changes in the composition of product—that is, they hypothesized that with an equal rate of increase in the outputs of two industries, the one with higher productivity increase will require fewer additional workers. Having found no evidence that either income increase or productivity differentials explain the growth rate of schooling, they concluded that demand forces cannot explain changes in the labor force's level of education. This is also the working hypothesis of this chapter, and should lead one to expect a decline in the relative wages of L_{ED} as its supply increases.

Evidence to the contrary is provided by Amir (in Chapter 6 of this volume), who shows that they did not change much on average: they declined in the public sector and rose both in education-intensive manufacturing and in the financial and business sector. Much of the growing wage gap between the business and public sectors is a result of the substitution of women for men in the public services; women's relative wage, which was low to begin with, decreased even further (see also Klinov, 1984, tables A-14 and A-15). This is consistent with demand forces working in education-intensive manufacturing (through exports) and in the financial and business sector (through inflation), and with a general oversupply of L_{ED}, which is absorbed by the public sector. If inflation were to subside and nothing else were to change, the excess L_{ED} supply might even grow larger. The simulations in my 1984 study (table A-12) show a general decline in the relative wage of L_{ED}. The fact that it did not occur evenly, but was concentrated in the public sector and among women, may be at least partly due to imperfections in educational, occupational, and intersectoral mobility *within* the L_{ED} group.

There are additional indications of the role of the government as an absorber of excess labor supply. After 1973 Israel experienced a slowdown in growth, much like other countries, but hardly any increase in unemployment. The expansion of the public sector in the same period, accompanied by a reduction in its relative wages, can be interpreted as the absorption of excess labor. Finally, the government's emphasis on education as a means of social integration commits it not only to a higher supply of educational services but also to the creation of jobs for the graduates of educational institutions.

Conclusion

There are two broad sets of explanations for the high and increasing share of nontradables, and particularly of public services in employment and product. One stresses the exogeneity of the import surplus and derives from it both demand elasticities and supply substitution forces sufficient to account for the initial level. Without denying the plausibility of this explanation, this chapter presents an additional approach, which tries to explain the changes in the 1960s and 1970s and emphasizes the lack of connection between balance-of-payments changes and the internal structure of production. This alternative approach provides a reasonably satisfactory explanation of the growth rates and the changes in relative prices of the tradable sector and of construction, but underpredicts all services. In the future a better overall explanation may be achieved by integration of the two approaches.

The discussion stresses the roles of changing factor endowments and of differential productivity growth. In particular, it argues that before 1973, productivity growth differentials increased the real product of the tradable sector relative to nontradables and more than offset the increasing concentration of production factors in nontradables. This offsetting effect was much weakened after 1973, while the rapid increase in the "educated" labor force accelerated. The result was an increase in public, financial, and business services, which are largely nontradable. Inflation was another contributing factor. The only tradable sector that gained from the change in factor endowments was education-intensive manufacturing.

There is evidence that the government has operated as an absorber of excess labor, but this is debatable: how can one *prove* that the expansion of public-sector employment was supply- rather than demand-induced? The public sector may have expanded its services for reasons unconnected with the increasing availability of the appropriate labor force. My simulations do not *prove* the contrary, but they do suggest that if one ignores supply-side considerations it becomes necessary to assume an inordinately high income elasticity to account for an increase of one-third in civilian public service employment during a decade of stagnant growth.

In evaluating the role of L_{ED} it is essential to take note of the very high level of aggregation involved in the grouping of the *total* employed with 13+ years of schooling, and implicitly assuming complete mobility within this category. This approach, therefore, does *not* ascribe the halt in the expansion of the tradables sector to lack of mobility by L_{ED} into the "right" professions, although lags in adjustments may still be a contributing factor. The issue raised here is the overall size of higher education rather than its composition.

Is there, then, overeducation in Israel? I rather doubt it. Educational systems are long-term phenomena, and an attempt to observe them from a trough in the business cycle is bound to be misleading. During the pre-1973 period, marked by rapid growth, there was no excess supply, and a resumption of growth, rather than a deceleration in education, is probably the long-term solution.

Last, the share of tradables can be increased by a real devaluation, that is, by discontinuing the artificial isolation of internal structural changes from Israel's external debt.

6

Educational Structure and Wage Differentials of the Labor Force in the 1970s

Shmuel Amir

The educational structure of the Israeli labor force has changed considerably since 1948, declining from an unparalleled high level to a much lower one in the early 1950s (because of mass immigration with a high proportion of people with little schooling) and rising continuously since then. The process accelerated in the 1970s: the proportion of employed persons with 13+ years of schooling rose from 12.3 percent in 1963 to 17.0 percent in 1971 and to 26.1 percent in 1979 (Table 6-1). This chapter analyzes the development of the educational and wage structure of the Israeli labor force in the 1970s.

The educational level of the labor force at any time reflects accumulated effects. In the 1970s, current conditions affected the education level of young people entering the labor force and the amount of investment in on-the-job training; most of the stock of human capital in the labor force and norms of educational investment, however, originated earlier: previous demographic trends, migration patterns, and economic conditions appear to have determined most of the changes in the educational structure in the 1970s. Since there is no way of distinguishing between currently and previously determined factors, the increased supply of educated labor in the 1970s will be considered exogenous to the 1970s labor market.

In the 1950s and 1960s, the demand for education was pushed up by a rapidly rising standard of living and by social measures designed to absorb the large number of immigrant children into the public school system, so that investment in education increased gradually. The demand for educated manpower was increased by the rapid expansion of public services, which are on the whole human-capital intensive. That expansion was itself the result of the rapid and sustained economic growth until the early 1970s and the high rate of population growth. The demand for educated manpower was probably also augmented by high investment in physical capital, which continuously raised the capital intensity of

TABLE 6-1. Educational level of employed persons, 1963–1979 (percentages and 000s)

Years of schooling	Employed persons[a]			Change (in percent)	
	1963	1971	1979	1963–1971	1971–1979
Men					
0–8	58.3	50.2	34.4	–8.1	–15.8
9–12	30.4	35.2	43.1	4.8	7.9
13+	11.3	14.6	22.5	3.3	7.9
13–15	—	6.8	10.7	—	3.9
16+	—	7.8	11.8	—	4.0
Total	100.0	100.0	100.0	0	0
Total (000)	598	695	792	97	97
Women					
0–8	45.4	33.9	20.7	–11.5	–13.2
9–12	39.8	43.0	45.8	3.2	2.8
13+	14.8	23.1	33.5	8.3	10.4
13–15	—	16.7	21.3	—	4.6
16+	—	6.4	12.2	—	5.8
Total	100.0	100.0	100.0	0	0
Total (000)	211	300	436	89	136
Both sexes					
0–8	54.8	45.4	29.7	–9.3	–15.7
9–12	32.9	37.6	44.2	4.7	6.6
13+	12.3	17.0	26.1	4.7	9.1
13–15	—	9.7	14.3	—	4.6
16+	—	7.3	11.8	—	4.5
Total	100.0	100.0	100.0	0	0
Total (000)	809	995	1,228	186	233

Source: CBS, *Labor Force Surveys*, 1963, 1971, 1979.

a. Excluding residents of the administered areas employed in Israel. If these are included, the total number of employed persons rose in 1971 and 1979 to 1,028 thousand and 1,301 thousand respectively, and the corresponding percentage of employed persons with 13+ years of schooling was 16.5 and 24.6 percent, respectively.

production. This rise in demand probably explains the sustained high level of educated workers' relative wages in the 1960s while the relative supply of these workers was gradually increasing. The high profitability of investment in education, combined with the rising income level, explains the growing enrollment ratios in secondary, postsecondary, and higher education, a trend that began in the 1960s and leveled off only in the mid-1970s. Against this background, several other factors at work in previous years accelerated the rise in the education level in the 1970s.

1. The baby boom of the late 1940s and 1950s increased the share of younger people in the working-age population during the 1970s; the accelerated replacement of older, less-educated workers by younger and better-educated ones thus steadily raised the education level of the labor force. The proportion of employed men age 14–34 was about 40 percent in both 1963 and 1971, but by 1979 it was 44.3 percent. The age composition of employed women did not change much; since the labor force participation rate of older women had been very low in the past, the change in the age structure of the population had less effect on the age structure of employed women (see Ben-Porath, 1983).

2. The labor force participation rate of women rose, especially among those with partial secondary education or more (see Table 6-1). Women's labor force participation in Israel is principally determined by their level of education; the positive effect of schooling on participation more than offsets negative income effects, and the increase in the general education level explains most of the rapid increase in women's participation—from 27.3 percent in 1960 to 29.8 percent in 1971 and 34.9 percent in 1979 (see Ben-Porath, 1984; Gronau, 1981, pp. 15–17; and Bank of Israel, *Annual Report 1980,* pp. 63–64 and 76–77). Moreover, because men's participation had been declining since the mid-1960s, the proportion of women increased even faster—from 25.6 percent of the total employed in 1960 to 30.0 percent in 1971 and 35.6 percent in 1979 (women contributed 23.5 and 27.5 percent of total worker hours in 1971 and 1979 respectively).

3. The education level of immigrants was above the local average in the 1970s, mainly because of the arrival of 250,000 Soviet Jews. Altogether, the weight of the group with 13+ years of schooling in total employment rose by 9 percentage points from 1971 to 1979 (Table 6-1). Roughly 50 percent of this increase represents the rise in women's participation combined with the rise in their education level. Employed men have a lower education level than employed women, and the decline in men's share of employment would in any case raise the average level; in addition, the men's education level has risen; together, these changes account for another 35 percent of the increase. Finally, 15 percent is ascribable to immigrants entering the labor force.[1]

There have been similar structural changes in the United States and other Western countries since World War II. As investment in education grew, the education level of the labor force rose gradually, but the relative wages of educated manpower and rates of return to education were not affected until the late 1960s. In the 1970s the supply of educated manpower began to grow much more rapidly, reflecting the postwar baby boom and the increase in university enrollment. In consequence, the relative wages of employees with higher education diminished, as did returns to education. When economic activity slowed down in the mid-1970s, the relative employment conditions of educated manpower deteriorated and they experienced severe occupational downgrading (see Freeman, 1982). In Israel there was little change in the employment opportunities of the better educated (relative to those of the less educated). Wage differentials were also affected differently by the increased supply of educated manpower; they narrowed for women but not for men.

Changes in the Wage Structure

The rapidly accelerating inflation of the 1970s caused large fluctuations in nominal and real wages—in the public and private sectors, in industries and occupations. These short-term fluctuations arose mainly from institutional factors such as the discontinuity of wage indexation, changes in indexation regimes, and the phasing of wage contract schedules. In order to focus on long-term economic factors and to minimize institutional biases, the analysis of trends in the 1970s is based on two three-year periods, one at the beginning and one at the end of the decade. Observations from the annual CBS *Income Surveys* for 1970–1972 and for 1978–1980 are pooled into two cross-sections centered on mid-1971 and mid-1979 respectively. The resulting samples are quite large: 6,730 men and 2,720 women employees for 1970–1972, and 9,390 men and 5,690 women employees for 1978–1980.[2]

The top section of Table 6-2 compares the wage structures of the total labor force in the early and late 1970s. In the 16+ and 13–15 years-of-schooling groups, men's wage differentials widened (12 years of schooling = 100) by 1.4 and 10.4 percent respectively; women's declined by 8.4 and 4.5 percent respectively. (The lower part of the table shows a similar trend for the wage differentials when measured in relation to the wages of the 9–12 years-of-schooling group.) For the two sexes combined (weighted by input in worker hours) relative wages declined by 1 percent for the 16+ group but increased by 7 percent for those with 13–15 years of schooling. At the other end of the schooling range (0–7 years of schooling) the relative wage rose.

The lower part of Table 6-2 shows that in the public services, relative wage levels of those with university and postsecondary education did not change significantly for either men or women. In the business sector, relative wages of men with postsecondary education (9–12 years of schooling = 100) increased 14 percent,

TABLE 6-2. Wage differentials by years of schooling, sex, and sector (adjusted for experience), 1970–1972 and 1978–1980[a]

	Years of schooling					
	16+	13–15	12	9–11	8	0–7
	Total (index: 12 years of schooling = 100)					
Men						
1970–1972	142.1	112.0	100.0	83.4	70.0	61.6
	3.1	2.6		1.5	1.3	1.1
1978–1980	144.1	123.7	100.0	84.5	73.1	67.1
	2.7	2.5		1.4	1.3	1.4
Women						
1970–1972	169.6	145.3	100.0	80.2	62.7	58.8
	6.6	4.3		2.2	1.9	1.8
1978–1980	155.4	138.7	100.0	81.6	64.7	63.2
	3.8	2.9		1.7	1.8	2.1
	By sector (index: 9–12 years of schooling = 100)					
	16+	13–15	9–12		0–8	
Men						
1970–1972						
Public services	160.9	132.8	100.0		76.0	
	4.8	4.5			2.0	
Business sector	160.0	120.9	100.0		72.5	
	5.5	3.9			1.8	
Total	158.1	124.8	100.0		73.2	
	3.1	2.5			0.9	
1978–1980						
Public services	160.0	137.0	100.0		79.5	
	4.5	4.4			2.3	
Business sector	163.2	137.8	100.0		77.1	
	4.8	3.9			2.1	
Total	157.3	135.3	100.0		78.6	
	2.7	2.4			1.1	
Women						
1970–1972						
Public services	179.3	155.8	100.0		66.8	
	9.2	6.4			3.1	
Business sector	183.5	148.2	100.0		73.0	
	15.0	7.9			2.7	
Total	194.4	166.3	100.0		69.8	
	6.5	4.5			1.6	
1978–1980						
Public services	168.6	154.3	100.0		74.7	
	6.5	5.5			3.5	
Business sector	157.5	135.0	100.0		69.6	
	8.6	5.8			2.9	
Total	173.7	154.5	100.0		69.5	
	4.4	3.4			1.6	

Source: Amir (1983), tables 4, 5, regressions 1 and 2 in table A-1, and regression 3 in table A-2.

a. Small numerals are standard errors of the coefficients.

while for women with university and postsecondary education they declined 14 and 9 percent.

Considering the sharp increase in the weight of the higher educational groups in the labor force, the failure of wage differentials to narrow suggests a sizable concurrent expansion of both the relative demand for and supply of educated labor, which canceled the expected supply effects on wages and employment. The remaining sections of this chapter examine this hypothesis.[3]

In looking for factors that might raise the relative demand for educated labor, I shall consider two of the factors discussed by Welch (1970) as being typical.

Growth industries. The most rapidly expanding industries are the most education intensive. An education-intensive growth pattern might be caused either by expanding demand for education-intensive products or by expanding supply, when the production costs of education-intensive products for which demand is price-elastic decline. In the case of Israel the relative wages of educated labor did not decline, so that a demand-side explanation might be the more relevant.

Nonneutrality in production. If nonlabor inputs, such as physical capital, are educated-labor enhancing, an increase in their relative quantity of quality would raise the demand for labor; nonneutral technological change, with increments in technology raising the relative productivity of educated labor, would have the same effect. There is, however, no clear distinction between the two, since changes in the quality of nonlabor inputs can be viewed as technological change.

Assuming that physical capital raises the productivity of educated labor, an increase in the relative demand for it might be explained by an increase in the physical-capital intensity of industries or in the quality of their capital—if it occurred in the 1970s—due to exogenous factors (see Layard and Fallon, 1975; Welch, 1970; Griliches, 1970).

Changes in Industrial Structure in Education Intensity and in Demand for Educated Manpower

This section examines how the increase in the education level was reflected in the industrial structure.[4] Was there any education-intensive growth (a process that might be viewed as specialization when occurring in tradable industries), and if so, how much? To investigate this question, I broke down the overall change in the education intensiveness of the labor force into two general components. One reflects the contribution of the relative growth of education-intensive industries (interindustry change). The other reflects the contribution of intraindustry educational change.[5]

Table 6-3 shows this breakdown in a nine-industry aggregation (one-digit) for the 16+ schooling level. The resulting estimates show that roughly three-quarters of the change in the education intensity of the labor force can be attributed to the

TABLE 6-3. Changes in education intensity and industrial structure of employed persons (1-digit aggregation), 1971–1979 (16+ years of schooling)

Sector	Industrial structure		Percent of employed with 16+ years of schooling		1979–1971		Decomposition of total change ($\Delta b = 4.05$)[a] percentage of persons with 16+ years of schooling			
	1971 (1)	1979 (2)	1971 (3)	1979 (4)	Industrial structure (2/1)	Percent of 16+ (4/3)	Within industry (7)	Between industries (8)	Interaction (9)	Total (7+8 +9)
Agriculture, forestry, fishing (0)	8.96	6.39	1.02	2.24	0.71	2.20	2.7	–0.7	–0.8	1.3
Manufacturing and mining (1+2)	23.80	24.18	3.96	6.73	1.02	1.70	16.5	0.4	0.3	17.2
Electricity and water (3)	1.08	0.86	4.62	10.45	0.80	2.66	1.6	–0.3	–0.3	1.0
Construction (4)	10.29	8.92	1.70	2.39	0.87	1.41	1.8	–0.6	–0.2	1.0
Commerce and catering (5)	12.42	11.49	2.64	4.29	0.93	1.63	5.1	–0.6	–0.4	4.1
Transport, storage communications (6)	7.23	6.57	1.97	3.62	0.91	1.84	3.0	–0.3	–0.5	2.2
Financial and business services (7)	5.51	7.41	20.58	22.01	1.35	1.07	2.0	9.8	0.7	12.5
Public and community services (8)	23.58	28.12	16.99	22.71	1.19	1.34	33.8	19.3	6.5	59.7
Personal and other services (9)	7.14	6.06	2.63	4.66	0.85	1.77	3.6	–0.7	–0.6	2.4
Total	100.00	100.00	7.06	11.11	–	1.57	70.2	26.4	3.4	100.0

Sources: Unpublished data from CBS *Labor Force Surveys, 1971* and *1979*

a. Change in percentage points: e.g., $\Delta b = 4.05 = 11.11 - 7.06$ (see columns 3, 4).

intraindustry increase in education intensity and only one-quarter represents an increase in the weight of education-intensive industries.[6] The interindustry component consists almost entirely of the large increase in public and financial and business services, whose combined weight in the (civilian) labor force rose from 29.1 percent in 1971 to 35.6 percent in 1979.

The contributions of the inter- and intraindustry components to the change in the education level of the labor force depend on the industrial classification used: the greater the degree of aggregation, the greater the ratio of the intraindustry to the interindustry component. To check the sensitivity of the decomposition to this aggregation bias, I repeated the breakdown for fourteen two-digit manufacturing industries (see Amir, 1983, table 7, pp. 26–27). The estimates show that only 17.5 percent of the relative increase in the 16+ years-of-schooling group and only 11.5 of that in the 13+ group can be attributed to interindustry differences in growth rate. There is no information about the character of the intraindustry changes in educational levels. Further research is needed on this question.

There are obvious reasons for the increase in the demand for public services in the 1970s. Per capita income was on the average 50 percent above that of the 1960s, and the income elasticity of demand for public service is assumed to be high. Furthermore, in the 1970s the standard of living rose much more rapidly than output (65 percent versus 44 percent respectively in 1971–1979), and this growth in the standard of living came at the expense of national savings. It is reasonable to assume that the rising demand for public services reflected this excessive growth of consumption. Demand for public services was also pushed up by changes in defense requirements (beyond any increase in military manpower) and by a rapid change in the age composition of the population, with the proportion of the services-demanding old and young age groups increasing considerably. (For a different explanation of the rapid increase in public services, see Chapter 5.)

The demand for financial and business services might have risen for different reasons (see Ofer, 1967). Accelerating inflation (from 12 percent in 1971 to 78 percent in 1979)[7] increased the volume of financial transactions of firms and households alike, and the demand for financial services rose accordingly. The demand for business services increased mainly because of the diffusion of computer services.

One of the most important determinants of the relative demand for educated labor was, presumably, changes in demand for quality. On the one hand, the ratio of imports and exports to GDP rose in 1971–1979 (exports from 35 to 47 percent, imports from 66 to 71 percent). The export increment consisted chiefly of the more sophisticated products, which are on average more education intensive than goods produced for domestic use.[8] At the same time, demand for higher quality for both public and private consumption affected local industry. Thus, for example, the defense establishment, with its increasingly sophisticated requirements, substantially raised its demand for locally produced goods.

Goods and services of better quality can be assumed to be more education intensive in production, and in most cases also more physical-capital intensive. The factor market has been affected by direct public intervention, as well as by changes in final demands. In the 1970s the government subsidized investment by grants and loans whose grant equivalent grew rapidly as inflation accelerated;[9] and indeed the relatively high rate of investment in physical capital was not affected by the signs of productivity decline and excess capacity in the 1970s. Assuming complementarity in production between physical and human capital, the increase in the quantity of physical capital due to subsidization should have raised the demand for educated labor.

To obtain supporting evidence for these strong assumptions, I examined the correlation between the rise in the education intensity of industries and a number of variables, including the rate of increase of the ratio of physical capital to labor, research-and-development (R&D) expenditure, the ratio of exports to revenue, and the growth rate of real product. For seven main industries there is a positive correlation of 0.7 (significance level = 0.07) between the increase in educated labor force intensity (both 13–15 and 16+ years of schooling) and the increase in the ratio of physical capital to labor in 1971–1979 (Amir, 1983, table A-8). For fourteen manufacturing industries there is a positive correlation of above 0.5 (significance levels between 0.02 and 0.06) between the increase in the percentage of university-educated employed persons and a number of important variables, namely the growth rates of (1) physical-capital intensity, (2) real product, (3) the proportion of revenue exported, and (4) the R&D–revenue ratio (between 1972/73 and 1979/80) (Amir, 1983, table A-8). Furthermore, the increase in the weight of university-educated employed persons was positively correlated with (5)—the 1972/73 R&D–revenue ratio of those industries. Note that (3) also correlates positively with (2) and with (4), and, in line with these results, (5) correlates with (2) and with the 1971 percentage of university graduates employed in each industry.

These results are consistent with the assumption that there has been specialization in human- and physical-capital-intensive goods, and that the process was connected with the rapid increase in the proportion of output exported. The strong positive correlation between the increase in the percentage of university-educated employed persons and both the growth rate of physical-capital intensity and R&D outlays is consistent with the assumption that both physical and technological change might have both been educated-manpower enhancing. This change could explain some of the sharp increase in demand for university graduates that seems to have occurred in manufacturing.

These correlations for the 16+ years-of-schooling group do not recur for the 13–15 group. This result might indicate that although physical capital and educated labor are complementary in the economy as a whole, in manufacturing there is complementarity only for the highest education level.

Wage Differentials and Industrial Composition of the Labor Force

The pattern of change in wage differentials and in the industrial composition of the labor force sheds some light on factors of importance in the labor market. Table 6-4 presents estimates of the main changes in the distribution of employed persons with 16+ and 13+ years of schooling. The percentage employed in public services dropped in all groups, but the shift was stronger among men than among women and in the 13–15 group than in the 16+ group. In the business sector, the largest increment for men is in manufacturing, and it is drawn from public services, reinforced from financial and business services in the 16+ group and from other industries in the 13–15 group. For women the pattern is similar but more moderate, except for an increase in the proportion of the 16+ group employed in financial and business services. Finally, the various changes are much more pronounced for the groups under age 35, which one would expect to have a more elastic response to demand factors.

Table 6-5 presents estimates of changes in wage differentials. The section on intersectoral differentials shows that relative business-sector wages rose in the 1970s for men and women alike. In the business sector (interindustry differentials), the strongest rise in men's relative wages was in manufacturing (for those with 13–15 years of schooling) or other industries (for those with 16+ years of schooling). For women (in both 13+ educational groups), the most pronounced rise was in financial and business services, with some rise in manufacturing (for those with 13–15 years of schooling), while in other industries there was a decline.

Tables 6-6 and 6-7 show a clear positive correlation between changes in industrial composition (reallocation) and changes in relative wages. This result suggests that demand factors are dominant, with lags in the intersectoral adjustment of supply to the changes in the demand for educated manpower (see above). Specifically, the findings indicate that this demand increased in the business sector (especially in manufacturing) more than in the public services. Table 6-6 presents elasticities of the relative supply of educated manpower to the business sector, estimated on the assumption that there are adjustment lags.[10] The elasticity of relative supply of women's labor is greater for the 13–15 group. The high intersectoral substitutability probably reflects the fact that a high percentage of women in this schooling group work in similar clerical and administrative jobs in the two sectors. As expected, the relative supply of the corresponding younger age groups (under 35) is much more elastic, reflecting their small transfer costs.

Table 6-8 shows that relative to men's wages, the wages of women employees with 13+ years of schooling declined, with the decline being greater in the 13–15 group. In the 9–12 group, women's relative wages increased. Since there are considerably more women in the 9–12 group than in the 13+ group, the average relative wages of women rose (in 1979, 46 percent of employed women had 9–12

TABLE 6-4. Industrial composition of employed persons with 16+ and 13+ years of schooling, 1971 and 1979 (percentages)

	16+ years of schooling					13+ years of schooling				
		Men		Women			Men		Women	
	Both sexes	Total	Under age 35	Total	Under age 35	Both sexes	Total	Under age 35	Total	Under age 35
1971										
Manufacturing	13.4	16.5	18.9	4.5	5.3	11.5	17.6	16.5	5.8	5.9
Financial and business services	16.1	18.6	20.1	9.1	9.1	8.7	11.5	11.6	6.0	6.3
Public services	56.8	49.7	51.2	76.6	79.4	56.6	32.2	43.5	74.9	76.6
Other industries	13.7	15.2	9.8	9.8	6.2	23.2	33.8	28.5	13.3	11.2
Change from 1971 to 1979										
Manufacturing	1.2	3.7	5.7	0.5	–0.1	4.2	7.0	9.0	1.8	1.8
Financial and business services	–1.4	–1.1	–3.6	0.8	1.7	0.8	0.1	1.9	1.6	2.2
Public services	0.7	–2.8	–8.7	–0.6	–4.2	–4.2	–4.7	–12.2	–4.5	–6.1
Other industries	–0.5	0.2	6.6	–0.7	2.6	–0.8	–2.4	1.3	1.1	2.1

Source: Unpublished data from CBS, *Labor Force Survey 1971* and *1979.*

TABLE 6-5. Percentage changes in intersectoral and interindustry wage differentials, by sex and years of schooling (adjusted for experience), 1970–1972 to 1978–1980[a]

	Years of schooling			
Differentials	16+	13–15	9–12	0–8
Intersectoral				
Men	5.3	13.3[b]	2.6	4.5
	5.0	6.2	3.0	5.0
Women	2.8	3.7	12.6[b]	–4.0
	10.0	9.0	6.5	9.0
Interindustry				
Men				
Manufacturing	7.7	18.8[c]	1.4	5.7
	8.0	7.0	3.2	5.0
Financial and business services	–7.4	9.4	5.4	2.2
	9.0	8.5	4.8	7.0
Other industries	12.4[d]	9.9[d]	–0.1	3.9
	8.0	7.0	3.2	4.2
Women				
Manufacturing	3.7	10.1[d]	16.4[b]	–1.0
	17.0	8.0	7.5	8.2
Financial and business services	26.7[b]	14.5[d]	15.4[b]	–5.4
	3.0	10.0	7.2	13.0
Other industries	–12.6	–6.6	4.8	–9.2
	12.6	10.0	7.2	8.0

Source: Amir (1983), table 10, regression 3 in table A-2, and regressions 6 and 7 in table A-3.

Note: Percentage change in ratio of wages in business sector or specified industry group to public services wages. The following is a sample calculation of the intersectoral differential for men with 16+ years of schooling:

(1) Ratio of business-sector to public-sector wages:

1970–1972 — 1.039
1978–1980 — 1.094

(2) Percentage of change of the ratio –

$$\left(\frac{1.094}{1.039} - 1\right) \cdot 100 = 5.3.$$

a. Small numerals are standard errors of the coefficients.
b. Significant at the 5 percent level.
c. Significant at the 1 percent level.
d. Significant at the 10 percent level.

TABLE 6-6. Elasticities-of-supply adjustment between public services and the business sector[a]

	All age groups		Under age 35[b]	
	i = 16+	i = 13–15	i = 16+	i = 13–15
Men				
α	11.9	23.0	41.9	69.0
β	5.3	13.3	5.3	13.3
$\sigma = \alpha/\beta$	2.3	1.7	7.8	5.2
Women				
α	3.4	25.5	27.9	36.0
β	2.8	3.7	2.8	3.7
$\sigma = \alpha/\beta$	1.2	6.9	10.0	9.7

Source: Tables 6-4 and 6-5; Amir (1983), table 10.

a. α and β calculated as $(\theta_{79}/\theta_{71} - 1)100$, where for $\alpha - \theta_\alpha = N_b/N_p$ and for $\beta - \theta_\beta = W_b/W_p$. ($b, p$ index, respectively, business sector and public services).

b. The wage differential for all age groups is used, because for this age group it is not significantly different from the differential.

years of schooling and 34 percent had 13+ years; see Table 6-1). These findings presumably reflect the supply effect of the large increase in the proportion of women in the 13+ group (from 40.9 percent in 1971 to 45.6 percent in 1979), compared with a more modest increase in the 9–12 group (from 34.6 percent in 1971 to 36.9 percent in 1979). These findings are also consistent with the general narrowing of women's wage differentials at the higher educational levels (compared with those in the 9–12 group; see Table 6-2). As Table 6-8 shows, women's relative wages may have decreased slightly in the public services; in the business sector, however, the decline is pronounced for the 13–15 group. At the same time there is a strong increase for the 9–12 group. These changes are reflected in the elasticities of substitution between men and women presented in Table 6–9:[11] the higher elasticities of the 16+ group (relative to the 13–15 group) suggest a large measure of occupational compatibility between men and women at the professional and academic level. At the postsecondary technical level, the distinction between men's and women's jobs is more pronounced, especially in the business sector (except in financial and business services); at this level women are predominantly employed in clerical and administrative jobs while men more commonly work in technical and industry-specific jobs. These gender-based differences are confirmed by the much lower elasticity of substitution for the 13–15 group in the business sector.

TABLE 6-7. Reallocation of educated manpower and change in relative wage in four industry groups, 1971–1979[a]

	16+ years of schooling			13–15 years of schooling		
	Industry *i*			Industry *i*		
Industry *j*	Manufacturing	Financial and business services	Other industries	Manufacturing	Financial and business services	Other industries
Men						
Public services						
Wages	7.7	−7.4	12.4	18.8	9.4	9.9
Reallocation	29.2	−0.6	7.4	60.5	15.1	6.3
Manufacturing						
Wages	—	−14.0	4.3	—	−8.0	−7.5
Reallocation	—	−23.1	−16.9	—	−28.3	−33.8
Financial and business services						
Wages	—	—	21.0	—	—	−18.5
Reallocation	—	—	8.1	—	—	−7.7
Women						
Public services						
Wages	3.7	26.7	−12.6	10.1	14.5	−6.6
Reallocation	11.0	9.6	−6.3	39.3	34.0	8.4
Manufacturing						
Wages	—	22.0	−8.0	—	4.0	−15.2
Reallocation	—	−1.3	−15.6	—	−3.7	−22.2
Financial and business services						
Wages	—	—	−31.0	—	—	−18.5
Reallocation	—	—	−14.5	—	—	−19.1

Source: Tables 6-4 and 6-5; Amir (1983), table 10.

a. Calculated as $(\phi_{79}/\phi_{71} - 1)100$, where $\phi_w = W_i/W_j$ for change in relative wages, and $\phi = N_i/N_j$ for the change in allocation.

Conclusions

In the 1970s the education level of the Israeli labor force rose markedly, mainly as a result of exogenous factors. Unlike the experience of many Western countries in this decade, the rapid increase in the supply of educated employed persons did not on average depress the relative wage level of those with more schooling and did not markedly worsen their employment conditions in comparison with those of peo-

TABLE 6-8. Ratio of women's to men's wages, by years of schooling and sector (adjusted for experience), 1970–1972 and 1978–1980[a]

	Years of schooling			
	16+	13–15	9–12	0–8
1970–1972				
All employees	0.927	1.005	0.754	0.719
Public sector	0.978	1.030	0.873	0.771
Business sector	0.793	0.854	0.697	0.701
1978–1980				
All employees	0.861	0.890	0.780	0.690
Public sector	0.927	0.986	0.850	0.776
Business sector	0.744	0.749	0.754	0.655
Percentage change				
All employees	−7.0[b]	−11.4[c]	3.4[d]	−4.0[b]
	5.0	3.4	1.9	2.8
Public sector	−5.2	−4.3	−2.6	0.6
	5.5	5.2	3.2	6.0
Business sector	−6.2	−12.3[d]	8.2[d]	−6.6[d]
	9.0	6.4	3.8	4.0

Source: Amir (1983), regressions 2 and 4 in tables A-1 and A-2 respectively.
a. Small numerals are standard errors of coefficients.
b. Significant at the 10 percent level.
c. Significant at the 1 percent level.
d. Significant at the 5 percent level.

ple with secondary education. On the whole, the changes in the wage structure were consistent with a rapid rise in the demand for educated labor concurrent with the increase in supply. One source of rising demand is evidently an increase in the relative demand for education-intensive public and financial and business services. But the rapid growth of these education-intensive services contributed only about one-quarter of the total increase in education intensity of the labor force. Three-quarters of it was due to the rise in education intensity within (one-digit) industries. This large contribution may reflect increased demand for more sophisticated goods and services, whose production is also more education intensive. Such a change in the demand structure probably did occur during the 1970s, reflecting specialization in trade and changes in demand for domestic goods and services.

Demand for educated manpower also seems to have been enhanced by a continuous rise in the ratio of physical capital to labor. A policy of heavy government

TABLE 6-9. Elasticities of substitution between male and female employees[a]

	Total labor force	Public services	Business sector
16+ years of schooling			
α	59.7	67.7	55.5
β	–7.0	–5.2	–6.2
σ	8.5	13.0	9.0
13–15 years of schooling			
α	4.2	12.3	14.5
β	–11.4	–4.3	–12.3
σ	0.4	2.9	1.2

Source: Amir (1983), tables 10 and A-6.

a. α and β calculated as $(\theta_{79}/\theta_{71} - 1)100$. ($\theta_\alpha = N_F/N_M$ and $\theta_\beta = W_F/W_M$, where F, M index respectively female and male employees).

subsidization in the 1970s may have induced private investment, which maintained a high level despite a severe slowdown in economic activity. Industries with a rising ratio of physical capital to labor tended to employ an increasing proportion of educated manpower; this correlation confirms the hypothesis that physical and human capital are complementary. In manufacturing, this relationship seems to be confined to the 16+ years-of-schooling group.

The clear positive correlation between changes in relative industrial allocation and changes in interindustry wage differentials indicates the trends of the demand factors at work and suggests that the supply of manpower adjusts with a lag. This lag might be consistent with the lengthy training needed for academic and technical occupations and with the cobweb structure of their labor markets. Thus relative demand for educated employees rose in the business sector; the rise was particularly pronounced in manufacturing. The decline in the relative wages of educated women is consistent with the sharp increase in their relative supply of labor during the 1970s.

7

Diversity in Population and in the Labor Force

Yoram Ben-Porath

The diversity of the Israeli population and labor force partly reflects trends observed in other countries, but also factors unique to Israel: the immigration of Jews with a multitude of social and economic backgrounds, and the existence of an Arab minority. This chapter discusses some of the major changes in population and the labor force, including ethnic factors when relevant.

Of the 4.1 million people living within Israel's pre-1967 borders as of 1982, 3.4 million were Jews and the rest mostly Arabs. Of the Jews, 1.4 million were born outside Israel: 0.8 million in Europe and America (EA) and 0.6 million in Asia and Africa (AA). With the Israeli-born (ISAA, ISEA) added to the respective groups of foreign-born, there were 1.5 million Jews of Asia-Africa origin and 1.3 million of Europe-America origin. Only half a million Jews are second-generation Israelis. Of the Arabs, 78 percent were Muslim; the rest were Christians and Druze.

The economic and social significance of demographic change in the Jewish population derives from the deliberate policy of building the nation through Jewish immigration. Macroeconomic policies have been largely affected by the government's desire to provide full employment in general or to solve the employment problems of particular groups, out of sensitivity to the effects of employment on immigration and emigration. The desire to mitigate social splits along lines of origin has been at the top of the national agenda from Israel's earliest days: a great deal of effort and many resources were aimed at closing the gaps between Jews in the hope of achieving rapid integration and equalization. This social policy has been reflected in Israel's particular development as a welfare state, both in terms of the transfers system and in terms of the structure of public consumption.

In contrast to the continuing efforts to reduce diversity within the Jewish population, Arab-Jewish differentials have not been a direct policy target. Many of the developments in the Arab sector have occurred only as a consequence of changing conditions in the Jewish sector. This refers both to the tremendous increase in income and in standards of living and to fluctuations in the level of employment and the industrial structure.

The share of Arabs living within Israel's pre-1967 borders declined from 13 percent in 1948 to 11 percent in 1952 because of mass Jewish immigration. It remained at this level until 1967, with Arab natural increase more or less balancing Jewish immigration. As a result of East Jerusalem's incorporation into Israel and the decline in Jewish immigration, this share rose to 17 percent as of 1982.

In 1982 there were 1.2 million Arabs in the West Bank and the Gaza Strip. The population of Israel *plus* these territories was 5.3 million, and the share of Arabs was 36 percent. This ratio has been more or less stable since 1967. The discussion here excludes the population and economic activity of the territories except when they relate to the situation within Israel.

The following analysis of the Jewish population refers to aggregation by continent of origin. Although this approach masks large variations among countries, it expresses the major elements of internal diversity. The different characteristics with which immigrants arrived, plus the economic conditions and policies at the time of immigration, determined people's economic and social development and current differentials. One important issue is the transmission of inequality from one generation to the next—the extent to which the initial endowments and trajectories of the Israeli-born are differentiated by origin.

Fertility

Fertility is a good indicator of long-term social differences as well as a major determinant of the age structure. Table 7-1 shows that in 1951 and 1955 levels of total fertility (a sum of the age-specific birth rates) among the various population groups ranked as follows, in descending order: Muslims and Druze, AA Jews, Christians, Israeli-born Jews, EA Jews. The EA fertility level was half that of AA. The trajectories were very different: within thirty years the AA immigrants' level of fertility declined by half and came within 10 percent of the EA group's fertility level, which increased somewhat. The initial gaps between ISEA and ISAA fertility were smaller, and the differences were almost eliminated by 1980. Within the non-Jewish population Christians showed the earliest decline in fertility, with a reduction as sharp as for the AA Jews; by 1980 the Christians' fertility level converged with that of the Israeli-born Jews of both groups. Among Muslims and Druze, however, there was an initial increase, with a rapid decline only since 1965. In 1980 the fertility level of Muslims and Druze was similar to that of AA Jews thirty years earlier. The Muslim-Druze distance from the Jewish population as a whole, from the AA Jews in particular, and from Christians first increased, peaked in 1965 (or 1970), and then declined.

TABLE 7-1. Total fertility by continent of origin and ethnicity, 1951–1980

	1951	1955	1965	1980
Jews	4.00	3.64	3.47	2.76
Mother born in				
Asia-Africa	6.31	5.68	4.58	3.04
Europe-America	3.16	2.63	2.60	2.76
Israel	3.56	2.83	2.88	2.76
Father born in				
Asia-Africa	—	—	2.86	2.80
Europe-America	—	—	2.60	2.68
Israel	—	—	4.24	2.64
Muslims	—	7.96	9.87	5.98
Christians	—	4.85	4.74	2.66
Druze and others	—	6.58	7.61	6.09

Source: CBS, *Statistical Abstract 1983*, pp. 99–100.

The mother's education level is the dominant explanatory variable for cross-section differentials in fertility. Its negative effect on fertility tends to be stronger at very low levels. The improvement in schooling among AA and non-Jewish women indeed occurred initially at the lower levels of schooling (with the elimination of illiteracy). This combination was an important factor that contributed to the narrowing of differentials over time. Studies based on data for the 1960s show that there were also significant "unexplained" differences by origin and length of residence in Israel (see, for example, Ben-Porath, 1973c). These residual variables represent differences in and transition between widely different equilibria associated with child mortality, attitudes to contraception, women's status and careers, and the like. There is convergence of the trajectories over time, and certainly a very important convergence between generations.

The onus of past and present differential fertility is most heavily felt in the transmission of inequality across generations. The negative association between number of children and investment in children (Becker, 1981) reinforces the direct correlation between the education levels of parents and children. The fact that a large fraction of ISAAs were born in the 1950s to low-income, poorly educated parents and had many siblings may explain some of the persistence in schooling and occupational status differentials between ISAAs and ISEAs (see below). Likewise, the recent reduction of the ISAAs' fertility level to convergence with that of ISEAs, together with the rise in cross-origin marriages (approximately 25 percent of marriages in 1983, compared with 12 percent in 1955), suggests a likely convergence of human capital endowments.

Age and Dependency: Coping with Large Cohorts

The age structure of the Jewish population has undergone some long-term changes. The massive immigration directly after the establishment of the state reduced the share of the working-age population (15–64) from 67 percent in 1950 to 61.7 percent in 1955, the approximate level at which it has remained. The sharp decline in the 1950s is mostly a consequence of the rise in the share of children (age 0–14) from 30 to 36 percent and in the share of the elderly (age 65+). The fairly stable share of the 15–64 age group after its initial sharp decline reflects a decline in the share of children (to 31 percent in 1980) and an increase in the share of the elderly (from 3.4 percent in 1950 to 9.2 percent in 1980). In the period 1950–1980 the number of the elderly increased almost eightfold, and the number of people age 15–64 more than doubled. More recently the share of the very old (75+) within the elderly population has increased. Obviously, the combination of the swing in the share of children and the trend in the share of adults tilted the burden of dependence "backward." The rising share of old-age support in the transfer system (see Chapter 10) and the pressure on various social services for the elderly reflect this demographic change. Still, Israel has a smaller proportion of elderly persons than does Europe or the United States.

Ethnic differences are an important factor in the age structure. Among non-Jews and Jews of AA origin, the share of the elderly is extremely low (2.8 and 5.0 percent respectively), while the share of children is almost half among non-Jews and over one-quarter among Jews of AA origin. The total dependency ratio among Jews of EA origin is similar to that of the AA Jews and thus significantly lower than among non-Jews, but it is much more heavily weighted toward the elderly than in either of the latter groups (CBS, *Statistical Abstract 1983*). Non-Jews account for almost one-quarter of the total population of children and for only 6 percent of the elderly. AA and ISAA Jews account for about half the children and for only one-quarter of the elderly.

From the viewpoint of the transfer system, these numbers imply that the heavy emphasis on child allowances benefits mainly AAs and non-Jews. Indeed, these allowances were probably chosen as a major redistributive instrument to narrow the income gap between AA and EA Jews, and not only because of the negative association between family size and income. The Arab population, with an even larger number of children per family, benefited from this redistributive device; this spillover, however, was checked by the application of a lower allowance to Arabs, on the ground that they do not serve in the army. Old-age support, on the other hand, benefited EAs more than others.

The apparently smooth movements in age structure conceal a more dramatic transformation, brought about by a sharp change in the size of cohorts, which was associated with the mass immigration of 1948–1951 (see Friedlander, 1975; Kop,

1980).[1] Owing to a combination of factors, cohorts born after the late 1940s were more than 70 percent larger than earlier cohorts, and as the larger cohorts grew up they caused sharp changes in the age distribution and in the growth rates of the age groups. In the 1950s and early 1960s they exerted tremendous pressures on the elementary and secondary school system. In 1955–1960, for example, when the total Jewish population grew 21 percent, the 10–14 age group grew 74 percent. The rapid expansion of the educational system in response to these pressures, and its failure to decelerate when the pressure subsided, provide an example of how aggregate public expenditure can increase because of asymmetric response to changing needs.

In the late 1960s this "bulge" reached adulthood, embarking on army service or higher education or entering the labor market. The ratio (in the Jewish population) of the 15–29 age group to the 30–64 age group rose from 54.5 percent in 1960 to 85.3 percent in 1975, and to 78.2 percent in 1980. This trend is comparable to the baby boom in the United States, where the same age group increased its share from 50.2 to 72.1 percent in the same period (Easterlin, 1980). Entry into the labor market was delayed: while the male population age 18–24 increased 49 percent in 1965–1970, this group's share in the civilian labor force rose only 18 percent. In effect its participation in the civilian labor force declined from 52.6 to 41.8 to 34.9 percent successively from 1965 to 1970 to 1975. (The participation of men age 25–34 also dropped 6.4 percentage points in 1970–1980). The total number of employed men age 18–24 in 1973 was the same as it had been in 1965.

The most important factor in this delayed entry was the increase in the size of the army, associated with the 1967 and 1973 wars, both through a prolongation of service and an expansion of the career army. Although expansion was required by external events, the demographic conditions at the time were also favorable. Another factor was the expansion of higher education. In 1965–1975 the number of university students and faculty almost tripled, and the share of students in the 20–29 age group almost doubled. These two factors, along with (perhaps) some increase in leisure, delayed entry into the labor market and cushioned the impact of the increase in cohort size. (In the United States, too, a high proportion of the baby boom generation went into universities and the army.)

For those age 18–24 who entered the labor market, earnings relative to those of men age 35–64 dropped steeply, from 60 to 40 percent in 1970–1981. There was also a significant decline in the relative earnings of older men and women (65+). In the same period the annual earnings of men age 25–34 declined a few percentage points, while their relative share increased from 40 to 60 percent. Thus the first of the large cohorts to enter the labor market in the early and mid-1970s suffered less than the smaller cohorts who reached the labor market in the late 1970s only to find the entry points filled with the large cohorts that had preceded them. Young employees also suffer more in terms of both earnings and unemployment when the general employment situation deteriorates, as it did in the late 1970s. These findings conform to trends in the United States (see Wachter, 1976; Freeman, 1979; Welch, 1979).

As the discontinuity in the age structure moves with time, small cohorts of elderly persons will enjoy the support of larger cohorts of providers. Only in the first quarter of the next century, when the large cohorts themselves become dependent, will the issue of old-age support emerge with greater force.

Schooling

Education is a key determinant of changes in human productivity and of economic and social differences.

The overall education level of the Jewish population was exceptionally high before 1948. It declined drastically in the period of mass immigration, stayed low in the 1950s, increased in the 1960s, and increased further in the 1970s.[2] The overall level was changed by immigration, the domestic school system, and the changing composition by origin of the immigrants and the population. A special survey in the 1961 census yields some idea of the gap in new immigrants' education levels. The survey covered men who were less than 60 years old at the time of the census and 25–54 years old when they immigrated. Among AA men 28.3 percent had arrived with no schooling at all, and only 6.2 percent with 13+ years, whereas the corresponding shares for EA men were 1.6 and 17.2 percent. Evaluated according to mean earnings by schooling in 1969, the difference between the values of the schooling distributions of new EA and AA immigrants was 19 percent (25 percent for pre-1947 immigrants and only 14 percent for 1948–1954 immigrants; see Ben-Porath, 1973a). The immigrants of the 1960s, and more so those of the 1970s (most of them from the USSR), raised the level of schooling.

Over time, however, the relative importance of immigration declined. In the domestic educational system enrollment rates of all groups rose sharply. The increases at the elementary and then secondary levels have been higher for children of AA origin, although the gaps at the university level have not been narrowed. The EA-AA gap has narrowed at lower levels of schooling but widened at the top of the scale (Table 7-2). The overall gap in the EA and AA levels of schooling (evaluated by the earning differentials associated with schooling in 1982, with EA as the base) was 14 percent in 1961, 1972, and 1982. More striking is the finding that the gap between ISAAs and ISEAs is equal to the gap between their respective parental groups and has not changed throughout this period (in fact it is slightly greater when all distributions are standardized by age). The advantage of the Israeli-born over their foreign-born parents (in the value of education) is equal for AAs and EAs for 1961, 1972, and 1982: 10–11 percent. This finding suggests that despite a significant improvement in schooling for all

TABLE 7-2. Years of schooling for both sexes by continent of origin and ethnicity, 1961–1982 (percentages)

	1961			1972			1982		
	0–8	9–12	13+	0–8	9–12	13+	0–8	9–12	13+
AA	77.8	19.2	3.0	67.5	27.5	5.0	53.7	36.3	10.0
EA	48.7	38.5	12.7	41.4	39.3	19.3	32.2	39.2	28.6
Israel	30.4	54.2	15.3	21.4	60.1	18.5	11.6	63.2	25.2
ISAA	60.9	34.5	4.5	35.7	59.3	5.0	17.0	71.7	11.3
ISEA	15.7	64.6	19.6	9.3	61.7	29.0	5.0	51.9	43.1
Jews	55.5	34.6	9.8	44.1	41.7	14.2	28.9	48.7	22.4
Non-Jews	90.9	7.6	1.5	81.8	15.5	2.7	59.2	32.8	8.0

Sources: CBS, *Statistical Abstracts 1964*, p. 525; *1973*, p. 625; *1983*, pp. 643–44.

groups, gaps have been transmitted from the immigrants to their children born in Israel, and the advance made during one generation is a bit smaller than the current (and persistent) gap.

There is no doubt that the state has made a conscious effort to close educational gaps, first at the elementary level, and then at the secondary level, where vocational education absorbed disproportionately more AA pupils. At the same time, the rapid expansion of the university system (which tripled in 1965–1975), largely at government expense, served first of all the EA and ISEA youth, who achieved close to universal academic secondary education and were thus ready to benefit from this service, and who were perhaps more motivated because of parental background. Thus the overall government effort in education, combined with the different characteristics of the origin groups, had conflicting effects on the ethnic gap.

The Arab population in the 1950s had an even lower level of schooling than AA Jews, but rising school attendance has gradually reduced illiteracy, and in the 1970s the number attending university increased. As a result, the gap between all Jews and non-Jews, which widened from 12 percent to 17 percent in 1961–1972, narrowed to 14 percent in 1982, equaling the gap between AAs and EAs and the gap between ISAAs and ISEAs.[3]

Men and Women in the Labor Force

From 1955 to 1982 the labor force participation rate of men (age 14+) declined from 80.1 to 63.4 percent, while that of women rose from 26.5 to 36.1 percent (Table 7-3). Thus the gap in participation between men and women narrowed to

TABLE 7-3. Labor force participation rates by sex and age, 1955–1982 (percentages)

	1955	1965	1970	1982
Men				
All	80.1	76.1	69.2	63.4
14–17	42.2	38.1	27.3	16.2
18–24	80.9 (18–34)	76.2 (18–34)	46.0	40.3
25–34			91.1	84.2
35–54	96.4	96.4	94.9	90.4
55–64	82.3	91.0	88.5	79.4
65+	38.3	39.7	33.8	25.0
Women				
All	26.5	29.4	29.3	36.1
14–17	31.7	27.1	18.1	9.7
18–24	32.2 (18–34)	37.5 (18–34)	44.9	38.4
25–34			32.6	53.7
35–54	26.2	30.9	32.8	48.7
55–64	17.0	22.9	22.1	25.1
65+	5.1[a]	6.0[a]	5.0	6.4

Sources: CBS, *Statistical Abstracts 1974*, table XII/5; and *1983*, table XII/4.
a. Small sample.

less than half its 1955 level and the share of women in the labor force rose from one-quarter to two-fifths.

Half of the decline in the participation rate of Jewish men from 1960 to 1970 is explained by the entry into young adulthood of the larger cohorts with low rates of participation. Most of the change, however, is a consequence of change in the age-specific rates of participation. Initially (1955–1965) the decline in participation was moderate and concentrated among the young, whereas there was a significant increase in the participation rate of men age 55+. Both delayed entry into and delayed exit from the labor force meant a shift in the age profile of participation that would be expected to occur with increased schooling. But in the mid-1960s the decline intensified and embraced all age groups. In 1965–1975 participation declined 14 percentage points, that of men age 14–24 approximately 20 percentage points, and that of men age 65+ 10.5 percentage points. Thus the cross-section age profile of participation was squeezed at both ends, by a further delay in entry (partly associated with more schooling) and by earlier retirement. At the same time there was a milder reduction in the participation rate of men in the major working age group, 25–64.

The overall level of participation of men in Israel is lower than in the United States and the developed countries of Europe, especially for the 14–24 age group. The low participation of young men is partly due to army service and to high rates of school and university attendance. On the other hand, Israeli men age 55+ have higher participation rates than in other countries. The decline in participation in the last two decades was much milder for this group in Israel than in other countries. The rate for Israel in 1980 was similar to that in Europe or the United States in 1960.

There are large differences in the age profile of participation by ethnicity and origin. Non-Jews both enter and retire from the labor force earlier than most Jews. The same is true for AAs compared with EAs (Table 7-4). These differences reflect to a large extent differences in education and market opportunities, but they may also be associated with effects of public and family support systems.

Women's participation increased 3 percentage points in 1955–1970 and 7 percentage points in 1970–1982.[4] This increase, combined with the changes in men's participation, caused women to contribute close to two-thirds of the growth of the labor force after 1965, compared with one-third in earlier years.

The sharp increase in women's education levels accounts for the aggregate increase in women's participation. In 1980 women constituted about half of the highly educated labor force. Most of the change took place in the 25–44 age group, which increased 20 percentage points in 1970–1982. This increased partic-

TABLE 7-4. Labor force participation rates by continent of origin, ethnicity, and sex (selected age groups), 1983 (percentages)

	All IS	ISIS	ISAA	ISEA	AA	EA	Non-Jews
Men							
Total	55.8	47.7	50.1	66.4	73.0	65.1	66.9
14–17	12.4	16.5	11.9	8.8	21.8[a]	14.6	19.8
18–24	33.1	26.4	35.1	31.5	44.3	31.6	73.1
55–64	83.8	84.8	69.1	89.3	73.0	83.8	57.5
65+	30.0	25.1	—	33.6[a]	15.4	28.5	6.4[a]
Women							
Total	47.7	40.0	42.1	57.8	33.9	37.3	10.2
14–17	10.0	12.1	9.0	9.8	15.7[a]	8.4[a]	—
18–24	42.8	38.0	44.1	41.7	46.6	38.7	—
55–64	40.5	28.9[a]	22.4[a]	56.0	16.7	33.2	—

Source: CBS, *Statistical Abstract 1984*, p. 328.

a. Small sample.

ipation occurred among mothers and cannot be ascribed to an increase in the proportion of unmarried or childless women. The growing employment of mothers was facilitated by an increase in part-time jobs (mainly in the services sector) and greater availability of childcare services.

Whereas women of earlier cohorts worked before bearing children, then withdrew from the labor force, and reentered it when their children grew up, the new (average) pattern shows increased participation throughout the peak childbearing period, and the familiar M-shaped curve relating participation to age gives way to an inverted-U curve. This transformation occurred first among EA women and only recently among AA women. The pattern is similar to the one observed in Europe and the United States. The participation of non-Jewish women is still very low: 10 percent compared with 40 percent for Jews in 1982.

Broadly speaking, the entry of women into the labor force was not associated with a decline in their relative wage. Highly educated women are an exception—their earnings have declined relative to those of men and of less-educated women. Women entered their traditional sectors—service industries, both public and private. In the 1970s public and community services increased their share in employment from 23.9 to 30.6 percent. (Among women with higher education the public sector provides three-quarters of employment.) The share of women in public services increased from 44.4 to 57.5 percent; financial and business services also rose from 5.2 to 8.8 percent of total Jewish employment and women's share in this sector rose 9 percentage points.

The reduced participation of men and the higher participation of women has narrowed the gender-based division in labor whereby women are relegated to the household and men to the labor market. There is, however, occupational and industrial differentiation (including almost complete feminization of certain occupations), reflecting the weight of gender-based comparative advantages, tastes, or biases.

The expansion of employment in the public sector could represent an endogenous response of the public sector to the growing supply of educated women (see Chapter 5). The public sector provided the increase in education that brought more women into the labor force, provided childcare services to facilitate participation by mothers, and also became their employer. The highly educated women are mostly EAs, so they were the major beneficiaries of this policy.

Occupation and Industry

The general industrial and occupational structure of Israel exhibits some universally familiar trends (a decline in the share of agriculture and an increase in the share of service industries and of white-collar occupations) coupled with certain oddities (such as an excessive level of services for its level of per capita income, and a high share of workers in construction). This section focuses on the particular roles played by different groups in the population.

Some insight into the occupational structure of immigrants comes from information on immigrants' occupations prior to their arrival (obtained in the 1961 census) and on their initial allocation in Israel (Ben-Porath, 1973a). AA and EA groups prior to immigration differed mostly in their shares in professional, managerial, and clerical occupations (17 percent for AAs, 28 percent for EAs). Both groups underwent significant occupational change in Israel, but the change for AAs was more radical: they were initially directed into agriculture. Thus the initial gap in occupational level in Israel (evaluated by relative earnings in Israel) was larger than it had been abroad (Table 7-5). In the 1960s and 1970s the value of the distribution of both groups increased, though more for EAs than for AAs. Upward mobility for AAs in the 1960s took the form of exit from agriculture and entry into blue-collar and some white-collar occupations. For EAs upward mobility meant entry into the top white-collar occupations and exit from all others. For both groups in the 1970s, the share of white-collar occupations increased, mostly at the expense of blue-collar occupations and only marginally at the expense of agriculture, which continued to decline.

The gap between the ISAAs and ISEAs in the occupational level was somewhat larger than the one between their foreign-born fathers, and grew wider—from 14 percent in 1972 to 16 percent in 1982—that is, cross-generation upward mobility was more marked in the group that was more advanced to begin with. The gap expresses the concentration of ISAAs in blue-collar occupations versus the concentration of ISEAs in top white-collar occupations (more than the foreign-born EAs). In the 1970s the share in white-collar occupations increased for both ISEAs and ISAAs, but the gap between them widened. The ISEA group is older than the ISAA group, and my calculation does not adjust for the difference in the life-cycle stage of these groups. However, the difference in occupational status reflects not only age differentials; Matras and Bar-Haim (1984), in studying the educational and early work careers of the Israeli-born cohort of 1954, found that this allocation to blue-collar/white-collar occupations rests on the allocation to tracks within the school system.

Nahon (1985) shows that among highly educated men, the gap by origin in the share employed in "high" white-collar occupations has declined and has actually disappeared among the young. The concentration of medium-educated (9–12 years) AAs in blue-collar occupations has increased. The overall resilience of the gap in occupational status is thus a consequence of the patterns of convergence and divergence in the educational distributions, and of the occupational allocations within schooling categories. This resilience, which was transmitted to the second generation of immigrants, is of great social importance.

The gaps in the occupational level between AA and EA women widened in the

TABLE 7-5. Indicators of occupational change and differences by origin and ethnicity, 1961–1982

Percentage change in total employment of specified group

	Men in white-collar occupations[a]			Men in agriculture			Women in white-collar occupations[a]	
	From abroad to Israel[b]	1961–1972[c]	1972–1982[d]	From abroad to Israel	1961–1972[c]	1972–1982[d]	1961–1972[d]	1972–1982[d]
AA	−2.0	3.3	6.1	22.8	−12.5	−2.0	8.1	13.8
EA	3.5	3.7	7.8	4.9	−3.6	−1.7	6.2	13.0
IS	—	−0.6	6.3	—	−3.4	−3.3	0.9	9.2
ISAA	—	—	8.3	—	—	0.1	—	19.8
ISEA	—	—	10.8	—	—	−6.3	—	5.3
Jews	—	1.4	7.3	—	−5.7	−1.5	6.6	13.9
Non-Jews	—	0.2	7.2	—	−23.9	−3.9	4.1	17.5

Differences in value of occupational distribution[e]

	Men					Women			
	1961 abroad[b]	1961 Israel[b]	1972[c]	1972[d]	1982	1961 Israel	1972[c]	1972[d]	1982
EA – AA	3.8	11.6[f]	13.3	12.1	13.0	16.1	20.4	16.3	15.5
ISEA – ISAA	—	—	—	14.8	16.1	—	—	22.1	17.6
AA – ISAA	—	—	—	−1.0	−0.1	—	—	−3.6	−6.3
EA – ISEA	—	—	—	−4.3	−3.8	—	—	−11.2	−9.1
Jews – non-Jews	—	14.0	12.4	11.9	11.4	3.8	−2.6	3.8	5.7
AA – non-Jews	—	6.3	4.8	4.6	3.9	−13.5	−21.4	−11.4	−8.4

Sources: CBS, *Labor Force Survey,* 1972, tables 37 and 38; CBS, *Statistical Abstract 1983*, tables XII/9, XII/18, and XII/29; CBS, *Employees Earnings, 1968–1972,* Special Publications Series No. 435, table B/2; CBS, (1961), Labor Force, Part IV, "Occupation Abroad," tables 1 and 3; Labor Force, Part II, "Labor Force Characteristics and Employed Persons, by Educational Attainment and Literacy," tables 9 and 14.

a. Includes in the 1961 classification: professional, scientific, and related workers plus administrative executives, managerial and clerical; in the 1972 classification: scientific, academic workers, other professional, and related workers; administrators and managers, clerical workers. Sales or trade workers are excluded from all classifications.

b. Figures based on the 1961 census include men age 25–54 at immigration, under 60 in 1961.

c. 1972 figures are based on the 1961 occupational classification.

d. 1972 and 1982 are based on the 1972 occupational classification.

e. Occupational distributions weighted by hourly earnings in occupations; 1971 figures for Jewish men and women were used to evaluate the distributions in 1961 and 1972; 1982 figures were used for 1972 and 1982.

f. For purposes of comparison to 1972, the correct figure here is 11.7.

1960s. In the 1970s there was a slight decline in the gaps among the foreign-born and a sharp decline among the Israeli-born.

The Arab population experienced a rapid growth in income, much of it as a result of entry into the Jewish labor market. In the 1950s there were barriers to the entry of Arabs into the Jewish sector, which was coping with the employment problems associated with mass immigration (the Arab population was subjected at the time to military rule, and movement required licenses). But by the early 1960s about half of Arab men were employed outside their places of residence, which in most cases meant that they worked in the Jewish sector. This percentage has not changed much since then. Higher wages and more advanced industrial structure turned the agricultural labor force into a commuting proletariat. In the general economy they started at the bottom in terms of occupation and industry and climbed as the group above them (AA Jews) moved upward, maintaining a distance from the Jewish occupational structure. The structure of employment within the Arab sector proper has also changed. As a result of changes in the two sectors, non-Jews moved from agriculture to construction and to other industries, and in the 1970s they moved out of construction into manufacturing and services. The share of Arab men employed in agriculture, which was about 45 percent in the 1950s, declined 30 percentage points in the 1960s, the entire difference entering blue-collar occupations. In the 1970s the share of white-collar occupations rose, but by 1982 it had just reached the level of AA Jews in the early 1960s. With the rise in the share of Arab university graduates, the issue of their occupational

TABLE 7-6. Percentage of Arabs employed in Israel in agriculture and construction (both sexes), 1961–1982

	1961	1972	1982
All industries	7.5	14.1	15.7
Israeli Arabs	7.5	9.3	10.0
Arabs from West Bank and Gaza	—	4.8	5.7
Agriculture	22.3	33.1	29.6
Israeli Arabs	22.3	20.5	17.6
Arabs from West Bank and Gaza	—	12.6	12.0
Construction	12.4	42.1	57.3
Israeli Arabs	12.4	21.5	23.1
Arabs from West Bank and Gaza	—	20.6	34.2

Sources: CBS (1961), tables 4 and 6; CBS, *Labor Force Survey 1972,* table 23; CBS, *Statistical Abstract 1983,* tables XII/1 and XXVII/20.

status may become more acute. Interestingly enough, non-Jewish women have a low level of labor force participation but a higher level of occupational distribution than AA women, reflecting high selectivity into white-collar occupations (teachers, nurses).

The transformation in the industrial composition of non-Jews occurred much more rapidly than that of Jews. It reflects both the economywide changes and the changing roles of different minorities or subgroups. A similar process occurred in the Jewish population among different waves of immigrants: newer immigrants replaced their predecessors in agriculture in the 1950s as the latter moved upward. An analogous process for Israeli Arabs has involved the entry into the Israeli labor market of Arabs from the West Bank and the Gaza Strip, half of them into construction and approximately another third into agriculture and manufacturing (Table 7-6). They gradually replaced Israeli Arabs first in agriculture and then in construction. But even within this more recent group in the labor force, agriculture has been declining.

Earnings

Even in the stagnating 1970s real wages, earnings, and standards of living rose significantly on average. I focus here on differentials in income and standards of living. Their presence and the pressures to close them may well have contributed to the excessive rise in consumption.

The crude gap in monthly earnings between AA and EA groups declined from 37 percent (of EA earnings) in 1957–58 to 32 percent in 1963–64, and to 26 percent in 1968–69. Since 1968 a series of income surveys indicates that the gap in weekly earnings narrowed from 29 percent in 1968 to 20 percent by the end of the decade (Amir, 1984). A similar series for household incomes of wage earners shows some odd fluctuations in the late 1960s, a gap of about 26 percent in 1970–1973 narrowing to approximately 20 percent in 1975–1982 (CBS, *Income Survey 1984*). Until 1968–69 three-fifths of the gap is not accounted for by the standard explanatory variables. According to Amir (1985), the narrowing of differentials in the 1970s stemmed mainly from the shrinkage of this unexplained residual, which is associated with origin rather than with the predicted earning differentials. Amir's explanatory variables include education, age, and period of immigration. The unexplained residual may be associated with discrimination or with lower ability and quality of schooling. An earnings function based on 1972 data yields lower returns to schooling for AAs than for EAs (Ben-Porath, 1981).

The gaps between the earnings of ISAAs and ISEAs are at least as large as those between the earnings of the foreign-born groups. In addition, the earnings gaps between AA and EA women are as large or larger, and are fully explained by the standard variables in earning equations.

TABLE 7-7. Income differentials and selected demographic factors, 1972 and 1982

	EA – AA		ISEA – ISAA		Jews – non-Jews
	1972	1982	1972	1982	1982
Percentage gap[a] in:					
Household gross income	25.5	19.9	36.1	30.7	30.0
Head's earnings	25.3	18.2	35.2	34.5	33.8
Wife's earnings	63.0	44.7	65.8	43.1	77.7
Other earners	–90.3	–76.7	–91.7	–173.1	–99.3
Nonhead earnings	21.3	25.5	47.2	24.8	38.1
Institutional transfers	–133.0	–29.1	–198.2	–28.7	–35.0
Per capita income	54.0	44.0	45.7	36.2	54.1
Percentage share of gross family income[b]					
Wife's earnings	13.4/7.0	18.1/12.5	17.2/9.2	18.4/15.1	16.3/5.2
Other earners	4.8/13.3	3.4/7.5	2.3/6.9	1.7/6.7	4.6/13.1
Institutional transfers	1.1/4.4	4.9/7.9	2.3/6.9	3.5/6.5	5.6/10.8
Mean years of schooling of household head	11.1/8.1	12.1/9.6	12.9/9.5	13.8/10.8	11.4/8.2
Household size	3.1/5.0	3.2/4.6	3.4/4.0	3.5/3.8	3.8/5.8

Sources: CBS, *Income of Employees' Families, 1972–1974,* Special Publications Series, no. 510, pp. 32-33; CBS, *Survey of Income, 1982,* Special Publications Series, no. 734, pp. 48–49.

a. The first group in each pair equals 100.

b. Shares are listed for each group.

Table 7-7 summarizes the differentials in the income of wage earners' households and their relation to some demographic components. The origin-related income differences have narrowed over time. This also holds true for households headed by nonworkers (not shown) and is confirmed by data from the CBS *Family Expenditures Surveys* (1968, 1975, 1979), which also include urban households headed by the self-employed. In fact the size of the gap reported there is lower than the one reported here. Data on ownership of consumer durables show that whereas in the 1960s gaps were narrowed in basic commodities (refrigerators, cooking ranges, washing machines), in the 1970s convergence occurred in telephones, cars, and entertainment equipment. Differences in housing density also narrowed significantly.

Compared with EA and ISEA families, AA and ISAA families receive fewer contributions from the earnings of the household head's wife, and more from other earners and from social security. Over the decade most of these differences narrowed. With regard to per capita income, the difference in family size doubles the gap between the foreign-born (among the Israeli-born the gap in family incomes is upward biased and the gap in family size is downward biased because the ISAAs are younger than ISEAs). The gap in household size also narrowed over time, and as a result the gap in per capita income narrowed more than the gap in family income. The decline in the gap in family size (mostly children) *plus* the increased importance of old-age support for EAs accounts for the sharp decline in the advantage that AAs and ISAAs had over EAs and ISEAs in terms of institutional transfers. The gaps in schooling of household heads (counted in years rather than in value) narrowed somewhat over the decade.

The size of the sample of Arab urban wage earners and changes in the coverage of the sample precludes comparisons over time. On the whole, the direction and order of magnitude of the difference between non-Jews and Jews are similar to those described for AAs and EAs. Despite the difference in the levels of child allowances allocated to Jews and Arabs, the gap in the number of children is so large that the absolute volume of institutional transfers is 35 percent higher for an Arab family than for a Jewish family.

Conclusion

The Jewish population, composed of immigrants with diverse socioeconomic backgrounds, experienced rapidly rising standards of living and levels of income and schooling, all of which are intricately linked with these differentials. The rapid increases may have made the gaps more tolerable and helped create a reasonable degree of social cohesiveness. At the same time, the tensions, the attempts to close them, and the countervailing forces to maintain relative positions may have contributed to the upward pressures. The major protagonists were the government and nonprofit institutions, households, and firms. The major arenas were the labor market, the political system, and the nonmarket sector of educational and health services. The consequences are not only in terms of the variables. There were also macroeconomic implications, expressed in the maintenance of full employment and in the excessive growth of the civilian public sector (see Chapters 5 and 9), of the system of transfer payments (see Chapters 10 and 11), and even of aggregate consumption.

Despite deliberate government policies to close gaps in standards of living and in human capital (such as the provision of health and education services, the provision of housing, and direct intervention in the distribution of incomes through transfers and taxes), Israel has learned that some forces preserve inequality and transmit it from first to second generation. Some of these are embedded in households and their differential endowments, which do have self-perpetuating tendencies. The endowments with which workers enter the labor force are determined by the school system and by the family. Thus the extension of universal primary education in the 1950s and the subsequent expansion of vocational secondary education, which helped to close the gap at the base of the educational pyramid, was countered by the rapid expansion of higher education, largely serving the EA population. Similarly, the provision of public employment to women was more beneficial to the EA group than to others. In the transfer system, the emergence of an elderly population of EA origin and the decline in fertility differences between origin groups offset part of the impact of child allowances on the ethnic gap. In a country of immigrants experiencing rapid population growth, the advantages of the early arrivals come not only from priority in employment positions and the accumulation of country-specific skills, but also from capital gains on the early acquisition of real estate. The massive public involvement in housing is partly designed to offset this last phenomenon, but because it is built on complementary financing it has a somewhat restricted redistributive effect.

Although convergence of earnings was slow, it was faster than the convergence of educational and occupational distributions. Stormy labor relations in the 1970s, along with some shift of power from the central Histadrut headquarters to local blue-collar foci, might have contributed to this convergence. The market may have been even more effective in the case of the self-employed (who may have benefited from the general failure to enforce the income tax law).

Past tensions arising from inequality focused on income, standards of living, and government services for the poor. In the 1970s the locus of conflict moved as more of the AA population entered the middle class. This was expressed not only in labor relations but also in the political arena, where the strong (70 percent) identification of AAs with the Likud against the EAs' identification with Labor, the new balance between them, and the closer competition in the political market all affected economic policy.

The turning point in the macroeconomic situation implies that in the future it will no longer be possible to increase levels of public services and employment to cope with social problems. As a result it may be harder to narrow differentials in higher education. Against the persistence of gaps in schooling and occupational status among ISAAs and ISEAs one must note that their fertility has converged and their children are being raised in smaller families, in a much more similar environment, to literate parents, with presumably more homogeneous aspirations. Increased intermarriage and residential and school integration hold a promise for faster convergence in the second generation of Israeli-born.

Jewish-Arab differences are wider and more persistent. Differences in women's roles in fertility and in rural/urban attachment are still very large, and the two populations continue to live apart. Despite some narrowing of differentials in educational endowments, a rapid increase in incomes, and changes in occupation and industry, occupational and industrial differentiation persists. The Arab population has benefited from the major redistributive mechanism of child allowances despite their built-in ethnic differentiation. The residential segregation of Jews and Arabs, however, has contributed to the persistence of gaps in the provision of public services. The Arab population has far less access to public-sector benefits in housing, investments, and so on. Because the Jewish-Arab gap has not been an explicit policy target, the substantial improvement and the narrowing of gaps resulted mostly from market forces or the automatic extension of certain services.

Even more severe and complex from a political point of view is the issue of the Arab population of the West Bank and the Gaza Strip, which has lived under a separate administration since 1967. The longer these people remain Israel's responsibility, the less possible it will be to ignore the economic and social dualism between them and the Jewish population. Their problem is also likely to bring into sharper focus the issue of Israeli Arabs.

II

The Public Sector: Competing Goals

8

Defense and the Economy

Eitan Berglas

Throughout its existence, Israel has had to devote a considerable part of its economic capacity to defense. The study of the economic effects of defense expenditures is essential to an understanding of the Israeli economy and its development through time. A better understanding of these effects is also essential to appropriate decisions about how much is to be spent on defense.

Israel's defense expenditures are much higher than those of other Western countries. Barkai (1980) shows that since 1973 Israel has equaled the Netherlands and exceeded Sweden in absolute defense expenditure, which means that in per capita terms, Israel's are two to three times as large as theirs. In relative terms, the defense expenditures of these countries amounted to 3–4 percent of GNP in 1976–1977, compared with over 25 percent in Israel. The persistence of a high defense expenditure over a very long period makes Israel's situation unique. Since World War II the average rate for all Western countries has been below 10 percent, and except for the United States, below 5 percent. In Israel defense outlays have exceeded 10 percent of GNP since 1962 and 20 percent since 1969, averaging over 25 percent per annum in the period 1969–1981.

The study of the effects of defense expenditures in all countries suffers from a built-in scarcity of data. Owing to the dictates of military secrecy, much information is not collected and data that are collected are classified. Thus it is not surprising that research on the economics of defense is rare. For the same reason, general studies of the Israeli economy devote considerably less attention to defense than is warranted by the magnitude of its economic effects.[1]

Although this chapter does not deal with the defense expenditures of actual and potential enemy countries, their military efforts affect the Israeli economy through their effect on the level and composition of Israel's defense expenditure. Shefer (1983) shows that in 1979 the combined defense expenditure of Egypt, Syria, and Jordan exceeded Israel's by 25 percent, while Iraq alone spent 66 percent of the Israeli amount.[2] Such figures give an indication of the potential military threat to Israel and are appropriate to considerations of the desirable and appropriate levels of defense expenditure.

The Burden of Defense

The simplest definition of the defense burden is the total resources diverted to defense and thus precluded from other uses by residents of Israel. Thus expenditures by the defense sector for goods and services reduce the availability of these (or substitute) goods for other purposes. Workers hired by the defense sector are not available to other sectors and thus reduce nondefense output. Finally, foreign currency spent on imports of military equipment is not available for nonmilitary imports. For the time being I restrict the analysis to a narrow definition of "burden" (that is, the current defense expenditure). The final section discusses fiscal and dynamic effects.

In 1980 defense expenditures came to ISh (Israeli shekels) 1,978 million (at 1975 prices), or 23 percent of GNP. A defense outlay of this order would have imposed a very different burden on the economy in 1958, when GNP was ISh 1,967 million (again at 1975 prices). Defining the burden as the share of defense expenditures in GNP takes into account the change in the size of the economy. This definition also seems to be the most meaningful standard by which to compare expenditures in different years, given the background of a very rapid inflation. But it ignores the special role of (nondefense) unilateral transfers from abroad. Some of these go directly to the government, others to private individuals (which then increase government revenue to the extent that recipients purchase taxed commodities). Thus one may want to use the share in GNP *plus* unilateral transfers as the basis of comparison. Nondefense unilateral transfers have declined throughout the period 1955–1980 as a percentage of GNP, and ignoring them therefore understates the increase in the defense burden.

By the definitions above, defense expenditures financed by an earmarked unilateral grant (such as recent U.S. grants) do not constitute a burden on the economy if the grant would not have been forthcoming for any other use. Thus for the present purpose the appropriate definition of the defense burden is the share in GNP of total defense expenditure *minus* defense-specific grants. Because it is difficult to decide what part of unilateral transfers are defense specific, I first estimate total defense expenditures and then estimate the part not borne by Israelis.

The long-term series may be affected by several relative-price biases: the rate of exchange for defense imports was kept artificially low throughout the period, thereby reducing the reported share of defense; this bias was serious during the first two decades but became less so in the late 1970s. Military-equipment prices have also changed, and it is impossible to segregate changes in quality.

There have been three open wars during the period covered here (in 1956, 1967, and 1973). It is important to realize that many unrecorded expenditures are incurred apart from the direct battle expenditures included in the data. On one plane, there are those who lost their lives or remain handicapped; but there is a serious economic loss as well. Most of those killed were young; they had barely completed the stage when they were chiefly consumers and had just reached the age at which, in peacetime conditions, they would have contributed to production well in excess of their own consumption. Similar considerations apply to the wounded, who suffer temporary or permanent loss of economic capacity. Moreover, the loss of future output has been compounded by the need for long-term future medical-services outlays.[3] Finally, there was the loss of civilian output during each war. A quick analysis of the data seems to show that in wartime GNP does not deviate much from the regular trend. However, the labor component of the defense budget gives an indication of how much labor was diverted from civilian uses in 1967 and 1973. Studies considering these aspects have been conducted by the Ministry of Defense but have not been published. Another cost of frequent wars, which is even harder to measure, is their effect on potential investment from abroad and on the reliability (and hence competitiveness) of Israeli exports. The burden of defense as estimated here does not include the cost of wars and is thus an underestimate. The cost of wars is an important subject for further research.

Finally, a large proportion of defense outlays, typically over 50 percent, is spent in foreign currency. Foreign- and local-currency outlays may have very different effects on employment and inflation in the short run, and on the composition of national product in the long run. To distinguish between these factors economists frequently separate local and foreign expenditures.

The Data

Two long-term defense-expenditure series are available: the budget series (prepared by the Ministry of Finance), and the noncivilian component of public consumption as defined for the national accounts (prepared by CBS). There are some quite large differences between the two in particular years, but in the averages over longer periods (Table 8-1) the differences are much smaller.[4]

As Figures 8-1 and 8-2 show, the ratio of defense expenditures to GNP has varied considerably over the period. However, apart from the war years (1956, 1967, 1973), the annual fluctuations are dominated by long-term variations and the period can be subdivided, the defense burden increasing in what can be de-

TABLE 8-1. Published defense estimates, annual averages, 1955–1980

	1955–1961[a]	1962–1966	1968–1972	1974–1980
Millions of 1975 ISh				
GNP	2,090	3,416	5,456	7,489
Defense expenditures (CBS series)	197	372	1,224	2,088
Annual average rate of growth (percent)				
GNP	10.2	7.7	11.6	3.0
Defense expenditures (CBS series)	6.1	11.3	13.4	−1.0
Defense as percent of GNP (current prices)				
CBS series	8.3	10.1	21.7	27.8
Budget series	7.7	9.4	21.3	29.0

Source: Berglas (1983), appendix.
a. Excluding 1956.

scribed as a step function. In 1955–1961, the first subperiod in Table 8-1, defense expenditures were around 8 percent of GNP. What is significant in this period is that the Sinai campaign of 1956 was the only war of the three that was not followed by a sharp increase in defense expenditures. The ratio began to rise in 1962 and averaged close to 10 percent of GNP in 1962–1966. The steepest rise in the ratio followed the 1967 war, the average for 1968–1972 being over 21 percent. Since the 1973 war it has been close to 28 percent. The increase in the defense share throughout the period means that in real terms defense expenditures rose considerably faster than GNP. Thus in constant 1975 prices GNP rose by a factor of 6.3 and defense by a factor of 18.6 from 1954 to1980.

Table 8-2 provides a breakdown of defense expenditures into the domestic (that is, local-currency) and direct import components. Domestic expenditure on materials and equipment also has a significant import component (close to 25 percent on average for 1974–1980). Nevertheless, the direct import figures are significant because they closely approximate the dependence on imported military equipment and spare parts. Comparison of the subperiods shows that the increase in defense expenditures was associated with an increase in the share of imported equipment—as a percentage of total defense expenditures, as a percentage of GNP, and as a percentage of the import surplus. Despite this association, the rise in total defense expenditures was sufficient to allow the local production of mili-

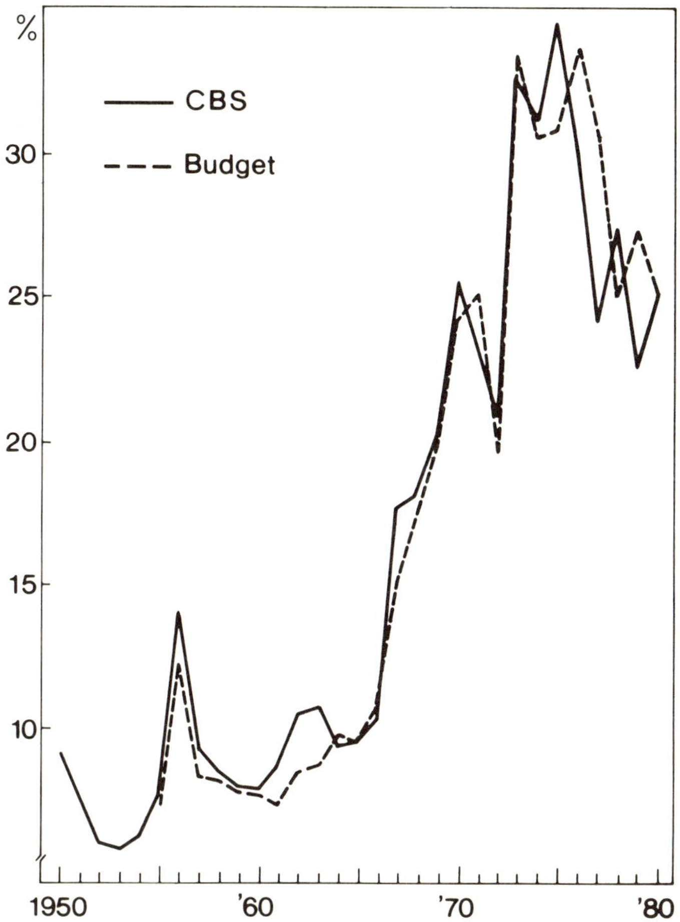

Figure 8-1
Share of defense in GNP, CBS versus budget series, 1950–1980.

tary equipment to grow very rapidly, and this growth acted as a major stimulus to the export of military equipment.

The annual figures show a jump in imports in 1967 and 1973, in each case followed by another peak two or three years later, due chiefly to the delivery of equipment ordered immediately after the war. Thereafter the share of local expenditures increases, reflecting the cost of absorbing the new purchases: when new and more expensive equipment is introduced, more manpower is needed and training and maintenance costs rise; there is also a gradual shift to local production of spare parts and ammunition for the new systems.

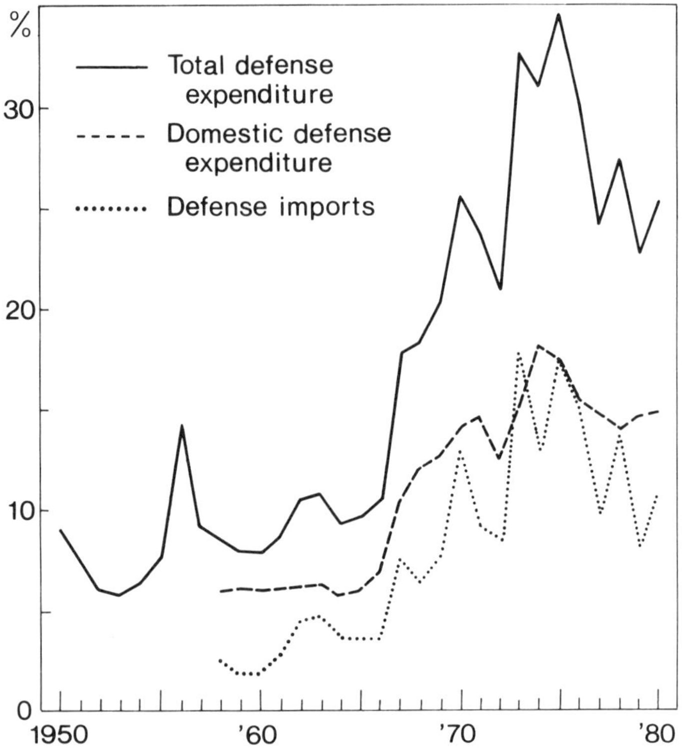

Figure 8-2
Domestic and imported defense consumption as a percentage of GNP, 1950–1980.

The Official Data Reconsidered

So far the analysis has been restricted to the official data. This section discusses expenditures that are misattributed to uses other than defense or are not reported at all.[5] The lack of data *ipso facto* precludes any definite estimation of the resulting biases, but it is nevertheless important that rough estimates be made whenever possible; in any case these estimates should at least be discussed.

Conscription. Conscripts receive only nominal pay in addition to their maintenance, and only the direct outlay is recorded in either of the two official sources. The understatement is equal to the income forgone by the conscripts.

Evaluation of the real cost of the conscript army involves estimating the number of service personnel and their forgone earnings, and then deducting their actual pay (including maintenance). For lack of official figures, the following considerations may provide a reasonably good estimate. The ratio of conscripts to the adult working population can be calculated from the length of conscription —

TABLE 8-2. The import component of defense expenditures, 1958–1980 (percentages)

	1958–1961	1962–1966	1968–1972	1974–1980
Direct defense imports as percentage of:				
GNP	2.2	3.9	8.6	12.4
Defense expenditure	26.7	38.6	39.6	44.6
Import surplus	12.0	18.9	37.5	39.5
Indirect defense imports as percentage of GNP	—	1.2	3.0	4.2
Total defense imports as percentage of defense expenditure	—	50.6	53.5	59.7
Defense expenditure as percentage of available resources (GNP *plus* import surplus)	7.0	8.4	17.7	21.2

Source: Berglas (1983), appendix.

three years for men, two for women. Thus Jewish men age 18–20 account for 10.2 percent of Jewish men age 21–65 (8.8 percent when the denominator includes non-Jews). The corresponding figures for women are 6.2 (5.3) percent. With the ratio of men to women in the labor force used as weights, the corresponding ratios for both sexes are 8.5 (7.3) percent (CBS, *Statistical Abstract 1981*, p. 52). This is, of course, only an estimate. Some people do not serve in the army, and some do not participate in the labor force. Several systematic biases are discussed in Berglas (1983).

Estimation of the forgone earnings is by no means a simple matter,[6] and the effect of three years of army service on lifetime productivity is far from clear. Allowing for several corrections, one might say that the unreported cost of conscription could be as high as 5 percent of GNP. It is borne by the youngsters who serve in the army. This may be an efficient way of collecting taxes, but it seems inequitable—those who serve in the army also pay for it. In this case GNP is also underestimated.

Reserve duty. Persons on reserve duty receive their regular wage or salary from the National Insurance Institute. These payments are included in the CBS but not in the budget series.[7] However, the amounts included by the CBS understate the true cost (see Berglas, 1983).

Reserve duty also has direct unrecorded effects on productivity: for example, what happens on a farm when the farmer is away for a month? Does his family make up for his absence or will he lose an entire season's crop, or much more than a month of output? How are firms affected by the absence of skilled workers, and what is the effect on schools when teachers are away?

Pensions. Government employees enjoy a budgetary pension; that is, no contributions are accumulated during the employee's working life. Pensions to former employees of the defense sector (civilian or regular army) do not appear in the defense budget, and they are treated as transfer payments in the national accounts along with other government pensions. This procedure of course understates both the GNP and the GNP share of defense and civilian public consumption.

The understatement of defense outlays due to underestimation of the cost of reserve duty and the exclusion of pensions may amount to 1–2 percent of GNP.

Casualties. The indirect cost of loss of life and earning capacity is not recorded at all. Expenditures such as medical costs and disability pensions are only partly recorded in the defense budget, and not at all in the CBS defense series (most of these items are considered as transfer payments in the national accounts). The expenditures included in the defense budget for such purposes are close to 1 percent of GNP.[8]

Stockpiling (fuel and essential foodstuffs). Stockpiles are kept above the economically desirable level. The cost of excess stocks includes installations, maintenance, and interest. These costs are borne by the users through higher prices. Aside from its direct cost, this system raises questions of efficient resource allocation. Consider the case of fuel: as a result of the need to keep large reserves, the user cost of fuel (and electricity) is significantly higher than it would otherwise be, with a direct effect on the comparative advantage of Israeli industry.[9] The fact that neither the army nor the Treasury finances the stocks is conducive to excess stockpiling.

The quantities and cost of emergency stockpiles are not made public. However, some idea can be gained by a rough calculation. In the late 1970s total oil imports to Israel came to approximately 12 percent of GNP. At a conservative estimate, emergency stockpiles for, say, three months would cost about 0.5 percent of GNP, taking account of amortization of storage capacity, maintenance, and interest on oil inventories and installations. Such stockpiles may raise the cost of fuel to the consumer by 4 percent. This is, of course, an example of an implicit tax. Larger stockpiles will increase the burden proportionately. The same considerations apply to stockpiles of other commodities, but their order of magnitude is smaller.

Civil defense. A large part of these expenditures is financed directly by the private citizen. Every residential building must contain a shelter constructed to army specifications, which again may be of too high a standard. The annual cost of shelters is close to 0.5 percent of GNP. Other civil defense expenditures are financed by the municipalities or the central government but are not included in the defense budget.

Land. The army and the industries run by the Ministry of Defense hold sizable areas, some of them in the most expensive parts of the country. The lost rental value is an estimate of the current cost to the economy of these lands.

Other expenditures. Numerous items recorded as government civilian expenditure should be ascribed to defense, among them part of the secret service; police operations concerned with the war against terrorism; expenditures on antiterrorist precautions by individuals and institutions; compensation to victims of terrorism; and a significant part of the investment in infrastructure such as roads, communications, and standby medical services. There are no estimates of the cost of these activities, but they provide a partial explanation of the large size of the civilian public sector.

Although it has not been possible to assign even a rough order of magnitude to all the items mentioned, it emerges from such figures as I have been able to suggest that the missing amounts (unreported or not ascribed to defense) come to more than half of reported local-currency expenditures. Moreover, in some cases the institutional setting may, as already indicated, have an adverse effect on the decision process that determines their magnitude and composition. Last but not least, many of these factors have a considerable effect on the productivity of the private sector, resulting in a significant underestimate of the implicit productivity of the labor force. Moreover, in all the cases considered in this section, the costs are of course borne by the whole population; yet they do not appear as part of the official tax revenues. This fact implies the existence of considerable concealed taxes.

These unreported elements have increased continuously. The period of conscription has been lengthened, as has the annual spell in the reserves, and the regular army has been enlarged. The increase in terrorist activity has prompted increased expenditures on countermeasures. Thus the major increase in local defense expenditures that followed the 1967 and 1973 wars certainly understates the actual increase.

Defense Imports and External Aid

The defense budget is divided into two separate parts: one in U.S. dollars and one in local currency.[10] The defense authorities are restricted in shifting between the two parts. The rationale behind the restrictions on convertibility was the recognition that in the short run local expenditures have a stronger inflationary effect; thus, at times of acute inflation, the tendency was toward stronger restrictions on local-currency expenditure. The most extreme example was a 1979 agreement with firms constructing airfields, which encouraged them to use as many imported components as possible (a policy reversed at a later stage). Another explanation for the special treatment of foreign currency arises from the fact that American aid is given to finance imported equipment and, with few exceptions, prohibited from use for local purchases. This arrangement sometimes led to importation of equipment that could have been manufactured more efficiently in Israel. At other times, the shortage of foreign exchange was regarded as severe, and the defense sector was encouraged to increase its local-currency purchases even when they were more expensive than imports. This situation was more common before 1973. Such policy switches mean that the shadow price of foreign currency to the defense sector is not correctly represented by the official rate of exchange.

Direct defense imports are translated into local currency by the official rate of exchange. Government policy has resulted in a consistently overvalued local currency.[11] As long as defense imports were exempt from import taxes (that is, until the late 1960s), the exchange-rate understatement of defense expenditures was of the order of 1.5 to 3 percent of GNP, depending on the effective exchange rate used; since 1970, defense imports have paid duty, and this bias has declined.

Table 8-3 provides the data for alternative definitions of the amount of foreign aid that should be deducted from the defense burden. U.S. military aid in the form of subsidized loans began in 1967 and in the form of grants in 1973. Despite their unprecedented level, the defense grants did not cover the increase in military expenditures in either 1968–1972 or 1974–1980. In 1974–1980 grants defined as military aid by the U.S. government financed 32 percent of direct defense expenditure in foreign exchange. If one includes economic with military aid, on the grounds that it was in fact forthcoming because of military needs, it follows that foreign aid covered the increase in foreign-currency expenditures for defense in 1974–1980, while the increase in local-currency expenditures was financed from other sources.

In the case of U.S. military aid, Israel was (with minor exceptions) obliged to use aid funds to finance imports of U.S. equipment. There are clear indications that Israel would prefer to use part of these funds in other ways, mainly to finance local production of equipment, which is frequently less expensive and sometimes also more effective. American aid has thus helped Israel to increase its defense effort and expenditures on equipment, and has induced increased use of U.S. equipment, thus reducing the use of other—in particular locally produced—equipment. In some cases American aid has impeded the development of more effective local alternatives. Another effect of foreign aid is the restriction of the recipient country's political freedom, which also affects its defense posture.

The definition of foreign aid as grants (including the grant component of loans) has a sound economic meaning. A major part of U.S. military aid has taken the form of loans. U.S. government loans granted on terms similar to those available to Israel in the financial markets constitute an economic burden. Loans given on easier terms, on the other hand, contain a substantial grant element (Table 8-3).[12] The fact that some of the aid was in the form of loans is not unimportant. The amount of U.S. military aid (including loans) has had a significant effect on the

TABLE 8-3. Defense imports and foreign aid, annual averages, 1964–1980 ($ million)

	1964–1966	1967	1968–1972	1973	1974–1980
Defense imports					
Direct	108.1	285.5	436.6	1,180.0	1,419.0
Indirect	37.7	71.0	151.4	277.0	481.1
Total	145.8	356.5	588.0	1,457.0	1,900.1
Foreign grants					
U.S. government grants					
Defense	—	—	—	820.0	616.4
Defense, including grant component of loans[a]	—	9.8	66.0	898.2	774.8
Civilian	28.8	13.8	10.0	50.4	417.6
Total	28.8	23.6	76.0	948.6	1,257.7[b]
Institutional transfers including grant component[c]	114.3	357.0	273.8	817.0	477.4

Sources: Bank of Israel, *Annual Report 1979*, pp. 186–87 (Hebrew version) and underlying data, as corrected and updated by the Bank of Israel Research Department.

a. The grant component is an estimate of the implicit current value of the subsidy in subsidized loans. Technically, it is the difference between the actual loans received and the present value of the debt schedule (interest and principal repayment) based on the market interest rate on loans of similar duration.

b. Including grant component implicit in economic aid loans.

c. The grant component implied by the low interest rate on Israel bonds.

level of defense imports. Since 1973, imports of military equipment have been restricted to the funds available as military aid (including loans). The servicing of debt is not included in the defense budget but imposes a heavy burden on the economy. Debt servicing and debt retirement will exceed the level of new loans in the 1980s, and thus will make financing of defense expenditures more difficult even if the current level of aid is continued.[13]

Contributions through Jewish organizations have declined in terms of constant dollars; relative to the level of defense expenditures, the decline is even greater. Nevertheless, 1967 and 1973 are striking examples of the availability of this source when it is really needed.

The External Economies of Defense

From the outset, the armed forces and the Ministry of Defense undertook activities beyond their direct military responsibilities. Some examples are education, absorption of immigrants, agricultural settlement, and the development and manufacture of weapons and equipment (which are also exported). Moreover, the army, by training young people as mechanics, drivers, and so on, provides skills that are useful in civilian life. Quantitative estimates are needed to shed light on the economic effects of these factors, but since the necessary data are not available, some qualitative comments may help suggest how the economic value of these externalities should be estimated.

Education

The armed forces carry out some important educational functions, both formal and informal.[14] University teachers are well aware of the difference between Israeli and foreign students; a large part of this difference is commonly attributed to military service, although this is hardly susceptible to measurement. Nor is it easier to assess the effect of military experience on productivity (it may, of course, also be negative, through the acquisition of bad work habits).

Industrial Development

Israel's military industry was started before 1948 in underground conditions. To this day, its development is partly due to the need for weapons that cannot be acquired abroad for political reasons. But this factor has declined in importance, and the defense industry (a term used here to include all enterprises that produce military equipment, regardless of ownership) has developed into the country's fastest-growing industry and has also become a major exporter. Production of military equipment is concentrated in three major manufacturing industries: metal products, machinery, and electrical and electronic equipment. Production statistics for these industries are a good indicator of the development of the military industry. From 1965 to 1977 their share in the total value added of industry (excluding diamonds) increased from 18.9 to 29.8 percent (CBS, *Statistical Abstract 1981,* pp. 418, 420, 429; Bank of Israel, *Annual Report 1980,* p. 23). During the same period, industrial production multiplied by a factor of 2.48. Put differently, the real annual rate of growth of the three industries was 12.0 percent compared with 7.9 percent for total industrial production. Some of the additional output was for local use, but there was also a major increase in exports. By 1980 the three industries exported 46.4 percent of their output compared with 40 percent in the industrial sector as a whole.[15]

Studies comparing various locally produced weapons systems with their imported counterparts suggest that local costs are in most cases reasonably low. Several factors contribute to low costs or to a comparative advantage in the production of military equipment.

1. Locally developed and produced equipment is better suited to the climate, terrain, organization, and scale of Israel. On the other hand, the major powers develop equipment that is adapted for use all over the world and is thus usually more expensive.
2. Israel has more experience than most countries in the continuous operation of equipment in combat conditions, experience that helps to debug existing equipment and to introduce improvements.
3. The market for weapons systems has oligopolistic characteristics; thus prices often considerably exceed costs.
4. Even in larger countries production runs of military equipment are relatively short. In a few items, Israel has production runs that are sufficiently large to enjoy economies of scale.
5. The scientific and technological level of Israel's institutions of higher learning and research and the composition and quality of its labor force (both civilian and military) make research and development there relatively inexpensive.

Political considerations also play a part in the weapons markets. Self-sufficiency in military equipment is often advocated as a means of reducing political dependence. It is now obvious that self-sufficiency, even in crucial systems, is an illusory goal, since for a small country that needs the most advanced systems the cost is prohibitive. Even large European countries such as the United Kingdom, France, and West Germany find it necessary to combine their efforts in developing major systems; and they also continue to use imported equipment. Although absolute self-sufficiency has always been unattainable, it is meaningful in a restricted sense. All countries shroud their most advanced systems in secrecy. Some of these systems can be (and have been) developed locally; what is perhaps no less important, once it is clear that local production is feasible, foreign countries are more ready to export their systems; possible examples are air-to-air missiles and electronic countermeasures. Last but not least, political measures are used in the weapons markets to achieve economic as well as political advantages. This situation may lead to the opening of certain markets that prefer Israeli exports for political reasons, but more often the opposite is true. The most obvious example is the case of the Kfir interceptor; political intervention prevented the export of this very effective aircraft.

All these factors explain the impressive development of the defense industry and its success as an exporter. In the case of systems that would be developed regardless of the existence of export markets, exports help to cover some of the sunk cost; in such cases exports may be exceptionally profitable. In other instances, the production of some kinds of equipment can be justified only by the existence of a potential export market.

How does the defense industry contribute to reducing the burden of defense? To the extent that the local industry succeeds in reducing the cost of military equipment, this success is reflected in a more efficient army for a given cost. In other words, if Israel had not succeeded in developing an efficient defense industry, the same defense effort would have implied a higher burden.

The effect of defense exports on the measurement of the burden as defined above needs to be examined carefully. If Israel had had no comparative advantage in military equipment, other export industries would have been developed.[16] However, the defense industries do create a positive externality, although it is somewhat difficult to measure. In principle, one would like to compare actual productivity (which may be measured by total real wages and profits) with the hypothetical output of an economy without a defense industry. A more practical procedure would be to regard as an externality (or a reduction in the burden of defense) the excess of real value added produced by factors of production employed in the defense industry over their alternative value outside it. This excess may be negligible or nonexistent for most weapons systems, but it may be considerable for some. However, it is important to note that a large part of the defense industry's profits is ploughed back into the defense sector (for example, into research and development). Thus they have in fact already been deducted from the burden.

Another externality is connected with the large number of people trained in the defense industry who subsequently move to the civilian sector. Some of the country's more sophisticated private businesses have been developed by entrepreneurs and workers who acquired their skill and experience in industry and the research institutions of the defense establishment. Finally, the defense sector has created a demand for high-quality products that has had a marked effect on civilian production.

The Financing of Defense Expenditures

This section surveys the financing of defense expenditures first through an analysis of the government budget, and then through an analysis of national resource allocation.

The Government Budget

Defense expenditures have increased throughout the period. There are four ways of financing the increase: reduction of other expenditures, increased taxation,

TABLE 8-4. Public expenditure and taxation as a percentage of GNP, 1957–1980

	1957–1961	1962–1966	1968–1973	1974–1980
Total defense expenditure	8.4	10.1	21.7	27.8
Local defense expenditure	6.0	6.1	13.0	15.5
Civilian public consumption	10.9	11.1	10.8	11.9
Tax revenue	31.7	35.5	36.0	45.4
Transfer payments	10.9	11.3	16.1	31.4
To individuals	5.1	6.7	8.7	16.2[a]
To firms (subsidies)	4.7	2.7	4.3	10.0[a]
Domestic debt servicing	1.1	1.9	3.1	5.2
Taxes net of transfers	20.8	24.2	19.9	14.0

Source: Berglas (1983), appendix, and Chapter 11 of this volume.
a. Including subsidy component in government loans.

foreign aid, and deficit financing. As Table 8-4 shows, the increase in defense expenditure was not associated with a reduction in civilian public consumption. Taxes were raised considerably, but at the same time transfer payments rose even faster. Consequently, net taxes—defined as taxes *minus* transfer payments—declined considerably. The growing gap between expenditures and net taxes was financed to some degree by grants and to a large degree by borrowing, both locally and abroad. Chapter 11 provides a detailed study of the development of the various instruments of government finance during the period; a summary will suffice here.

Until 1966 taxes were sufficient to finance total domestic government expenditures (including civilian consumption, transfer payments, and local-currency defense expenditures). Figure 8-3 shows that a gap then developed and increased further after 1974, when a 2.5 percentage-point increase in the ratio of local defense expenditures to GNP was associated with an increase of 1 percentage point in public civilian consumption, 15 points in transfer payments, and only 9 points in taxes. A comparison of a 1968–1973 with 1962–1966 reveals a similar pattern: defense expenditures rose by over 11 percent of GNP; nevertheless, civilian expenditures and taxes, as measured by the share in GNP, remained essentially unchanged, while transfer payments rose from 11 to 16 percent of GNP.

Thus in the two periods of major changes the increase in defense expenditures was not accompanied by any attempt to divert resources from the rest of the economy; on the contrary, the government increased other expenditures at the same time. Even without an analysis of annual policy fluctuations, it is safe to say that the government's resort to deficit financing has had serious effects on the

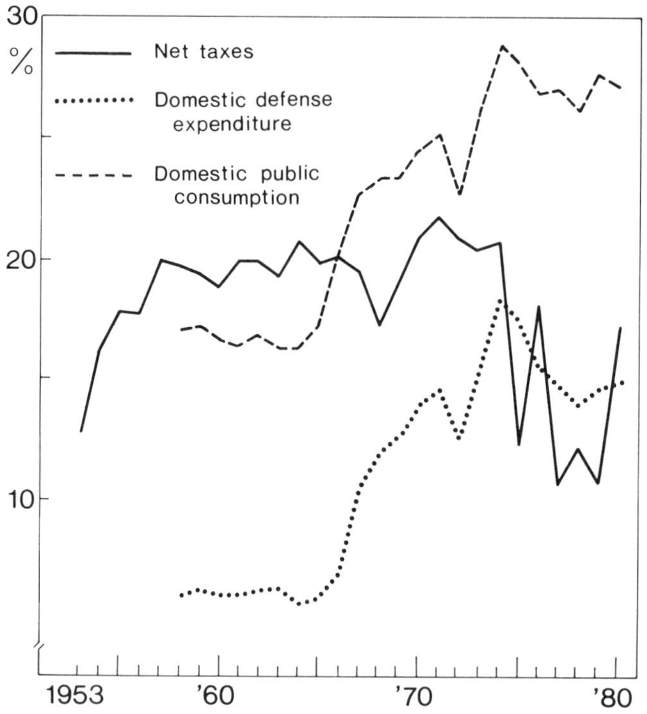

Figure 8-3
Domestic defense expenditures, public consumption, and net taxes as a percentage of GNP, 1953–1980.

financial markets and the import surplus and is a major cause of the instability that has characterized the Israeli economy since the 1970s.

The Allocation of National Resources

How does a change in defense expenditures affect inflation, investment, growth, and foreign debt? It is often maintained that an increase in defense expenditures is the cause of unfavorable developments in these variables; that a larger foreign debt and slower growth affect the country's long-term defense position; and that these external effects of increased defense expenditures are often ignored, or at least not sufficiently considered, by myopic policymakers. Although this question deserves further investigation, the discussion here is confined to the first aspect, namely, the effects of changes in defense expenditures on several major economic variables. This issue alone is quite complex; it is very difficult to isolate the effects of, say, the increase in defense expenditures after 1973 on the growth of inflation. An analysis of these effects requires both a reliable model of the economy and consideration of the effects of the accompanying policies. Clearly, the economy would have behaved differently had the increase in defense outlays after 1973 been accompanied by a reduction in other government expenditures, including transfer payments. The following paragraphs analyze the effects of changes in defense expenditures together with the policies actually implemented to finance them (see Berglas, 1983, for a more detailed discussion).

Table 8-5 compares the situations in the two years preceding the 1956, 1967, and 1973 wars and in the five years that followed them.[17] There are major differences among the three periods, which reflect changes in policy and exogenous factors. Each period can be seen as dominated by one or two major events. Thus the exceptionally rapid growth rate of 1954–1955 and the declining rate of inflation that followed the major switch in economic policy of 1952–53 had a considerable effect in the period after 1956. The period surrounding the 1967 war is associated with the depression of 1965–1966 and the occupation of the West Bank in 1967, which resulted in the low inflation rate of the four years after the war (see note b to Table 8-5). The period after 1973 is dominated by oil prices, other terms-of-trade effects, and changes in world economic activity. These are reflected in a sharp decline in the rate of growth after 1973, as well as in the mounting inflation.

The data for the three "normal" prewar periods reveal two major longterm trends for 1953–1972: a decline in the GNP share of private consumption and a similar increase in the share of defense expenditures. Changes in other variables were relatively small; the share of civilian public consumption in GNP fell somewhat, while the share of investment increased slightly. The ratio of import surplus to GNP fell significantly in the decade after 1956 and rose somewhat in the early 1970s. Although the GNP share of private consumption declined until 1972 because of the rapid growth rate of GNP, private consumption grew absolutely throughout the period and there was no per capita decline. The growth rate of real total and per capita consumption, however, declined throughout the period.

The only postwar shift in resource allocation common to the three wars was a marked contraction of investment, which, after the 1956 war, exceeded the increase in defense expenditures so that the import surplus could be reduced. Investment dropped much more after 1967 and 1973, but not nearly enough to accommodate the increase in defense expenditures. Nevertheless, the import surplus–GNP ratio hardly rose after the 1967 war, thanks to the rapid growth rate, made possible by the excess capacity created by the 1965–1966 depression and stimulated by the opening of the West Bank. By the early 1970s, however, it was clear that the economy had reached a point at which, without a change of policy, a faster-growing import surplus and slower growth could be foreseen (see Berglas, 1970). Moreover, in 1971 and 1972 the inflation rate was double that of the preceding decade.

With regard to growth rates, the indications seem more consistent. The growth

TABLE 8-5. The allocation of resources before and after wars, 1954–1978

	1954–1955	1957–1961	1963–1964[a]	1968–1972	1971–1972	1974–1978	Change		
							1954–55 to 1957–61	1963–64 to 1968–72	1971–72 to 1974–78
Percent of GNP (annual average)									
Private consumption	74.6	71.1	69.9	61.6	56.7	63.3	–3.5	–8.0	5.7
Civilian public consumption	11.8	10.9	10.4	10.5	10.5	11.6	–0.9	0.4	1.1
Defense expenditure	7.0	8.5	10.0	21.6	22.2	29.4	1.5	11.6	7.2
Investment	31.2	29.0	32.0	28.9	32.4	29.2	–2.2	–3.1	–3.3
Import surplus	24.6	19.5	22.0	22.9	22.8	33.0	–5.7	0.9	10.7
Annual average rate of growth									
Real GNP	16.8	9.0	10.6	11.5	11.7	3.1	–7.8	0.9	–6.6
Real private consumption	11.6	8.9	10.4	8.1	7.8	4.9	–2.7	–2.3	–3.3
Real private consumption per capita	8.3	5.1	6.0	4.8	4.4	2.3	–3.2	–1.2	–2.1
Inflation	9.0	3.9	5.8	7.1[b]	12.4	39.1	–5.1	1.3	26.7

Source: Berglas (1983), appendix.

a. Figures for 1963–1964 are used because 1965 and 1966 were years of recession.

b. This average number is misleading. The annual rates for the years 1968 through 1972 were 2.1, 2.5, 6.1, 12.0, and 12.9 respectively.

rates of real output, private consumption, and per capita consumption have been falling, as a comparison of the pre- and postwar periods makes clear. Private consumption, total and per capita, grew much more slowly after wars than in the years preceding them, a result that needs careful interpretation. Scrutiny of the per capita consumption series shows that even when the downward trend is eliminated, the rate of growth of per capita consumption declines after each war. The change in the ratio of consumption to GNP is determined by the interaction of the changes in the rates of growth of output and per capita consumption.

So far, it can be said that the government has still not found an economic policy that would reconcile a large defense expenditure, price stability, and a manageable import surplus.

9

Public Spending on Civilian Services

Gur Ofer

Since the end of World War II most countries, both developed and less developed, have experienced a sharp rise in the level of activity and in the share of their public sectors in the provision of social services (see, for example, OECD, 1976, 1984a–c). Despite its obvious benefits, this expansion is regarded as one of the factors contributing to declining growth and to the development of stagflation in many industrialized countries. The bureaucratic nature of the public sector, high deficits and taxation, and ambitious welfare programs have all been blamed for inefficiency; for crowding out productive investments, fanning inflation, and creating disincentives to work. Israel has been a leading participant in the trend to expand the public sector, and although special circumstances can be cited to justify the need for more public services in Israel than elsewhere, one cannot ignore the many ills associated with this process. This is especially true with regard to the period under consideration here—from 1968 to the early 1980s, a period sometimes referred to as the "third decade."

This chapter deals with one aspect of the development of the public sector, namely, public civilian services (education, health, economic services, and the like). It does not cover defense (see Chapter 8) or income maintenance and welfare programs, which consist mainly of transfers to households rather than the provision of services (see Chapter 10).

As Israel entered its third decade of statehood, the level of activity of its public services was already high by international standards. Given its level of economic development, Israel employed a higher proportion of its labor force in public (civilian) services than did many more developed Western industrialized countries, and these services absorbed a higher share of Israel's GNP (see Ofer, 1967, and Chapter 2 of this volume). In the course of the third decade a number of forces joined in what should have made the further expansion of publicly financed public services very difficult. These forces, in order of appearance, were the stepping up of defense expenditures, the launching of an ambitious income-maintenance program by the government at the turn of the 1960s, and, finally, following the 1973 war, a sharp decline in the rate of growth of the economy. The defense budget grew to absorb Israel's entire foreign aid receipts or import surplus while internal resources generated by growth dwindled to a tiny flow. The government was forced to seek alternative means of finance—such as inflation. As defense also drew off more tax revenues, and as taxes were indeed being raised, the share of net taxes in total government resources (net of transfers) actually declined.

Considering the facts that transfers substitute for some of the functions of direct supply of services and that the initial (1968) level of public services was high to begin with, one might expect the share of public services at least not to rise under such conditions. But spending on civilian public services did rise from 1968 to the early 1980s, from 17 to 20 percent of GNP, and the share of those employed in civilian public services (CPS) rose from 22 to around 30 percent of the *civilian* labor force. The relative rise in the GNP share of CPS is quite significant, especially under the circumstances described above; the increase in its employment share is very significant under any circumstances (see Chapter 5). Complicating matters further, in addition to the general growth in public services, the relative burden on public and government funds to finance them also increased substantially (see below). This chapter first describes the rise in absolute and relative spending on public services and then analyzes the forces that pushed for expansion under the worst of circumstances.

Table 9-1 presents data on the role of civilian public services in the Israeli economy in 1960–1983. Most of the data are presented as relative shares in GNP. The rise in the share of CPS in GNP, from 17 to 20 percent, is shown in line 10. As shown, CPS consists of services supplied by the public sector (including national and local government agencies as well as various departments of "national institutions" such as the Jewish Agency) and by nonprofit public organizations (NPOs). Traditional national accounting practices in Israel and elsewhere classify NPO activities under private consumption (as in line 5a in the table). This practice is debatable everywhere, but more so in Israel, where some NPOs, notably the sick funds that provide health insurance to almost the entire population, antedated the state as seminational institutions, where dues paid to quasi-NPOs are considered as virtual taxes, and where the government provides the lion's share of support to so many NPOs (including those in the public sector as shown in line 5b in Table 9-1; see also Table 9-4).[3] As can be seen from Table 9-1, NPOs have been providing about a third of all CPS; only lately has their share reached 40 percent (lines 8 and 9) of the total.

Next, Table 9-1 shows the "pincer movement" encircling public services. The defense burden on the economy is discussed in great detail in Chapter 8. Here it is presented in juxtaposition to the import surplus. Assume that defense has first

TABLE 9-1. Resource use of taxes as percentage of GNP, 1960–1983

	1960–1965	1966–1967	1968–1972	1973–1975	1976–1979	1980–1983
1. Import surplus	20	15	23	38	28	26
2. Defense expenditures	10	14	22	33	25	24
3. "Civilian surplus"	10	1	1	5	3	2
4. Gross investment	31	20	24→32	33	26	24
5. Private consumption (a)[a]	69	68	66→57	61	64	65
(b)[a]	63	62	60→51	55	57	57
6. Gross taxes (a)[b]	28	30	38	44	48	49
(b)[b]	27	29	37	43	47	48
7. Net taxes (a)[b]	20	20	19	17	14	14
(b)[b]	23	23	22	20	18	18
8. Civilian "government" consumption	11	12	11	11	12	12
9. Consumption of non-profit institutions	6	(6)	6	6	7	7
10. Total civilian public consumption	17	18	17	17	19	20
11. Total civilian public expenditure (including investment)[d]	19	20	19	20	21	21
Annual growth rates						
12. GNP (1975 prices)	9	1→2	11	4	3	3
13. Prices (consumer price index	6	8→2	2→13	20→39	39→79	120→152

Sources: Lines 6b, 7b, 9: Bank of Israel, *Annual Report*, various years, chapter on NPOs or on the Public Sector; line 11: CBS, *Statistical Abstract 1983*, table X/2, p. 267; all others – updated from Berglas (1983), appendix.

a. (a) includes and (b) excludes consumption of nonprofit institutions (NPOs) in private consumption.

b. In (a) taxes on NPOs are included and in (b) excluded from gross taxes.

c. In (a) transfers to NPOs are included and in (b) excluded from total government transfers to the economy.

d. Investment in education and health only.

claim on the import surplus, and that only the remainder is "civilian surplus" (line 3) available for civilian needs. This "civilian surplus" shrank from 10 percent in the mid-1960s to a mere 1–5 percent since 1966–1967. Foreign aid was only barely able to keep up with increasing defense needs. Even small civilian surplus shown since 1973 overstates the true situation, both because the actual defense burden on GNP is higher than shown in the national accounts and because the import surplus figures are higher over the past ten years than the normal stream of foreign aid acquired. The government financed part of the surplus by increasing the volume of short-term loans to finance part of the expansion of public services, but reliance on outside sources of credit was severely limited.

Lines 6 and 7, which summarize gross and net taxes, present a second part of the picture. The differences between the corresponding figures in lines 6 and 7 are government transfers to households and businesses. The transfers consist of various income-maintenance programs, subsidies to basic food items and services, support for production and exports, interest on the domestic debt, and capital gains by the private sector on nonindexed government loans in a period of accelerating inflation. The most striking feature is that while the share of gross taxes in GNP rose sharply from less than 30 percent to almost half of GNP, the share of net taxes actually declined by 6 percentage points, reflecting the steep rise of transfers from 4–8 to 30–35 percent of GNP in the late 1970s and early 1980s. This is a real revolution in the financing of the public sector during Israel's third decade (see Chapter 10). The upshot is that fewer free resources in terms of GNP shares should have been left over for CPS.

As shown in lines 4 and 5 of Table 9-1, the brunt of the macroeconomic pinch was borne during the first half of the decade by private consumption, whose share declined 9 percent in 1968–1972; but in the second half of the 1970s and in the early 1980s it was borne by investment, whose proportion of GNP declined 9 percent, to 24 percent. It is worth noting that the decline in the share of private consumption occurred while GNP was growing rapidly (line 12). When the growth rates of GNP dropped after 1973, private consumption managed to keep growing by raising its share in GNP. As a result, the investment rate—strongly influenced by government investment and direct support of private investment—had to give way. As already mentioned, the declining rate of economic growth since 1973 should have dried up the final source for CPS expansion. During the first half of the decade, when overall rates of GNP growth were high, the GNP share of CPS did not rise. But it did rise when growth decelerated, and pressures to continue to develop CPS did not cease. In this respect the development of CPS (at least its direction) is similar to that of private consumption.[1]

Which public services were responsible for the expansion of the entire sector? Table 9-2 presents data on the internal structure of CPS in terms of GNP shares and employment shares. The two groups of services whose shares expanded most are education and health: from half the total expenditure in the early 1960s their combined share grew to 65 percent of total CPS by 1983. Similarly, of all persons employed in CPS, education and health services accounted for 54 percent in 1962 and for 58 percent in 1980. At the other end of the scale are economic and general services, whose share in total expenditures declined from 27 percent of CPS in

TABLE 9-2. Expenditures and employment in public services, 1962–1981 (percentages)

	1962/63	1968/69	1974/75	1980/81
Shares in GNP				
National expenditure	20.3	21.1	20.6	22.1
Education	6.0	7.2	8.2	8.2
Health	5.5	5.4	5.9	7.6
National consumption	18.7	19.1	18.8	20.7
Public consumption	17.1	17.5	16.8	19.6
Education	26	32	33	38
Health	23	22	22	29
Welfare	51	18	20	17
Economic and general		27	25	16
Shares in Civilian Employment[a]				
Public services	20.4 (100)	22.4 (100)	25.7 (100)	28.1 (100)
Education	6.7 (33)	7.4 (33)	9.6 (37)	11.1 (40)
Health	4.3 (21)	4.2 (19)	4.4 (17)	5.1 (18)
Welfare	0.9 (4)	0.9 (4)	0.9 (4)	0.9 (3)
Administration and others	8.5 (41)	9.9 (44)	10.8 (42)	11.0 (40)

Sources: GNP weights: Bank of Israel, *Annual Report 1982*, table E/5, p. 89, and corresponding tables in previous issues; labor force: CBS, *Statistical Abstract 1983*, table XII/10, pp. 356-57 and corresponding tables in previous issues.

a. Figures in parentheses are the percentage of total civilian employment in public services.

1968 to 16 percent in 1980–81, with almost no decline in their employment share. In the middle are various welfare services (including immigrant absorption), whose share remained stable. The decline in the GNP share of general and economic services reflects returns to scale in the regulation of a growing economy, some transfer of functions (both bona fide and artificial) from the public sector to the business community (such as banks), a decline in direct government intervention in the economy, and a decline in the relative wage of employees in these services (see Chapter 5). The stability in welfare and absorption services may reflect the shift that took place during the 1970s from welfare services to direct income transfers to households under universal legislation — a less bureaucratic-intensive operation.

The Rise in Expenditures on Education and Health

The rising share of CPS, and particularly of education and health services in GNP, is translated into comparative annual rates of growth over the period under discussion (Table 9-3). Changes in a sector's GNP share (in current prices) are the product of differences in real rates of growth and changes in relative prices.[2] Such products (referred to as "total burden") are presented in lines 4 (education) and 8 (health) of Table 9-3. The rising shares of both services in GNP are due to higher rates of growth of total burdens; these were much higher than those of real GNP over the entire period 1962–1979, and only slightly lower since 1979. It is interesting to note that the most significant difference between the rates of growth of services and GNP occurred when the latter declined sharply, after 1974. Total burdens, however, especially those of health, continued to grow. Only around the end of the 1970s did the growth rates of services seem to succumb to budget constraints and stop growing.

What explains the rise in the shares (or burden) of education and health services? The first important distinction is between growth in the volume of real output and a rise in the relative price of the service. There may be various justifications for such a rise in prices, but if that increase is genuine, there is no added service rendered. The problem with the distinction between price and output changes in services is that in the absence of any firm output measures the distinction assumes zero increase in the services' productivity. Under such an assumption output can be measured by inputs, and changes in prices by the rise in input prices relative to the general price level. Based on this assumption, the figures in Table 9-3 show that the rise in relative service prices explains about one-quarter of the increase in the education and health burdens during the 1970s, with most of the impact concentrated in the second half of the period.

It is, however, farfetched to assume that no increase in productivity took place in the provision of these services. Advances in all spheres of medicine and the significant rise in the level of schooling of teachers are only two cases justifying the rejection of the zero-productivity assumption. Thus if one assumes that productivity in these services equaled that of the private sector, then almost all the registered rise in relative prices in 1962–1980 would be transferred to increases in real output. Put differently, the registered rise in real output in Table 9-3 should be considered as the lower boundary of the rise and the figures for total burden as the upper limit.[3]

But even by the conservative and conventional measures, in 1968–1978 real expenditures on health services more than doubled and those on education in-

TABLE 9-3. Annual rates of growth of public services, 1962–1981 (percentages)

	1962/63–1968/69	1968/69–1974/75	1974/75–1980/81	1968/69–1980/81
1. GNP	7.7	8.5	3.1	5.8
2. Population	3.4	3.1	2.3	2.7
3. GNP per capita	4.2	5.2	0.8	3.0
4. Input productivity in private sector	2.1	4.6	0.7	2.6
Education				
5. Total burden[a]	11.6	9.7	3.9	6.8
6. Relative price	4.5	1.5	2.8	2.1
7. Real growth	6.8	8.1	1.1	4.6
8. Real growth per capita (7/2)	3.3	4.8	−1.3	1.9
9. School-age cohorts	3.6	2.8	2.2	2.5
10. Students	3.5	3.8	3.4	3.6
11. Cost per student	3.3	4.1	−2.2	1.0
12. Current elasticity (5/1)[b]	1.5	1.1	1.3	1.2
13. Real elasticity (7/1)[b]	0.9	1.0	0.4	0.8
Health				
14. Total burden (15 X 16)	9.1	10.4	7.0	8.7
15. Relative price	3.5	0.6	4.4	2.5
16. Real growth	5.4	9.7	2.5	6.0
17. Real growth per capita (16/2)	1.9	6.4	0.2	3.2
18. Current elasticity (14/1)[b]	1.2	1.2	2.3	1.5
19. Real elasticity (16/1)[b]	0.7	1.1	0.8	1.0
20. Population age 65+	6.7	6.4	4.0	5.2

Sources: CBS, *Statistical Abstracts 1980* through *1983*, chapters on population, GNP, education and health; line 4: Bank of Israel, *Annual Report 1983*, table F/1, p. 114.

a. The total burden of a service is the rate of growth of expenditures in current prices deflated by the general price index. It includes changes in real spending and in the relative price of the services.

b. All elasticities are GNP elasticities with respect to spending on a given service. In "current" elasticity the numerators are changes in the total burdens of the service, that is, including changes in its relative prices. In real elasticity the numerators are changes in real spending on a service.

creased by some 90 percent, at annual rates of 7.7 and 6.5 percent respectively. In both cases expansion was much more rapid in the first half of the decade than in the second, reflecting the sharp decline in the growth of GNP. After 1978 there was a further decline in the expansion of these two services to rates not much above zero.

The second distinction relevant to the justification of expanding services is the one between expansion designed to maintain a given standard of service per capita at the level prevailing at the beginning of the period concerned, and real expansion of the service per capita. In times of strict budgetary limitations it is harder to justify the expansion of services per capita than it is to press for maintaining existing standards.

In 1968–1978 the population of Israel increased 31.5 percent. Hence the expansion of health and education services at this rate (and assuming zero productivity growth) would only have maintained existing standards of service per capita. In practice, real health services expanded at more than twice that rate, so that more than two-thirds of this growth went into raising the standard of service per capita, which improved by some 60 percent. Real educational services expanded by approximately 80 percent, and in these too the growth was reflected chiefly by a higher average standard of educational services per capita. It should be noted that most of the rise in expenditure per capita occurred before 1974, and was very fast. Since 1974 expenditure per capita on health services has risen at the still respectable annual rate of 2.5 percent, but expenditure per capita on education has risen only 0.8 percent per annum. After 1978 the standard of educational services per capita actually declined for the first time.

The measure of service per capita is, of course, a very crude one; it conceals changes in the structure of the population and in the relative weight of those sections within it with specific demand for the service: school-age children for education, and elderly people for health services. Thus it is necessary to go into a more detailed breakdown of the factors underlying the rise in the level of service per capita.

Education

The rise in expenditures on educational services per capita was not due to an increase in the size of the learning-age groups (3–17 and 21–25). These groups made up some 41 percent of the total population in 1968 and 40 percent of the total population in 1978 (compare lines 2 and 9 in Table 9-3). The rise in service per capita was achieved by an increase in the rates of school attendance and in the cost per student. In 1968–1980 overall attendance rose from 69.5 to 78.8 percent. The increase in the number of pupils averaged 3.6 percent annually, whereas the population grew only 2.7 percent annually.

A particularly dramatic increase occurred in the rate of kindergarten attendance, from 59 percent in 1968 to 92 percent in 1979. In the higher grades of secondary schools, attendance rose from 48 percent in 1968 to 64 percent in 1979. The increase was smaller in the 21–25 age group (postsecondary studies)—from 19 percent in 1968 to 25.5 percent in 1979. These three changes reflect an intensification of the educational system. In each of the age groups concerned, Israel is ahead of many—perhaps not all—developed countries, and all three rate increases must face critical review of their justification.

Cost per student over the third decade grew, on average, at a marginal rate of 1 percent annually. Most of this growth was concentrated in elementary education, where numerical expansion slowed down following a period of rapid growth, and in secondary education. In the two most rapidly growing subsystems—kindergartens and postsecondary education—there were, respectively, decline and stagnation in costs per student. This negative correlation between extensive and intensive expansion may reflect either inertia and rigid budgets or a policy that regards simultaneous expansion across broad fronts as unproductive (see Chapter 7).

Part of the rise in the average cost per student was due to a reform in the educational system that began in the late 1960s, whereby the top two grades of the eight-grade elementary school system were transferred to the secondary school system, creating an intermediate section in the latter. The primary motive of this reform was the desire to promote ethnic integration.

Finally, part of the growth in the average expenditure per pupil was due to the increase in the number of pupils in the secondary and postsecondary system, where the outlay per pupil is much higher than in the lower grades.

An analysis of the factors causing the rise in expenditure per pupil in the elementary school system indicates that the chief factor there was the higher cost per hour of instruction, with only a small part of the increase resulting from additional hours of instruction or from a reduction in the number of pupils per classroom. In the secondary education system, on the other hand, the increase in the number of hours of instruction played a decisive role in raising expenditure per pupil, while expenditure per hour of instruction decreased somewhat.[4]

Health

Of the two major medical services offered to the population—clinics or doctors' visits on the one hand and hospitalization on the other—Israel is relatively clinic intensive. An average Israeli visits a doctor about 10 times a year and spends approximately 2.3 days a year in hospital. The corresponding figures for the average OECD citizen are 4.25 visits and 2.9 days in hospital (see OECD, 1977).

The increase in hospitalization costs per capita is largely due to the rising expenditure per person hospitalized. This expenditure increased by 55 percent during the 1970s and accounted for over three-quarters of the rise in total hospital expenditure per capita (the remainder is due to a 15 percent increase in the total number of hospitalizations per capita). The increase in the cost of individual hospitalization occurred entirely in the first half of the third decade, whereas the increase in the number of hospitalizations occurred entirely in the second half.

The first phenomenon is characteristic of a period when the infrastructure of the hospital system—beds and medical staff—is being expanded; the second may reflect a response by the public and the medical system to the increase in supply. The rise in hospitalization costs might have been much greater had the length of the average hospitalization period not decreased—from 19 days in 1968 to 15.3 days in 1978 and to 14.4 days in 1980. The reduction in the average period of hospitalization was made possible by the stable level of hospital beds per capita (about 7 beds per 1,000 people) and of hospitalization days per capita (2.3 days).

Perhaps one-half of the increase in the number of persons hospitalized can be ascribed to the rise in the proportion of elderly people in the population, since the elderly use hospitals at least three times more than the average citizen (OECD, 1984b, based on statistics from Australia). In 1968–1980 the proportion of elderly in the population rose from 6.5 to 8.5 percent.

The rise in the cost of individual hospitalization (and of each day of hospitalization) in the first half of the period was caused by the sharp increase in the input of doctors, nurses, and equipment per hospitalization day and—to a lesser extent—by a slight decrease in the average utilization of hospital capacity. In hospitals belonging to the General Sick Fund, the proportion of doctors per 1,000 hospitalization days rose from 0.38 to 0.83, and that of nurses increased from 1.41 to 2.56.

There was a parallel rise in other material costs of hospitalization. The nature of hospitalization (or of the hospitalization day) became much more medically intensive than in preceding decades. This increased intensity partly reflects the shortened duration of hospitalization: patients now receive fuller treatment in fewer days in hospital, with the result that the cost of hospitalization per day is higher.

Some of the phenomena mentioned above—the intensive use of clinics, the low number of hospital beds, and the high input of doctors per hospital day—may be related to the fact that Israel has one of the highest ratios in the world of doctors to population. There are more than 25 physicians per 10,000 people, compared with 15–18 in most other developed countries (only in Eastern Europe and in the USSR are the figures typically above 20). Similarly, the ratio of doctors to other medical workers and to hospital beds is higher than in most countries. The chief source of the large supply of doctors is immigration, but professional preference may also play a role (pay rates are lower than in other countries). The production of medical services in Israel may account for the relative abundance of doctors and substitute doctors for beds (by making greater use of clinics and doctors in hospitals). It is not easy to determine the effect of such a substitution on the quality of medical services, but it may explain the different pattern of development.

Despite the above-mentioned disparities, the overall development of medical services in Israel in the 1970s was fairly similar to that in other developed countries.

There is no way to determine whether the rise in the volume of education and health services over the period was "necessary," but one can gauge this necessity through methods of program evaluation, and of normal or reasonable economic behavior, with the help of international comparisons.

The survey above demonstrated that the increase in health and education services was mainly the result of a rise in the level of service per capita, not only for the population at large but also for service-specific groups of clients. One may wonder if, under conditions of both overall resource and government budget constraints, such expansion was warranted. There seems to be agreement in Israel that raising the quality of elementary education was a top national priority in the 1970s following a rapid expansion during the 1950s and 1960s. The rapid expansion of kindergarten education was advocated on educational grounds but was also essential in a period when mothers' participation in the labor force rose sharply (see Chapter 5). The large expansion of secondary and postsecondary education is defended on grounds of social integration and, of course, human-capital considerations. The educational reform, mentioned above, is the only major program that is considered neither fully justified nor successful. In the sphere of health services, the expansion of hospitalization costs is under constant criticism, as it is everywhere, and there is a general feeling that the clinic system is cumbersome and inefficient.

To determine the merit of any of the major elements responsible for the expansion of services, a much more detailed investigation is required. The second test of (necessarily crude) international comparisons is carried out here with the averages of OECD countries. The comparisons are made in two spheres: the levels of activity in public services at various points in time, and the rates of change and their explanations. Around 1980 or 1981 the OECD share of public expenditure on education was 5.7 percent of GDP and the share on health was 5.6 percent of GDP. The corresponding figures for Israel in 1980–1981 were 7.8 and 5.9 percent respectively. Israel's national expenditure on education and health is lower in this comparison since in Israel public involvement in these services is somewhat higher than in the OECD. Higher spending on education in Israel is explained by a higher proportion of school-age children in the population, by somewhat higher attendance rates of school-age children—especially in kindergartens and in postsecondary institutions—and by higher levels of service per student in terms of GNP units. The surplus is even larger if levels of GNP per capita are standardized and if one accepts the general assumption that the share of public services in GNP is positively correlated with GNP per capita. The similarity between Israel and OECD in shares of health services results, on the one hand, from somewhat lower coverage and copayment and less clinic activity per patient in OECD and, on the other hand, from the lower level of hospitalization in Israel. Still, the level in Israel would be somewhat higher if one were to adjust for the lower level of GNP per capita and the lower proportion of elderly people in the population. (In Israel the proportion is 8.4 percent, compared with 12.5 percent in OECD.)

The comparative levels of 1980 were achieved by a faster growth of public services (that is, as shares in GNP and per capita) in OECD than in Israel over the period. Overall growth—total burden and total real growth—were almost uniformly faster in Israel, which experienced much higher rates of growth of both GNP and population (and also of GNP per capita). OECD, on the other hand, experienced higher expenditure and real GNP elasticities of public services. Whereas current price expenditure elasticities in OECD were typically around 2 and real elasticities well above unity, corresponding elasticities in Israel were just above 1 and below 1 respectively (for Israel, see Table 9-3).[5] The conclusions are, first, that the dynamic burden of growth of public services in OECD was heavier than in Israel, and, second, that the shares of public services in GNP back in 1960 were much higher in Israel than in OECD: the combined share of education and health services in Israel in 1960 was 11.5 percent compared with about 8 percent in OECD. In a way, the pressure of raising the share of public services in Israel was lighter in the last two decades than it was overall in OECD. This difference may be either a result of the much stricter budget constraint imposed on Israel, or a manifestation of the fact that some of the expansion in OECD since the early 1960s occurred even earlier in Israel. One additional restraining factor in Israel was a somewhat better control over the expansion of hospital care—a main source of increase in the cost of health care in the West over the past two decades.

In conclusion, the verdict on the expansion of education and health services in Israel remains rather inconclusive; Israel has lower income elasticities in the international comparisons, but higher initial levels and concentration on raising service levels.

Financing Public Services and Some Policy Implications

As noted at the beginning of this chapter, the expansion of public services was accompanied by a more-than-commensurate increase in the share of their financing from public funds (especially from the government budget and the taxpayer at large). This section offers a more detailed consideration of that trend in the financing of education and health services (most other services are fully financed by the government, by definition). Table 9-4 summarizes the data.

In 1968 the government (together with the Jewish Agency and the local authorities) financed three-quarters of the country's education services—half directly, and one-quarter through transfer payments to nonprofit and other educational institutions. By 1978 the government's share in financing education had risen to 84.5 percent—an increase of 10 percent. Most of the increase in the government's share occurred during the first half of the period, but the trend continued through-

TABLE 9-4. Financing of public services, 1968–1981 (percentages)

	1968/69	1974/75	1978/79	1980/81
Education				
Government and local authorities	74.7	82.4	84.5	84.0
Jewish agency	20.2	10.7	7.6	—
Nonprofit institutions	15.8	14.6	14.8	16.0[a]
Foreign sources	7.5	5.9	7.0	—
Private and other	9.5	5.0	1.7	—[a]
Total financed by foreign sources[b]	27.7	16.6	14.6	—
Health				
Government	52.8	59.2	58.5	62.0
Jewish agency	21.7	0.9	0.8	—
Parallel tax[c]	16.5	15.7	16.2	—
Nonprofit institutions	38.4	33.8	33.5	38.0[a]
Own resources	34.6	29.5	30.6	—
Foreign resources	3.8	4.3	2.9	—
Total foreign sources	(25.5)	(5.2)	(3.7)	—
Direct private financing	8.8	7.0	8.0	—[a]

Sources: CBS, *National Expenditure on Education* and *National Expenditure on Health*, National Accounts Statistics Series, 1968–1980

a. Includes direct private financing.

b. Sum of Jewish Agency and foreign sources.

c. Medical insurance premiums paid by employers on behalf of their employees. The "tax" is collected by the National Insurance Institute and transferred to the sick funds that provide medical services.

out the period. What made the situation even graver was that in 1968 the Jewish Agency financed some 20 percent of the total national expenditure on education from foreign aid funds, whereas in 1978 its share contracted to only 7.6 percent and has decreased further since. The result is an additional burden on the Israeli taxpayer, equal to some 22 percent of the national expenditure on education. Throughout this period, nonprofit institutions financed about 15 percent of the cost of education (compared with about one-quarter in the early 1960s), approximately half the funds at their disposal being unilateral transfers from abroad. Direct private financing of educational expenditures contracted from 9.5 percent of the total to only 1.7 percent during the third decade. The decisive factor in this reduction was the institution of free, compulsory secondary education in the late 1970s.

The general picture in health services is similar: the government's share rose from approximately 53 percent in 1968 to 62 percent in 1980. Along with this development, there was an even sharper decrease in the Jewish Agency's participation, from 20 percent of the total national expenditure on health in 1968 to nearly zero in 1980. Here, too, the increase in the burden of government financing from internal sources over the decade is about 30 percent, and again it must be stressed that this represents a growing proportion of a rapidly increasing volume of expenditure. Moreover, the contribution of nonprofit institutions to health services decreased from approximately 40 percent to less than 33 percent, while the volume of direct private financing dropped from 10 percent to less than 8 percent.

The trend in both health and education reveals two almost identical processes: a transition from foreign financing to financing from internal resources, and a switch from direct private financing and independent fund-raising by nonprofit institutions to the imposition of a greater burden on the central fiscal system. Altogether, during this decade the fiscal framework had to absorb 30 percent of the growing outlays on health and over 20 percent of the growing outlays on education. Annual rates of growth of government financing of these costs were therefore much higher than those of the expansion of the services themselves.

The high proportion of foreign aid until the mid-1960s may also explain the readiness and ability to expand health and education services. For as long as such an expansion can be implemented without direct levies on citizens or even by taxes, its political price is low. Indeed, it is quite possible that part of this expansion would not have been regarded either as essential or as effective if it had had to be paid for from internal sources. The contraction of aid from abroad created the need to continue previously expanded service systems under less favorable conditions of financing and economic growth. The availability of foreign resources provided an incentive to initiate new projects and obtain government approval for their implementation. For example, the availability of donors ready to finance new hospitals (in Jerusalem) and universities (in all parts of the country), as well as a long list of nonprofit institutions serving various purposes, was conducive to the creation of these institutions (or the construction of their buildings). Sooner or later, however, most of these institutions appeal to the government for the major part of their budgets. Such donations, which often cover only part of the construction budget, create long-term obligations that the government would not have approved (or would have postponed) had the original partial donation not existed.

Like the increasing share of public services in GNP, the rising proportion of financing through third parties or through the central fiscal system is a common phenomenon in Israel and most other countries, and has similar implications and problems. But Israel is a special case because of past foreign aid and the very heavy burden on the central fiscal system.

Under these circumstances the question that naturally arises is how to deal with the level and growth needs of public services under both universal and particular conditions facing the Israeli economy. The options are restraint on the existing volume and further growth of these services and the transfer (back) of some of the burden of financing these services to the private sector or at least to outside the central tax system. Such means, together with possible organizational reforms, may raise the level of efficiency in the provision of services and pare down the supply of services to the most (or more) vital ones.

Education services were found by international comparison to be excessive in Israel. But before a cut is recommended one has to take account of Israel's special needs for a larger educational system. The main special need stems from the facts that more than 50 percent of the current adult population was born abroad and very few spoke any Hebrew before coming to Israel, and that a majority of immigrants arrived with low levels of education. Educational attainment correlates with social and ethnic divisions, and the burden of social integration also falls largely on the educational system. Finally, as a country poor in natural resources, Israel should invest relatively more in human capital than richer countries. Some of this extra demand is certainly being offset by the massive "brain gain" as a result of immigration to Israel from many developed countries. The extent of this offset is difficult to calculate, but the brain gain clearly also increased the demand for education by setting high educational norms for the second generation of immigrant professionals; it may also have generated higher demand for jobs in educational institutions. All in all, there may be objective justification for a somewhat higher level of education services in Israel. The main doubt concerns the extent of university education, where most of the brain gain is concentrated.

The strategies adopted to alleviate the pressure to increase expenditures on education will have to include restraint in the expansion of costs per student and a rise in the self-sufficiency of education (especially higher education and auxiliary educational services). Higher education more than other levels of education is considered by students as an investment, and the public financing of its costs has a regressive effect on income distribution. A system of targeting and selective assistance to low-income candidates should be instituted.

In the sphere of medical services Israel has a smaller comparative excess, if any, and by now, as distinct from the period of mass immigration, its medical needs could be considered normal. As in many other countries, the expansion of hospitalization and its costs have been the main causes of the rise in medical costs in Israel. The main forces behind these worldwide trends are considered to be: the rapid technological advances in medicine; the rise in third-party financing of individuals' medical expenses—through insurance and government support; and doctors' complete control over the nature of treatment combined with payment per services rendered; the latter adds a material incentive to doctors' natural curiosity and interest to provide perfect service rather than an optimal or reasonable one.[6] A number of solutions for some of these problems are advocated all over the world:

1. A shift from collecting a fee per service rendered to charging a fee for undertaking complete responsibility for the client's health over a specified period of time, or for life. This change would encourage suppliers to optimize rather than maximize the amount of service.
2. Overall budget constraints on medical costs of public organizations combined with joint decisionmaking over medical treatment by doctors and medical administrators.
3. Some contribution by patients toward the specific costs of medical treatment.
4. A check on the use of full hospitalization—the "hotel" element—and a shift to outpatient clinical treatment in hospitals.

One organization that combines many of these elements is the health maintenance organization (HMO), which charges a fixed fee for overall medical responsibility and also assumes financial responsibility (thus incorporating elements 2 and 4 above) and implement other means of savings. Under such a system the quality of medical services must be assured by some degree of competition between HMOs and a good deal of public comparative information on their performance.

Israel instituted some of the above-mentioned optimizing elements years ago. The system of sick funds was established in the 1920s, and they function essentially like an HMO. In addition, as noted earlier, hospital expansion was checked by budget difficulties and by the availability of a large supply of doctors as substitutes. The system is thus basically sound and, provided its flaws are remedied, can provide the infrastructure for good cost-conscious medical care. The two major flaws in the system are, first, the lack of competition (the major sick funds treat more than 80 percent of all insured) and of a real free choice of sick fund on the basis of the quality of medical services. Some competition, however, does exist among smaller sick funds and in the relatively small private medical sector. The second flaw is the failure of sick-fund fees to cover all of the medical treatment; the effect is to erode both the financial responsibility of the organization and the direct interest of the members in the efficiency of their fund. Finally, there are structural, organizational, and accounting problems impeding better coordination between the system of clinics and hospitals and a better use of existing hospitals by members of different funds or programs. The advocated solutions are to reduce most government support for the sick funds and in any case to make the support a fixed sum rather than a deficit-covering type. The difference should be borne by members partly as increased dues and partly by some degree of self-participation in the cost of services provided. Support for medical expenses should be on a selective principle, for the needy, rather than universal. A larger degree of competition between funds and inside each fund should be encouraged and a scheme for more economical use of hospitals worked out. These are relatively small changes compared with those needed in other countries, and they can assure better medical care at somewhat lower costs, especially to the central fiscal system.

It is generally agreed in Israel that the public sector is too big and that the tax system cannot cope with the demands made on it. There is a feeling that some aspects of the activities of the public sector are superfluous and that others are provided at unacceptably low levels of efficiency. On the other hand, it must be generally accepted that the social value and the value for the individual of most medical and educational services provided by the public sector is higher than the value of many goods and services consumed as private consumption. The apparent distorted preferences, which may be more strongly pronounced in Israel under its resource and government budget constraints, are explained by the fact that these services are provided free of charge or at far less than cost and are (or were) paid for by a distant third party or even by a general tax. Thus the appropriate move would be not to cut those public services but to reduce the gap between payment and service by presenting households with a set of relative prices somewhat closer to real relative costs. If successful, this strategy will force families to make choices in favor of public services and away from private consumption, it will increase the budgetary responsibility both of managers of programs and of their clients, and it will do all this with a lower general tax burden. Such steps will also streamline inefficiencies and unwanted services. Finally, the principle of universality of providing services to all and collecting the costs through a progressive tax system cannot work in Israel for the time being, both because of the reasons specified above and because of the weakness of the tax-collecting apparatus. Israel, like many other countries that expanded their public services beyond their ability to finance them with a reasonable tax burden, must return to the selective principle of providing aid only to the needy.

10

The Development of the Transfer System and the Redistribution of Income

Yehuda Geva and Jack Habib

The Israeli transfer system faced a number of major challenges in the early 1970s. For one, the population of Israel had begun to age significantly: the population over age 65 rose from 5 percent in 1960 to 6.8 percent in 1970 and was expected to age further. Most of the elderly were totally dependent on the income-maintenance system, since they had immigrated late in life and had had no opportunity to accrue savings and work-related pensions toward their retirement. A second challenge was the transfer system's influence on income gaps among the major ethnic groups in the Israeli population. The combination of lower levels of education, Asian or African origin, and greater family size created gaps in economic status between ethnic groups. The system of income redistribution could serve as an instrument to narrow these gaps.

Israel has a highly skewed family-size distribution. In 1970, 14 percent of all families had four or more children. This posed a special challenge for the income-maintenance system, since many low wage earners with large families found it difficult to achieve minimally accepted income levels even when fully employed. Provision for children within the income-maintenance system could thus play a particularly important role in shaping the system's redistributive impact.

These concerns gained prominence in the early 1970s when a number of reports indicated that overall inequality had grown in the 1950s and had stabilized at a new plateau in the 1960s. The findings no longer qualified Israel for a place among countries with a uniquely low level of inequality, and there did not seem to be any automatic inequality-reducing forces at work apart from outright government intervention. The same was found to be true of the ethnic disparities (see Committee, 1971; Habib, 1979; and Achdut and Carmi, 1981). The early 1970s also saw the first attempts at measuring the extent of poverty. Although the proposed "poverty standard" raised considerable controversy, it became a common means of measuring the adequacy of the income-maintenance system.

The poverty rate was particularly high among the elderly and among large families. Moreover, in almost half of all poor families the head of household was of working age and participated in the labor force. This fact focused attention on the working poor—a previously unrecognized group both in Israel and elsewhere. In 1969 the transfer system reduced the number of families below the poverty line by only one-third, and was particularly ineffective in alleviating the conditions of the working poor. Concern was also expressed at the fact that 46 percent of all poor persons were under 18 years of age.

Several essential features shaped the impact of the transfer system at the beginning of the 1970s. In the 1960s old-age pensions provided a flat-rate benefit unrelated to preretirement wages (these benefits accounted for 44 percent of all public transfers). This benefit was not sufficient to provide an income above the poverty line after retirement. A supplementary income-tested benefit was therefore instituted within the social security system, whereas the provision of wage-related pensions was left to collective bargaining arrangements.

Provision for working-age families was the responsibility of the welfare system, whose benefits tended to be low and, moreover, bore a distinct social stigma. A 100 percent penalty was imposed on any earned income, severely reducing the incentive to work. Therefore, the actual number of recipients was quite low and the sums involved were only a small part of total transfers.

A second instrument for providing income support to the working poor was child allowances. In the early 1970s the sums per recipient were small and coverage was incomplete. However, because allowances were provided to all income groups and there was a large number of children in Israel, child allowances represented a significant share (27 percent) of total transfers. An even more important form of benefits for children was an income-tax exemption granted for each child. Furthermore, unlike child allowances, the value of these exemptions rose as family income increased.

Programs for the disabled were organized by disability categories and represented 17.2 percent of all transfers in 1970. Persons disabled at work or while serving in the army benefited from generous programs; on the other hand, no special programs were available for persons whose disability stemmed from other causes, and welfare was their major source of support. Another group for whom coverage was limited was the unemployed: there was no program of unemployment insurance.

Against this background, several critical questions emerged as Israel moved into the 1970s. What should the response be to the increasing proportion of elderly persons in the population? Should support for the working poor and for large families be expanded? How could these aims be best achieved: through reform in the welfare system or through an increase in child allowances? Should programs be developed to extend coverage within the social security system to groups for whom programs were as yet unavailable?

The 1970s was a period of significant structural change and quantitative increase in the transfer system. Support levels and coverage for the elderly were significantly expanded. Greater emphasis was placed on expanding the adequacy of income-tested benefits to the elderly poor. Benefits for the working poor were also raised considerably. The policy was to emphasize a more universal strategy of support for the working poor by substantially increasing child allowances, which became part of a broader shift in the structure of direct taxation, accompanied in 1975 by the elimination of tax exemptions for children. Along with the elimination of personal exemptions, the progressiveness of marginal tax rates was reduced and the tax base was expanded to include a large number of previously tax-exempt forms of income. These changes represented a fundamental shift, both in the strategy adopted to achieve horizontal and vertical equity within the tax structure, and in the division of labor between the tax and the transfer systems in providing child-related benefits (Ben-Porath and Bruno, 1977).

The welfare system was also overhauled to provide a better safety net for persons with weaker labor-force attachment. New programs of disability insurance and unemployment insurance were introduced, and benefits in all existing disability programs were expanded. All this meant a significant increase in transfers, which grew in real terms at an annual rate of 13 percent; the share of transfers in GNP rose from 3.3 percent in 1970 to 6.6 percent in 1980. The growth in transfers as a percentage of the civilian budget was somewhat more moderate (from 12.4 to 17.4 percent); transfers rose from 24.9 to 31.9 percent of total social welfare expenditures (that is, income-maintenance, health, education, and personal social services).

As a result of the elimination of exemptions, the level of child benefits changed little over time. The elimination of exemptions increased the average tax burden, and there were further increases in average tax rates in the second half of the 1970s.

The total tax burden rose from 30 to 50 percent of GNP in the 1970s. Taxes on wages rose even more steeply due to an increase in both income taxes and National Insurance (NI) contributions. The share of the latter in total taxes rose from 13.9 percent in 1970 to 15.5 percent in 1978 (Yitzhaki, 1983).

Several questions arise concerning the nature and magnitude of the impact of these changes on income distribution. Did the taxes and transfers substantially increase inequality? Were there reinforcing or offsetting shifts in the distribution of pretransfer income? What were the implications of these developments for major demographic groups and ethnic gaps? Did demographic changes during the decade influence the redistributive impact of the growth in transfers? Of particular interest are the changes in family-size distribution and the weakening of the relationship between family size, income, and ethnic background. The rise in the share of the elderly also influenced the redistribution of transfers and their differential effect on ethnic groups.

In the following sections we discuss the methodology and data sources used to measure changes in income distribution, document the trends in pretax, pretransfer inequality, and analyze the impact of taxes and transfers, and the trend in the net income distribution. In evaluating the impact of taxes and transfers we distinguish between changes in their rate and in their efficiency in reducing inequality; efficiency is defined as the redistributive effect per unit of taxes or transfers. We speculate on some of the structural changes that affected the trend in efficiency. We then proceed to examine the implications of the developments over the decade for various subgroups, and conclude with a discussion of some of the decade's developments in a macroeconomic context.

Data Sources and Methodology

The following analysis of trends in income distribution is based primarily on the CBS *Family Expenditure Surveys* of 1968, 1975, and 1979. These surveys exclude the agricultural sector and the major part of the non-Jewish population because it resides predominantly in small towns and villages. Thus our analysis is based on the urban Jewish population only. We adjust family income for family size by employing a commonly used equivalence scale that assumes considerable economies of scale and measures needs in units of standardized adults.[1] The Gini Index was calculated on the basis of population deciles defined as 10 percent of all persons, and on the percentage (in each decile) of total income per standard adult summed over all persons. The underlying criterion of equality is that average income per standard adult (weighted by the number of persons in the family) be equal across deciles.

To assess the impact of taxes and transfers, we calculated the change in the measures of inequality between pre- and posttax and transfer incomes. In calculating taxes, we included only the employees' share in NI contributions so as to avoid assumptions regarding the incidence of employers' shares. This exclusion leads to an underestimate of the absolute increase in the tax burden and may also somewhat bias the trend in inequality, although the direction is not clear. Two factors are involved: less progressivity in NI contributions than in income taxes, so that an increase in the weight of NI contributions in relation to income taxes renders the average tax less progressive; and the extent of change in the structure of NI contributions.

Over the decade the overall rate of NI contributions rose, but so did that of income taxes; thus their relative volumes did not change appreciably. Similarly, the structure of NI contribution rates did not change appreciably from 1970 to 1980; the maximum income subject to social security contributions was about the same percentage of the average wage in both years. But this picture changes if 1968 is taken as the base year: in that year the maximum was at its lowest point, and a steep increase in 1970 caused a sizable increase in the progressive distribution of the system compared with the 1960s and a marked rise in total contributions. These two factors operate in opposite directions: the regressive effect of the rise in the relative role of NI contributions could offset the progressive effect of the increase in taxable-income ceilings.

The Trend in Pretax, Pretransfer Inequality

Information on the distribution of pretax, pretransfer income has been available since 1968. Only posttransfer (or net income) data are available for earlier periods. These data indicate a rapid increase in inequality in the 1950s, which must have resulted mainly from an increase in pretransfer inequality. If anything, the growth in transfers in that decade should have reduced inequality. In the 1960s there was little or no discernible trend (Committee, 1971). In the 1970s there was a decline in pretransfer inequality as measured by the Gini or Atkinson indexes (Table 10-1). However, the pattern over the decade is not uniform: the Gini Index de-

TABLE 10-1. Income inequality as measured by the Gini Index and Atkinson Inequality Index (AII), 1968, 1975, and 1979[a]

	Atkinson Index		Gini Index
	e = 2.0	*e* = 1.2	
Pretransfer income			
1968	0.887	0.423	0.395
1975	0.548	0.371	0.364
1979	0.560	0.382	0.376
Posttransfer income			
1968	0.554	0.260	0.358
1975	0.229	0.186	0.314
1979	0.260	0.214	0.337
Net income			
1968	0.379	0.195	0.314
1975	0.182	0.147	0.278
1979	0.192	0.157	0.280

Sources: CBS, *Family Expenditure Surveys*, 1968, 1975, 1979.

a. The Atkinson Index explicitly incorporates an assumption about the social welfare function in the form of *e*, the inequality aversion parameter. As *e* rises, inequality aversion increases. In the calculation of the Atkinson Index, zero incomes were assigned a value of 1 in 1969 and for all subsequent years a value proportional to the rise in average incomes. The average income per standard adult of each unit was weighted by the number of persons in the unit.

clined from 0.395 in 1968 to 0.376 in 1979; there was a steeper decline until 1975 (the Gini is 0.364) and a subsequent increase.

A second source of data on income distribution is the CBS series of annual income surveys. Although while the basis for obtaining the income data is not identical with that of the *Family Expenditure Surveys,* and the populations surveyed are different, the pattern of inequality over the 1970s in the survey reveals a similar decline and subsequent rise. This confirms that the pattern is not idiosyncratic to the particular years compared in Table 10-1. In the income survey, the rise at the end of the decade is such that inequality returns to the levels recorded at the beginning of the decade.

The sources of the trend in pretransfer inequality have not been studied in detail. Wage differentials appear to be one source, as they follow the pattern of overall inequality. For example, the ratio of weekly wages of workers with 16 or more years of schooling to workers with 5–8 years of schooling declined from 1.9 to 1.6 in 1968–1975 and then returned to 1.8 in 1979. Amir, in Chapter 6, attributes this pattern to a policy that succeeded in temporarily narrowing wage differentials in the public sector in the mid-1970s.

The Impact of Taxes and Transfers

The impact of taxes and transfers is implicit in the difference between pre- and posttransfer distributions presented in Table 10-1. Table 10-2 summarizes these differences.

Given the rise in the share of taxes and transfers in GNP, one would expect to find an increase in their redistributive impact. Inequality in net income declined over the decade (8 percent for the Gini Index and 20 percent for the Atkinson Index). This decline, however, is almost entirely due to a decline in pretax, pretransfer inequality. The impact of net taxes on the Atkinson Index even declines over the decade. The change in the influence of net taxes is due to opposing changes in the impacts of taxes as against transfers: the impact of transfers increased quite substantially in 1968–1975, but for 1968–1979 the increase was rather small. Taxes reveal the opposite pattern: their impact declined steeply in the first half of the decade, but over the decade as a whole there was a 9 percent rise in their impact on the Gini Index while the effect on the Atkinson Index was somewhat lower. These trends are in part the result of integrated changes in the tax-transfer structure and should be viewed as inherently related.

How did changes in the *level* of transfers and taxes as opposed to changes in their impact per unit of transfer or taxes affect their redistributive impact? Here, the per unit impact is the redistributional efficiency of taxes and transfers; the lower the efficiency, the greater the amount of redistribution required to achieve a given change in inequality.

TABLE 10-2. The rate, total impact, and per unit impact (efficiency) of taxes and transfers, 1968, 1975, and 1979

	1968	1975	1979
Transfers			
Percent of pretransfer income	5.2	8.3	6.8
Impact on Gini Index			
Total	0.037	0.050	0.039
Per unit	0.007	0.006	0.006
Impact on Atkinson Index			
Total	0.163	0.185	0.168
Per unit	0.031	0.022	0.024
Taxes			
Percent of pretransfer income	17.8	20.0	30.3
Impact on Gini Index			
Total	0.044	0.036	0.048
Per unit	0.0025	0.002	0.002
Impact on Atkinson Index			
Total	0.065	0.039	0.057
Per unit	0.004	0.002	0.002
Net transfers			
Total impact			
Gini Index	0.081	0.086	0.087
Atkinson Index	0.228	0.224	0.225

Source: CBS, *Family Expenditure Surveys,* 1968, 1975, 1979.

Table 10-2 presents the efficiency measures. To compare changes in efficiency over time, it is necessary to standardize the units of transfer or taxes across periods. We have done this by calculating the efficiency in each year in relation to the rate of transfers or taxes in pretransfer income. Thus we calculated efficiency by dividing the total impact of transfers or taxes—on a measure of inequality—by the rate, so as to obtain a measure of the consequences of transferring or taxing 1 percent of pretransfer income. It must be emphasized, however, that this measure reflects the average efficiency of total taxes or transfers, and not necessarily the *marginal* impact of a change in the rate of transfers or taxation.

The transfer rate rose rapidly in the first part of the 1970s, but over the entire decade the increase was only 31 percent. The efficiency of transfers declined by almost as much, so that the overall increase in the impact of transfers was quite small. The cumulative increase in the tax rate over the entire period was 70 percent; but the decline in the efficiency of taxes—36 percent for the Gini Index and 49 percent for the Atkinson Index ($e = 1.2$)—considerably reduced the impact of the increase. These findings indicate that changes in the average efficiency of taxes and transfers played a major role in moderating the impact of the rise in tax and transfer rates.

The efficiency of the transfer system depends on the differential progressiveness of its various programs and on the relative weights of the programs within total transfer payments.[2] The following paragraphs first consider the possible impact of changes in the composition of transfers and then the changes in the efficiency of specific programs.

Previous studies (Habib, 1979; Achdut and Carmi, 1981) have revealed distinct differences in the redistributive impact of various programs. In particular, old-age assistance has been shown to have a more progressive distribution by population income deciles than child allowances.

The following explanation of the pattern of transfer efficiency emerges for 1968–1979. In the first half of the decade, the rise in the weight of child allowances in total transfers and the decline in the correlation between income and family size served to reduce the efficiency of total transfers. Over the decade as a whole there was a decrease in the relative number of large families and in the strength of the relation between family size and income. For example, a regression of the number of children on income reveals that the estimated income coefficient decreased from −0.477 in 1968 to −0.413 in 1975 and to −0.282 in 1979. In addition, the multiple coefficient of correlation, though very low for all periods, declined over the decade (from 0.046 in 1968 to 0.04 in 1975 and to 0.02 in 1979). In the second half of the decade there was a reverse shift in transfer composition that appears to have counteracted the consequences of the declining correlation.

The efficiency of taxes declined primarily in the first half of the 1970s, apparently because of a more regressive rate pattern. This is in part an inevitable result of integrated tax-transfer changes; after the elimination of family-size exemptions in 1975, the tax system made no allowances for family size. Child allowances were included as part of the transfer system. This shift certainly increased the regressive distribution of tax rates. A second possible factor was the expansion of various forms of nontaxable income in 1968–1975, which tended to reduce effective tax rates, particularly at higher income levels. The tax reform of 1975 expanded the tax base to include such hitherto untaxed incomes, but there was a corresponding decrease in the progressiveness of marginal tax rates, designed to maïntain the prereform degree of tax progressiveness.

Inequality and Population Subgroups

Table 10-3 shows the pattern of change in overall inequality in terms of three components of the Atkinson Index: between-group inequality, within-group in-

TABLE 10-3. Within-group, between-group, and demographic change components of the Atkinson Index, 1968 and 1979

	Within group	Between group	Demographic change
1968–1979			
Pretransfer	161.0	–7.1	–54.3
Posttransfer	74.7	13.1	12.2
Net	75.1	11.9	13.0
1975–1979			
Pretransfer	238.9	–142.4	3.4
Posttransfer	63.8	60.1	–23.9
Net	58.3	104.2	–62.5
1968–1975			
Pretransfer	91.1	32.8	–24.0
Posttransfer	69.6	30.4	0.0
Net	71.2	29.7	0.9

Sources: CBS, *Family Expenditure Surveys*, 1968, 1979; Bruno and Habib (1976).

equality, and changes in the composition of families. Ten groups were defined by sex, age, marital status, and number of children.

Virtually the entire change in inequality resulted from within-group changes. This result reflects several underlying factors. One is that changes in demographic composition were relatively small and largely offsetting. The most important changes were a rise in the percentage of units headed by elderly persons (high within-group inequality) and a decline in the number of families with six or more children (low within-group inequality).

The absence of more significant between-group changes has its roots in the fact that the growth of transfers was very widespread, embracing all population groups. As noted, over the decade as a whole there was little change in the relative share of old-age support and child allowances in total transfers. The one group that registered significant gains was units headed by elderly men; their relative net income increased almost 20 percent, both through an improvement in their pretransfer position (notably through an increase in work-related pension entitlements) and through larger redistributive gains. In contrast, the most disadvantaged group was units headed by elderly women; they made almost no gains in relative income, and although they benefited considerably from redistribution, their pretransfer position deteriorated and largely offset these gains. The size of this group, as a percentage of all families and of all elderly units, grew considerably.

Of particular interest in the Israeli context is the fact that there was only a moderate narrowing of income gaps by family size. Three factors help to explain this pattern. One is that the expansion of child allowances, while increasing the relative benefit levels of large families, extended coverage to small families that had not been previously eligible. Second, the overall increase in total benefits to children was much more moderate than the increase in child allowances, owing to the simultaneous elimination of tax exemptions for children. A third factor is the decline in the value of child allowances in the latter part of the decade. Child-related benefits (exemptions and allowances) for a family with average earnings were 8.9 percent of the average wage for a family with two children in 1968, 8.8 percent in 1975, and only 5.6 percent in 1980. Larger families gained in 1968–1975, with the benefits for a family with four children rising from 18.7 to 27.4 percent; but by 1980 their value had dropped to 17.7 percent. Because of the shift from allowances to exemptions, the decline in the value of child-related benefits was even greater at above-average income levels, while low-income groups experienced a net increase (Achdut and Carmi, 1981; Yitzhaki, 1983).

Continent of Origin

The goal of reducing social and economic differences among various cultural and continent-of-origin groups has been a consistent part of Israeli social policy. These groups are not explicit targets of transfer programs, but because of the correlation among origin, income, and demographic traits they are differentially affected by changes in the degree of overall redistribution or in the distribution of transfers among demographic groups. Attempts to support large families are, in particular, viewed as directed at ethnic disparities.

The relative position of persons born in Asia or Africa (AAs) improved somewhat over the decade. Their net income rose from 72 to 77 percent of the average. The pattern of this rise does not, however, conform to the earlier reported pattern of overall inequality: there was only a modest rise in the relative income of the AA group in 1968–1975 (from 72 to 74 percent), followed by a larger rise in 1975–1979 (from 74 to 77 percent), despite the increase in overall inequality in the latter period.

The explanation is to be found in the pattern of relative income by family income (unadjusted for family-size differences) and in the pattern of change in average family size by continent of origin. Whereas the family-income gap remained constant at around 0.92, the family-size gap narrowed in 1975–1979. Average family size in 1968 was 4.65 for the AA group and 2.86 for those of Europe-America (EA) origin; in 1979 the corresponding figures were 4.30 and

2.74. The trend toward smaller family size accounts for the rise in the relative income per standard adult among AA families. The lack of improvement in family income even in 1968–1975 is apparently related to the fact that although AA families are overrepresented among large families, who gained during this period, they are underrepresented among the elderly, who also improved their income position considerably. Benefits in this program are quite progressively distributed. Finally, the decrease in the family-size gap between ethnic groups reduced the efficiency of child allowances as an instrument for narrowing ethnic disparities.

The Macroeconomic Context

In the early 1970s the growth in transfers in relation to GNP paralleled the growth in their redistributive impact. Until 1973 the Israeli economy was growing fairly rapidly and the rate of inflation was relatively low. Beginning with the Yom Kippur War and the oil crisis, the economic situations changed radically: inflation accelerated rapidly and there was little growth in GNP. Yet transfers continued to grow rapidly until 1977, and no serious attempt was made to adjust them to prevailing economic conditions until late in the decade. After 1977, transfers declined sharply in relation to wages, as did their redistributive impact; yet their share in GNP fell only slightly, remaining well above the levels recorded at the beginning of the decade.

There are two possible explanations for this disparity. One is that the per-unit impact of transfers (efficiency) was lower at the end of the decade than in the early 1970s. The other is that despite the stagnation of GNP, real wages rose very rapidly. As a result, transfers dropped much more in relation to wages than in relation to GNP.[3]

Total expenditures on transfers in relation to GNP remained below the average in OECD countries (6.7 compared with 12.2 percent); the gap at the beginning of the decade was even larger (3.2 compared with 8.7 percent). The major reason for this difference was the smaller share of old-age support in GNP in Israel than in OECD countries, primarily because the percentage of population over retirement age in Israel is considerably smaller than the European average (in 1974 it was 74 percent of the OECD average). Moreover, benefit levels are also lower because wage-related pensions are not part of Israel's social security system and are, in any case, not widely prevalent among the retired population. The share of disability benefits in GNP is also considerably lower in Israel, while the share of child allowances in GNP is higher than the European average. In 1974 the average pension benefit as a percent of GNP in Israel was 80 percent of the OECD average.

The major cause of the decline in benefit rates in the late 1970s was the accelerating rate of inflation. Although benefits were adjusted twice a year, these adjustments did not suffice to prevent a decline in the value of transfers under accelerating inflation. Basic old-age benefits, for example, declined from 15.9 percent of the average wage in 1975 to 11.6 percent in 1979.[4]

These indexing arrangements served as automatic stabilizers, reducing or increasing the rate of transfers in an inverse relation to the rate of inflation. They also provided policymakers with a relatively convenient way of allowing transfer rates to decline without resorting to policy initiatives or new legislation.

The value of child allowances declined even more steeply in relation to average wages in the same period. Real wages increased rapidly, and although allowances were automatically linked to prices, they were not linked to wages. In 1975–1979 the value of child allowances for a family's first child dropped from 4.4 to 2.8 percent of the average wage, and for a family with four children from 27.4 to 17.7 percent.

The policy with respect to child allowances must be seen in a relation to the adjustment of the parameters of the tax structure during this period. The level of child allowances was linked to the level of tax-credit points granted each taxpayer and spouse. These credits, together with the lowest tax bracket, set the minimum taxable income. During the 1970s neither credit points nor tax brackets were adjusted to increases in real wages. The taxable-income threshold declined from 57 percent of the average wage in 1975 to 38 percent in 1979; the boundary of the lowest tax bracket went down from 125 percent of the average wage to about 80 percent in the same period. This trend accounted for the entire increase in average tax rates (Yitzhaki, 1983). As a result, net wages increased far more slowly than gross wages.

Several possible interpretations can be offered for the decline in the real value of transfers by the end of the 1970s. One is that the decline reflects a deliberate policy aimed at reducing the level of transfer benefits and the total cost of transfers, in part as a response to the slowdown in GNP growth and to the economy's inability to control the growth of real wages. Thus it was easier to let inflation erode the value of transfers and to increase average tax rates than to control wage increases. The other interpretation is that the failure to maintain the relative value of benefits was more a reflection of the delayed response of the linked-adjustment arrangements to the accelerating rate of inflation, and was largely unintended.

It is impossible to choose between these two explanations with any degree of certainty. The early 1980s saw public attention increasingly drawn to the consequences of a decline in real transfers and an increase in tax rates for the redistribution of income, especially with reference to the welfare of the poorest groups in the population. The political climate also changed, and as a result, benefit rates were restored to the levels of the mid-1970s. The major exception is child allowances, whose value continued to decline as part of a persistent policy (since the 1975 tax reform) designed to avoid adjusting the tax system according to changes in real wages.

11

Taxes and Transfers in an Inflationary Decade

Eitan Berglas

Israel's tax system underwent far-reaching changes during the 1970s as a result of increases in government expenditures, incomes, social tensions, economic involvement in international trade, and, more than anything else, inflation. Two committees appointed to reform the tax system in this decade introduced substantive changes by combining the tax and the transfer-payment systems, but failed to neutralize the effects of inflation on the tax structure. As of 1985 the policymakers in charge of the tax system were still seeking a solution to the problem of taxation in an inflationary environment.

Because the tax system is merged with transfer payments, I refer to taxes and transfers as components of an integrated system, distinguishing between gross taxation and net taxation (that is, gross taxation minus transfer payments), the latter being the sum available to the government for financing public services.

The Public-Sector Budget

An intelligent discussion of taxation proper requires an understanding of the framework within which all government activities are carried out. Table 11-1 summarizes the development of the public-sector budget since 1961.[1] All the data appear as percentages of GNP rather than as absolute figures because galloping inflation renders the presentation of such data in nominal (or even real) terms meaningless. Furthermore, because GNP shares represent the burden of financing borne by the public, they can indicate the extent of government intervention. GNP shares must, of course, be analyzed with the growth rate of product in mind. The last line of the table therefore gives the annual rate of growth of gross national product. This line clearly shows the continuous steep decline in the annual growth of GNP, from 10.1 percent (in real terms) in the early 1960s to 1.6 percent in the early 1980s.

TABLE 11-1. The public-sector budget as a percentage of GNP, 1961–1983 (annual averages)

	1961–1965	1966–1970	1971–1975	1976–1980	1981–1983
Expenditures					
Domestic public consumption	15.9	21.6	25.0	25.7	27.3
Domestic public investment	4.6	4.3	4.8	4.0	3.4
Public consumption of imports	5.2	9.2	13.1	11.9	8.4
Interest in foreign currency	0.9	0.7	0.9	1.8	2.7
Total	26.6	35.8	43.8	43.4	41.8
Income					
Net taxes	23.6	22.2	21.3	17.8	17.2
Growth of money base	1.9	1.6	3.0	2.4	2.1
Increase in net internal debt	−3.6	0.6	5.4	4.4	7.0
Increase in external debt	0.8	7.5	5.1	7.0	6.7
Foreign grants	3.8	3.8	9.1	11.9	8.9
Growth of GNP (annual rates, percent)	10.1	7.7	7.2	3.0	1.6

Source: Meridor (1985).

Rising GNP shares such as are shown in Table 11-1 indicate that government expenditures grew far more rapidly than product. The sizable jump in the second half of the 1960s can be ascribed entirely to the increase in defense outlays, which also contributed significantly to the further increase in the 1970s and to the decline in the beginning of the 1980s (see Chapter 8).

Taxation did not suffice to finance the increase in government spending. Gross taxes did indeed increase, but net taxes declined continuously during the period. The government therefore had to resort to alternative sources of finance. Foreign grants increased until 1980 but lagged behind the increase in government spending, and even more so behind the ever-widening gap between the latter and government tax revenues. The increase in the money base (printing money) covered only a small part of the deficit; the major source was borrowing from the public and from abroad, which increased in volume throughout the period.

Table 11-1 shows another significant change in the composition of government finance: until the mid-1970s there were no sizable gaps between the public sector's income and expenditures in foreign currency; from the mid-1970s on, however, foreign sources were resorted to more and more frequently to finance domestic spending. In other words, the government borrowed abroad and sold foreign currency to Israeli residents in order to finance its local expenditures.

A comparison between the extent of financing by new loans and the growth rate of product is illuminating. Whereas in the early 1960s the government repaid net debts, in the second half of the 1960s it took on new loans (net of repayment) that amounted to 8 percent of product each year while product itself grew at the same rate. In the 1970s government reliance on new loans as a percent of GNP exceeded the annual GNP growth rate. This growing gap resulted both from a sizable decrease in net taxation and from the slowdown in economic growth. In the beginning of the 1980s the government increased its debt by almost 14 percent of product each year, while product itself grew by less than 2 percent annually.

Two extremely difficult problems result: a heavy debt-servicing burden and finding sources of credit. The growth of the debt relative to product means that the GNP share of interest payments is growing. Only part of the increase in interest rates on foreign credit is reflected in Table 11-1 (interest payments in Israeli currency are included in net taxation in Table 11-1; see also Table 11-2.)[2] Interest payments on local and foreign-currency debts already constitute a heavy burden on the budget and are expected to remain at approximately 10 percent of GNP throughout the 1980s even if the debt proper does not increase substantially.[3]

Taxes and Transfer Payments

Table 11-2 summarizes the annual development of taxation and Table 11-3 the pattern of transfer payments for 1960–1982.[4] Taxes as a percentage of product grew from 32.5 in 1960 to 36.8 in 1970 and to 45.0 in 1980. Because product grew by 65 percent in constant prices between 1970 and 1980, total taxes collected in that period more than doubled in real terms.

The 1970s can be divided into two halves: until 1975 and from that year on. The difference betwen them is the combined result of the income tax reform of 1975 and the introduction of a value-added tax in 1976.

Table 11-4 highlights the steep increase in total tax collection. In the second half of the 1970s the tax system collected approximately 47 percent of product, compared with 35 percent in the 1960s and 41 percent in the first half of the 1970s. This rise occurred mainly in direct taxes and taxation of domestically produced goods, while taxes on imports declined.[5]

The gross taxation rate has a direct bearing on the distortions caused by the tax system. Every tax system, besides levying taxes and incurring direct expenditures

TABLE 11-2. Taxes as a percentage of GNP, 1960–1982

Year	Direct taxes: Total	Direct taxes: Wage-earners	Direct taxes: NI	Taxes on domestic production: Total	Taxes on domestic production: VAT	Import taxes: Total	Import taxes: VAT	Compulsory loans	Total taxes	Net taxes
1960	11.5	—	2.9	13.6	—	7.4	—	0.1	32.5	20.3
1965	16.2	—	2.9	12.5	—	6.2	—	1.5	34.9	23.4
1970	19.7	5.3	4.7	10.6	—	6.4	—	2.9	36.8	21.2
1971	21.9	5.3	5.4	10.5	—	8.7	—	4.5	41.1	23.9
1972	20.0	4.8	5.0	10.0	—	8.6	—	4.0	38.6	21.4
1973	20.7	5.3	5.2	9.5	—	9.0	—	3.8	39.3	20.1
1974	21.5	5.0	5.3	9.8	—	11.3	—	5.0	42.6	20.6
1975	21.9	5.0	5.3	11.3	—	9.0	—	3.4	42.3	19.3
1976	25.0	6.3	6.2	13.6	1.5	10.5	1.0	1.6	49.1	23.1
1977	24.0	6.6	6.6	13.3	3.0	9.6	2.1	1.3	46.8	19.7
1978	23.8	6.1	6.8	13.3	4.4	7.9	3.2	1.3	45.0	21.0
1979	25.2	7.2	6.8	13.4	5.1	8.7	3.3	1.4	47.3	24.7
1980	25.5[a]	8.2	7.2	13.3[b]	5.0	6.2[c]	2.9	0.1	45.0	23.0
1981	25.2	7.8	7.5	11.7	5.1	6.9	2.7	0.0	43.7	15.8
1982	26.2	7.8	7.2	12.3	6.1	8.7	3.5	1.1	47.2	19.6

Sources: Bank of Israel calculations based on CBS data; taxes and product in current prices. Bank of Israel, *Annual Report 1983*, tables E-1A, E-9, E-10.

a. Total direct taxes in 1980 consisted of income tax (71.5 percent), National Insurance (28.3 percent), and a tax on stocks (0.2 percent). Income tax was levied on wage earners (44.7 percent), corporations (19.5 percent), self-employed (11.9 percent), company directors and cooperative members (9.2 percent), deductions at source (14.7 percent). National Insurance covered both wages (93.3 percent), and nonwage earnings (6.7 percent).

b. Total indirect taxes on domestic production in 1980 consisted of VAT (value-added tax)(19.3 percent), purchase tax (7.3 percent), fuel tax (6.9 percent), employers' tax (14.0 percent), other operating taxes (7.8 percent), property taxes (5.9 percent), local authorities' taxes (8.0 percent), and other taxes (10.8 percent).

c. Total taxes on civilian imports in 1980 consisted of VAT (42.5 percent), and purchase and other taxes (32.5 percent).

in doing so, also affects the public's behavior; that is, it encourages attempts by the taxpayer to ease the burden of taxation by reducing the supply of labor, by directing savings and investments to tax-free channels, or by tax evasion. All these reduce the efficiency of the economic system. A proportionate increase in tax rates causes a considerably larger proportionate increase in the excess burden. The excess burden of taxation—that is, the economic damage caused in terms of the efficiency of production—rose considerably in the 1970s. It is unfortunate that there has been little research in Israel on this important subject. There are too few estimates of the excess burden of various taxes in Israel, or of how they affect one another. The only source is the study by Yizhaki (1982), according to which the excess burden of personal income tax in Israel in 1975–1978 was approximately 23 percent of total personal income tax collections. The excess burden that would result from raising the existing tax rates is far higher—Yitzhaki's study shows that if all income tax rates were increased 1 percent, the additional excess burden would exceed 45 percent of the additional tax collected. And these figures still underestimate the true cost, since they ignore the mutual interaction between other taxes, collection costs, intersectoral distortions, and tax evasion. Further inquiry into this subject in Israel is essential to the formulation of a rational tax system.[6]

The steep increase in gross taxation was accompanied by a rise in transfer payments to the public; the latter grew even faster than tax payments. If the

TABLE 11-3. Transfer payments as percentage of GNP, 1960–1982

	To individuals		To domestic production		To exports			Total	
Year	Transfers	Implicit subsidy through credit	Transfers	Implicit subsidy through credit	Transfers	Implicit subsidy through credit	Interest on internal debt	Excluding Subsidized credit	Including Subsidized credit
1960	5.5	—	2.4	—	2.9	—	1.4	12.2	—
1965	7.0	—	2.1	—	0.5	—	1.9	11.5	—
1970	8.4	0.4	1.7	—	2.3	—	3.2	15.6	—
1971	8.9	0.9	1.7	—	3.3	—	3.3	17.2	—
1972	8.8	0.7	1.7	—	2.8	—	3.9	17.2	—
1973	10.1	1.7	2.3	—	2.8	—	4.0	19.2	—
1974	11.9	3.0	2.1	—	3.7	—	4.3	22.0	—
1975	12.9	1.6	2.7	3.2	3.0	—	4.4	23.0	27.8
1976	14.1	2.2	3.3	4.9	3.5	—	5.1	26.0	33.1
1977	14.4	1.9	3.1	4.3	4.1	—	5.5	27.1	33.3
1978	14.4	1.7	3.3	3.5	0.1	1.3	6.2	24.0	30.5
1979	14.0	2.6	3.4	4.2	0.2	2.7	5.0	22.6	32.1
1980	14.3	1.9	2.8	3.8	0.1	3.5	4.8	22.0	31.2
1981	13.9	1.0	6.5	3.1	0.7	2.8	6.8	27.9	34.8
1982	14.4	0.9	4.6	2.7	1.4	1.9	7.2	27.6	33.2

Sources: Bank of Israel calculations based on CBS data. No data are available on the subsidization of credit to domestic production before 1975 and to exports and households before 1978.

TABLE 11-4. Taxation and transfers as percentage of GNP, 1961–1982

	1961–65	1966–70	1971–75	1976–80	1981–82
Taxes					
Direct taxes	14.3	16.5	21.2	24.7	25.7
Income tax on wage earners	—	—	5.1	6.9	7.8
National Insurance	2.8	3.5	5.2	6.7	7.4
Taxes on domestic production	13.9	11.6	10.2	13.4	12.0
VAT	—	—	—	3.8	5.6
Taxes on civilian imports	6.8	5.6	9.3	8.6	7.8
VAT	—	—	—	2.5	3.1
Total taxes	35.1	33.6	40.8	46.6	45.5
Compulsory loans	1.3	1.5	4.1	1.1	0.5
Transfer payments					
To households and non-profit institutions	6.3	8.3	10.5	14.3	14.1
Subsidization of credit to households	—	—	1.6	2.1	0.9
Subsidization of domestic production	2.0	2.0	2.1	3.2	5.6
Subsidization of credit to domestic production	—	—	—	4.1	2.9
Direct support of exports	1.1	1.7	3.1	1.6	1.1
Subsidization of credit to exports	—	—	—	1.5[a]	2.4
Interest on internal debt	1.8	2.2	4.0	5.3	7.0
Total excluding credit subsidization	11.2	14.2	19.7	24.4	27.8
Total net taxation excluding credit subsidization	23.9	19.4	21.1	22.2	17.7
Net taxes after deduction of implicit subsidization of credit	—	—	—	14.5	11.5

Sources: Tables 11-2 and 11-3.

a. The subsidization of credit for exports occurred in 1978–1980, during which period it accounted for an annual average of 2.5 percent of product.

implicit subsidization of credit is ignored the share of gross taxation *minus* transfer payments in total product remained fairly stable, at around 20 percent. However, deducting the subsidy element in credit brings net taxation down to about 15 percent of product in the second half of the 1970s, compared with about 24 percent in the early 1960s.[7]

The steep decline in net taxation coincided with increasing government expenditures during the decade. The rise in the government's deficit was reflected in Israel's growing public debt and the interest payments on it. These interest payments, which are also transfer payments, contributed to the sizable increase in transfer payments toward the end of the decade.

During the 1970s the tax system and transfer systems became even more closely interrelated. In the first half of the decade, a system of child allowances was worked out to complement income tax exemptions for children. The 1975 tax reform abolished these tax exemptions and replaced them with child allowances. Changes of this sort increased both gross taxation and transfer payments. For example, after the 1975 reform the share of child support in transfer payments doubled, and in 1975–76 it was 2.6 percent of GNP. Thus part of the increase in gross taxation since 1975 is tied directly to the increase in transfer payments and is not reflected in net taxation.

The Structure of Direct Taxes

The 1970s saw far-reaching changes in the structure of income tax. Some of these resulted from the work of two tax-reform committees—the Asher Committee and the Ben-Shahar Committee—in the first half of the decade; many others stemmed from gradual developments in the tax base and in the tax schedules that in turn were caused by the rise in real wages and, most of all, by rapid inflation. The tax brackets were revised several times during the decade, usually with a view to correcting the shifts of the tax schedules due to inflation, but these revisions were invariably only partial.

Other studies provide a full description of the changes in the tax schedules (Berglas, 1971; Committee, 1975b; Gabbay, Haroeh, and Cukierman, 1976; and Ben-Porath and Bruno, 1977). Table 11-5 presents data, for selected years, on tax rates for a wage earner with a spouse and two children and distinguishes among:

a. Income tax—income tax as a percentage of an employee's wages.
b. Net tax—definition (a) above plus the employee's payments to the National Insurance Institute (NI) *minus* child allowances.
c. Net tax including employer's contribution—definition (b) *plus* the employer's payments to NI.

Definition (b) thus represents the tax from the employee's point of view, and definition (c) presents the employer's point of view.

TABLE 11-5. Tax rates paid by one wage earner with a spouse and two children, 1970–1980 (percentages)

					Rate of change in coefficient of disposable income[b]		
	1970	1975	1980	1980[a]	1970–1975	1975–1980	1975–1980[a]
Average wage							
Income tax	9.0[c]	11.8	18.6	16	0.97	0.92	0.95
Net tax	12.3	6.3	17.5	14	1.07	0.88	0.92
Net tax including employer's contribution	21.7	18.3	29.4	28	1.04	0.86	0.90
Double the average wage							
Income tax	24.0[c]	21.8	31.2	28	1.03	0.88	0.92
Net tax	27.3	20.7	33.0	29	1.09	0.84	0.90
Net tax including employer's contribution	35.0	30.9	42.7	39	1.06	0.83	0.88

Sources: For 1980, Internal Revenue Administration data. For other years, Bank of Israel, *Annual Report 1983*, table B-1.

a. These columns present the tax paid by a family that earned the same real wage in 1980 as in 1975. Comparison of these columns with 1975 shows the effects of inflation and the revision of tax tables on tax payments; comparison with the data for 1980 shows the effect of real wages on tax payments.

b. The rate of change in the coefficient of disposable income is the change in the percentage of disposable income. For example, the effect of net taxes on disposable income for 1970–1975 is given by (100 – 6.3)/(100 – 12.3) = 1.07. The rate of change in gross income times the rate of change in the coefficient of disposable income yields the rate of change in disposable income.

c. In 1970, in addition to income tax and NI dues, individuals were required to pay compulsory loans at 5.9 percent of an employee's wage (average wage level) and 6.6 percent of wages that were twice the average level.

A comparison of 1970 and 1975 shows that the tax reform reduced net taxes both on average incomes and on incomes that were twice the average level. Disposable income rose 7 percent in 1970–1975, faster than the increase in the gross income of persons with average income, and 9 percent for persons with twice the average income level. Hence the tax reform appears to have benefited lower-income groups less. But this description ignores the major change introduced by the Ben-Shahar Committee—the considerable expansion of the tax base in 1975—

which had a greater impact on high-income groups, although it was partly offset by reduced tax rates. The fact that total tax collection did not decline after the reform is evidence of the substantial effect of this expansion and may also indicate some deepening in tax collection in the early days of the reform.

Table 11-5 ignores compulsory loans that were in force until 1975. These loans bore lower interest rates than the market rates and were not liquid for a considerable length of time. Compulsory loans raised approximately 20 percent of income-tax collections. Taxation through compulsory loans has many disadvantages: the public may regard them as taxes pure and simple, and one may assume that their distortive effect on resource allocation is similar to that of any other tax. Persons without liquid assets found compulsory loans particularly onerous. Moreover, repayment of these loans often fell due in years when the government had serious liquidity problems of its own. Most compulsory loans were therefore abolished by 1975.[8]

The period 1975–1980 saw no further reforms in the tax structure. Nonetheless, Table 11-5 reveals a sizable increase in the tax burden. The average net tax, from the employee's point of view, rose from 6.3 to 17.5 percent for average income earners and from 20.7 to 33.0 percent for persons with twice the average income. This increase was due to the rise in nominal incomes, only part of which reflected a change in real incomes.[9] During this period, the rise in disposable income amounted to 88 percent of the increase in the nominal income of average income earners. The effect on high-income earners (double the average level) was even more dramatic—their disposable income rose by only 84 percent of the increase in wages. When the taxes levied on employers are added, the disposable income of an average employee rose by only 86 percent of gross wage increases, and that of an employee with twice the average wage by 83 percent.

When tax schedules are denominated in nominal currency, tax payments increase whenever nominal wages increase, regardless of whether or not the increase also entails a real wage increment. Furthermore, when the tax is progressive, tax payments rise more rapidly than nominal wages, so that the tax burden increases. For the tax burden to increase along with nominal income, the marginal tax rate must exceed the average tax rate.[10]

Table 11-5 shows that in 1975–1980 the tax burden on higher-income groups grew heavier; that is, their disposable income increased more slowly. This phenomenon of disposable income increasing at a slower pace the higher the income applies to more than 90 percent of all income tax payers. For them inflation can be said to have made the tax system more progressive. For the highest income earners the marginal tax rate approaches the average rate (close to 60 percent), at which stage the tax burden hardly grows at all as inflation rises.

The 1975 tax reform commission did not recommend full linkage of the tax brackets. Linkage was set at 70 percent of the rise in the consumer price index

(CPI) and was performed only once a year. Consequently, the real value of each tax bracket decreased by some 35 percent between 1975 and 1980 (Bank of Israel, *Annual Report 1982,* p. 98 [Hebrew version]); this trend raised the real tax level even for persons whose real income did not change during the period. According to Table 11-5, a family with an average income in 1975 that managed to maintain its real income level until 1980 suffered an 8 percent drop in its disposable income as a result of the partial linkage of the tax brackets. A family whose 1975 income was double the average level took a 10 percent loss in disposable income. Table 11-5 also highlights the fact that in 1975–1980 about two-thirds of the increase in the tax burden stemmed from the effects of inflation, and the remaining third from a change in real income. In other words, the tax system has become more burdensome and progressive since 1975.

Adding employers' contributions to NI to both wages and taxes leaves the general picture unchanged: in 1975–1980 the tax burden increased and became more progressive. Adding the employers' contribution emphasizes the sizable increase in the burden of direct taxation.

A major share of payments to NI is made by employers, whose contribution rose from 12 percent of wages in 1970 to 16.9 percent in 1980.[11] In the same period, total NI receipts rose from 4.7 percent of GNP to 7.2 percent. The large share of NI receipts is especially noteworthy when their collections are compared with those of income tax from wages. In 1976–1980 total NI receipts from wages totaled more than 90 percent of income tax collected from wages.[12]

In view of the quantitative importance of NI, one should not ignore the combined effect of these two taxes in calculating the tax schedules and the marginal rates, and the distortive effects of the tax system. Any increase in the NI tax rate, and especially any increase in its ceiling, has a significant effect on the marginal tax. The tax-reform committees in Israel always accorded great importance to the maximum tax rate in the tax table (see, for example, Ben-Porath and Bruno, 1977). After the 1975 reform, this rate was reduced from 80 to 60 percent. At that time the NI tax ceiling was well within the 35 percent tax bracket; that is, for incomes whose marginal tax rate was 45–60 percent the NI tax did not increase the marginal rate. Because the income tax brackets were not fully linked, and because the NI tax ceiling was linked to wages, the result was that since the end of the 1970s the NI tax ceiling has been within the 60 percent marginal tax bracket, resulting in a considerable span of incomes on which the full marginal tax rate—including NI deductions—amounts to around 70 percent.[13]

Child Allowances

During the 1970s there was a significant change in the structure and size of child allowances. These started out in 1959 as payments to families with a large number of children (payable from the fourth child on). From 1965 on, employers also paid allowances for a wage earner's first child. In the early 1970s the NI paid allowances for the third child, and since the 1975 reform the NI has paid the allowance for all children. Total child support rose continuously: in the first half of the 1970s it stood at 1.3 percent of total product, and in the second half at 2.6 percent of GNP.

The 1975 reform not only increased child allowances quantitatively; it also introduced a qualitative change. The reform abolished all tax exemptions granted to families according to the number of their children, with a view to maintaining the approximate gap between the tax burdens borne by families with different numbers of children.

The use of child allowances both as a substitute for tax exemptions and as a means of helping large families—many low-income families have a large number of children—is a constant source of confusion. The debate on what the desired allowance structure should be has apparently only just begun.[14]

The shift from tax exemptions for children to child allowances led to another basic change: the connection between tax payments and tax benefits for children was severed. For families whose income was not taxable, child allowances were, in effect, negative income tax; before 1975 these families had not enjoyed either the tax exemptions or the allowances paid by employers. But while the shift to child allowances undoubtedly makes the tax system more progressive, it also has undeniable drawbacks. On the one hand, it intensifies the contrast between taxpayers and tax evaders, since the latter do benefit from child allowances and did not benefit from personal tax exemptions. In addition, the gap between earnings from work and income from other sources grew wider. Even for persons whose net income did not change, earnings from work declined while income from the NI increased—creating a disincentive to work. These and other changes in the tax structure (such as unemployment insurance) affect structural unemployment in the Israeli economy; these effects, as noted earlier, have not been sufficiently thoroughly investigated in Israel.

The Effects of Inflation

The subject of taxes and inflation has occupied economists both in academic circles and in the tax administration throughout the 1970s. At first the deliberations centered on the linkage of personal tax brackets. The Asher Committee recommended several revisions of the tax table, and from 1975 on the brackets were linked once a year to 70 percent of the rise in the CPI. This rate was justified on the grounds that it was the same rate at which cost-of-living (COL) allowances to wage earners were linked. The logical link between tax brackets and the COL allowance is not quite clear; the connection may have been motivated by a desire to maintain the built-in flexibility of the tax system, that is, to ensure that real tax collection would automatically increase along with inflation. Because inflation accelerated more rapidly than anticipated by the reform committee, the revision proved insufficient. By 1980 the tax brackets were being revised four times a year and were fully linked to the CPI.

All the linkage schemes failed to solve the central problem—that income tax is based on an annual calculation. Income tax does not distinguish between a shekel received as income or paid as tax on the first or the last day of the tax year. Under inflationary conditions, the result is a serious distortion, favoring those who receive most of their income early in the tax year and who can put off paying their taxes until the end of the tax year. Self-employed taxpayers enjoy an advantage over wage earners in that they can to some extent manipulate the timing of receipts and outlays (including tax payments).[15] The advantage of the self-employed over wage earners is reflected in the fast rise in the share of taxes paid by wage earners in total income tax since the beginning of the 1970s (see Table 11-4).

While the treatment of individual income tax concentrated on updating tax brackets, corporate tax was treated as several distinct issues, with no coherent conceptual framework. During the 1970s various contradictory arguments were raised: inflation was said to cause overtaxation of corporations and erosion of equity capital; it was also said to create tax havens enabling firms to avoid taxes. Evidence exists in support of both arguments. A comprehensive treatment of all such examples is a complex task that cannot be attempted here. (For a more comprehensive treatment see Aaron, 1976; and, for Israel, Bronfeld and Souari, 1980; Berglas, 1980; and Committee, 1980). Discussion here focuses on some of the more controversial issues. The tax-haven argument rests on the practice of financing the purchase of government bonds (whose linkage differentials and interest were tax exempt) by loans. Interest paid on such loans was tax deductible, and their volume grew as nominal interest payments increased with inflation. When this specific loophole was closed, firms switched from government bonds to shares, especially bank shares that offered essentially similar benefits.

As for the inventory argument—under the prevailing circumstances, whereby purchases are deductible at cost, overtaxation will occur if purchases are financed out of equity capital, but not if they are financed through credit. A similar situation prevails with respect to equipment. When only nominal depreciation is tax deductible, overtaxation results if equipment is purchased with equity capital (for additional details see Berglas, 1980). The fact that the extent of tax distortion depends on the source of finance makes it impossible to find partial solutions. The tax authorities have tried to cope with these distortions by granting extra exemptions for inventories and allowing accelerated depreciation on equipment. These concessions eased the tax burden on firms that financed their expenditures out of equity capital. But they also granted an economically unjustified—and therefore distortive—advantage to firms that financed their transactions through loans,

TABLE 11-6. Corporate taxes as a percentage of GNP, 1975–1982

	1975	1980	1982
Total corporate taxes as percentage of product	4.0	3.5	3.3
Taxes on nonfinancial corporations	2.8	2.2	1.9
Tax on financial corporations	1.2	1.3	1.4

Source: Internal Revenue Administration data.

especially linked loans, because linkage differentials were allowed as a tax-deductible expense at the time they were incurred. Thus loan financing became advantageous from the tax viewpoint and encouraged the financing of investments out of borrowed funds, with considerable effects on the structure of firms' capital and government revenues from corporate taxes.

Under such circumstances it is not surprising that total tax collections from firms as a percentage of product shrank as inflation increased. This result does not imply that all firms and industries were equally capable of reducing their tax burden. Inflation created tax discrimination between different industries and thus contributed to the distortion of resource allocation in the economy. Partial data taken from the Internal Revenue Administration and summarized in Table 11-6 demonstrate that while the tax burden on nonfinancial firms gradually declined, the burden on the financial sector increased.

As the existing laws had obviously failed to solve the problem, a new law was promulgated in the early 1980s to cope with corporate taxation in inflationary periods. This law was an (unsuccessful) attempt to solve the basic difficulty entailed in keeping annual accounts denominated in a currency whose value fluctuates; in addition, it granted many tax benefits to preferred types of expenditures.

Taxes on Domestic Production

The major change in taxes on domestic production during the 1970s was the introduction of a value-added tax (VAT) of 8 percent in 1976, raised a year later to 12 percent and in 1982 to 15 percent. The tax base includes all purchases by consumers of both domestically produced goods and imports. Exports and investment goods are exempt (excluding construction of dwellings). The VAT base is consumption *plus* housing; it is not levied on fruit and vegetables but is levied on imports. Israel's VAT has a broader and more uniform base than other countries', which facilitates its collection.

Taxes on production include, in addition to VAT, purchase tax, fuel tax, employers' tax, property taxes, and taxes levied by the local authorities. As shown in Table 11-2, the share of these taxes in total product declined gradually while the share of VAT went up. By 1980 VAT accounted for 5 percent of product while other taxes on domestic production totaled about 8 percent, compared with 11 percent in 1970. Among the other taxes on domestic production, the share of employers' tax (introduced at the same time as VAT) grew to 2 percent of product in 1980. Thus, by the end of the period the relative weight of purchase and property taxes had dropped to only about 6 percent of product.

The shift to a broad-based VAT, its relatively low rate, and the declining weight of high purchase taxes occurred with no notable shocks. From the legislative and adminisrative viewpoint, the introduction of VAT may be considered a success.

VAT also turned out to be less sensitive than income tax to inflation. Because collection is from current sales, the tax base is adjusted continuously. When inflation accelerated, it became evident that even a two-month lag in collection causes considerable erosion in tax revenues. Since 1983, VAT has been collected on a monthly basis, reducing this erosion but raising the costs of collection both to taxpayers and to the tax authorities. A 1985 proposal to shift to a cash basis will, if adopted, further reduce the sensitivity of VAT to inflation.

Taxes on Imports

VAT on civilian imports totaled 2.5 percent of product in the period 1976–1980.[16] Total import taxes declined in the second half of the 1970s while the VAT component rose to 2.5 percent; thus there was a significant decline in import duties and purchase taxes on imported goods. Since VAT is levied on an extremely broad base, while import duties and purchase tax have a narrow base, this process is related to a drop in the discriminatory taxation of imports. The gradual reduction in tariffs in the second half of the 1970s was reversed in the early 1980s.

At the end of 1977 the government announced the liberalization of foreign currency, involving considerable relaxation of foreign currency controls, a move to a floating exchange rate, and the abolition of subsidies for exports. Tables 11-2 and 11-3 show how the liberalization affected the system of taxation and transfers. Direct support of exports, which peaked in 1977 at over 4 percent of GNP, sank to 0.1 percent in the following year and remained at this low level until 1980; in the early 1980s direct support again grew sizable. Direct support was replaced from 1978 on by indirect support in the form of subsidized credit, which gradually reached the volume of direct support given before the liberalization.

Indirect support through subsidized credit has the disadvantage of being less immediately related to the sector that the authorities seek to support. The extent of support granted to value added depends on the level of value added and on the length of the production process. Thus it can be said that the liberalization did not reduce the level of support to exports and even worsened its structure. It should be noted, however, that in the same period the share of exports in product grew as well, so that the subsidy as a percentage of the value of exports actually declined moderately. The share of exports in GNP was 25.2 percent in 1970 and 44.9 percent in 1980; hence support to exports (including subsidized credit) was 9.2 percent of total exports in 1970 and 8.0 percent in 1980. As for imports, there was a 20 percent drop in taxes on these during the period following the liberalization. Furthermore, a large and growing share of taxes came from VAT. The decline in import duties and their partial replacement by VAT represent the limited success of the liberalization policy. In the early 1980s there was a partial withdrawal from this policy.

Transfer Payments

Sokoler (1984) and Chapter 10 of this volume provide a comprehensive analysis of transfer payments and their contribution to the weaker economic strata. This section concentrates only on their significance as part of the Israeli government's taxation policy.

The increase in transfer payments embraced all components. The rise in direct support reflects in part the shift in the tax structure from tax exemptions to child allowances. The latter were first applied in the first half of the 1970s and were expanded in the second half. Child allowances accounted for 1.3 percent of GNP in 1971–1975 and for 2.3 percent of GNP in 1976–1980. In the latter period there was also an increase in transfer payments by around 1.5 percent of product due to the inclusion of sick-fund dues in NI payments. But these two elements explain only part of the increase. Generally speaking, the 1970s were years of considerable expansion in personal transfer payments following legislative amendments, the adjustment of rates, and demographic developments. NI pension payments to the elderly and other survivors, which had been 1.5 percent of product in 1970, rose to 3.3 percent in 1980.

The growth of direct subsidies in the second half of the 1970s, which peaked in the early 1980s, represents the combined effect of new policies and unanticipated inflation. This period was also characterized by a sizable increase in subsidized credit to firms and to exports.

A large increase in transfer payments occurred in interest payments on the domestic public debt. Estimates of this item should be treated with caution—interest as calculated by the CBS is based on actual payments, with no distinction made between nominal interest (which sometimes constitutes repayment of principal) and real interest.[17]

The deficient estimates of interest payments in Israel lead to the undesirable avoidance of discussions on the problem of the public debt. The cumulating government deficit has created a large internal debt that exceeds gross product, and an external debt of over half the product. The very existence of such a debt involves sizable interest payments and presents a very serious economic problem. Even if the data are not accurate, there is no doubt that interest payments have grown substantially, and that adjustment to rapid inflation will cause further increases in debt servicing.[18]

The effect of inflation on transfer payments is of great interest. At first glance, the picture seems inconsistent: the method of updating figures as inflation accelerates leads to inflationary erosion of direct transfers. For example, child allowances that are fully linked to the CPI decline in value owing to the infrequency of revisions and the increase in the rate of inflation. The real value of child allowances in 1980 was already 25 percent lower than in the period from July 1975 to March 1976—the first period after the 1975 tax reform.[19] In the early 1980s, when revisions for various allowances were made more frequently, the erosion was smaller despite the increase in inflation, but remained quite sizable nonetheless.

The lag in revisions that reduced the value of transfers had the opposite effect on support for goods and export credit. In this area the acceleration of inflation is closely related to an increase in transfers. The reasons for this are political: once the government undertakes to support certain prices, it sets controlled price levels and thereafter finds it difficult to revise them. Thus, despite government decisions to prevent subsidies from exceeding a certain level, they invariably do so. This pattern is even more evident in the case of subsidized credit. When the government sets the level of subsidized credit it not only delays revising the interest rate, it does so only for new loans, so that the implicit subsidy to past loans rises beyond the level originally planned.[20] The main lesson from such a situation—which has yet to be learned—is that since the rate of inflation cannot be anticipated, the government should avoid policy measures whose cost depends on that rate. The volume of subsidization granted in Israel to goods and credit in the 1970s reveals the enormous cost of implementing such a policy and its destabilizing effect through raising costs precisely when inflationary pressures increase.

Income Tax, Consumption Tax, and Wage Tax

Among the important changes in taxation during the 1970s were the introduction of VAT, which is primarily a tax on consumption; a sizable increase in NI dues; and the introduction of an employers' tax, which are taxes on wages. Income taxes on wages rose more than taxes on profits. More exemptions were granted to taxes on savings, such as the tax exemption to "complementary training funds" and the partial exemption to pensioners. These changes raise the question of the economic differences among taxes on income, on consumption, and on wages. Recommendations to switch from income tax to consumption tax (also known as expenditure tax) are gaining public and professional support. Similar recommendations have been made by committees in the United Kingdom and in the United States.[21] This section compares the various types of taxes and the development of Israel's tax base in the 1970s.

The economic literature includes several equivalence therorems that have a direct bearing on such a comparison, covering the following taxes: A proportional tax on

a. Consumption *plus* legacies bequeathed
b. Wages *plus* legacies inherited
c. Wages
d. Income *minus* net interest receipts
e. Consumption
f. Income *minus* savings

From the individual's point of view, tax (a) is equivalent to tax (b), tax (c) is equivalent to tax (d), (e) is equivalent to tax (f).[22]

These equivalence theorems are important to the present discussion, for they imply that in a world with no legacies (or when their value is small in comparison with one's lifetime earnings) proportional taxes on wages, on consumption, on income (with net interest receipts exempt), and on income with savings exempt are equivalent. The equivalence results remain unchanged under progressive taxation, provided that lifetime income is used as the tax base. In reality, given the use of annual income as the tax base and of progressive tax schedules, the equivalence is not complete but can still serve as a useful background for the following analysis.

The 1970s were characterized by a steep increase in taxes on wages. The share in GNP of total direct taxes (income tax and NI dues) rose by 5.8 percent, and these taxes on wage earners alone grew by 5.4 percent. The employers' tax, introduced in the mid-1970s, accounted for 1.9 percent of product. In contrast, the product share of direct taxes on nonwage income hardly changed.

From the equivalence theorems it follows that in the absence of taxes on legacies, income taxes that exempt interest receipts are equivalent to taxes on wages.[23] Estate taxes were abolished in Israel in the late 1970s, and a large part of the returns to savings are also tax exempt. Examples of exemptions include interest on government bonds, savings schemes, pension and provident funds, and imputed income from housing. The decline in corporate[24] and property taxes, the rise in taxes collected on wages, and the widespread exemptions for savings all indicate that income tax in Israel is gradually becoming a wage tax.

Alongside the exemption granted to returns to a large part of savings, gross savings also enjoy tax benefits. This point warrants some explanation, using provident funds as an example. Payments made into provident funds are deducted from the taxpayer's taxable income. The savings accumulated in the provident funds are invested in special government securities bearing high, tax-free returns. Benefit payments by the funds are also tax exempt. Severance-pay schemes enjoy a similar status. In the second half of the 1970s these schemes were joined by the complementary training funds, which resemble provident funds (although the minimum saving period is shorter, six years instead of fifteen).[25] These funds considerably expanded the possibilities of tax-deductible savings. As for pension plans, a compromise in the early 1970s made 35 percent of payments made by the pension funds (with a fairly high ceiling) tax exempt, even when the payments into the pension funds and the accumulated interest were tax exempt too.[26]

Taxation of savings is completely devoid of any unifying principle, and it is extremely difficult to explain the attitude taken by legislators. Exempting the complementary training funds from taxes has turned them into the government's most expensive source of finance and has led to considerable discrimination between taxpayers who are entitled to save in such funds and those who are not. Since eligibility to save in such funds is determined in wage contracts, they have turned into nonuniform tax benefits extended to privileged groups of employees.

Measuring the effects of the differential treatment of various savings schemes on wages, profits, and the performance of the capital market requires the analysis of a very complicated general equilibrium model. In the case of certain savings schemes such as pension and provident funds, severance-pay funds, and complementary training funds, the tax benefits go far beyond what such schemes would have received if the government had taxed consumption rather than income. These benefits lack any economic rationale. They introduce a distortion between various savings schemes that reduces the efficiency of the capital market. They discriminate between various types of taxpayers according to their eligibility for certain savings plans. A reform in the tax treatment of various savings plans is long overdue, and it is important that it be carried out in conjunction with a general reform of the capital market.

The changes that occurred in direct taxation were a move in the direction of a tax on wages, and a partial move toward a tax on consumption. The base of the VAT, introduced in the mid-1970s, is essentially consumption. Therefore, the tax is close to being a proportional consumption tax. The major change in Israel's tax system in the 1970s was not the result of a comprehensive tax reform. A reevaluation of the appropriate tax base and the desirable mix of income and product taxes, a considerable reduction in transfer payments, a possible reduction in taxes, and, finally, the appropriate handling of the problem of inflation continue to be needed in the mid-1980s.

III

Crises in an Open Economy

12

Perspectives on the Balance of Payments

Nadav Halevi

This chapter surveys the main developments in Israel's balance of payments, with special emphasis on the last decade. Balance-of-payments developments and policy are closely entwined with general macroeconomic developments and problems, some of which are discussed in detail in other chapters in this volume. The first major section presents an overview of Israel's trade and balance of payments and the major instruments of balance-of-payments policy. The second section discusses the structure and development of trade. The third section deals with the import surplus, the way it is financed, and the implications for economic dependence.

Overview

Trade and the Balance of Payments

Trade enables different economic agents and regions to exploit their comparative advantage, thereby increasing economic welfare. The larger a country, the more varied its economic agents and regions, and the smaller the share of trade that must cross national boundaries. It is therefore not surprising that a small country such as Israel, with neither diverse natural resources nor large enough domestic markets for efficient large-scale production of a wide variety of goods and services, should be highly reliant on foreign trade.

Several indicators of the importance of trade are shown in Figure 12-1.[1] One is the ratio of total imports of goods and services to GNP. Annual fluctuations were in the 30 – 40 percent range in the 1950s, usually in the 40 – 50 percent range in the 1960s, and have been around 70 percent since 1973.[2]

Whereas for most countries imports and exports are more or less of comparable size, Israel has had a large and persistent deficit, that is, an import surplus. With

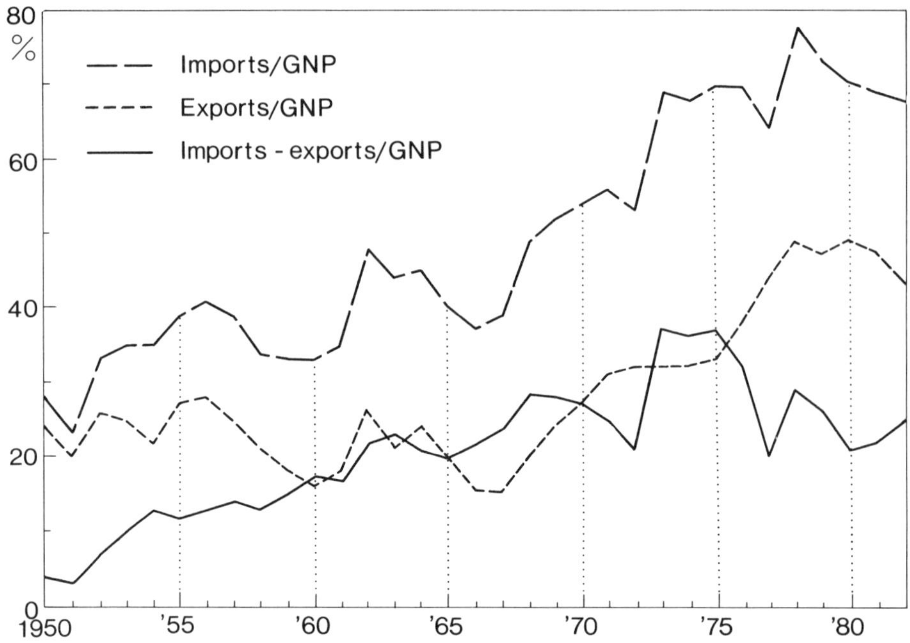

Figure 12-1
The relative importance of trade, 1950–1982. (Halevi, 1983b.)

the export-GNP ratio used to measure the importance of trade, Israel's share does not seem relatively high until 1977, when it began to be in the 40–50 percent range. However, the discrepancy between imports and exports points up a second major aspect of reliance on foreign trade: the addition of resources to the economy, as shown by the relative importance of the import surplus, measured as the ratio of these additional resources to GNP. This ratio has fluctuated over time, with the additional resources provided by the import surplus ranging between one-fifth and one-third of GNP. The addition to resources has played a crucial role in Israel's economic development: it made possible the very high investment ratio that characterized the economy (at least till the 1970s) and explains much of the growth of per capita income. It also made possible high levels of public expenditures for defense and for social capital, without the painful necessity of severe sacrifices in private consumption.

The three ratios presented in Figure 12-1 and the balance-of-payments summary in Table 12-1 point out the major developments in the goods and services side of Israel's balance of payments: a high and growing reliance on imports, an even faster growth in exports, but a persistent import surplus. Although the import surplus has not increased in relative importance, it has grown tremendously

TABLE 12-1. Summary balance of payments: 1952-1982 ($ million)

Year	Goods and services[a]			Unilateral transfers, net credit	Long-term capital			Short-term capital, net credit
	Credit	Debit	Net credit		Credit	Debit	Net credit	
1952	86	392	–306	191	137	30	107	9
1953	102	365	–263	173	90	23	67	4
1954	141	373	–232	263	135	57	78	–77
1955	145	432	–287	210	80	7	73	2
1956	178	536	–358	241	145	66	79	28
1957	223	558	–335	249	157	88	69	18
1958	235	573	–338					
1958	216	561	–345	264	189	116	73	–6
1959	267	586	–319	251	174	89	85	–23
1960	336	682	–346	311	207	100	107	–39
1961	397	840	–443	343	291	110	191	–91
1962	472	933	–461	326	348	129	219	–112
1963	577	1,017	–440	340	483	214	269	–123
1964	619	1,183	–564	327	485	178	307	–78
1965	711	1,234	–523	321	415	187	228	–46
1966	834	1,283	–449	289	420	236	184	19
1967	911	1,447	–536	521	526	221	305	–274
1968	1,150	1,806	–656	438	468	274	194	54
1969	1,290	2,175	–885	464	528	311	217	265
1970	1,402	2,664	–1,262	650	982	300	682	–12
1971	1,875	3,096	–1,221	792	1,001	369	632	–268
1972	2,222	3,316	–1,094	1,059	1,217	482	735	–745
1973	2,812	5,376	–2,564	2,190	1,443	503	940	–548
1974	3,559	6,754	–3,195	1,718	1,108	532	576	1,254
1975	3,687	7,536	–3,840	1,770	1,591	558	1,033	616
1976	4,400	7,469	–3,069	2,210	1,907	660	1,247	57
1977	5,479	7,850	–2,380	2,071	1,778	745	1,033	–556
1978	6,621	9,741	–3,120	2,246	2,060	969	1,091	–386
1979	8,030	11,687	–3,657	2,784	2,221	1,027	1,194	549
1980	9,791	13,567	–3,776	2,967	2,467	1,260	1,207	206
1981	10,439	14,768	–4,329	2,936	2,563	1,330	1,233	587
1982	10,165	14,885	–4,720	2,621	2,450	1,219	1,231	161

a. Until 1958, the goods and services accounts were based on c.i.f. recording of merchandise imports. Since 1958, recording has been based on f.o.b.

in absolute dollar terms, especially since 1972. The persistence of the deficit reflects the fact that means were found to finance it. Israel was very fortunate in being able to mobilize large sums in the form of unilateral transfers; these have financed from half to as much as two-thirds of the import surplus. The remainder was financed by foreign loans and investments. The very large deficits of the last decade were accompanied by large increases in Israel's foreign debt.

Instruments of Balance-of-Payments Policy

When the state of Israel was first established, it was faced with a foreign exchange problem. Whereas the currency of Mandatory Palestine had been fully backed and convertible into sterling, Israel's domestic currency could not be automatically exchanged for internationally acceptable means of payment. It was clear that exports could not provide sufficient foreign exchange to meet all demands, at least not in the short run. A shortage in foreign exchange can be dealt with by decreasing the quantity demanded or by increasing the quantity supplied, or both. There are different ways of achieving these objectives, and Israel's policymakers have employed a number of major measures concurrently, with emphasis shifting among them.

One was exchange control, the framework for which had been established since World War II. Administrative controls rationed expenditure and required all receipts to be handed over to authorized foreign-exchange dealers. Over the years the administrative controls were gradually eased, then replaced by fiscal controls for imports of goods not viewed as competitive with local production, for imports of services, and, between 1962 and 1968, for all imports.[3]

In October 1977 a major reform of controls was announced. This reform abolished or eased what controls still remained on payments for goods and services, particularly for foreign travel and for incoming capital movements; however, despite the announced abolition of exchange control, the framework has remained in force, particularly with regard to capital movements.

The main instrument affecting international transactions via the market mechanism is the rate of exchange. A distinction must be made between the formal or official rate and the effective rate, that is, what purchasers of foreign exchange actually pay per unit, and what sellers receive. Until late 1977, Israel had an adjustable peg system. Except in 1952–1954, when three formal rates were employed simultaneously, an official rate was in force that was changed from time to time by decree.

Until 1975, changes in the formal rate of exchange were infrequent, usually long overdue, viewed as a sign of weakness, and frequently heralded as the "last" devaluation. Because of the need to adjust the exchange rate more frequently than the system was designed for, subsidies and taxes were used to create a difference between effective and formal rates. Such nonformal components of the exchange rate served a dual purpose: first, they could be adjusted as often and as unobtrusively as necessary; second, they permitted a multiple effective rate system, discriminated between various types of receipts and expenditures. As a result there were often wide deviations in the rates between and among imports and exports of goods, and since subsidies were only occasionally given to exports of some services (notably tourism and transportation) and certain types of unilateral transfers (such as personal restitutions from Germany), there was often great divergence in rates between trade in goods and other international transactions. When this diversity became very large, it would create pressure on the authorities to devalue the formal rate and, at least temporarily, sharply decrease the size of the informal component of the exchange rate.

The much higher domestic inflation that followed the 1973 war required more frequent adjustments of the exchange rate than the existing system could handle. In mid-1975 Israel adopted a crawling peg system, which essentially allowed for monthly devaluations of 2 percent, and equal increments to subsidies. This system not only permitted more rapid adjustments of relative prices but also made devaluation an acceptable, nondramatic measure.[4]

As a whole the period 1955–1977 was marked by divergences between formal and effective rates, divergences between effective rates on exports and imports, and fluctuations in the rate of "real" devaluation—that is, changes in effective rates and in foreign prices, deflated by changes in domestic prices. Figure 12-2 shows the developments in relative effective rates and real devaluation for this period.

The adoption of a fluctuating rate system in October 1977 was a major departure from all previous experience: rates could change daily and could go down as well as up. Although a fluctuating rate conjures up visions of free-market forces at play—and indeed, this was heralded as the main advantage of the system when it was announced—the Bank of Israel replaced the Ministry of Finance as the determining agency. Because the private sector buys more foreign exchange than it supplies on basic balance account (that is, goods and services, unilateral and long-term transfers), the way the Bank of Israel allows the difference to be made up affects the exchange rate. After a period of minimal intervention, during which there were highly undesirable foreign short-term inflows and exchange rate appreciation, since March 1979 the Bank has permitted daily fluctuations but steered the exchange rate along the trend desired by policy.

A comparison of the combined effects of changes in foreign prices and in exchange rates for industrial sectors with the domestic price index for manufactures shows that purchasing power parity declined from mid-1979 on.[5] This trend reflects the dilemma of choice between rapid depreciation for balance-of-payments purposes and dampened depreciation to minimize cost inflation. As a

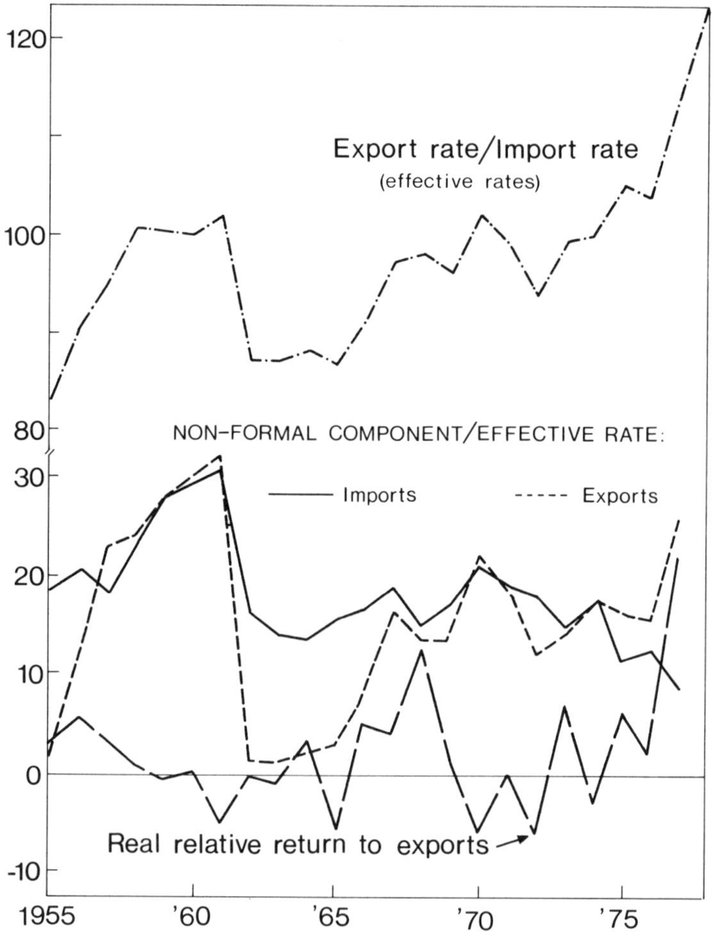

Figure 12-2
Effective rates and changes in real exchange rates, 1955–1977. (Halevi, 1983b.)

result, there was a reemergence of export subsidies, mainly through cheap credits. Inclusion of these subsidies in an index of annual relative return to exporters with 1977 = 100 yields the following: 97 in 1978, 105 in 1979, 109 in 1980, and 105 in 1981. Thus, after 1979 relative competitive power of exports was maintained, at least through 1981 (such data were not computed after that year).

Although manipulation of the exchange rate was used over the years to curb excess demand and affect supply, it was never the sole, and often not even the major, instrument of balance-of-payments policy, for three reasons (whose relative importance was not constant). First, it was assumed that at least in the short run the supply of foreign exchange was price inelastic; therefore, achieving equilibrium through the price mechanism alone would primarily entail curbing demand. Second, such rationing of limited supplies would not accord with official priorities. Finally, the process of devaluation could lead to inflationary cycles, thus rendering real devaluation impossible to achieve.

When the balance-of-payments problem seemed to become acute, drastic measures were taken. In addition to the occasional large devaluation, another major measure used was restrictive fiscal and monetary policy, designed to curb total effective demand and thus both decrease the demand for imports and stimulate exports by depriving potential exporters of the more attractive domestic market. Such policies were used in 1952–1953, 1966–1967, 1975–1977, and in 1980. In these years, other major policy objectives, economic growth and full employment, were sacrificed in favor of immediate improvements in the balance of payments. These, of course, are short-term measures and were always viewed as such.

Even when the most drastic measures were taken, it was recognized that there was no quick way to achieve balance between autonomous receipts and expenditures. Consequently, the long-term objective has been to achieve structural changes in the economy in the form of biased growth, that is, a faster development of exports and import substitutes than of nontradable goods and services. The exchange rate can be a major instrument of such biased growth. Even more important has been the government's development policy, a major element of which has been the Development Budget; the development of exports and of import substitutes has always been given high priority. In addition, concerted efforts were made to mobilize unilateral transfers and long-term capital to finance the import surplus, and thereby provide the resources for development that would eventually decrease the relative importance of the deficit.

Trade in Goods and Services

The Structure of Imports

Israel's trade statistics classify imported goods into four major categories: finished consumer goods, investment goods, petroleum products, and other raw materials or semiprocessed goods. The three major balance-of-payments services categories are transportation; investment income (in this case, interest and dividend payments or accruals); and, until 1958, "government n.e.s.," because it included direct defense imports. From 1958 on, direct defense imports have been shown as a separate commodity import category.

The share of finished consumer goods in total imports of goods and services declined rapidly in the 1950s to about 5 percent in the 1960s and then to less than 4 percent in 1975–1980, rising somewhat to over 5 percent in 1982. The share of investment goods fluctuated considerably, generally between 10 and 15 percent until the early 1970s, but has been less than 10 percent since 1974. During the 1950s the falling share of finished goods was matched by the growing share of semiprocessed goods and raw materials (excluding petroleum products), which reached 40 percent. No such trend is evident after 1960; in fact the shares of both finished goods and raw materials declined from 1967 on. This decline is explained mainly by the growth of direct defense imports, whose share fluctuated considerably from year to year, between 10 and 24 percent, whereas it was less than 10 percent before 1967. A second explanatory factor is the relative growth of petroleum products since 1974; by 1982 these accounted for more than one-tenth of total imports—twice as much as finished consumer goods. Despite the relative growth of these items, the share of all commodity imports declined gradually, from about 75 percent in 1959 to 60 percent in 1982.

Among the services, technically the most important item is transportation.[7] Its share tended to decline from 1958 to 1973, rose again thereafter, and has been about 9 percent in recent years, mainly as a result of higher fuel prices. The most dramatic growth item, and since 1973 the largest service item, is "investment income," which is interest on foreign loans and dividends paid or accruing to foreign investors. Israel's foreign debt increased throughout the period, particularly in 1973–1982. As a result of this, and of rising interest rates, the share of investment income rose slowly (though not steadily) from less than 5 percent in the 1950s to over 18 percent in 1982. Foreign travel (Israeli tourism abroad) became a significant expenditure item only from the 1960s on, with the easing of controls and rising prosperity. By 1982, tourism accounted for about 4.4 percent of total imports, close to the level of all finished consumer goods. The share of the remaining services has fluctuated between 5 and 8 percent.

The instability in the shares of two items—defense imports and investment goods—is particularly noteworthy. Fluctuations in defense imports are, of course, strongly affected by political considerations—both defense needs and special financing available—but part of the fluctuation results from the timing of balance-of-payments accounting. The fluctuating share of investment goods clearly reflects changes in the economic climate.

With most imports being inputs for domestic production of final goods and services, it is of interest to allocate imports of goods and services to final uses. This is an extremely complicated task and subject to many qualifications because it relies on input-output coefficients that are not constant over time. Given these limitations, the results, which reflect the changes in final uses, are quite striking.[8] The share of total imports (excluding direct defense imports) going to private consumption was 27 percent in 1971 and 33–34 percent in 1975 and 1980. About 10–11 percent of imports went to public consumption (excluding direct defense imports). The share going to fixed capital formation fell from 29 percent in 1971 to 23 percent in 1975 and to only 17 percent in 1980. In contrast, the share going to production of exports rose considerably, from about 30 percent in 1971 to 42 percent in 1981.

The Structure of Exports

The rapid growth and diversification of Israel's exports have been outstanding features of the economy. Until the late 1950s agricultural exports, dominated by citrus fruit, accounted for more than one-quarter of all exports. They shrank to about 10 percent of the total in the 1960s, and were less than 6 percent in 1982. The share of cut and polished diamonds rose to over 20 percent by the mid-1970s but has generally declined since then. Other industrial products have grown in relative importance, from about 23 percent in 1958 to 37 percent in 1982.

Ever since Bruno (1962) applied input-output data to analyze the factor content of Israel's exports in 1958 and concluded that Israel tended to export goods that are capital intensive, the question of factor content and comparative advantage has been of interest to Israeli economists (for example, Hershkowitz, 1973). In recent years the importance of human capital has been stressed in explanations of Israel's trade patterns, particularly in manufactured goods.

If the factor content of each industrial branch is assumed to be the same for both its exports and its total product, estimates of factor content for each branch can be weighted by its shares in exports and in total product to yield total industrial exports and product averages.[9] Such estimates show that the ratio of capital to labor was higher in exports than in product throughout the 1970s, but that the difference declined during the decade.[10] Similar estimates by Tsiddon (1982) for human capital, measured by the percentage of academic and professional workers in total employment, show that although there was no substantial difference between exports and total product as regards skill intensity in 1970, this pattern changed in 1973–1982; in 1975 exports were 10 percent more skill intensive than total product, and in 1980 the difference was 20 percent.

In a recent study of human capital intensity in Israel's manufacturing, Baruh (1983) found that three alternative measures of human-capital intensity in Israel's exports and import substitutes all show that even though imports are still more skill intensive than exports, the gap narrowed considerably in 1972–1980.

Baruh also compared factor intensities in Israel's trade in manufactures with more developed countries, the United States and Western Europe, and with less developed countries. His findings conform with those of an earlier study (Fishelson, Hillman, and Hirsch, 1980) based on 1971 and 1975 data: Israel imports skill-intensive goods from the more developed countries and exports skill-intensive goods to less developed countries.

The growth of Israel's industrial exports in the 1950s and 1960s was primarily the result of investment in export industries. Regression results have found exports to be price elastic (for example, Halevi, 1972; Pomfret, 1976); however, the real rate of exchange was not changed sufficiently to make it the dominant factor in export promotion.

During the 1950s and 1960s Israel's industrial development was heavily concentrated in nonsophisticated industries producing import substitutes such as food, textiles, clothing, and rubber and in the exploitation of mineral resources such as cement, potash, and phosphates. These were also the major export branches. The traditional, less sophisticated industrial branches accounted for more than 60 percent of total industrial exports as late as 1970. Thereafter their share dropped to about 45 percent in 1975 and to less than 36 percent in 1980, with more sophisticated products growing in relative importance. Particularly dramatic in the last decade has been the growth of chemicals, metal products, electrical and electronic products, and transport equipment.

Is this increase in the relative growth of sophisticated exports a result of changing comparative advantage arising from growing abundance of human capital? Baruh (1983) found that interindustry changes in manufactured exports during the 1970s were positively related to changes in human capital. In another study of industrial exports, Halevi, Teubal, and Tsiddon (1983) found that the standard factor-intensity approach seemed inadequate to explain the growth of sophisticated exports. This study proposed that sophisticated exports require a significant learning process. And indeed, regressions run on pooled time series and cross-section data, using cumulated past exports as a proxy for an experience term, suggest that the increased export share of the sophisticated industries in the 1970s is in part explained by the accumulation of export experience.

As in the case of imports, there is no economic justification for viewing exports of goods as preferable to exports of services. In fact all the service categories together have generally accounted for between 40 and 50 percent of total exports. The major service exports are transportation, investment income, and tourism. The share of transportation in total export receipts fluctuated around 15 percent throughout the period and evidenced no relative growth. The share of investment income rose, surpassing citrus in the 1970s. For investment income, exports and imports are related: both are affected by the trend of rising interest rates, and the growing indebtedness was frequently accompanied by growing interest-bearing foreign exchange deposits. Tourism is of special interest because it is viewed as an export industry with potential for great growth. To date, tourism has shown abrupt shifts to higher levels rather than a steady trend; its share was about 5 percent in the 1950s, 7–8 percent in the 1960s, and 8–10 percent in the 1970s. Clearly, the hoped-for levels have not yet been achieved.

The export figures show gross receipts; they do not reflect the foreign exchange cost of the various categories. The net return, or value added in foreign exchange, has varied from as little as 20 percent (for diamonds) to over 80 percent (for tourism and agricultural exports). Industrial exports vary widely in the share of value added, averaging some 50–58 percent. Average value added fell in the 1950s and early 1960s, as the share of citrus in exports fell and that of diamonds and industrial exports rose. As the relative importance of industrial exports and tourism continued to rise, the share of value added gradually increased. During the 1970s, higher value-added industries grew more than others, but this favorable trend was more than offset by worsened terms of trade: prices of imported inputs rose more than export prices; consequently, average value added for all exports fell from 52 percent in 1972 to 46 percent in 1976 and remained close to that level in 1977–1981 (estimates by Nachmani, 1983).

The Geographic Structure of Trade

After 1948 it was natural for Israel to maintain strong economic ties with the United Kingdom. Gradually these ties weakened, and in the 1950s imports were affected by the sources of finance: U.S. grants and loans tended to finance imports from the United States, German reparations led to growing reliance on trade with Germany, and various bilateral trade agreements were quantitatively significant.

Since the 1960s, the geographic pattern of imports has reflected more basic economic considerations. The United States has been Israel's main supplier. By the late 1970s, Germany and the United Kingdom each supplied slightly more than one-tenth of Israel's imports, the rest of the EEC about one-fifth, and the United States close to one-quarter. Thus a small number of developed countries provided 70 percent of Israel's imports.

The pattern of exports is not identical. The U.K. share has steadily declined, from close to 30 percent in the early 1950s to less than 10 percent since 1970. Germany and the other EEC countries grew in relative importance until the mid-1960s, at the expense of other European countries and the United States. Despite the existence of commercial and preferential agreements with the EEC between 1964 and 1975, replaced in 1975 by a free trade area agreement, there has been no increase in the EEC share since the mid-1960s. The United States has remained a major buyer, particularly of diamonds.

A detailed geographic breakdown of the services items is not available. However, it can be assumed that the pattern of services closely connected to trade in goods, such as transportation and insurance, is fairly similar to that of merchandise trade.[11] Interest payments are mainly to the United States. Tourist transactions are distributed differently from merchandise trade. In earlier decades, tourists to Israel were predominantly from the United States, but during the 1970s Europe—chiefly the EEC countries—surpassed the United States as a buyer of this export service. Israeli tourist expenditures abroad have grown greatly with the rise in standards of living and the easing of currency restrictions. The main destination is Europe, although there has been some growth in travel to the United States and to more exotic and expensive destinations.

Since 1967 Israel has had increasing trade relations with the territories occupied as a result of the Six Day War. By 1980, exports of goods and services to these areas had grown to some $700 million, or about 7 percent of total exports. Imports were only about $500 million, less than 4 percent of the total, and about half of this amount represented wages to Arab workers employed in Israel (estimates by CBS Balance of Payments Division). Thus, these territories have only a marginal impact on Israel's balance of payments, although in trade with them Israel has an export surplus. On the other hand, Israel is the main trading partner of the occupied territories, although its importance is greater in the territories' imports than in their exports.

The Terms of Trade

Prices of imports have always fluctuated, sometimes considerably, as in the early 1950s as a result of the Korean War, and after the closing of the Suez Canal in late 1956. But strong rising trends were not evident before the Yom Kippur War, and it was acceptable to show balance-of-payments figures and compute rates of change in nominal dollar prices. However, given the worldwide inflation of the 1970s, set off by the dramatic increase in oil prices, ignoring price changes is liable to lead to serious misinterpretation of the trade statistics.

Commodity prices rose considerably after 1973, with the main impetus coming from the tremendous increase in oil prices in 1974 and again in 1979–1980. Commodity import prices in 1980 were more than three times as high as in 1972, then declined a bit in 1981–82. Commodity export prices caught up for a while in 1978, but the commodity terms of trade for 1973–1982 averaged about 90, with the main deterioration occurring in 1974–75. The terms of trade computed for all goods (including defense imports) and services (excluding investment income) also fell, but by less, never falling below 90.

Such changes in the terms of trade obviously affect the size and composition of exports and imports, which are influenced by price fluctuations and by uncertainty regarding price changes. No less important an effect is welfare gains or losses, particularly in an economy so reliant on trade and on an import surplus. Conceptually, three types of gains or losses are involved: (1) since exports are a means of paying for imports, a given quantity of exports can buy more or less imports when export and import prices do not change at the same rate: (2) given that unilateral and long-term capital transfers are mobilized to finance a deficit in goods and services, there is a loss involved to the extent that such sums are determined before a rise in import prices: (3) a net debtor can gain from the fact

TABLE 12-2. Estimated gains and losses from changes in terms of trade, 1973–1982[a]

Year	Gain or loss from export	Loss from long-term transfers	Gain from interest payments		Total annual gain or loss		Total annual gain or loss (–) as percent of imports	
			A	B	A	B	A	B
	(1)	(2)	(3)	(4)	(5)	(6)	(7)	(8)
1973	–104.0	–751.2	34.8	34.8	–820.3	–820.3	–0.15	–0.15
1974	–127.8	–628.6	63.3	110.4	–693.1	–646.0	–0.10	–0.10
1975	–70.7	–169.5	20.3	182.3	–219.9	–57.9	–0.03	–0.01
1976	61.7	–58.8	7.8	200.9	10.7	203.8	0.00	0.03
1977	177.1	–257.6	11.4	231.8	–69.1	151.3	–0.01	0.02
1978	115.1	–418.3	63.0	374.3	–240.2	71.1	–0.03	0.01
1979	–289.2	–716.0	103.1	557.7	–202.1	–447.5	–0.08	–0.04
1980	–219.5	–706.3	154.5	1,168.8	–771.3	243.0	–0.06	0.02
1981	75.9	145.9	–29.2	958.9	192.6	1,180.7	0.01	0.08
1982	269.9	223.4	–63.8	1,137.4	429.5	1,630.7	0.03	0.11

Note: A includes gains from interest payments from price changes during year; B includes gains from interest payments from cumulative price changes.

a. Columns 1–6 are expressed in millions of dollars.

that if interest changes are determined and fixed, a rise in the price of imports means that the real cost of interest payments decreases in terms of forgone imports. The total gain or loss should therefore take into account all three of these components.[12]

Estimates of gains or losses from changes in terms of trade depend on somewhat arbitrary assumptions and must be interpreted with caution. Given these limitations, Table 12-2 presents some estimates. Column 1 shows the gain or loss computed by asking "What could last year's exports have bought this year?"[13] Column 2 shows the gains and (usually) losses in import buying power of predetermined unilateral and net long-term capital transfers.[14] Gains from fixed-interest payments are based on the assumption that short-term interest rates adjust rapidly, whereas only one-third of interest charges on long-term debt are readjusted and two-thirds were set in 1972. Column 5 measures total gains or losses from price changes in the current year, whereas column 6 takes into account—for each year—cumulated effects on interest payments.[15]

There were losses from exports in the early 1970s, and more gains than losses thereafter. Long-term transfers were worth less in every year before 1981. Fixed interest charges usually gave annual gains, and cumulative gains covered most other losses. Thus net losses were significant only in 1973 and 1974, when they were equal to 15 and 10 percent of imports respectively. As debts get renewed at higher interest rates, the net loss situation will change.

The Import Surplus and Its Financing

The large and persistent import surplus has been a distinguishing feature of the economy. It has been both a blessing and a problem. The size and financing of the import surplus are discussed first, and then the concept of Israel's economic dependence.

The Import Surplus

As shown in Table 12-1, imports exceeded exports throughout 1952–1982. In the 1950s the import surplus (deficit in goods and services) fluctuated between a high of $364 million (in 1951) and a low of $232 million (in 1954). In the 1960s the trend was upward: despite the fact that exports grew more rapidly than imports in most years, the difference was not sufficient to counteract the absolute difference in size between imports and exports. During most of the decade the deficit was $450–550 million, but toward the end it rose and by 1970 it had exceeded $1 billion, remaining close to that level until 1973 war. Since then, both the absolute levels and fluctuations have been much higher. The import surplus rose to $4 billion in 1975, declined to less than $2.4 billion in 1977, then rose again to $4.7 billion in 1982.

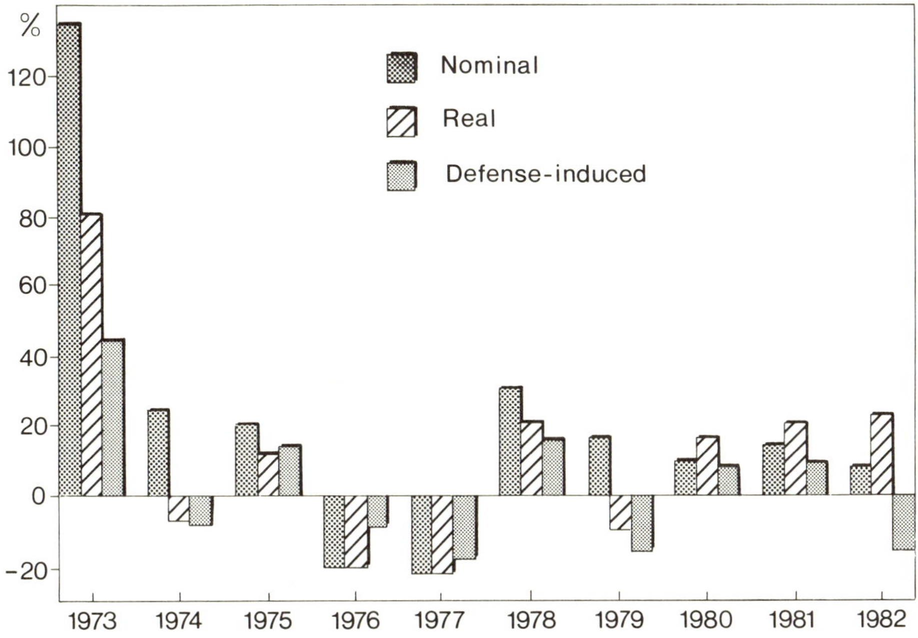

Figure 12-3
Annual change in deficit: Goods and services, 1973–1982. (Table 12-1.)

Two factors have been the major contributors to the growth of the dollar deficit in the last decade. One is the increased levels of defense imports. Direct defense imports remained at a high level after the Yom Kippur War, fluctuating between $1 billion and $2 billion. The second factor is the annual rise in import prices since 1972, discussed above.

Figure 12-3 shows annual percentage changes in the nominal import surplus, in the real import surplus, and the contribution to the change in the real deficit accounted for by real direct defense imports.[16] Clearly, the largest change was in 1973–134 percent in nominal and 80 percent in real terms. Nominal deficits rose significantly in 1974–75 and in 1978. Real deficits rose significantly in 1979, 1981, and 1982. In 1980–1982 improved terms of trade caused nominal deficits to increase by less than did deficits in constant prices.

Increased defense imports accounted for much of the increase in the real deficit in 1973; thereafter, their contribution to changes in the real deficit was not large. However, the very much higher average nominal deficits of the last decade—and these are what have to be financed—are in large part due to the higher levels of defense spending. Thus Israel was unable to compensate for the higher nominal financial burden of defense spending and rising prices.

Types of Financing

Although the deficit in the goods and services account means additional resources, it has been viewed with concern, primarily because of the way the deficit has been financed. The most important economic distinction among types of financing is between unilateral transfers and capital transfers; the latter imply both interest (or dividend) payments and eventual repayment.

Figure 12-4 shows the proportion of the deficit financed by net unilateral transfers, net long-term capital, and the remainder, which by definition includes short-term capital and errors and omissions. Israel has been fortunate in having always been able to finance a significant proportion of its deficit by mobilizing unilateral transfers. Only once (in 1951) did these cover less than 40 percent of the deficit; in most years they covered 60–75 percent.

Net long-term capital flows were almost always considerably smaller than unilateral transfers, but they were substantial additions to total resources. The two together—which I shall call "long-term inflows"—were not sufficient to cover the deficit in 1949–1953; what remained of the deficit was financed primarily by foreign-exchange reserves, most of which were built up and held in London as backing for the Palestine currency. A "consolidation loan," arranged in 1954,

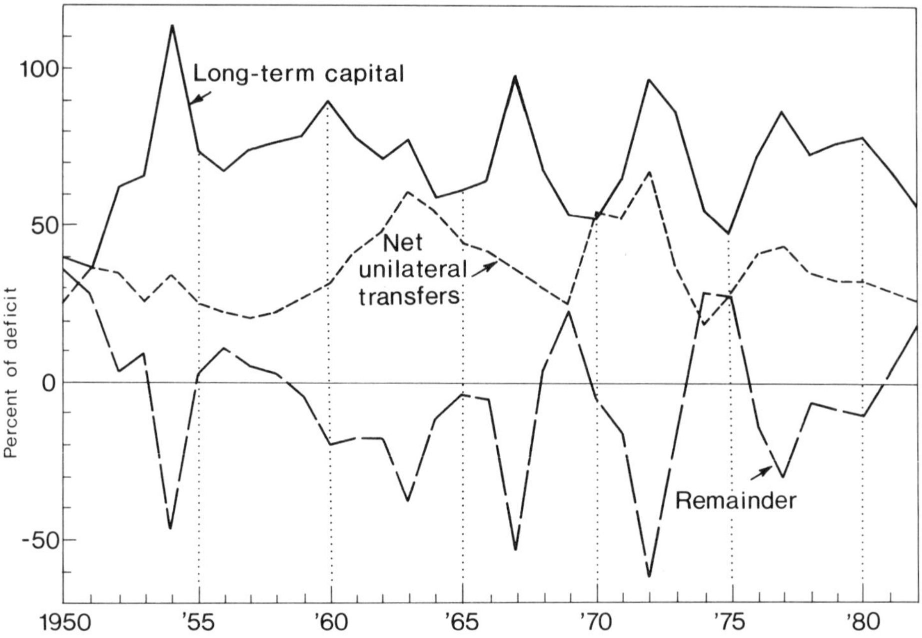

Figure 12-4

Types of funds financing the import surplus, 1950–1982. (Halevi, 1983b.)

allowed Israel an extra portion of unilateral transfers at the expense of future receipts and temporarily solved the then crucial foreign-exchange situation. However, only from 1958 on did long-term inflows reach such levels that they not only fully financed a higher level of annual deficits but also permitted the accumulation of short-term assets. Particularly noticeable is the (then) record inflow in the war year of 1967, which exceeded the deficit by 54 percent (in dollar terms, by almost $300 million).

During the 1970s the absolute figures rose dramatically for deficits, unilateral transfers, and capital inflows. The deficit in 1972, though double that of 1971, was almost entirely covered by grants alone, and the total inflow greatly helped build up reserves. However, the growing deficit in 1974–75 was not matched by long-term inflows, and reserves were brought down sharply. Lower deficits in the next two years permitted improvement in the short-term asset position, and the larger deficits of 1978–1980 were slightly more than covered by long-term inflows; but in 1981 and even more in 1982, when the share of unilateral transfers fell sharply, long-term inflows fell short of requirements, and large-scale short-term borrowing became necessary.

Sources of Financing

Israel's three major sources of financing have been world Jewry, the U.S. government, and the government of West Germany.

World Jewry. Financial support from this source comes in several forms. Funds raised abroad by institutions connected to the World Zionist Organization and by smaller philanthropic institutions have been reliable sources, increasing in periods of crisis. In recent years these have averaged about $500 million a year.

Private transfers, including immigrants' remittances, became relatively important only in the 1970s; in recent years they have approached institutional transfers in size, perhaps because they include repatriation of funds held abroad by Israelis.

Since 1952, with the sale abroad of State of Israel Bonds, organized Jewish fundraising has included loans as well as gifts. Bearing far lower interest rates than those of similar long-term financial instruments, the bonds have obviously incorporated a grant element, but being repayable they are not unilateral transfers. Quite important till the 1970s, bonds sales in recent years have also averaged about $500 million annually, but redemptions have risen to such levels that net receipts are relatively small.

U.S. government. The United States has given Israel loans and grants since 1949, starting with an Export-Import Bank loan of $100 million and followed by substantial grants in 1951–1954. Thereafter grants almost disappeared, and the main type of U.S. aid until 1972 was via the agricultural surplus program. In addition, there were hard-currency loans from different specialized agencies.

Since 1973, U.S. aid in the form of grants and loans, both for defense imports and as economic aid, have grown to be the major source of financing, averaging almost $1.9 billion annually in 1973–1982.[17] Owing to the fact that this aid has accompanied, and in large part been tied to military needs, some analysts have suggested that direct defense imports should not be counted in computing the deficit, since they are in a sense self-financing (see Chapter 8). Since 1973, official grants alone have covered more than half of defense imports, and in most years much more. Since 1976, total aid (including grants and loans) has exceeded defense imports, substantially so in most years. The ratio of total aid to the import surplus increased to about two-thirds in 1980, then dropped sharply in 1981, and again in 1982, to only about 46 percent.

German reparations. In accordance with the Reparations Agreement, the Federal Republic of Germany provided Israel with some $815 million in the form of goods in 1953–1965.[18] During that period these transfers were a major source of foreign exchange. As with receipts from bonds sales and U.S. aid, the local-currency counterpart of the foreign-exchange receipts was earmarked for development projects. In 1963 Germany agreed to provide some loan capital as a substitute continuation of aid.

In 1954 Israeli residents began receiving personal restitution in the form of lump-sum payments or pensions from the German government. From 1974 on, lump-sum payments declined, but pensions continued to increase. By 1982 annual restitution payments were close to $450 million.

Of the three major sources of finance, world Jewry has been the most consistent, its share of long-term transfers generally ranging between 30 and 50 percent, rising significantly in 1967–1969 and falling to about 25 percent from 1978 on. Germany's share was about 40 percent in 1957–1961, around 30 percent in the next five years, and in recent years it has averaged only about 13 percent. The U.S. role was important in 1949–1953 but declined thereafter to levels of less than 10 percent. With the aid program adopted as a result of the 1973 war and its aftermath, the United States has accounted for over half of all long-term and unilateral transfers. In fact it is the growth in U.S. aid that has reduced the relative share of the other major sources, and not a decline in the latters' transfers.

Israel's Foreign Debt

The use of loans to finance part of the deficit in goods and services is reflected in Israel's continuously growing foreign debt. Table 12-3 presents data on foreign-exchange assets and obligations.[19] Until the 1970s, most obligations were long term and were assumed or guaranteed by the government. The government is still the major debtor, and its long-term debts reflect borrowing from the U.S. government and sale of Israel Bonds. Since 1970, short-term obligations have increased

TABLE 12-3. Foreign exchange assets and obligations, 1953–1982 ($ million)

	Obligations				Net obligations	Net assets	Reserves held at the Bank of Israel
	Long term (1)	Short term (2)	Total (3)	Assets (4)	(3 – 4) (5)	(4 – 2) (6)	(7)
1953	329	81	410	41	369	–40	—
1954	382	49	431	80	351	31	—
1955	419	47	466	89	377	42	51
1956	452	62	514	86	428	24	56
1957	483	58	541	82	459	24	53
1958	519	66	585	130	455	64	94
1959	569	66	635	168	467	102	124
1960	599	121	720	270	450	149	383
1961	700	126	826	365	461	239	503
1962	820	161	981	506	475	345	416
1963	940	174	1,114	626	448	452	515
1964	1,076	192	1,268	666	602	474	540
1965	1,214	273	1,487	779	708	506	634
1966	1,298	304	1,602	756	846	452	612
1967	1,580	273	1,853	968	885	695	695
1968	1,772	334	2,106	916	1,190	582	647
1969	2,110	413	2,523	729	1,794	316	381
1970	2,698	609	3,307	849	2,458	240	350
1971	3,203	1,558	4,761	1,585	3,176	27	548
1972	3,737	1,885	5,622	2,838	2,784	953	1,116
1973	4,599	2,320	6,919	3,872	3,047	1,552	1,761
1974	5,527	2,815	8,342	3,191	5,151	376	1,071
1975	6,573	3,578	10,151	3,548	6,603	–30	1,040
1976	7,993	3,738	11,731	4,079	7,652	341	1,156
1977	9,080	4,524	13,604	4,994	8,610	470	1,359
1978	10,256	6,171	16,427	7,208	9,219	1,037	2,242
1979	11,502	8,093	19,595	8,498	11,096	405	2,781
1980	12,543	9,627	22,170	10,233	11,937	606	2,854
1981	13,423	11,082	24,505	11,153	13,352	71	2,847
1982	14,495	13,464	27,959	12,453	15,506	–1,011	2,994

Sources: Column 7: Bank of Israel, *Annual Report*, various issues; all other data: CBS, Balance of Payments Division.

tremendously as a result of Israel's worsening foreign-exchange position and the growing involvement of Israel's banking sector in world financial markets.

The private banking sector borrows and lends abroad, and since 1975 it has been a net borrower from foreign banks.[20] It has also used large deposits from foreigners to finance imports and local transactions. These deposits grew from $528 million at the end of 1971 to $1.5 billion in the mid-1970s and stood at $6.5 billion by the end of 1982.

Column 5 of Table 12-3 shows total obligations net of total (recorded) assets. These were less than $500 million until 1964, exceeded $1 billion in 1968, and grew rapidly after 1973 to over $15 billion by 1982. The short-term net asset position—what can be called the economy's (as opposed to the official) net foreign-exchange reserves—is shown in column 6; these reserves were very low in the 1950s, close to $500 million during most of the 1960s, and fluctuated widely in the 1970s. Although they averaged $570 million over the entire period, they dropped to *minus* $1 billion in 1982. Clearly, the official reserves held by the Bank of Israel, which grew from close to $1.25 billion in 1972 to almost $3 billion in 1982, are to a very large extent balanced by net short-term obligations of other sectors.

During the 1970s the growth of world liquidity, swelled by petrodollars, created a vast pool that Israel was also able to tap; in fact it borrowed relatively less than many other industrialized countries. In the early 1980s much of the increased short-term indebtedness of the banking system was undertaken to prevent foreign-exchange reserves from falling to dangerously low levels.

Economic Dependence

Israeli economists have long been concerned about Israel's economic dependence on other countries. A country that is as open as Israel is not economically independent. The term *dependence,* as used in Israel's economic discussions, refers to the import surplus.[21] This dependence, however, is viewed as a justifiable price for the benefits of trade.

Table 12-4 presents various indicators of economic dependence. Two basic approaches underlie these ratios. One reflects concern with the question how the economy would be affected if the import surplus were to be sharply reduced; the second focuses on the future burden imposed by the persistence of an import surplus.

A reduction in the import surplus would decrease total available resources by at least the same amount. Line 1 shows that despite fluctuations in the share of resources (in current prices) provided by the import surplus, there has not been a trend; the share is usually about one-fifth. A large decrease in the import surplus could mean a decrease in essential imports, and thus lower domestic product.

TABLE 12-4. Ratios indicating economic dependence in selected years, 1952–1982

	1952	1958	1964	1970	1975	1980	1982
1. Import surplus/resources	0.21	0.17	0.19	0.21	0.27	0.17	0.20
2. Exports/imports	0.22	0.34	0.52	0.53	0.49	0.72	0.68
3. Debt-financed import surplus/resources	0.07	0.04	0.08	0.11	0.15	0.06	0.09
4. Interest/exports	0.14	0.13	0.09	0.10	0.11	0.09	0.11
5. Interest and debt repayment/exports	0.49	0.67	0.37	0.31	0.26	0.22	0.23
6. Gross investment/import surplus	1.30	1.41	1.96	1.09	0.87	1.08	0.96

Sources: Lines 2, 4, and 5: Computed from detailed balance-of-payments data; lines 1, 3, and 6: computed from CBS National Accounts Statistics and balance-of-payments data computed at average effective exchange rate.

Line 2 shows that the share of imports covered by exports has increased substantially, though not steadily, over time; therefore, in this respect, dependence has decreased. Available foreign-exchange reserves and short-term borrowing can also temporarily maintain a deficit in the face of declining long-term transfers.

The possibility of a sudden fall in the import surplus is a function of the dependability of long-term transfers and foreign confidence in the Israeli economy. Although neither aspect is reflected in the table, the tremendous growth since 1973 in the U.S. share of long-term transfers and the relative growth of short-term obligations clearly indicate increased dependence and greater vulnerability.

The view of the import surplus as a burden arises from the fact that current deficits involve interest charges and debt repayment. Line 3 of Table 12-4 shows the ratio of the part of the import surplus that was financed in a "burden-creating" manner to total resources. This ratio was relatively low throughout most of the period simply as a result of the availability of large unilateral transfers, and shows marked fluctuations.

Lines 4 and 5 also reflect the burden of debt arising from balance-of-payments deficits: the first shows the ratio of annual interest charges to exports; the second includes gross capital payments (that is, it does not allow for refunding). The ratio of interest charges to exports reveals no clear-cut trend. The total capital repayments measure shows a generally falling trend in the 1960s, which halted in the more recent years of growing deficits and debts. The effects of these developments will become apparent in the ratios some time in the near future.

A more fundamental approach to the future burden would concentrate on the contributions of past and current import surpluses to economic development. One relevant indicator of such an approach is shown in line 6. In the 1950s and 1960s, gross domestic investment was well in excess of the import surplus, whereas since 1970 this ratio has been much lower. Net investment figures would show high rates of dissaving in the last decade.[22]

Conclusion

After the turbulent early years of organizing a foreign-exchange regime and relying on severe foreign-exchange controls, Israel's balance of payments developed fairly steadily over the next two decades. Trade expanded rapidly, and although exports grew faster than imports, the balance-of-payments deficit tended to grow absolutely. Unilateral transfers financed most of the deficit, and the difference was made up by loans and investments at favorable terms. On several occasions, when the deficit or the way it was financed caused growing concern, more drastic—though temporary—policy actions were taken: either a large devaluation of the exchange rate of deflationary fiscal and monetary measures.

Since 1973, the situation has changed in several basic ways. Worsening terms of trade and a higher level of defense spending were the major factors in creating a much larger import surplus. Despite large inflows of grants, the larger deficits were accompanied by ever-increasing foreign indebtedness.

The frequent adjustment of exchange rates—introduced by the crawling peg system of 1975 and intensified by the switch to a fluctuating rate in late 1977—was both made necessary by and contributed to the high inflation rates. The easing of exchange controls in late 1977, and in particular the widespread use of foreign-exchange-denominated, highly liquid accounts and the integration of Israel's banks in the world financial markets, also intensified inflationary pressures and complicated policymakers' efforts simultaneously to decrease inflation and to improve the balance of payments.

Israel's failure to prevent increases in the import surplus in recent years and the concomitant growth of foreign indebtedness and increased reliance on short-term obligations have brought it to a precarious position. On the one hand, projected debt repayments in the near future are so high as to make it unlikely that enough net additional lending can be mobilized to permit continued deficits at existing levels. On the other hand, Israel's financial position is more reliant on foreign confidence and, paradoxically, more influenced by its own current deficits and indebtedness than by the tremendous development that has occurred in its export industries. Clearly, these balance-of-payments problems will be of major importance in the years to come.

13

The Energy Sector in the 1960s and 1970s

Haim Barkai

Energy, Income, and Prices

During the 1960s Israel's energy consumption grew rapidly, as it did in other industrialized countries—crude oil consumption, effectively Israel's only source of primary energy through 1980, almost tripled, per capita energy consumption more than doubled, and the energy input coefficient rose by more than 25 percent (Table 13-1). Yet the ratio of the value of oil imports to GNP hardly changed, because of the drop in the real cost of oil imports during the 1960s.

Lower real energy cost may have indirectly affected the growing energy intensity in GNP and per capita terms (Tables 13-1 and 13-2). The direct price, whatever its impact, reflected changes in domestic energy prices that were only tenuously linked to the real cost of energy to the economy. Over the 1960s these fell at a substantially higher rate than the cost of energy, as indicated by the comparative pattern of the Inverse Energy Terms of Trade series and the domestic energy (relative) price index.[1] By 1970 Israel's real unit cost of primary energy was about 13 percent lower than it had been in 1960, and its domestic energy prices were 33 percent lower.

Total consumption of primary energy rose only 57 percent between 1970 and 1980. The intensity coefficients (Table 13-1, column 5) of the late 1970s and early 1980s underline the slowing of the persistently rising trend for over two decades. The indexes of per capita energy consumption (Table 13-2) still suggest an increase of about 18 percent, but compared with a 122 percent rise in the 1960s, it is insignificant.

This slowdown, and even reversal, however, was limited to the *physical* magnitudes—energy units per capita and per units of GNP. The time trend of *values* tells an altogether different story. Because the ratio of energy consumption to GNP remained fairly constant at somewhat less than 1 percent throughout the 1950s and the 1960s, the energy sector was of little macroeconomic significance.

TABLE 13-1. Oil imports, energy consumption, and aggregate energy coefficients, 1960–1983

	Energy imports		Energy consumption[c]		Aggregate energy coefficient[d]	Prices	
	Oil[a] (MTOE)[b]	Millions of current $	Millions of current $	Index (1970=100)		Domestic energy relative price[e]	Inverse of energy terms of trade[f]
Year	(1)	(2)	(3)	(4)	(5)	(6)	(7)
1960	2.92	34.1	19.5	36.0	2.28	148.9	115.7
1961	2.87	33.6	21.9	40.4	2.32	138.0	114.5
1962	3.40	39.6	24.5	45.3	2.36	138.7	115.7
1963	3.80	44.6	26.6	49.1	2.30	130.8	110.7
1964	3.98	46.6	30.3	55.9	2.39	126.9	110.7
1965	4.54	53.8	34.3	63.4	2.65	117.5	106.1
1966	4.98	58.9	36.6	67.2	2.56	109.6	101.0
1967	4.72	55.9	38.3	70.2	2.65	109.8	103.0
1968	4.34	63.8	43.4	79.5	2.93	106.4	104.0
1969	5.94	70.2	48.2	88.5	2.85	108.1	99.0
1970	6.09	70.1	54.5	100.0	2.87	100.0	100.0
1971	6.26	85.3	73.7	108.9	2.90	106.9	119.8
1972	6.33	93.8	87.6	118.9	2.88	112.3	121.2
1973	8.69	195.7	143.9	128.6	2.83	114.6	173.8
1974	6.94	585.5	548.3	130.6	2.70	202.5	552.5
1975	7.69	628.3	535.2	131.8	2.67	255.7	510.1
1976	7.47	687.1	611.7	133.6	2.67	258.9	563.8
1977	7.69	743.2	677.0	138.4	2.74	250.5	510.7
1978	8.17	777.6	698.1	147.1	2.77	248.7	395.6
1979	8.85	1,373.6	1,200.5	153.9	2.77	268.9	572.7
1980	8.95	2,138.3	1,957.3	156.9	2.76	312.4	840.5
1981	8.70[c]	2,029.4	1,964.5	160.7	2.71	310.0	852.0
1982	9.26[c]	1,853.4	1,808.7	168.0	2.82	327.8	769.8
1983	8.69[c]	1,607.0	—	169.3	2.79	—	—

Sources: Barkai (1984), tables 1, 3, and 5, and sources cited there.

a. Oil imports and residual fuel. Data for 1960–1969 calculated from import values and prices paid per ton of imported oil; figures adjusted to the 1970 entry.

b. Includes 0.24, 0.66, and 1.28 MTOE (Million Tons Oil Equivalent) of coal for 1981, 1982, and 1983 respectively.

c. Gross domestic consumption excluding bunkering, exports of fuel to the administered territories, and use of solar energy for heating water. The latter two are of negligible quantitative significance.

d. Tons per ISh. 100,000 at constant 1970 prices.

e. Aggregate energy price index deflated by GNP implicit price deflator.

f. Oil import prices deflated by export prices.

TABLE 13-2. Energy intensities: Israel and selected industrialized countries, 1960–1980

	United States	West Germany	United Kingdom	France	Greece	Italy	Israel
Per capita energy consumption[a]							
1960	100.0	48.2	58.9	35.7	8.2	17.8	13.8
1970	100.0	48.1	48.0	38.4	13.9	28.1	21.1
1980	100.0	54.3	44.9	43.8	—	31.5	24.9
Index of per capita energy consumption							
1970 (1960= 100)	144.6	144.4	117.9	155.5	243.5	228.0	222.0
1980 (1970= 100)	100.0	112.8	93.6	114.1	—	111.8	117.8
Energy intensity per unit of GNP[b]							
1960	100.0	93.6	105.4	69.4	82.4	56.9	53.7
1970	100.0	77.2	100.0	58.8	75.9	60.9	51.4
1980	100.0	45.6	64.2	42.1	57.5	55.1	62.3
Index of GNP energy intensity							
1970 (1960= 100)	100.8	101.4	120.2	120.6	136.0	114.9	192.2
1980 (1970= 100)	94.1	90.0	89.6	92.0	92.6	106.5	95.2

Sources: British Petroleum, *Statistical Review* (1980), p. 32; World Bank, *Atlas*, various issues 1960–1981; Barkai (1984), table 1, column 2; Ministry of Energy (1981).

a. Based on oil-ton equivalent per capita.

b. Based on oil-ton equivalent per GNP unit.

c. Constant 1975 prices.

By the time the dust of the first OPEC price hike settled in 1974, it stood at the then unbelievable level of 4.55 percent of GNP, turning energy into a major macroeconomic variable practically overnight. The second oil price hike of the late 1970s pushed the energy-GNP ratio even higher, to 11 percent, and the primary energy imports—total imports ratio from 2 percent in 1970 to over 14 percent in 1980.

The rise in the real price of energy to Israeli consumers seems to be the only factor that can explain why the GNP input coefficient peaked in 1971. Israel's domestic energy prices continued to lag behind its energy terms of trade. Nevertheless, the slow rise in the early 1970s and the threefold rise in domestic (relative) energy prices through 1982 undoubtedly contributed to the substantial slowdown in both the growth rate of energy consumption and its intensity in production and consumption.

Income, Relative Energy Prices, and the Demand for Primary Energy

The figures for 1960–1972 suggest that energy consumption is highly sensitive to changes in income, and the data from the 1970s suggest the possible relevance of prices. The data do provide some insight into the responsiveness of the aggregate demand for energy to income and prices. This is derived from estimating an energy consumption function in which income and prices are the independent variables and crude consumption serves as a proxy for the dependent energy variable: the deflated energy price index and real GNP per capita are proxies for the independent price and income variables respectively. Other estimates, presented in Table 13-3, introduce lags that permit the derivation of short- and

TABLE 13-3. Income and price elasticities of demand for primary energy[a]

	$E_t(1)$	$E_t(2)$	$E_t(3)$	$E_t(4)$
Number of observations	21	20	20	20
R^2	0.94	0.97	0.96	0.99
D.W.	1.69	2.50	1.29	1.82
α	1.32	0.39	0.51	0.22
	0.10	0.19	0.23	0.12
α_1	—	—	0.805	—
			0.25	
β	−0.12	−0.07	−0.17	−0.06
	0.05	0.03	0.04	0.02
γ	—	0.69	—	0.795
		0.14		0.09
Price elasticities				
Short-term	−0.12	−0.07	−0.17	−0.06
Long-term		−0.23		−0.20
Income elasticities				
Short-term	1.32	0.39	0.51	0.22
Long-term		1.26	1.32	1.07

Sources: Prices: Barkai (1984), table 3, column (1); energy consumption: table 13-1, column (1); product: Bank of Israel, *Annual Report*, various years 1960–1980.

Note: $E_t(1) = A \times y_t^{\alpha} \times \pi_t^{\beta}$ $\quad$ $E_t(3) = A \times y_t^{\alpha} \times y_{t-1}^{\alpha_1} \times \pi_{t-1}^{\beta}$

$E_t(2) = A \times y_t^{\alpha} \times \pi_t^{\beta} \times E_{t-1}^{\gamma}$ $\quad$ $E_t(4) = A \times y_t^{\alpha} \times \pi_{t-1}^{\beta} \times E_{t-1}^{\gamma}$

Small numerals are standard deviations.

a. Proxies for variables in demand-function estimates are: energy: per capita oil consumption; income: per capita income; prices: aggregate energy (relative) price index (table 13-1, column 6).

long-term elasticity coefficients. The annual crude consumption, price, and income data cover the period 1960–1980.[2] The coefficients in Table 13-3 show that the long-term income elasticity of demand for energy was greater than unity. Price elasticities are very low indeed in the short run, and in the long run range between 0.2 and 0.23. Estimates of demand functions for specific energy products and for electricity (not presented here), which reflect *actual* behavior in energy-product markets, yield similar values for income and price elasticities, supporting the findings on demand for *energy* as an aggregate.

A 60 percent increase in per capita income in the 1960s, with an income elasticity of about 1.3, implies an increase of more than 80 percent in per capita demand for energy; a 34 percent drop in relative energy prices, with a price elasticity of −0.2, would raise per capita energy consumption by about 7 percent. Combined income and price effects could therefore explain a rise of about 85–90 percent in per capita energy consumption in this decade. Because it actually rose by about 120 percent (Table 13-2), these factors explain 75 percent of this increase and (presumably) of the corresponding rise in GNP energy intensity as well. The balance can probably be attributed to energy-enhancing changes in the industrial structure and in consumption patterns such as the rapid penetration of consumer durables into Israeli households.

Similarly, price developments and income patterns in the 1970s explain the small (18 percent) rise in per capita energy consumption and the downswing in the input intensity of energy. The comparatively small increase in per capita income (about 24 percent) over the decade, and the 1.3–1.4 income elasticity coefficients, would have been expected to generate a 35 percent increase in per capita energy consumption. But consumer prices, which rose by about 200 percent over the decade, and the −0.2 estimate for price elasticity suggest a 40 percent reduction in per capita energy consumption, which is more than the income-induced rise in consumption. The actual increase in per capita energy consumption was positive, though quite small (Table 13-2). This finding suggests that other factors, exogenous in the models' specifications (such as the major expansion of the petrochemical industry at the very same period in which the price of its feedstock was skyrocketing), might have pushed primary energy demand upward.[3]

A long-run price elasticity estimate might also overstate a *reversal* in the direction of the price effect. Among other things, the high equipment intensity of energy use suggests a weaker response to a rise than to a fall in energy prices. That this may indeed have been the case is indicated by the lower price elasticity coefficient in Table 13-3, where the price variable is specified with a one-period lag and yields a price elasticity of around −0.10. If this coefficient is used for calculating the total (negative) price and (positive) income response, the result is quite close to the actual change found in per capita consumption (Table 13-2).

Israel's Position in an International Energy-Consumption Array

This reading of the events depends on the validity and relevance of the elasticity estimates derived from the models. One way to check on them is to compare them with similar estimates of other countries, taking into account Israel's position in the array of per capita income, and in the array of per capita consumption and energy input intensity.

Table 13-2 shows that since 1960 Israel has been located at the lower end of the array of industrialized countries in terms of both per capita energy consumption and GNP input intensity. The large differences between the input intensity of energy and the per capita energy consumption of the United States and the European countries suggest that income differences might be an important—though not exclusive—factor. The much lower real energy prices in the United States, which for many oil distillates were less than half the corresponding European prices, undoubtedly contributed to the comparatively high level of U.S. energy consumption. These data and direct estimates of income elasticities suggest that the income elasticities of several European countries were as high as 1.15 (Germany) and 1.25 (Italy)—and even the lower-income countries had income elasticities that were greater than unity—while the U.S. coefficient was somewhat less than unity. In view of Israel's significantly lower per capita income levels, the estimated 1.15–1.30 elasticity coefficients are fully consistent with the income elasticities derived for the industrialized EEC and U.S. economies.

The findings derived from the Israeli data, which suggest low price elasticities of demand for energy in the aggregate, are also consistent with the estimates for the industrialized countries. Nordhaus (1977) suggested a short-term price elasticity of about −0.3 and a long-term elasticity of −0.7 for the United States; for the seven industrialized countries, he put the long-run elasticity at −0.66.[4] Israel's position in the array of per capita income is thus fully in line with Nordhaus's findings on differences in elasticity coefficients between higher- and lower-income countries, and countries in which consumer energy prices are higher or lower. The findings here, which imply that Israel's long-term income elasticity of demand for energy was and is substantially higher than unity, and that the long-term price elasticity is about −0.3, are accordingly a reasonable approximation of reality.[5] This result suggests that these characteristics of demand for energy are an inherent element in Israel's economic structure for, say, the decade to come.

Macroeconomic Significance and Current-Account Burden

With energy consumption less than 1 percent of GNP and imports at about 2 percent of the import bill, Israel's energy sector was of minor macroeconomic significance through the end of the 1960s. As in other oil-importing countries, the first oil price explosion jolted both the ratios of primary energy consumption to GNP and of primary energy imports to total imports. The first rise to 4.3 percent of GNP and to an oil bill of close to 8 percent of total imports occurred in 1974 and 1975. The second price coup beginning in 1978 pushed the same ratios to an all-time high of 11 and 14 percent respectively, and it became obvious that energy would henceforth play a major macroeconomic role, both in its impact on the balance of payments and on tax revenues, and in its effect on prices.

The first OPEC price hike dealt Israel's balance of payments a heavy blow. The annual cost of crude oil imports, which had been less than $100 million in 1972, was close to $600 million in 1974 (Table 13-1). Reducing the inflow of crude was out of the question: it would have severely muzzled economic activity. Despite the fact that almost half of Israel's primary energy intake was used for electricity generation, its power stations in the 1970s had no dual-firing capability, so that the option of a partial switch of the primary energy intake to coal was not a viable proposition in the 1970s. (The first dual-firing capability came into operation in 1982). Substitution of alternative fuels for gasoline is, of course, even less feasible than using coal for electricity generation. Consequently, a reduction in the growth rate of primary energy consumption and, correspondingly, in oil imports was the only response that could be expected to the price shocks. Oil prices, which rose by a factor of about 2.6 between the last quarter of 1978 and the end of 1980, together with a moderate (10 percent) growth in crude consumption in the three years ending in 1981, brought the current-dollar value of the oil import bill to $2 billion. This increase coincided with the return of Sinai to Egypt, which also involved turning over the new oil fields developed by Israel. By that time these were supplying 25 percent of Israel's oil consumption, so that about $500 million or 40 percent of the annual *increase* in the cost of primary energy between 1978 and 1981 was due to the relinquishment of the Sinai oil fields. Thus, between 30 and 40 percent of the deterioration in Israel's balance-of-payments position—and the increase from $1.2 million (1972) to $4.5 million (1981) in the import surplus—may be attributed to the mainly exogenously determined impact of the energy sector.

Welfare Effects of the Deteriorating Energy Terms of Trade

Changes in the energy terms of trade have obvious welfare implications. Yet as long as the energy sector is small, these are not likely to have much immediate macroeconomic significance or a meaningful welfare effect. Thus the decline in the price of oil between 1960 and 1970 reduced the real annual cost of Israel's total primary energy consumption in 1970 by about 0.25 percent of GNP. In other words, if in 1970 Israel had paid the 1960 (real) price of oil for the quantity it consumed in 1970, it would have paid, in terms of its export flow, approximately 0.25 percent more of its 1970 GNP than it actually paid.[6] By 1972, the reversal of the price trend wiped out this cumulative decade-long gain. A comparison of the 1974 energy terms of trade by a similar calculation shows that the annual welfare cost of the first OPEC price hike was 3.12 percent of GNP. The impact of this shock (whose estimate gives the lower boundary of the loss) was particularly severe because of its abruptness. Reference to Israel's growth rate yields a full appreciation of its significance: this turnaround of prices imposed an additional *annual* cost for primary energy higher than the average annual growth of GNP for 1973–1983.

The middle years of that decade (1975–1978) saw a slight improvement in the energy terms of trade. But this partial recovery of the welfare loss was canceled altogether by the first stage of the second oil price explosion in 1979. By the end of 1980 the welfare cost due to higher prices climbed to almost 4.5 percent of GNP based on the corresponding 1978 figures. By then it exceeded 7 percent of GNP if the basis for comparison is 1972 prices, and almost 7.5 percent on the basis of 1970 prices. The 1981–82 price reversal mitigated the welfare loss but did not push it below about 5 percent of GNP on the basis of 1972.[7]

The larger welfare loss following the second oil price shock, although the price hike itself was substantially smaller than in 1973–74, reflected the fact that the *total* cost of energy was by now a dominant fraction of the import bill, and a major input. As a result, changes in policies—particularly price policies—have become of substantial macroeconomic significance.

Domestic Energy Prices and Inflation

The obvious candidates for bearing the added burden of deteriorating energy terms of trade are the direct consumers of oil distillates and electricity—households and businesses. Long-term resource allocation considerations suggest that the changes in real energy costs required a reduction of energy intensity in production, and that these changes would in turn generate corresponding changes in the pattern of comparative advantage of industrial branches. Households, too, should have been induced to save energy. Thus, raising the domestic price of energy products in line with the rise in the real cost of crude to the economy would have been the most obvious way to start controlling its economic effects.[8]

Prices were indeed raised, but the increased costs were not passed on in full. Israel adhered to the pattern set in the 1970s in other industrial countries, many of which used tax and regulatory devices to dampen the impact of rising (marginal) energy cost on domestic prices. This strategy is apparent from a comparison of the two relevant price series—the relative price of an "energy basket" in terms of the GNP basket "paid" by Israeli consumers, and the inverse of the energy terms of trade (the cost of oil in terms of Israel's export basket) presented in Table 13-1. Although both series moved in the same direction in the 1960s and 1970s, their rates of decline in the 1960s and increase in the 1970s differed considerably, reflecting the screen between world oil prices and the energy prices paid by Israeli consumers. This price screen was set up, maintained, and from time to time adjusted by government fiat.

The effective (though not necessarily articulated) energy price policies pursued in the 1960s thus entailed a substantial reduction in domestic energy prices, almost 2.5 times more than the reduction in the economy's unit cost of primary energy. In the 1970s, domestic energy price policy could not but follow the trail of the rising unit cost of primary energy, but even the 330 percent increase in (relative) domestic energy prices between 1970 and 1983 amounted to roughly 40 percent of the rise in costs.

The wide gap between the rise in the index of domestic energy prices and the real cost of primary energy also reflects an attempt to restructure the peculiar relative-price/relative-cost pattern of fuels and electricity that evolved in the 1950s and 1960s. The government tried to bring relative consumer prices closer to the relative refinery-gate cost of fuels and, of course, to the real cost of electricity by changing the mix of taxes and subsidies. Yet simultaneously it used its control over energy prices as a device to contain inflation, which inevitably reduced government revenues.

A closer study of the association of energy prices and the price level suggests that the popular (and populist) notion that the trend of the former largely dictates the trend of the price level is erroneous. Neither the turning point of 1970, when a minor annual inflation rate of about 2 percent rose toward a double-digit rate within one year, nor the several further steps, by which inflation accelerated to the triple-digit (annual) rate toward the end of the decade and beyond, are explicable in terms of energy prices. Causation, whatever its strength, runs the other way, from the price level to energy prices. The attempt to contain inflation by manipulating energy prices proved largely ineffective in the long run. Dampening efforts, whatever their force, proved temporary at best, and over the decade they had to be abandoned time and again, generating a stop-go energy price cycle, all at a heavy cost to the exchequer.[9]

Taxes, Subsidies, and Fiscal Absorption

The tax/subsidy policy, reflected through the 1960s in the substantial differences between relative refinery-gate costs of distillates and their relative prices, was guided mainly by revenue considerations. Their importance stems from the significant contribution of the energy sector to tax revenues in this period. Net energy taxation accounted for 6 percent of total tax revenues in 1962, and though lower at the end of the decade (4.7 percent), it was still higher than in any year throughout the 1970s and 1980s. It was also by far the highest single tax-yielding "product" whose cost of collection was negligible.

Net fiscal absorption from the energy sector was, accordingly, 1.5 percent of GNP in 1962 and at the end of the decade, and reached an all-time high of 2 percent in 1975 when the tax base, due to the OPEC price explosion, was much wider than in the 1960s. Given that the ratio of the value of primary energy consumption to GNP in the 1960s was about 1 percent, the *average* tax rate per unit of primary energy (oil) consumed was close to 150 percent, while the corresponding 1975 rate was only 50 percent.

Average tax ratios can offer some insight into the tax burden and the importance of the energy sector as a source of revenue. A better understanding of the significance of the tax burden and its time pattern involves a discussion of specific tax rates. Throughout the 1950s and 1960s, only gasoline was taxed; middle and heavier distillates were differentially subsidized. Thus about 85 percent of the gross tax was net government revenue—the fiscal *absorption* figures above reflect the net revenue figures. Gasoline, however, accounted for only about 10 percent of the crude consumed in the country; thus over time the gasoline tax rate was at a (varying) level of several hundred percent. At the same time, middle distillates were sold below cost at varying rates of subsidy, while fuel oil used to generate electricity was the most highly subsidized product—the Israel Electric Company paid only about 60 percent of its refinery-gate cost.[10]

This structure of energy tax rates and relative energy prices began to crumble in the early 1970s, and the OPEC price explosion eventually brought about its effective demise by the early 1980s. The allocative distortions created by the exorbitant tax rates on gasoline and heavy subsidies to other fuels became common knowledge. By the late 1960s, when the price of gasoline relative to other fuels reached an all-time high, it spurred the conversion of virtually the entire taxi fleet and even small trucks to diesel fuel. What might finally have forced the authorities' hand was the rapid increase in private car ownership and the natural resentment of this rapidly growing constituency to the high tax rates on gasoline.

The significantly lower gasoline tax rates initiated in the early 1970s did not, however, entail lower fiscal absorption through the decade. The reduction of subsidies on heavier fuels partly compensated for this loss of revenue. But it was the rapidly growing effective tax base, due to substantially higher refinery-gate costs, that helped maintain the policy of using energy taxation as a substantive source of government revenue. The level of net fiscal absorption from the energy sector peaked at 2 percent of GNP in 1975.

The attempt to maintain this level of fiscal absorption was abandoned in 1977 with the change in government and the steadily increasing rate of inflation, which by the end of that year exceeded 50 percent. The (unsuccessful) attempt to combat runaway inflation by means of government-controlled price ceilings on commodities reduced energy tax revenues. From 1977 on, fuel and electricity prices were adjusted at infrequent intervals, while the shekel cost of the primary input—crude oil—rose steeply in the wake of continuous devaluation. This time lag proved costly in terms of fiscal absorption. By 1979 the energy sector—which had always been a source of net government revenue, and in 1975 and 1976 provided 3–4 percent of net taxes—drew a subsidy of more than 1 percent of net tax revenues. In GNP terms, the energy sector changed from a net absorption of 2 percent of GNP in 1975 to a *negative* absorption level of about 0.6 percent in 1979. By 1981, the delays in the adjustment of fuel prices led to an effective subsidy from general revenues to the energy sector of close to 4 percent of net taxes (a net negative absorption of 1.7 percent of GNP). Thus, within five years the net expansionary effect of the energy sector on disposable income changed by about *4 percent of GNP.*[11]

The obverse image of this boost to disposable income is the deficit in the government's (domestic) budget, which has been at least 10 percent of GNP since 1975 (17 percent in 1981). Thus, if the 1976 levels of absorption from the energy sector had been maintained to the end of the decade, the government's real domestic deficit would have been about 25 to 35 percent lower, with a corresponding significant (lagged) impact on aggregate demand and inflation. As mentioned earlier, the attempt to combat inflation by focusing on cost-push effects of energy prices proved futile, and in the longer run was indeed counterproductive. It had little effect on the price level through 1978, and even less thereafter, but by generating substantial budget deficits it increased the impact of demand effects on the dynamics of the inflationary process.

Supply-Side Considerations

In terms of demand factors, the government seems never to have conceived, and has certainly never articulated, an overall energy policy. Supply considerations, however, have always received attention. The cost advantage of oil over coal for electricity generation in Palestine was significant even in the 1920s and 1930s and continued so after World War II, since Israel has no coal deposits. The possibility of using nuclear energy to generate electricity was intensively studied—and rejected—in the early 1960s. Israel's demand for electricity was simply too small for cost-effective use of nuclear energy, even at the relatively low capacities of such generating plants at that time. As a result, generating plants put into operation in the 1960s and 1970s were entirely oil-fired; dual-fired capacity was planned for only after the OPEC price coup and came on line in 1981.

Ensuring a continuous flow of crude and maintaining a sizable strategic reserve have been core objectives of government supply policy since Israel's inception.

Because the proximity of Persian Gulf crude made it cheapest for Israel, Iran was Israel's main supplier from 1949 through 1978. Political considerations (no doubt supported by profit considerations) led to the construction of a pipeline from Eilat to Ashkelon in the late 1950s. Immediately after the Six Day War it was enlarged to a fifty-inch line, used mainly to pipe Iranian oil to Mediterranean markets. The throughput of this line, 0.65 million barrels per day (with 1 million bpd planned for at a later stage), was to serve as a ("costless") strategic reserve of oil. The pipeline started operating in the early 1970s and was used through 1978.[12] It also carried crude from the Sinai oil fields, whose minuscule output in 1967 was increased by a factor of approximately 20 in the 1970s. By 1980 these wells (including wells in new fields) supplied 25 percent of Israel's oil. A politically significant agreement on the supply of oil was an integral element of the 1978 peace treaty with Egypt and carries obvious cost advantages for both countries. The weakness of oil markets improved Israel's—and all other oil-consuming countries'—stance in this ongoing economic relationship, which was initially strongly affected by political considerations.

The dominance of political factors made direct government involvement in decisions on sources of oil supply inevitable. Actual implementation of purchases was, and is, carried out by three companies that were given franchises and specified shares of the market for the distribution of oil products. These firms buy crude, refine it, and sell it at their own expense, but all these operations require government approval, and accordingly involve official cartel arrangements and the setting of product prices by a regulatory authority.

Electricity is generated and distributed by a government monopoly, the Israel Electricity Corporation. Not only does the top management consist of government appointees, but electricity prices are set by government fiat (subject to parliamentary approval), and in view of the sizable investment required to generate electricity, the government—represented by the Ministry of Energy and the Treasury—is also involved in decisions on building up capacity.[13]

The foreign policy considerations inevitably entailed in the reliable supply of primary energy do indeed require substantial government involvement, especially given Israel's unique vulnerability to disruptions in supply. But the need to maintain a large strategic reserve of crude and the politics of world oil supply do not require the present cartel arrangements for the distribution of energy product. Nor do they necessitate government involvement in the purchase of crude and the "approval" of refinery production costs, based on an outdated Persian Gulf formula devised in the 1960s. Western European markets, which are an alternative source for distillates, offer a relevant price benchmark to refinery-gate pricing decisions, hence to greater efficiency in oil purchasing and refining operations and lower fuel prices for electricity generation.

14

External Shocks and Domestic Response: Macroeconomic Performance, 1965 – 1982

Michael Bruno

In retrospect, the period beginning in the mid-1950s and ending in 1973 may be considered the golden age of Israel's economic development. Except for a brief slump in 1966 – 1967, these years were characterized by very rapid growth: in 1960 – 1972 real GDP grew at 10 percent annually (13 percent in 1968 – 1972), capital stock at 9 percent, labor input at 4 percent (7 percent in 1968 – 1972), and total factor productivity at 4 percent (6 percent in 1968 – 1972).

This period was also marked by relatively harmless changes in the price level, with inflation running at an annual rate of 6 – 7 percent and with workable institutional solutions to its potential distortive effects (wage and savings indexation). Even the balance of payments did not seem to pose an insurmountable problem. By 1972 exports financed about two-thirds of imports (compared with one-seventh in 1950, and one-half in 1960), with the remaining third easily covered by abundant foreign capital in the form of unilateral transfers and well-phased long-term loans. These were accompanied by a renewed surge of immigration during the post-1967 euphoria, and combined with a very flexible labor market (once the Israeli labor market was opened to Arab workers from the Gaza Strip and the West Bank in 1968) that permitted the continued rapid expansion of industry, directed particularly toward export markets.

The only signs of impending trouble were internal and social. An Israeli version of a Black Panther movement, formed toward the end of the war of attrition on the Suez Canal, drew increasing attention to hitherto neglected domestic problems. In the three to four years preceding the 1973 war Israel allocated an ever-increasing share of its domestic resources to the expansion of social services (education, health, and welfare) and developed one of the most advanced income-maintenance schemes in the world — while defense expenditures were rising. Little or no thought was given to the possibility of a major crisis that would turn internal political commitments into a heavy economic liability.

The 1973 war marked a watershed in almost all spheres of Israeli life, and certainly in economics. The broad aggregates for the period after 1973 seem to reflect an entirely different economy. Growth came to a virtual standstill; in almost no year did GDP grow by more than 4–5 percent, and usually by much less; inflation soared 30–40 percent annually in 1974–1977 and reached triple digits by 1980. The current-account deficit in current dollar prices quadrupled in 1972–1975, and although it fell sharply by 1977 it grew again in 1978–79, and again in 1981–1983. The foreign debt continued to grow—albeit at a slower rate, commensurate with the much reduced GDP growth. While the system for a time adapted to the phenomenal rates of inflation with relative ease, the ensuing economic and social frictions worsened considerably.

This chapter puts some of these developments in their proper perspective, especially in relation to the crisis affecting the entire industrial world. After describing the typical response of industrial countries to supply shocks, it examines developments in Israel in relation to this worldwide pattern. Such a perspective also helps avoid the pitfalls of placing all the blame either on external causes or on domestic blunders.

The first section provides an overview of the main developments in growth, balance of payments, and inflation in the context of worldwide stagflation. The second section establishes a theoretical framework in which the roles of supply and demand shifts are analyzed. The next three sections offer an empirical analysis of output, employment, and relative price changes by subperiod and related developments in the current account and in the inflationary process. The final section summarizes Israel's macroeconomic performance.

Israel's Brand of Stagflation: An Overview

The world economy suffered several serious shocks in the period 1965–1982. The first was the collapse of the Bretton Woods system of fixed exchange rates at the end of the 1960s, following the massive outflow of dollars from the United States in the wake of its military involvement in Southeast Asia. This collapse was followed by substantial monetary expansion in most OECD countries at a time of full employment, which generated worldwide inflationary pressures. Both of these trends had weakened by the beginning of 1973.

The second, heavier shock was the commodity price "explosion" at the end of 1973. The most significant factor was the oil crisis, but the combined increase in the prices of most other industrial raw materials also had a substantial, though less permanent, effect. Typically, the inflationary process in most Western countries started with a wave of price increases that crested in 1974 and 1975 (OPEC I) and then receded; by 1978 the inflation rate was almost back to its preshock (1970–1973) level just before another price hike (OPEC II, 1979–80). These waves hit all economies more or less simultaneously, but their amplitude and duration differed from one country to another.

The most striking feature of the 1970s was the fall in output and the doubling of unemployment that accompanied accelerated inflation in most countries, more or less at the same time. High unemployment rates persisted throughout the 1970s despite a modest remission in 1976–1978. The second oil shock and consequent contraction in economic activity in the industrial world brought about a further increase in unemployment. This time, unlike the OPEC I pattern, real interest rates in world capital markets rose substantially and remained high into the renewed upswing of economic activity in 1983.

The difference between these shocks and the familiar business-cycle fluctuations of the previous two decades lies mainly in their effect on the supply and real cost of productive factors: a real wage push at the end of the 1960s, steep increases in energy and raw-material prices in the 1970s (in face of rigid real wages), and sharp fluctuations in the real cost of capital. The typical response to an input price shock in a developed industrial economy is a rise in output prices and a fall in profitability, output, and employment. The slowdown in economic activity is further exacerbated by demand contraction, which may result from a combination of a direct terms-of-trade effect on real income, anti-inflationary (plus current-account motivated) internal contractionary macroeconomic policies, and intercountry repercussions of analogous developments among trading partners. Both the profit squeeze and stronger fluctuations in output reduce the demand for investment and thus also hamper the development of productive capacity.

While output, employment, and productivity in the industrial countries slowed sharply after 1973, many middle-income industrializing countries (MICs) continued to grow quite rapidly, enjoying a "free ride" on the recycled OPEC surpluses. They could finance their rising investments and corresponding government and external-account deficits by borrowing on the newly emerged private capital markets at low or negative real interest rates, while their domestic labor markets remained flexible, at least for a while. The cost of faster growth was deeper indebtedness and increased acceleration in inflation rates. But by the time the second oil shock set in (1979), conditions in these countries, too, had worsened substantially. Rising real interest rates on world capital markets and the growing real cost of domestic labor (and falling oil prices for some of the exporters) precipitated a series of financial crises in 1981–82.

Table 14-1 summarizes the main macroeconomic developments before and after 1973 for Israel, a group of nineteen OECD countries, and ten MICS.[1] The following initial impressions emerge:

1. Whereas in the 1960s and early 1970s Israel enjoyed much faster GDP and labor productivity growth than other MICs, its growth decelerated sharply to only slightly above the slow OECD rate of the more recent period. There is some

TABLE 14-1. Annual average rate of change, selected variables, Israel and major country groups: 1960–1973 and 1973–1980 (percentages)[a]

	Israel		19 OECD countries		10 MICs	
	1960–1973	1973–1980	1960–1973	1973–1980	1960–1973	1973–1980
1. Gross domestic product[b]	9.2	3.3	4.7	2.6	6.7	6.0
	5.7	2.5	1.8	2.2	4.9	3.8
2. Employment[b]	3.7	1.1	1.2	0.7	4.0	2.9
3. GDP per employed person	5.5	2.2	3.6	2.0	2.7	3.0
4. Gross investment	11.0	–2.9	6.4	0.4	8.9	6.6
5. Pubic consumption	15.1	–0.1[c]	4.8	2.3	9.9	6.6
6. Import/export prices	–0.5	0.8	–0.5	1.5	–0.5	–0.5
7. Consumer prices	7.4	57.8	4.7	10.8	6.3	18.5
	4.9	33.2	1.8	2.9	3.8	9.0
8. Ratio of current-account deficit to GDP[d]	18.5	19.7	1.5	0.9	3.9	8.0
	4.2	4.8	1.5	2.0	4.6	4.6
9. Unemployment at end of period	2.6	4.8	3.6	6.2[e]	—	—

Sources: Lines 1, 4–6, and 8: OECD, *National Income Accounts*; IBRD, *World Tables* (for MICs and Israel); line 2: ILO, *International Labor Statistics*; line 7: IMF, *International Financial Statistics*.

a. Small numerals are mean standard deviations.

b. Israel's data refer to the business sector; see Metzer (1983).

c. The corresponding figure for 1972–1980 is 5.5 percent (in the war year 1973 public consumption grew 4.5 percent).

d. Figures give percentage ratios in constant 1975 prices.

e. Unemployment at the end of 1982 was 8.8 percent.

indication (lines 2 and 3) that this slowdown may be closely linked to a sharp contraction in final demand.

2. Israel's inflation rate was only slightly above the MIC average in the first period, but rose to more than three times the MIC average (and to more than five times the OECD average) in the second period.

3. The real current-account deficit relative to GDP was on average minimal and hardly grew in the OECD countries while growing substantially in the MICs, reflecting their expansionary borrowing and growth policies in the 1970s. Israel's relative deficit, which was already very high by international standards in the earlier period, grew only slightly. As the fourth section will show, the response of

current-account policy to external shocks has a lot to do with the slowdown in overall economic activity and with the rise in inflation during part of this period.

4. Israel seems to have survived the crises with only a modest rise in unemployment, compared with the OECD average, and despite its sharp growth slowdown. As the third section will show, this apparent departure from the general pattern is misleading. The growth of employment in Israel's *business sector* contracted sharply (Table 14-1, line 2)—very much in line with the typical performance of other industrial countries—and the public sector took up most of the slack.

Figure 14-1 presents the main developments in growth and inflation in a quasi-Phillips-curve framework. Rather than plotting unemployment rates (which mean little in this context), it uses deviations from mean GDP growth in 1964–1981 as the horizontal measure of "capacity" growth; the vertical axis measures the rate of inflation of consumer prices. An argument could be made in favor of applying different capacity growth rates for the periods before and after 1973. However, in the case of Israel this procedure affects mainly the size of output deviations before 1972 without qualitatively changing the overall picture.[2] The procedure used here has the advantage of simplicity and, moreover, requires no prior information on capacity growth.

The OECD figures (dotted line) are here calibrated on the working assumption that Israel's "normal" growth and inflation rates were double the OECD average, so that a similar standard could be applied to the deviations from the average. The resulting visual impression does suggest a number of plausible hypotheses for further study and fits in with the following tentative economic history.

The period 1965–1967 was a very deep Keynesian recession: the implied Phillips curve is very flat, and its slope closely resembles the one implied by the OECD 1965–1969 group of points. Next comes an almost horizontal line from 1967 to 1969—a phenomenal output expansion with virtual price stability; in 1968 alone output in manufacturing grew 25 percent (capital only 3.6 percent), and in 1969 another 15 percent (capital 5.9 percent). The rest of the economy also expanded rapidly. This large jump occurred in a context of unusually high capacity reserves built up earlier and left idle during the recession, and of considerable slack in the labor market. By the beginning of 1967 unemployment had reached 12 percent, thus providing considerable reserve, followed after the Six Day War by renewed immigration and an inflow of Arab labor from the Gaza Strip and the West Bank. These phenomena temporarily made the labor market look like an epitome of Arthur Lewis's "economic development with unlimited supplies of labor." By 1969–70 there was almost full employment and although growth continued at a rapid pace, the strain of maintaining very high rates of public expenditure (on defense, on social services and income maintenance) was beginning to tell. The movement from 1969 to 1972 now suggests a very much steeper Phillips curve, though still with the "right" negative slope.

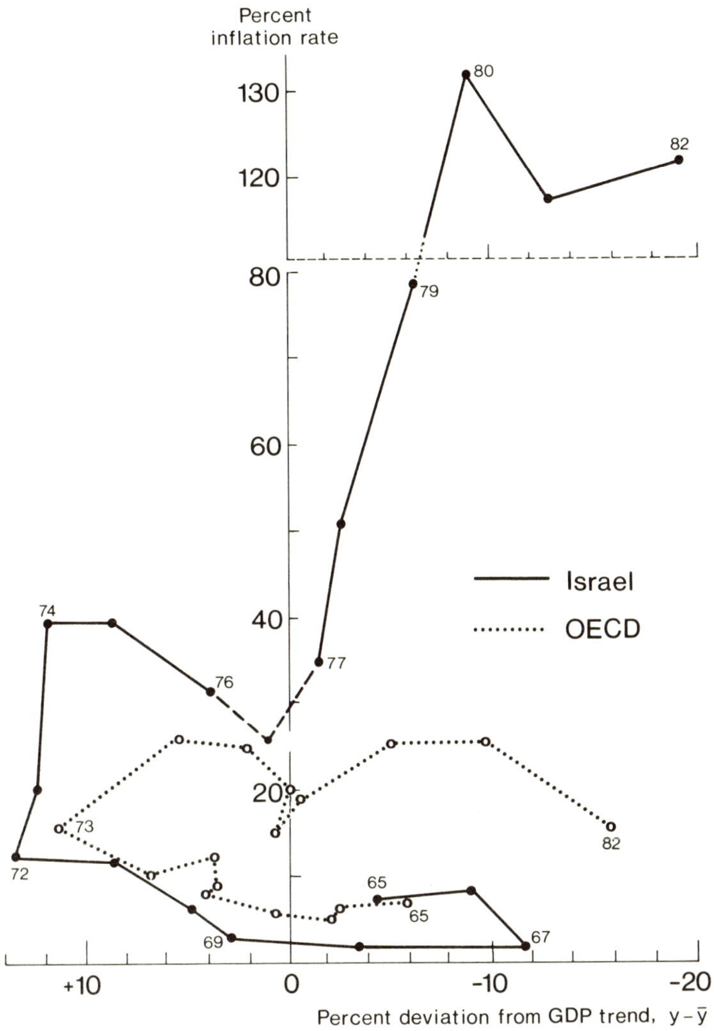

Figure 14-1
Inflation and output slack, Israel and OECD, 1965–1982 (real OECD figures ×2). (Table 14-1.)

The phenomenal growth spurt petered out by 1973. The next period (1973 to mid-1977) looks quite similar to the general bell-shaped curve shown for the OECD countries in Figure 14-1. The upward slope in 1973–74 may be understood in terms of the price shock impact, which in the case of Israel was exacerbated by a large devaluation and indirect tax measures, continued in the form of a crawling peg in 1975–76. The inflation of both periods can be fully accounted for within a conventional wage-price adjustment mechanism (Artstein and Sussman, 1977; Bruno and Sussman, 1979, 1980), discussed further in the fifth section.

The trend in 1975–1977 is associated with the stabilization policy adopted in 1976, which resulted in a real cut in the government deficit and a very stringent monetary policy whose most spectacular effect was on the current account (see below). Whereas the output slack of 1974 (and, in the case of Israel, part of 1975) reflects a shift in the aggregate supply curve, that of 1976–77 reflects primarily shifts in aggregate demand in response to the earlier supply shock. (Figure 14-1 includes a separate point for Israel in January–May 1977, not only because May 1977 marked a shift in political regimes, but because it clearly shows that inflation was then decelerating in a way that appears quite similar to that of the OECD reference curve).[3]

Any analysis of the main macroeconomic tradeoffs in an open economy would be incomplete without an examination of the main simultaneous developments in the external account. Inflation is, after all, a measure of the strain on internal (nontradable) resources. Excess demand in an open economy spills over into the tradable-goods sector and widens the import gap. The effects of the events of 1973–74 on the external accounts thus dominate the macroeconomic responses of a small country like Israel.

A convenient way of observing the developments in relative external dependence is to consider a quasi-Phillips curve diagram in which the vertical axis of Figure 14-1 is replaced by an "external dependence ratio," here measured as the ratio to GDP of either the total or the civilian current-account deficit (the total deficit *minus* defense imports, which are not directly related to economic activity). Interestingly, Figure 14-2 suggests an analogous time-phasing (shown in Table 14-2). The civilian deficit ratio fell sharply during the 1965–1967 recession (from 14.7 to 6.8 percent), then returned to the earlier level (13–14 percent by 1969–1971), illustrating an obvious tradeoff between growth and the current account.[4] This tradeoff was dominated by the key relationship between imports and domestic demand (discussed further in the fourth section). The end of the "euphoric" boom, 1972, is marked by an exceptionally low deficit ratio, largely accounted for by a remarkable export performance. Next came the Yom Kippur War/OPEC I shock,[5] again showing up as a "perverse" upward-sloping stagflationary shift.

Figure 14-2 illuminates the attempt made to move out of the crisis. In 1975–1977 the deficit ratio dropped sharply (from 36 to 22 percent in the total and from 21 to 12 percent in the civilian deficit), clearly at the cost of a sharp deceleration in GDP growth.

The most remarkable feature of Figure 14-1 may be Israel's departure from the OECD pattern after 1977. While the horizontal shifts in deviations from GDP

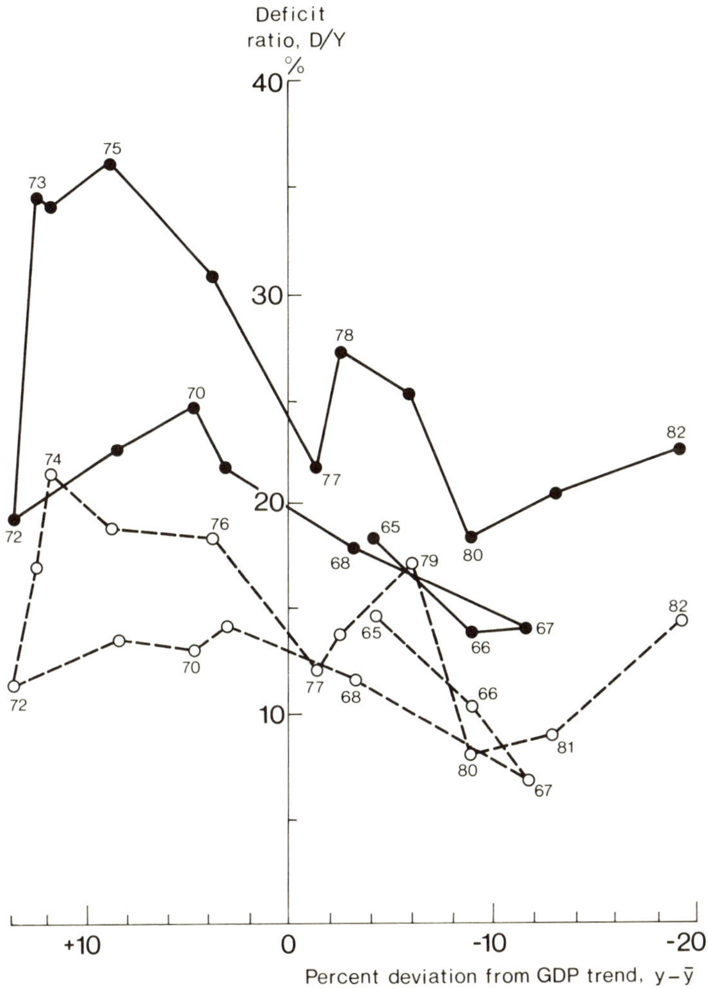

Figure 14-2
External deficit ratio and output slack, Israel, 1965–1982. (Table 14-1.)

trend remain quite similar, the vertical (inflation) coordinate seems to have taken on a life of its own, reflecting an almost complete dichotomy between the nominal and the real economy. The inflation from the end of 1977 onward may be viewed as an expectations-driven monetary "bubble," resulting from a change in the monetary regime. It seems to have relatively little to do either with external worldwide shocks or with real developments in the rest of the economy.

In Figure 14-2, the years after 1977 follow a zigzag path closely related to different policy regimes of three consecutive ministers of Finance: decontrol of

TABLE 14-2. Mean growth rates, 1960–1981 (percentages)

	1960–1965	1965–1967	1967–1972	1972–1975	1975–1977	1977–1981
Business sector						
GDP	9.4	–0.2	13.9	3.5	2.8	3.8
Capital stock	10.6	7.3	7.8	8.6	5.7	4.1
Manhours	4.4	–5.8	7.4	–0.5	–0.1	2.0
Product wage	6.0	11.3	0.9	3.0	7.6	1.5
Real rate of return[a]	14.3	9.6	21.6	19.5	16.3	16.3
National accounts						
Private consumption	9.7	2.1	8.1	5.4	4.0	5.8
Public consumption	9.9	24.6	10.3	19.5	–11.1	3.8
Investment	10.9	–19.3	24.5	1.8	–10.3	–1.7
Exports	12.7	10.4	17.8	4.3	13.6	4.7
Imports	12.0	6.9	15.2	14.1	–3.8	4.2
Import/export prices	–1.2	–1.3	0.0	3.3	–1.3	0.3
Key macro-economic targets						
Ratio of current account deficit to GDP (current prices)[a]	18.3	14.2	19.4	36.2	21.5	22.6
Unemployment rate[a]	3.6	10.4	2.8	3.2	4.1	5.3
Consumer prices	7.2	5.0	7.1	33.0	33.0	94.2

Sources: Business-sector data: based on Metzer (1983); other data: CBS, *Statistical Abstract*, various years.
a. End-of-period levels.

foreign capital flows by Ehrlich (a rise in the civilian deficit ratio from 12 to 17 percent in 1977–1979), the brief austerity regime of Hurwitz (a decline in the ratio to 8 percent in 1981),[6] and Aridor's ill-fated anti-inflation real exchange rate appreciation policy (the civilian deficit ratio rose to 14 percent in 1982, and to 16.5 percent in 1983).

Aggregate Supply and Aggregate Demand in the Short Run: A Theoretical Framework

An analysis of the effects of input price shocks on the economy must incorporate raw materials (n) as a separate factor of production of gross output (q) along with GDP (y), which in turn depends on conventional labor (l) and capital (k) inputs.[7] The determination of output and prices in a system like this can be described in terms of aggregate supply (S) and aggregate demand (D) schedules, as shown in Figure 14-3. For convenience net output is expressed in terms of GDP along the horizontal axis.[8] The vertical axis measures a *relative* price (π)—the price of final goods (p) relative to the domestic price of a competitive basket of goods, $p^* + e$,[9] where p^* represents the world price of final goods and e the exchange rate. π is also the reciprocal of the real exchange rate.

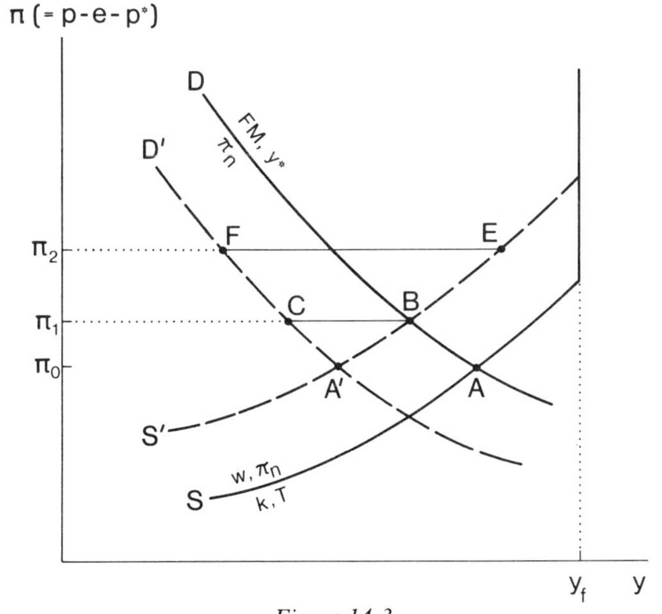

Figure 14-3
Aggregate demand and supply framework.

Two other relative prices play a major role in accounting for aggregate shifts in this system. One is the relative world price of material inputs ($\pi_n = p_n^* - p^*$), where p_n^* is the nominal world price of materials. The other is the real cost of labor in terms of output units or the product wage (w).

The aggregate supply of goods in the short run can be described as an upward-sloping curve, S, which represents the marginal short-term cost schedule. Along a given S the productive capacity (represented here by capital stock, k), the level of technology or total factor productivity (T), and the real cost of the two variable factors of production, materials and labor (π_n and w respectively), are held constant. Below a certain output level, as capacity becomes underutilized, the supply curve may be horizontal while at a certain maximum output level (y_f) S becomes vertical as full employment is reached. Under fairly reasonable assumptions it can be argued that an increase in the real cost of either materials (π_n) or labor (w) will shift the supply curve (S) up and to the left, while an increase in the capital stock (k) or in total factor productivity (T) will in the long run shift S down and to the right (see Figure 14-3).

The curve D marks the aggregate demand schedule for this economy. It can be derived from a conventional Keynesian open economy framework. Other things being equal, the demand for final goods (such as consumer goods or exports) rises with a fall in the relative final goods price (π). In D the relative price of materials (π_n) is again held constant because it may affect demand through real income and wealth, and not only through the supply side. When the real price of materials such as oil rises, a net importer of these goods suffers a real income loss while a net exporter (such as OPEC) benefits. For a country such as Israel a rise in the real cost of material inputs certainly shifts the aggregate demand schedule to the left (this is why π_n is placed on the left side of D in Figure 14-3). A rise in real world income (y^*), which affects export demand, or expansionary domestic fiscal and monetary policy (FM in Figure 14-3), which affects domestic demand for consumption and investment goods, will each shift the D curve up and to the right.

The first impact of rising input prices is a leftward shift of the aggregate supply curve from S to S'—rising real costs of inputs reduce profits and the output that producers will be willing to supply at each given relative price level. Suppose there is sufficient compensatory expansionary policy on the demand side to neutralize the contractionary effect of rising material prices on real income, so that the demand curve (D) stays put. In this hypothetical case, with everything else (including real wages) held constant, rising material prices cause the economy to move from the equilibrium point A to a new equilibrium point, B. There is a fall in output and employment, and a rise in prices—the essence of a stagflationary impact effect. A similar effect of a supply shock would be observed if there were an autonomous real wage push, exceeding productivity growth.

The size of a material price shock depends on the behavior of real wages. If they are downward flexible, mitigating the squeeze on profits, they may impart a compensatory rightward shift to the *S* curve. If wages are rigid (or rise) relative to productivity (T), the leftward shift in S, for a given upward push on material prices, will be more pronounced. The associated profit squeeze hampers investment and thus depresses capital growth (change in k), which may further strengthen the supply shock effect in the medium and long run. Such supply shock stands in marked contrast to a shift in aggregate demand, with the *S* curve held constant. In that case, prices and output would tend to move together (compare, for example, points A' and B).

On the demand side, other things being equal, a rise in raw material prices (π_n) depresses net importers' real income and demand, shifting the D schedule leftward and exerting further downward pressure on output and employment. Contractionary demand management policy (a fall in FM) and the mutual interaction of falling incomes in the export markets of other industrial countries (reducing y^*) cause further contraction of economic activity.

Suppose D shifts to D', with supply represented by S'. A new equilibrium in the commodity market, given in Figure 14-3, will be at point A', output having fallen further and the final goods relative price also falling in this case (a real depreciation) from π_1 to π_0.[10] The price *level* need not fall, however, since this level also depends on the world prices of final goods (p^*) and on the exchange rate (e). If π is downward rigid or there is a temporary real appreciation, production may actually take place at a lower level, C, where there may be a temporary disequilibrium between supply and demand.

A system such as this can be used to analyze the determinants of gross output in a subsector such as manufacturing or to determine GDP in the aggregate business sector. GDP or gross output can be expected to be inversely related to π_n and w, and positively related to all other demand and supply factors (FM, y^*; k, T). A labor-demand schedule can also be derived, depending on whether producers maximize profits on their normal supply schedule or whether production is effectively constrained on the demand side (see the earlier example of point C in Figure 14-3). Real wages will adjust gradually downward when for the whole economy GDP is less than y_f, that is, when there is unemployment in the labor market (see the subsequent discussion of the Phillips curve). Thus over time S' may shift back to the right.

One way of directly linking the commodity (and labor) market framework described to the current account of the balance of payments is to note (as is done in greater detail in the fourth section) that imports are positively linked to GDP (and possibly also to π) and exports are negatively linked to the relative price π and to domestic demand pressure. Thus any leftward movement along the horizontal axis or downward movement along the vertical axis of Figure 14-3 will also signal a reduction in the real external (civilian) deficit, and a movement in the opposite direction a deterioration in the deficit. In fact changes in the commodity market (such as a demand contraction) may be deliberately designed to achieve a current-account objective.

The system could be expanded further if an independent adjustment process were specified for the exchange rate, *e* (as a function of monetary policy, asset markets, and current-account imbalances), and for investment and capital stock (k) (a function of profits, credit policy, housing needs of immigrants, and so on). Although these may be important for a more complete picture of the adjustment process in a typical industrial economy, in the case of Israel these variables can be assumed to be determined outside the system.

The Internal Balance: Output, Employment, and Relative Prices

In its application to real data in this section, the framework outlined above is modified in two ways. First, the analysis of output and relative price determination is confined to the business sector (and occasionally to the manufacturing sector only) and the government sector is considered to be exogenous. Thus the vertical portion of the aggregate supply curve will represent "full employment" in the business sector, that is, after subtracting government employment. Second, since the emphasis is on short-term adjustments relative to trend, rather than on the trends themselves, Figure 14-4 shows deviations of the main variables from

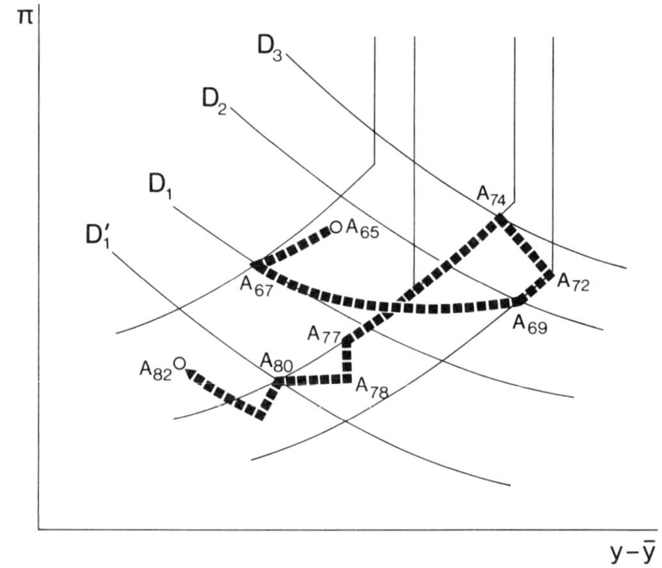

Figure 14-4
Stylized account of supply and demand shifts, 1965–1982.

TABLE 14-3. Annual growth in labor supply to the business sector, employment, and unemployment, 1960–1982 (percentages)

	1960–1965	1965–1967	1967–1973[a]	1973–1975	1975–1977	1977–1982
Sources of labor supply to business sector						
1. Population growth	5.2	1.0	4.1	2.2	3.2	3.3
2. Workers from administered territories	0.0	0.0	1.3	0.1	−0.2	0.3
3. *Less:* Employment in the public sector	−0.9	−0.2	−1.8	−2.6	−1.2	−1.3
4. *Equals:* Growth rate in labor supply (lines 1 *plus* 2 *plus* 3)[b]	4.3	0.8	3.6	−0.3	1.8	2.3
5. Growth in employment business sector	4.3	−3.7	5.4	−0.6	1.2	1.9
Aggregate unemployment rate (percent)						
6. Mean	3.0	9.8	3.9	3.0	3.9	4.3
7. End-of-period	3.8	11.6	2.6	3.2	4.1	5.0
8. Hypothetical[c]	3.7	10.4	4.6	7.5	9.0	11.7

Source: CBS, *Statistical Abstract 1960* through *1983.*

a. The final year 1973 was chosen, rather than 1972 because the definitions of the labor force were changed in that year.

b. Net labor supply to the business sector is defined as total labor force including workers from the territories, *minus* employment of the public sector.

c. Defined as end-of-period aggregate unemployment *plus* excess of public sector over 1969 percentage.

their respective mean trends—6.0–6.2 percent growth for GDP and domestic demand shifts (6.9 percent for foreign demand), 2.1 percent for the growth of labor supply, and 4 percent for the productivity trend in real wages.

Table 14-3 presents the growth in the business sector's labor supply in terms of three main components:

1. Population growth, whose main fluctuations are due to immigration: very high in 1960–1965 and 1967–1973, low during the recession of 1965–1967 and immediately after the 1973 war.

2. The influx of workers from the administered territories after the Six Day War. After 1973 their number remained at about 65,000–75,000, or 5–6 percent of the total labor force.

3. The potential growth of the business sector *minus* the part of the labor force entering the public sector. The share of the public sector in total employment rose from 20 percent at the beginning of the 1960s (it was still only 23 percent in 1967–1973) to over 29 percent at the beginning of the 1980s. The most rapid increase coincided with the exogenous supply shock of the mid-1970s. On average, in the decade 1973–1982 a potential employment growth of 1.5 percent annually in the business-sector labor force was thus diverted to public services. Comparison of lines 7 and 8 of Table 14-3 yields another indication of the importance of this factor, suggesting that if the share of the public sector in total employment had stayed constant at its 1969 level, unemployment would have reached 11.7 percent at the end of the period (1981)—more than the OECD average—rather than the actual level of 5 percent.[11]

Lines 4 and 5 of Table 14-3 summarize the growth of the net supply of labor and the actual growth of business-sector employment. A comparison of these data with the growth of the product wage[12] relative to trend (Table 14-4, line 2) indicates a positive real wage push in the early and mid-1960s, followed by a considerable slack in the labor market. The economy was recovering from an unprecedented 10 percent unemployment during the recession, accompanied by an increase in immigration and an inflow of workers from the territories. Thus, despite the very rapid output growth, full employment was probably reached only in 1973 (the unemployment rate of 2.6 percent was the lowest ever). From then on, employment growth was only slightly lower than that of labor available to the business sector.

Real wages were downward flexible in 1967–1972, 1974–75, and again in 1980. The real wage push of 1975–1979 can be partly accounted for by the increased pressure of public-sector demand for labor, and partly by the accelerated inflation, which in Elkayam's (1982) version of the Phillips curve (see regression 5 in Table 14-6) accounts for this particular increase.[13] Various regressions for nominal or real cost-of-living-deflated wages (Artstein and Sussman, 1977; Elkayam, 1982; Kondor, 1982) all point to the importance of labor-slack variables (overall unemployment as well as the share of workers from the territories) in accounting for aggregate real wage behavior during this period.

In Table 14-4 actual output and relative price data are associated with underlying shifts in supply and demand schedules. Lines 6–8 give output growth rates, relative to trend, for total GDP,[14] business-sector GDP, and gross output in manufacturing; all show more or less the same pattern. Line 9 gives the mean growth rate of the relative consumption to export price ratio, revealing a fall (that is, real depreciation) in the first and last two subperiods and an increase in the two middle periods.[15]

The upper part of Table 14-4 gives the data for various elements of the supply curve (capital stock, product wage, and relative import prices) and two measures

TABLE 14-4. Supply and demand shifts, output, and relative price changes, 1965–1981 (mean percentage growth rates relative to trend)[a]

	1965–1967	1967–1969	1969–1972	1972–1975	1975–1977	1977–1981	Mean trend
Supply shifts							
1. Capital stock	1.2	1.6	2.4	1.4	−1.9	−2.8	6.5
2. Product wage	7.3	−6.5	−0.9	−1.0	3.6	−2.5[b]	4.0
3. Relative import /export price	−1.3	0.1	−0.1	3.3	−1.3	0.3	—
Demand shifts							
4. Domestic (*G* + *I*)	−6.2	16.9	5.9	4.4[c]	−17.3	−4.1	6.1
5. Foreign (y^*)	−0.5	5.3	1.7	−2.1	2.5	−4.2	6.9
Output							
6. Total GDP	−4.4	8.1	4.4	−1.7	−4.8	−2.3	6.0
7. Business sector	−6.4	11.2	5.4	−2.7	−3.4	−2.4	6.2
8. Manufacturing output	−7.9	15.3	3.6	−2.8	−2.3	−3.8	7.0
9. *Relative domestic price* (π)[d]	−0.7	−5.4	0.8	0.7	−7.1	−2.5[e]	—

Sources: Business sector data: Metzer (1983); other data: CBS, *Statistical Abstract*, various years. Foreign demand variable (y^*): Bank of Israel, *Annual Report*, various years.

a. Except for lines 3 and 8, in which figures are not detrended.

b. For the subperiods 1977–1979 and 1979–1981 the shares are +0.5 and −4.5 percent respectively. In 1982–1983 the real wage again rose sharply.

c. If defense and aircraft imports are excluded the number is only 0.9 percent.

d. Measured in terms of domestic consumption over export prices.

e. 1979–1981: +0.6 percent.

of demand shifts: domestic demand (represented by changes in public consumption and investment, which are deemed quasi-exogenous) and world market demand. There are three subperiods with unambiguous supply shifts: negative in 1965–1967 (real wage push), positive in 1967–1969 (large real wage drop), and negative again in 1972–1975 (OPEC I input price shock). In other subperiods the various indicators give conflicting signals and are in any case small. The direction of demand shifts is almost always the same as that of the output shifts, except in 1972–1975, when domestic demand continued to grow for a while (mainly because of defense expenditures). The output contraction in that period is thus dominated by the supply shock.

Figure 14-4 shows the results of this impressionistic analysis most clearly. The 1965–1967 recession came as a reaction to an earlier boom (including a real wage explosion) and was largely a Keynesian demand (mainly investment) contraction. After the Six Day War there was a sharp positive supply shift (S_1 to S_2) in which unprecedented demand expansion (D_1 to D_2) could be sustained at no inflation, with a concommitant real depreciation.[16] In 1969–1972 demand continued to grow, with only slight (or no) additional supply reserves. Full employment was reached only around 1972 (see point A_{72}). Then came a negative supply shock (S_2 to S_2), while domestic demand continued to rise for a while (to D_3). The years 1974–1977 were dominated by a sharp demand squeeze and a series of nominal devaluations targeted at the current account.[17] No unemployment emerged as the public sector continued to grow (see earlier discussion and Table 14-3).[18]

The subsequent years, 1977–1981, are much harder to characterize in terms of the model. Runaway inflation probably affected the real side of the economy (productivity slowdown?) in ways that elude quantification. Detrending the main variables (output, demand, real wages) at the mean rate for 1964–1981 may bias the picture. One year for which a demand contraction can clearly be identified is 1980 (the Hurwitz austerity program). Throughout the rest of the period the fluctuations in Figure 14-4 are dominated by irregular relative price changes. There was a sharp temporary devaluation in 1978 (with Ehrlich's October 1977 turnabout); a real appreciation episode in the second half of 1978, followed by another import price shock and devaluation in 1979–80; an artificial deceleration of inflation during the 1981 election campaign; and a real appreciation episode in 1981–82. Although these fluctuations show up in the numbers for relative prices, it is not clear whether the associated output observations can be cast into the earlier mold of equilibrium supply-and-demand configurations. They seem, in part at least, more like temporary disequilibria (see the analysis in the preceding section).

With demand fluctuations dominating the scene, it is hard to suggest a simple formal econometric model for the aggregate economy that includes independent demand variables not inherently correlated with the GDP fluctuations they are supposed to "explain." A model incorporating the elements above can, however, be applied to a large subsector such as manufacturing. The equations shown in lines 1–3 of Table 14-5 follow the logic of this model by regressing gross output per unit of capital in manufacturing on two relevant real cost variables (real manufacturing wage relative to trend and the relative price of industrial inputs) as well as on the two demand variables shown in Table 14-4.[19] The signs and sizes of the coefficients are quite reasonable (except for the effect of foreign demand, which is relatively small and insignificant). When the last three years (1979–1982) are omitted, the regression results (line 1) improve substantially. This result supports the earlier argument and casts doubt on the relevance of the model to the more turbulent recent period.

Although the same model cannot be used for the aggregate business economy,

TABLE 14-5. Selected regressions for manufacturing

	$\bar{R}^2$	D.W.	Period
Gross output[a]			
1. $\dot{q} - \dot{k} = -0.10 - 0.62w^u - 0.57\pi_{n-1} + 0.29d^u + 0.17x^u$	0.37	2.75	1964–1979
0.09 0.36 0.22 0.15 0.11			
2. $\dot{q} - \dot{k} = -0.04 - 0.34w^u - 0.42\pi_{n-1} + 0.35d^u + 0.08x^u$	0.26	3.02	1964–1982
0.09 0.34 0.21 0.16 0.10			
3[b]. $\dot{q} - \dot{k} = 0.49w - 0.18\pi_{n-1} + 0.39d$	0.66	1.87	1964–1982
0.14 0.36 0.14			
Rate of return and total productivity[c]			
4. $r = 0.13t - 1.50w - 2.81\pi_n + 0.029j$	0.73	1.36	1965–1980
4.65 3.0 2.15 2.49			
5. $q - 0.4k - 0.6h = 0.05t - 1.21\pi_n + 0.019j$	0.99	1.80	1965–1980
14.3 2.64 3.88			

Source: Regressions 4 and 5: Bar-Nathan (1983b).

a. $\dot{q} - \dot{k}$ = rates of change. u = unanticipated change of variables. Small numerals are standard errors.

b. Regression run in log-levels with correction for autocorrelation.

c. Small numerals are t-values. The variable j is a demand-pressure proxy, measured by the intensity of hours worked.

TABLE 14-6. Selected regressions for the business sector

	$\bar{R}^2$	D.W.	Period
GDP[a]			
1. $\dot{y} = \underset{2.08}{2.07} - \underset{0.48}{1.05}(\dot{p}_m - \dot{p}_x) + \underset{0.07}{0.12}\Delta\dot{C}_r + \underset{0.25}{0.64}\dot{y}_{-1}$	0.23	2.17	1964–1981
2. $\Delta\dot{y} = \underset{1.31}{-0.29} - \underset{0.43}{1.37}\Delta(\dot{p}_m - \dot{p}_x) + \underset{0.07}{0.16}\Delta\dot{C}_r$	0.39	2.45	1964–1981
Rate of return (factor price curve)[a]			
3.[b] $\dot{r} = \underset{4.10}{7.09} - \underset{0.30}{1.60}\,\dot{w} + \underset{0.21}{0.92}\Delta\dot{y}$	0.81	1.69	1962–1981
Consumption wage (Phillips curve)[c]			
4.[d] $\dot{w}_c = \underset{6.3}{0.24}(1/u_{-1}) - \underset{2.7}{2.9}\ell_a$	0.34	1.38	1965–1981
5.[e] $\dot{w}_c = \underset{3.4}{0.60}\Delta\dot{p}_{c+1} - \underset{4.62}{0.53}\,\dot{w}_{c-1} + \underset{+\,4.32}{0.003}t$	0.54	1.97	1968:1–1980:1

Sources: Regression 4: Kondor (1982); regression 5: Elkayam (1982)

a. Small numerals are standard errors.

b. Regression corrected for autocorrection ($\rho = 0.63$).

c. Small numerals are *t*-values.

d. Here $\dot{w}_c$ is defined as change in nominal wage *minus* $(0.7\dot{p}_c + 0.3\dot{p}_{c-1})$. ℓ_a denotes the growth in labor from the administered territories.

e. Based on quarterly data. $\Delta\dot{p}_{c+1}$ is the expected acceleration in inflation.

regressions 1 and 2 in Table 14-6 represent a partial attempt, with the change in real credit (a quasi-exogenous variable; see Brezis, Leiderman, and Melnick, 1983) proxying for the pressure of demand and a significant and large coefficient for the terms of trade, probably catching both supply and demand side effects.

The behavior of the product wage and the fluctuations in output growth ($\Delta\dot{y}$ is the acceleration in GDP growth) give a good explanation of the changes in the rate of profit on capital for the business sector. The estimated factor price curve is presented in line 3 of Table 14-6 (note the high R^2 despite first differences). An earlier curve estimated for the manufacturing sector by Bar-Nathan (1983b) is reproduced in line 4 of Table 14-5. Bar-Nathan's basis is a gross output framework (rather than GDP), with wages deflated by the output price. Thus raw material prices appear separately in the regression. Demand fluctuations are proxied by labor intensity (hours per worker). The combination of the factor price and productivity equations (Table 14-5, lines 4 and 5) gives a reasonably good account of profit and productivity changes in manufacturing. Raw materials alone account for 35 percent of the slowdown in total productivity after 1973, the demand proxy accounts for another 24 percent, leaving 41 percent as an unexplained residual in Bar-Nathan's analysis. Recently, Bar-Nathan (1983a) has successfully estimated a similar model for the construction sector in Israel, where demand fluctuations have played a particularly important role.

The preceding analysis has shown that the behavior of output, employment, and the related real cost of raw materials (π_n) and of labor (w) conveniently fits into the framework of short-term supply and demand shifts outlined earlier. The demand shifts, especially in 1975–1977, were closely related to current-account developments, discussed next.

The External Balance on Current Account

The second section of this chapter suggested how developments in the commodity market may be linked with (or even driven by) the size of the current-account balance. Halevi (1983b) provides a detailed analysis of the external account; this section covers only the part that is linked with the domestic response to external shocks in the period 1965–1982.

A relatively simple way of analyzing the behavior of the current account is to consider both imports and exports as functions of a shift variable and of relative prices. With imports for defense and the import component of production for exports subtracted, the remainder is the import component of domestic uses. These imports (n) can be related to the growth of domestic uses (h) and to the relative price of imports ($p_n - p$), with elasticities γ_n and η_n, respectively.[20] Likewise, net exports (x) can be related to the expansion of Israel's external markets (z) and to the relative price of exports and domestic uses ($p_x - p$), with elasticities γ_x

and η_x, respectively. The change in the real civilian deficit (D) can thus be expressed in the following form:[21]

$$\dot{D} = N\gamma_n\dot{h} - X\gamma_x\dot{z} - [N\eta_n(\dot{p}_n - \dot{p}) + X\eta_x(\dot{p}_x - \dot{p})]. \quad (14.1)$$

The change in the real current account is thus broken down into three major components: the shift in imports in response to domestic demand, the shift in exports in response to external demand, and a third term (in square brackets) constituting the competitive factor—the response to changes in relative prices. This last term mainly represents the effective real depreciation or appreciation of the exchange rate.

In applying equation (14.1) to the data I used two alternative sets of coefficients. Set A assumes $\gamma_n = \gamma_x = 1$, $\eta_n = 0.25$, $\eta_x = 1$, and is based on earlier studies of import and export demand (see for example, Weinblatt, 1972, for imports and Halevi, 1972, for exports). Set B is based on a simple regression performed on the relevant data: $\gamma_n = 1.5$, $\gamma_x = 1.14$, $\eta_n = 0$, $\eta_x = 1.41$. In case B, imports are assumed to be price inelastic but with a considerably higher expenditure elasticity (probably unrealistically high—see below), and the export price elasticity comes out higher than in earlier estimates. However, the difference between the two models in the estimated role of the competitive factor is rather small.

Table 14-7 presents the results of this analysis for the two sets of coefficients. Line 1 gives the change in the current account at current prices; line 2 estimates the effect of changes in the external terms of trade, from which the residual, the civilian deficit at constant prices (line 3), is obtained.

The models differ in the extent of overall "explanation" by subperiod (for example, A gives a better fit in 1968–1972, B in 1973–1974), but both seem quite off the mark for 1978–1980. Most of this discrepancy can be traced to a larger-than-expected drop in the deficit in 1980.[22] Both models give very similar estimates of the role of relative competitiveness (lines 6 and 7). Comparison of the two price shock periods reveals that in both 1973–1974 and 1978–1980 the terms of trade cost almost $1 billion. The first period saw a worsening of the real deficit, primarily on account of continued import expansion. This trend was halted in 1975–1977 by the large domestic squeeze described in the previous section. During the second price shock (1979–1980) the large terms-of-trade loss was absorbed with greater ease.

The worst period in terms of macroeconomic performance seems to have been 1981–1982. Despite an improvement in the terms of trade (of about $300 million), the rise in domestic import demand and the substantial real appreciation greatly increased the deficit. The most marked development was the real appreciation of 1981–1982, which cost around $450 million in those years alone (and was further exacerbated in 1983), more than the total gain obtained earlier with real

TABLE 14-7. Components of change in civilian deficit, 1965–1982 ($ million, 1975 prices)

Component of change	1965–1967	1968–1972	1973–1974	1975–1977	1978–1980	1981–1982
1. Change in deficit at current prices	–203	370	1,433	–444	527	1,002
2. International terms of trade	28	–418	781	–108	993	–318
3. Change in deficit at constant 1975 prices	–231	788	652	–336	–466	1,320
Change in relative prices[a]						
4. A	42	–159	94	–204	–194	449
5. B	7	–126	77	–191	–128	441
Estimated import shift						
6. A	51	1,597	555	3	456	797
7. B	76	2,396	833	5	684	1,196
Estimated export shift						
8. A	–187	–691	–292	–377	–318	–205
9. B	–213	–788	–333	–430	–363	–234
10. Total explained A	–94	747	357	–578	–56	1,041
11. Total explained B	–130	1,482	577	–616	193	1,403

a. Mostly the effect of real depreciation or appreciation.

depreciation in 1974 and 1980. This was the price paid for a stabilization policy that did not pay off even in terms of disinflation (see below).

Although an import-export view of the current account seems to fit the short-term movements of the deficit reasonably well, in the long and medium run an alternative or supplementary savings-investment view is perhaps more instructive. Here the increase in net indebtedness is taken as financing net investment, with the difference being made up out of domestic savings. Table 14-8 shows that in both 1962–1967 and 1968–1972 the economy managed to finance, on the margin, 80–90 percent of its total net capital accumulation from domestic savings (line 4). When nonbusiness investment (mainly housing) is subtracted from both numerator and denominator, this ratio drops to 50 percent in the second period (line 4a).

The picture after 1973 is radically different: while annual investment dropped sharply, particularly in the business sector, the foreign debt continued to increase and domestic savings were negative, due to rising government deficits and falling private savings ratios (see Chapter 4). Defense imports fail to explain rising total indebtedness, since these were largely financed by grants. As line 5 of Table 14-8

TABLE 14-8. Annual investment and savings, 1962–1982 ($ million, 1975 prices)

	1962–67	1968–73	1974–77	1978–82	1962–82
1. Net domestic capital formation:					
1a. Total[a]	1,279	2,244	2,750	1,805	1,960
1b. Business sector	628	1,052	1,088	668	846
2. Increase in net foreign debt	125	536	1,433	770	645
3. Net domestic savings:					
3a. Total (1a – 2)	1,154	1,708	1,317	1,035	1,315
3b. Savings for investment in business sector (1b – 2)	503	516	–345	–102	201
4. Share of domestic savings (3a ÷ 1a)	0.90	0.76	0.48	0.57	0.67
4a. Share of business sector (3b ÷ 1b)	0.80	0.49	–0.32	–0.15	0.24
5. Defense imports net of grants	221	595	364	70	319

Sources: National accounts and balance-of-payments data expressed in dollars and deflated by Israel's export price for manufacturers. Line 5: See chapter 8 in this volume.

a. Includes investment in housing and public-sector buildings.

shows, the defense imports that had to be financed from other sources fell between the two periods. The price of a much reduced growth rate while consumption, particularly private consumption, continued to grow almost unabated, shows up most clearly here.

The net domestic savings ratio as a percentage of GNP plus transfers from abroad dropped sharply after 1972–1975, from around 15 percent at the height of the boom to an annual average of 2 percent in 1974–1981.[23] This drop is fairly evenly divided between a reduction in the private savings ratio after 1973 and a rise in the public-sector deficit, which first emerged during the recession. As shown in Chapter 8 of this volume, the public sector's sharply rising gross tax receipts (reaching over 50 percent of GNP in the late 1970s) failed to keep up with the rise in public outlays, mainly on account of transfers and subsidies (which reached 30 percent of GNP in the second half of the 1970s, compared with 12–15 percent in the earlier period).

Even though the foreign debt continued to increase after 1973, it grew much more slowly, though still faster than the growth rate of GDP. Compared with the group of LDCs whose average real debt grew 9 percent annually in 1972–1982, Israel's debt grew only 4.6 percent annually, in contrast to an annual rate of 13.6 percent in the preceding decade.[24] Having started from a very high debt level, Israel avoided the strategy followed by many other semi-industrialized countries. Whether voluntary or otherwise, the cost of the response to the external shocks in terms of growth and investment forgone was very high.

The Tradeoff between the External Balance and Inflation

Figure 14-1 shows the general similarity between the inflation-output tradeoff in Israel and in the industrial countries in 1965–1977 (although the OECD data are doubled in this figure). Also, during the OPEC I shock and its aftermath Israel's inflation was considerably higher than the preshock relative "norm" would suggest. However, the pattern of inflation during that period can be explained by the series of devaluations undertaken between 1974 and 1977 as part of the current-account targeted adjustment policy. In the face of quasi-full employment, growing public-sector outlays, and an already well-indexed economy, such large-scale devaluations (from 4.2 Israeli pounds per dollar before November 1974 to 10.5 Israeli pounds per dollar just before the devaluation of October 1977) were bound to result in an accelerated inflation rate, with only a very partial payoff in real competitiveness. The analysis of the relationship between exchange rate adjustments and the wage-price mechanism has been discussed in considerable detail elsewhere (for example, Bruno and Sussman, 1979, 1980). A much-quoted pair of wage and price equations estimated by Artstein and Sussman (1977) for annual data for 1955–1974 gives:

$$\dot{p} = -0.04 + \underset{(0.11)}{0.67\dot{w}} + \underset{(0.06)}{0.25\dot{p}_n} + \underset{(0.08)}{0.14(\dot{m} - \dot{y})} + \dot{t} \qquad (\bar{R}^2 = 0.94) \tag{14.2}$$

$$\dot{w} = -0.04 + \underset{(0.10)}{0.82\dot{p}} + \underset{(0.10)}{0.47(1/u_{-1})} - \underset{(11.88)}{20.76l_a^2} - \underset{(0.01)}{0.03d} \qquad (\bar{R}^2 = 0.95) \tag{14.3}$$

where p = the (log) consumer price index, w = the *nominal* wage, p_n = import prices, m = the log of narrowly defined money (M_l) (dots, as before, are time changes), t = the log of an indirect tax factor (1 + tax rate), u = unemployment, l_a = the share of workers from the territories, and d = a dummy variable for years of wage freeze.

Combining equations (2) and (3) yields a reduced-form equation:

$$\dot{p} = -0.14 + 70(1/u_{-1}) - 3087 l_a^2 - 0.04d + 0.56\dot{p}_n + 0.31(\dot{m} - \dot{y}) + 2.22\dot{t}. \tag{14.4}$$

The model gave a fairly accurate account of the inflationary process both for the earlier years of relative price stability and for the subsequent acceleration, including an out-of-sample forecast to 1975 and 1976.

The coefficients of equation (14.4) suggest that an increase in the annual rate of devaluation from 6.6 percent in 1967–1972 to 32.5 percent in 1974–1977 could by itself account for a 14.5 percent acceleration in annual inflation rates between the two periods. The drop in unemployment would account for a further acceleration of 3.5 percent. This combination of factors may have been all that was needed to account for the higher rate of inflation in Israel during the period, not counting the acceleration in money growth, on the one hand, and the mitigating effect of a 4 percent wage freeze (in 1974) on the other.[25]

As noted earlier, Figure 14-1 shows a very different pattern of accelerated inflation after 1977. The model above in its original form can indeed be shown to predict much less well for that period. The wage equation, in particular, has to be modified (see, for example, Elkayam, 1982), and the definition of "money" in the price equation would have to be changed. However, there is more to this matter than merely applying a set of updated coefficients. The data indicate an inherently different process associated with the change in the nature of the exchange rate regime (probably starting with the crawling peg in 1975—see Gottlieb and Piterman, 1982) and in particular with the liberalization of foreign-exchange control in 1977. Both this process and the explicit introduction of financial asset formation are discussed in detail in Chapter 17.

The tradeoff between the balance of payments and inflation via devaluations raises two obviously related questions: In what way is this a symmetrical two-way relationship? and has the exchange rate ever successfully served as a stabilizing device? These questions seem particularly relevant to the 1981–1983 real appreciation episode. The experience of both this and earlier periods suggests that the effect of upward and downward adjustments in the exchange rate is not symmetrical (see Bruno and Sussman, 1979, for earlier quarterly evidence on this asymmetry).

Conclusion

This chapter has tried to account for the macroeconomic developments throughout most of the period 1967–1982 within a rather simple macroeconomic supply-and-demand framework. The exogenous shocks of the 1970s came at the end of the unprecedented 1968–1972 boom and were particularly severe in Israel. The contractionary bias of domestic policy was at first dictated by the balance-of-payments squeeze. The results of the 1975–1977 effort were impressive in terms of improving the external balance, less so in terms of inflation, and quite poor in terms of long-term structural change. Public-sector employment continued to grow almost unimpeded, and investments in the tradable-goods sector did not return to their desired long-term level; these two factors prevented another successful shift of resources into manufacturing exports such as occurred in the 1960s and before the 1973 crisis.

Slowing down the growth of the public sector would have meant abandoning or delaying ambitious social programs undertaken at a time when the balance of payments seemed a remote issue. But indirectly this inflexibility must have taken its toll in terms of the subsequent loss of economic growth potential. Unlike some of the semi-industrialized countries mentioned at the beginning of this chapter, Israel could probably not have afforded to increase its foreign debt in the mid-1970s—its debt had already set a world record before this troublesome decade started. Israel thus suffered from the slowdown typical in industrial countries, without the accompanying overt signs of massive unemployment. At the same time, it did not display the internal flexibility of monetary and income policies that characterized small low-unemployment countries such as Austria. Nor could it afford the expansionary stance of countries such as Korea or Singapore.

The failures since 1977 are in some ways much more serious, mainly on account of Israel's rapid inflation. The most marked difference between the post-1977 inflationary "bubble" and the two-digit inflation of 1973–1975 is the loss of monetary control in the later period. Although the earlier period was highly inflationary by international standards, it could at least be argued that inflation was to some extent functional: it was a costly, and probably only partly avoidable, by-product of a conscious attempt to improve the country's competitiveness in the face of a severe foreign-exchange shortage. Nothing of the sort can be said for the period after 1977. By 1977 the foreign-exchange constraint had been alleviated at least temporarily, foreign capital markets were more accessible, inflation was receding, and an effort could have been made at that time to stabilize the economy further, restructure its productive system, and embark on a more rapid growth path even at the cost of some additional long-term borrowing.

In retrospect, 1977 was a crucial crossroads. During the two to three years before the next oil shock, the economy could have corrected its "structural" mistakes (as some other small European economies did; Finland, for example, embarked on a successful medium-term plan at about that time). Instead, the change of government brought only one institutional economic change, which proved disastrous. The opening up of the economy to short-term external capital flows (and the unnecessarily large devaluation that signaled its start) without any accompanying fiscal or liberalization measures, locked the economy into a new inflation-cum-low-growth pattern that seems unbreakable except by another major institutional reform.

15

Indexation in the Labor Market

Ephraim Kleiman

Israel's long-sustained inflation, dating back to before independence, resulted in the evolution of a widespread system of indexation that protected it from some of inflation's worst effects. But by making inflation tolerable, indexation may also have contributed to its perpetuation, if only by preventing the buildup of public pressure for its control. Moreover, indexation, especially of wages, has often been blamed not only for the transmission and perpetuation of inflationary pressures, but even for their creation in the first place.

Unlike some other countries undergoing rapid inflation, Israel has ex-post indexation: it takes the form of agreements made in advance to adjust nominal values retroactively to changes in the price level.[1] In financial markets such a contract usually cannot be renegotiated except by default.[2] In the labor market, however, indexation is only one of several contractual and other mechanisms regulating wages; and because the supply of the service contracted for is continuous, its providers retain real power over its renegotiation. Therefore, the role of indexation in this market cannot be considered in isolation from the operation of other wage-setting mechanisms.

The first and second sections of this chapter describe and analyze the mechanics of Israel's indexation apparatus. The third section discusses the 1975 reform of the system and its results; the fourth analyzes the relationship between indexation and other wage mechanisms. The final section briefly discusses the effects of wage indexation on economic stability.

The COLA System

Under the highly centralized structure of Israel's trade unions, wages are set by three separate mechanisms.[3] (1) Collective bargaining between the Histadrut (the Federation of Labor Unions), on the one hand, and the Israel Manufacturers' Association and the government as an employer, on the other, sets overall wage increases for whole industries, expressed as percentages of the existing tariffs. (2) Negotiations between management and employee committees in individual plants grade individual workers according to different tariff categories; such assignments, together with automatic seniority changes, usually result in further increases in the form of a "wage drift."[4] These two mechanisms determine the wages that would obtain in the absence of inflation. (3) The cost-of-living allowance (COLA) adjusts nominal wages to the rise in the price level. This last mechanism ensures that the real-term contracts arrived at through the first two are not vitiated by inflation.

The formal basis of the COLA is a periodically renewable agreement between the Histadrut and the Israel Manufacturers' Association, specifying the rules under which the COLA is to be calculated. But both the Histadrut-owned enterprises and the government—the two biggest single employers in the country—subscribe to it automatically, and other nonsignatories are made to comply by virtue of regulations issued by the Ministry of Labor. These agreements are contracted for periods of one or two years and continue in force even when not renewed by their expiration date.

Basically, the COLA mechanism periodically adjusts the nominal wage in line with increases in the consumer price index (CPI). In practice, the interval between adjustments has varied with the rate of inflation: from as often as monthly in 1952, when prices rose nearly 70 percent within twelve months, to quarterly adjustments in other periods—semiannually or annually in the mid-1960s, and quarterly again since 1980.[5] COLA payments are subject to a threshold clause (3 percent before 1975 and 5 percent in subsequent years); smaller price increases are accumulated until later adjustment dates.

The CPI, which serves as the basis for COLA calculations, is published monthly by the Central Bureau of Statistics, with a fortnight's lag: each month's index is announced on the fifteenth of the following month (the sixteenth, if the fifteenth falls on a Saturday). The COLA is based on the ratio between the average levels of the CPI in the two periods of equal length following and preceding the date of the last adjustment. Thus, it can be due even if prices in a given period were stable, provided they had been rising in the preceding one.[6]

For a long time no attempt was made to clarify the objectives of the COLA beyond its role in preventing the erosion of real wages by inflation, and it seems to have been regarded as a sort of social welfare measure. Since its inception in 1941, COLA payments have been subject to a ceiling, and until 1975 the latest COLA was also tax exempt (thereby increasing wage earners' net income by more than the inflation rate, depending on their average tax rate).[7] On some occasions, when doubts were raised as to whether the threshold had in fact been reached, or when prices rose rapidly early in the adjustment period, compromise arrangements provided for advance payments to low-income earners.

The weights used in the compilation of the CPI are derived from periodic surveys of the expenditure patterns of urban wage-earning households. They thus represent the consumption bundle of what is essentially a nonexistent "average" household. But in Israel's first two decades the rise in the cost of living tended to be fairly uniform across broad population groups (see Landsberger, 1963; Manzly, 1974). In addition, households in the two lowest income deciles, which are harder hit than others by occasional reductions in food and public transportation subsidies, are often compensated directly, through special grants by the National Insurance Institute.

As a rule, the COLA is calculated with reference to the price rise in all expenditure items (though, since 1975, not on the entire increase) except, in some periods, for imputed expenditures on owner-occupied housing. Because of the prevalence of owner occupation and of "key-money" leaseholds, this item sometimes accounted for more than 18 percent of all consumer expenditures in Israel; and in periods of rapidly rising housing prices it could contribute more than half the total increase in the CPI. Its exclusion in 1964–1975 was justified on the grounds that the cost of use of self-owned assets constitutes part of consumers' true income, as well as of their expenditure.

The broad basis of the CPI, its frequent updating, and its continuous price sampling render the index virtually immune to manipulation through short-lived subsidies to overrepresented items. Such "index juggling," common in the 1950s, has to be distinguished from the deferment of the COLA through subsidies, sometimes resorted to for political or social reasons, that really slow down CPI increases. The government has also been known to reduce real wages, at least tempo-

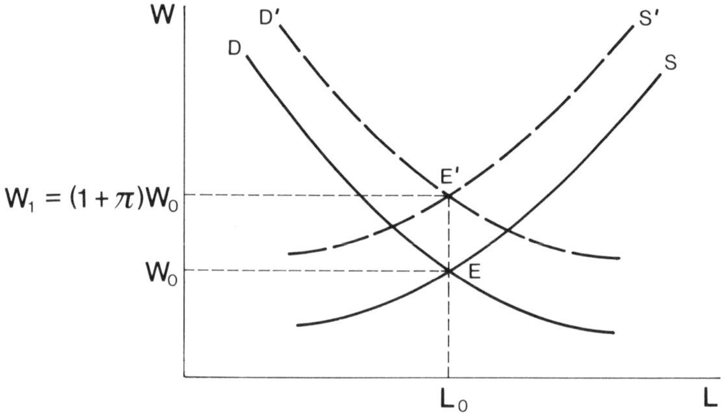

Figure 15-1
The effects of inflation on wages in a competitive market and under wage indexation.

rarily, by timing hikes in taxes or in government-controlled prices so that they fall close to either end of the COLA adjustment interval.

The evolution of the COLA system in the 1950s and 1960s was the result of numerous minor changes, introduced one at a time as various deficiencies of the system came to light. Although these changes were usually technical rather than substantive, they reflected a tug-of-war between the different attitudes of the parties to the COLA agreement, as well as of the government. The latter had a tradition of regarding wage indexation as the main transmitter, or even generator, of inflationary pressures, both on the cost and on the demand side. Similarly, employers often claimed that indexation raised real wages above their noninflationary level, an element of anticipated inflation being already taken into consideration in the wage increases agreed upon through collective bargaining. The Histadrut, on the other hand, regarded the COLA as the only way of protecting wages against erosion by inflation. Both these views seem to ignore the existence of other mechanisms in the labor market, and, as will be seen below, both are wrong.

Labor-Market Effects of Wage Indexation

The first step in evaluating the operation of wage indexation in Israel is to consider its role as a labor-market simulator. Figure 15-1 illustrates this role, with quantities of labor measured on the horizontal axis and the nominal wage on the vertical axis. Both demand for and supply of labor are assumed to be functions of the real wage only, those for some initial price level P_0 being denoted by the solid curves D and S, with an equilibrium nominal wage W_0 and a market-clearing quantity L_0. As the price level rises to $P_1 = (1 + \pi)P_0$, both curves shift upward by π, to D' and S' respectively. As the rise in the output price raises the value of marginal product of labor, at W_0 employers wish to increase their labor inputs beyond L_0, and competition among them continues until the stimulus extinguishes itself as the nominal wage rises to the new equilibrium nominal wage at $W_1 = (1 + \pi)W_0$, the equilibrium quantity remaining unchanged at L_0.

Such an adjustment has costs. Even if each employer ends up with the same amount of labor as before, the bidding process through which the wage rise is effected is accompanied by shifts of labor among employers. Similarly, in an organized collective-bargaining market, the industrial strife brought on by pressures to renegotiate existing wage contracts may be expected to result in a loss of labor inputs. A contractual agreement, made in advance, to raise the nominal wage by the same rate as the price increase will in this case yield the same result as that attained by market forces, but without the loss of inputs accompanying both the competitive process and organized industrial strife.

Figure 15-1 shows the case of a purely monetary inflation in a closed economy in which, by simulating the market mechanism, indexation simultaneously pro-

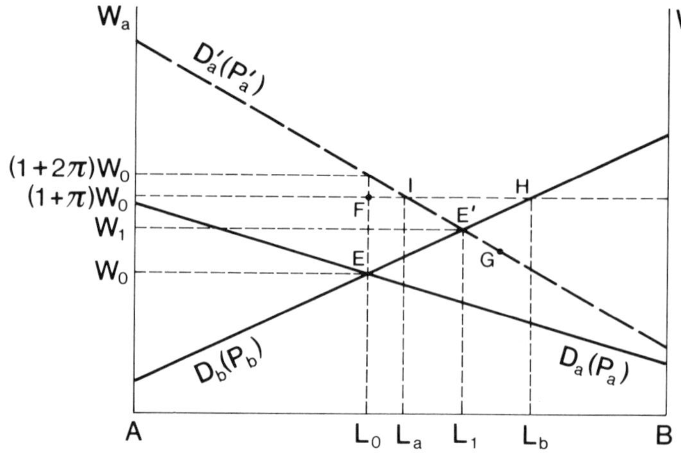

Figure 15-2
The effects of wage indexation with nonuniform price inflation.

tects real wages from erosion by inflation and neutralizes the latter's effect on the distribution of national income between wages and profits. This, however, will no longer be the case if, either because of the existence of foreign markets or because of structural changes accompanying inflation, the price rise is not homogeneous. Figure 15-2 shows the extreme case in which the entire price rise is confined to only one of two sectors. For ease of exposition, we assume labor supply to be given, so that the amount of it employed by one sector can be measured from A rightward, and the amount employed by the other sector from B leftward, along the horizontal axis. The demand schedules for labor in the two sectors, for given price levels of the corresponding outputs, P_a and P_b, are described by the curves D_a and D_b respectively. At their intersection point, E, the nominal wage W_0 equilibrates the allocation of labor between the two sectors at L_0.

Now let P_a rise by a rate of 2π while P_b remains constant, so that, with the two sectors sharing equally in output, the rise in the general price level is still π. The demand curve of sector A is now shifted equiproportionately, to D'_a, with a new equilibrium point at E', representing a reallocation of labor to L_1, in favor of the sector whose prices have risen. As drawn here, however, the corresponding equilibrium nominal wage is only $W_1 < (1 + \pi)W_0$: the change in the relative demand of the two sectors has resulted in an overall decline both in the aggregate demand for labor in the economy and, except for a *pari passu* decline in its supply, in the equilibrium real wage. At the nominal wage obtaining under indexation, $(1 + \pi)W_0$, the increase in the quantity of labor demanded by the expanding sector, $L_a - L_0$, would fall short of the decrease in that demanded by the shrinking one, $L_b - L_0$, resulting in a corresponding increase in unemployment.[8] This will happen whenever the demand elasticity for labor is smaller in the expanding sector than in the contracting one. On the other hand, had sector A's demand been elastic enough for D'_a to intersect D_b to the right of H, the equilibrium real wage would have risen above the level guaranteed by wage indexation.

The results obtained here for the one-sector price rise case hold, with minor modifications, for all nonuniform price increases. In particular, with sector B representing tradables and sector A nontradables, Figure 15-2 describes the effects of domestic inflation under a fixed exchange rate, and with the sectors reversed, those of inflation abroad. A special case is a rise in the prices of noncompeting imports, such as oil. Like all other price rises originating outside the economy's business sector—such as indirect taxes or exchange rate hikes—this will raise the domestic prices of all outputs using them, without increasing the nominal value added in their production. Provided no structural change takes place (as, for example, when import components and demand elasticities are the same in both sectors), both nominal profits and the nominal value of the marginal product of labor will remain constant, thereby decreasing in real terms. But with wages linked to an index of *output* prices, a rise by π in their level will raise the nominal wage to $(1 + \pi)W_0$, resulting in unemployment, represented by the distance between the points I and H. It will also change income distribution in favor of wages, the decrease in real profits exceeding that warranted by the price of imports. Coupled with an attempt by employers to recoup this extra loss, and accommodating fiscal and monetary policies aimed at preventing unemployment, wage indexation will then generate an inflationary spiral.[9]

As was hinted at earlier, if price increases are nonuniform, wage indexation may raise nominal wages by too little just as well as by too much. In the former case, the remaining upward adjustment may be easily attained via either of the two other labor-market mechanisms described earlier. But given the institutional character of collective bargaining, and even of the wage drift, their inherent downward stickiness rules out the possibility of a similar adjustment when indexation overshoots the equilibrium wage level.

Once structural changes occur, indexation can no longer eliminate the transition costs of the adjustment process. In the absence of indexation, these result from employees' leaving previous jobs to search for higher wages among employers competing for their services. But with nominal wages raised simultaneously for all employers, this search will be triggered by labor layoffs in sectors where relative prices have declined. In the former case, the resultant loss of labor inputs represents deliberate abstention from employment and may be expected to spread gradually over time, especially if labor is sector or employer specific. As the unemployment generated under similar circumstances by indexation is involuntary, the social burden of the transition costs might be heavier in the latter case, especially in the presence of labor specificity.

The 1975 COLA Reform

For the greater part of Israel's first two decades, expanding demand for labor, generated by rapid economic growth, practically obviated the danger of indexation's overshooting the equilibrium wage level. With relatively low inflation rates, any excessive indexation hikes accumulated within the span of the biennial collective agreements could be comfortably accommodated within the framework of these agreements and still leave scope for considerable wage increases. At the same time, the annual increments to the labor force were large enough to accommodate most structural changes without requiring much reshuffling of the existing stock. When deteriorating employment conditions in the second half of the 1960s made overshooting a real risk, the Histadrut agreed to forgo the payment of the COLA then due. The preference evinced for such a (presumably transitory) step to a reduction in wage tariffs suggests that, at least in the breach, indexation may have provided a less painful way to achieve occasional downward adjustments in the real wage than the other mechanisms of the labor market.

The growing frequency with which ad hoc changes were introduced in the mid-1960s made clear the necessity of a more systematic reform of the entire mechanism. A report by a committee of experts, appointed by the Histadrut and the Manufacturers' Association, took the view that most of the disputes over the COLA stemmed from the system's inability simultaneously to protect real wages and to neutralize the effects of domestic inflation on income distribution. Emphasizing the latter role, the report recommended that wages be linked to an index of domestic output prices rather than to the CPI, and that the COLA be paid on all labor earnings and be taxable at the wage-earner's average income tax rate. It also stressed the desirability of frequent adjustments and of avoiding ad hoc changes in the mode of calculation (see Committee, 1966). These recommendations were not implemented; changing economic conditions postponed the needed overhauling of the COLA system for nearly a decade.

As can be seen from the first two columns of Table 15-1, Israel's third decade began with rapid growth and negligible inflationary pressures. In 1968–1972 per capita GNP rose by an annual average of 8.4 percent, and no COLA payment was called for from January 1966 to January 1970—by far the longest such period ever experienced. But with the gradual exhaustion of the economic opportunities opened in the aftermath of the Six Day War and of the slack created by the 1965–1967 recession, the annual rate of price rises began to accelerate. In the wake of the Yom Kippur War and the 1973–74 energy crisis, growth nearly ceased, and the economy became firmly set on the inflationary trajectory that it is still traveling today. Coupled with tax-engineering practices designed to minimize tax payments, which resulted in a reduction in the share of COLA-covered "basic wage" in labor earnings, these developments revived the need for a thorough revision of the wage indexation system.

TABLE 15-1. Product, prices, real wages, and COLA wage protection, 1968-1982 (percentages)

	Annual rate of change					Effective wage protection	
			Average monthly real wage				
Year	Per capita GNP (1)	CPI (2)	Total (3)	COLA erosion (4)	Other (5)	Actual COLA (6)	100% COLA (7)
1968	11.7	2.1	1.7	–2.1	3.8	0	—
1969	9.6	2.5	2.6	–2.6	5.2	0	—
1970	4.6	6.1	2.6	–3.0	5.6	47.5	—
1971	7.7	12.0	2.6	–8.6	11.2	0	—
1972	8.9	12.9	1.5	–7.0	8.5	38.8	—
1973	0.8	20.0	5.9	–6.6	12.5	72.5	—
1974	2.4	39.7	–2.8	–13.2	10.4	53.4	—
1975	1.2	39.3	–2.1	–12.0	9.9	57.5	—
1976	–0.3	31.3	2.0	–11.0	13.0	54.0	61.0
1977	–0.1	34.6	10.3	–7.8	18.1	69.4	82.9
1978	1.2	50.6	1.6	–14.8	16.4	55.9	75.5
1979	1.8	78.3	9.4	–20.2	29.6	54.0	72.3
1980	0.3	131.0	–3.0	–16.1	13.1	75.2	90.6
1981	2.8	116.8	10.3	–9.4	19.7	82.5	116.6
1982	2.0	120.3	–0.3	–15.2	14.9	72.2	94.8

Explanations and sources: Columns 1 and 2: CBS, *Statistical Abstract, 1983*, tables VI/1 and X/1. Column 3: Index of monthly real wage obtained by dividing index of average monthly nominal wage per wage-earner post by the CPI for corresponding month. Rate of change calculated from annual averages of the monthly real wage index for adjacent years. Index of nominal monthly wage: CBS, *Israel Monthly Bulletin of Statistics*, various issues. Column 4: Monthly COLA effect defined as monthly COLA index divided by the CPI for the corresponding month, *minus* 1. Rate of change calculated from annual averages of monthly effect for adjacent years. Monthly COLA index from July 1975 onwards constructed from CBS, *Statistical Abstract, 1983*, table XII/48; for earlier years, *Statistical Abstract*, various years, introduction to chapter on Labor and Wages. Advance payments of COLA of given nominal values transformed into percentages by dividing by COLA "ceiling" for corresponding period. Column 5: Column 3 *minus* Column 4. Column 6: Annual increase in average of monthly COLA index divided by annual increase in CPI. Column 7: As for column 6, excluding advance payments but with all COLAs increased by 25 percent. Calculation for 1976 based on actual COLA paid in first half of 1975, and a 100 percent COLA thereafter.

The opportunity for such a revision presented itself with the reform of the personal income tax system in 1975 (see Committee, 1975b; Ben-Porath and Bruno, 1977). This reform, *inter alia,* introduced indexation of income brackets and, by abolishing various tax exemptions and rebates, made practically all wage earnings taxable at the same rate. The government's involvement in COLA arrangements was increased; it participated with the Histadrut and the newly formed Employers' Coordination Bureau in setting up a COLA reform committee and in carrying out the latter's recommendations. To reduce the now much-increased risk of wage overshooting, and to give the government a freer hand in its exchange rate and indirect tax policies, the reform committee limited the COLA to only 70 percent of the rise in the CPI and raised the threshold from 3 to 5 percent. At the same time, to prevent frequent disruptions of long-term wage agreements, it restored the COLA price base to include all items of expenditures covered by the CPI, with adjustments to be calculated at six-month intervals on a wage base incorporating all earlier allowances; the calculation was also modified so that the time lag involved would be shorter. Because income tax became indexed, the COLA was made taxable at regular income tax rates. Despite a recommendation to abolish it, the ceiling on COLA payments was retained.[10]

The main change introduced by the 1975 reform—the reduction of the indexation rate to less than the full rise in the CPI—was selected as an alternative to linkage to the GDP price index, which was regarded as impracticable. It was argued that the rate of 70 percent roughly corresponded to the rate effectively obtained in the past under a more limited price base, a longer time lag, and ad hoc adjustments. In fact it seems to have been dictated primarily by the suggestion of the same rate, a short time earlier, for the indexation of income tax brackets. The combination of these two reforms ensured that nominal disposable income would not rise by more than the COLA. But it also meant that in the case of undershooting, wage increases exactly compensating for it from employers' point of view would fail to restore real labor earnings to their *status quo ante* level.

Waiving 30 percent of the rate of price rise from the COLA computation reflected the optimism engendered by a short-lived lull in inflation.[11] This move was also accompanied by the forfeiture, at the transition stage, of some of the COLA payments then due under the previous system of indexation. When inflation accelerated to a three-digit level such a low indexation rate was no longer tenable, and in October 1979 it was raised to 80 percent.

The results of the 1975 reform are summarized in columns 4, 6, and 7 of Table 15-1. Column 6 shows the effective rate of wage indexation that actually obtained in 1968–1972, that is, the share of the annual price increase compensated for by the COLA. The great variation observed before 1975 reflects the less-than-complete price coverage, the various ad hoc practices described earlier, and the low inflation rates and labor-market conditions that made these practices acceptable.

With a formal indexation rate of 0.7 and semiannual adjustments, the effective wage protection offered by the COLA averaged less than 60 percent in 1975–1979, rising to over 75 percent with quarterly adjustments and to an 80 percent formal rate after that. Column 4 of the table shows the year-by-year erosion of real wages by measuring the change that would have occurred in wages had the COLA been the only mechanism for raising the nominal wage. This erosion was on average twice as high in the years after 1975 as in preceding years, amounting to as much as one-fifth in 1979. The erosion of real wages is determined both by the rate of inflation and by the rate of effective indexation; and the latter depends not only on the formal indexation rate but also on the direction of the inflationary process, the length of the COLA adjustment interval, and such ad hoc measures as advance payments.[12]

To isolate the effect of partial indexation introduced by the 1975 reform, column 7 presents the effective rate that would have obtained under 100 percent linkage of the COLA to the CPI. Because of the lag in COLA payments, full indexation will overcompensate wages when inflation is falling off, and under-compensate them when it is accelerating. It can be seen that, in practice, full indexation would have considerably raised the effective rate, not letting it fall below 0.72 in any single year from 1977 on. The fact that it would also have eliminated most of the erosion caused by inflation indicated that erosion was largely due to the reduction in the formal indexation rate. In only one year, 1981, would full indexation have resulted in overshooting—which its abandonment was intended to prevent.

Figures 15-3 and 15-4 provide a longer view of the effect of partial indexation, showing the cumulated wage developments in the ninety months before and after July 1975 respectively.[13] The lowest curves in both figures describe the real wage that would have obtained had the COLA been the only adjustment mechanism in the labor market. It can be seen that in both periods the COLA system, as practiced, would have resulted in a significant erosion of real wages by inflation; and that in the long run this erosion would have been much greater in the high-inflation years following the 1975 reform. The middle curve of Figure 15-4 describes the effect of a COLA based on a formal indexation rate of 100 percent. It shows that even with full indexation, real wages in the second period would have suffered a cumulative average erosion of over 3 percent per year. In any case the top curves of both figures show that real wages rose in 1975–1982, and at a much higher rate than in 1968–1975. Columns 3, 4, and 5 of Table 15-1 break down the annual rate of the total change in real wages into the change due to the COLA and a residual representing all other wage-setting mechanisms. The results show that the real wage increase due to the latter components was greater in all the years after 1975 than in any of the years before. The numbers in these columns indicate a lack of any positive association between the rate of change in real wages and the

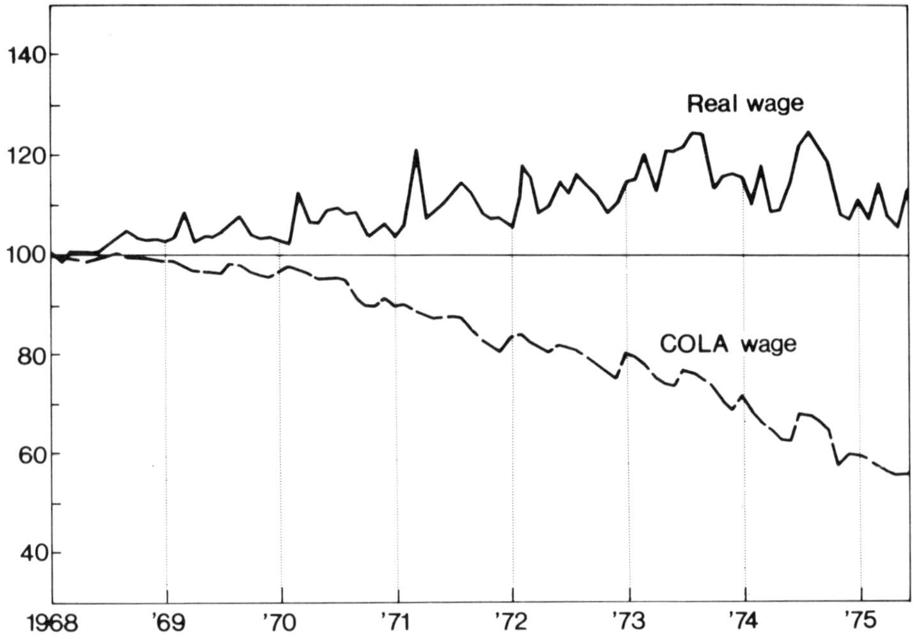

Figure 15-3
Real wages and the COLA effect, 1968–1975.

COLA's contribution. The more rapid increase in real wages in the later years seems to have been due to changes in the general conditions of the labor market rather than to the operation of the COLA system. The fear that the COLA would raise real wages above their equilibrium level is thus seen to have been unfounded. Such overshooting either did not occur or, if it did, was caused by mechanisms other than indexation.

Indexation Mechanisms in the Overall Wage-Setting Process

Figures 15-3 and 15-4 point out the importance of mechanisms other than the COLA in the development of real wages. The difference between the highest and lowest curves in these figures shows that the accumulated contribution of these mechanisms accounted for half the real wage by the end of the period ending in 1975, and for three-quarters of it by the end of the following period.[14] As shown, these cumulated effects of the other wage hikes include the COLAs paid on them subsequently. But the data in Table 15-1, where these contributions were calculated on an annual basis, also support this impression. In none of the years covered by the table would COLA payments have prevented the real wage from falling

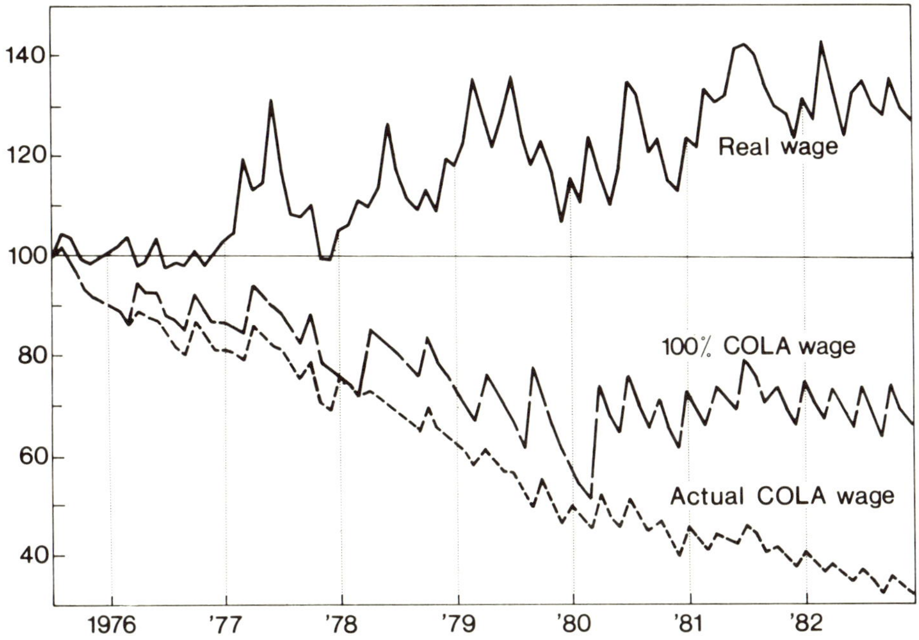

Figure 15–4
Real wages and the COLA effect, 1976–1982.

below its level in the preceding year. But in over two-thirds of these years this deficiency was more than made up for, sometimes quite considerably, by wage hikes stemming from other sources. The relative importance of these hikes is reflected in a positive correlation between them and the total annual rate of change in real wages; no such systematic association is discernible between the latter and the rate of wage erosion due to COLA insufficiency.

Table 15-1 shows that the non-COLA elements of wage changes were at least partly synchronized with the erosion of real wages by inflation. Columns 4 and 5 are negatively associated ($R = -0.746$), indicating either that 90 percent of the COLA erosion was compensated for within the twelve months by other wage mechanisms, or that 60 percent of the wage increases yielded by these mechanisms were wiped out within the year by the excess of inflation over the COLA.

An earlier study, covering the period 1957–1981, found the rate of COLA insufficiency to have a unidirectional influence on other wage changes one year later (O. Liviatan, 1981). As it referred to annual changes, the results of the above-mentioned study suggest that the substitution of other wage components for the COLA took place mainly through the collective-bargaining mechanism. Apparently this mechanism took the erosion of real wages systematically into

TABLE 15-2. Correlation coefficients between rate of COLA erosion and other contemporaneous wage changes, various intervals, 1968–1982

Observation interval	1968–1975[a]	1975–1982[a]	1968–1982[a]
Monthly	−0.250[b]	−0.571[c]	−0.514[c]
Quarterly	+0.092	−0.155	−0.119
Semiannual	−0.354	−0.213	−0.297
Annual	−0.752[b]	−0.429	−0.746[c]

Source: Worksheets (monthly data) underlying table 15-1.

a. Up to July 1975, or following that date. For annual observations, 1975 is included in both subperiods. For more detailed explanations see notes to Table 15-3.

b. Significant at the 5 percent level.

c. Significant at the 1 percent level.

account, either to compensate for its occurrence in the past or as a naive expectations model. However, the correlation coefficients presented in Table 15-2, which were calculated for changes at monthly, semiannual, and annual intervals, suggest that a number of mechanisms, operating with intervals of different lengths, may be involved. In particular, the negative association between the annual rate of COLA erosion and other contemporaneous wage changes tends to repeat itself in the monthly data but not in the semiannual or quarterly data. Furthermore, the fact that after the 1975 reform the monthly association became more pronounced and the annual one less so suggests that the relative roles of these mechanisms have not remained stable throughout the period covered here. On the one hand, in view of the high inflation rates of the late 1970s, compensation could no longer be delayed until the signing of new collective wage agreements, and ways had to be evolved to shorten the time lag considerably. On the other hand, the introduction of partial indexation, which allowed the government greater freedom in manipulating price hikes to counteract what it considered to be excessive wage increases, could have reversed the causal direction of the relationship between the COLA and other wage-setting mechanisms.

To establish whether the substitutability between the COLA and other wage mechanisms followed a similar pattern in the short and the long runs, I applied the Granger statistical causality tests used in the Liviatan study to monthly, quarterly, semiannual, and annual data.[15] To allow for changing economic and institutional conditions, I conducted the tests both for 1968–1982 as a whole and for two subperiods: February 1968–June 1975 and July 1975–December 1983. The results, presented in Table 15-3, indicate that whereas the short-term (monthly) influences over the period as a whole seem to have run in both directions, it was the erosion rate, *D*, that dominated other wage changes, *WO*. This impression is

TABLE 15-3. Granger tests for the direction of causality between COLA erosion, D, and other components of wage change, WO[a] (F-values)

Lag periods[b]	1968–1975[c]		1975–1982[d]		1968–1982	
	$D \rightarrow WO$	$WO \rightarrow D$	$D \rightarrow WO$	$WO \rightarrow D$	$D \rightarrow WO$	$WO \rightarrow D$
Monthly						
1–3	0.47	1.96	4.72[e]	1.59	5.68[e]	4.43[e]
1–4	0.37	1.01	3.16[f]	1.54	4.12[e]	2.86[f]
1–5	0.74	1.34	4.01[e]	1.75	3.93[e]	2.31[f]
1–6	0.84	1.07	4.32[e]	2.65[f]	4.33[e]	2.79[f]
1–7	0.91	0.87	3.57[e]	1.41	4.04[e]	1.84
1–8	0.81	0.88	3.25[e]	1.44	3.21[f]	1.92
1–9	0.98	1.37	2.97[e]	2.23[f]	2.46[f]	3.92[e]
1–10	0.95	1.32	2.38	1.89	2.14[f]	3.59[e]
1–11	1.63	1.19	1.61	1.64	1.68	3.22[e]
1–12	1.11	1.18	0.83	1.40	0.59	2.49[e]
Quarterly						
1–2	1.30	0.11	1.81	1.56	1.72	3.96[e]
1–3	2.00	3.89[f]	1.17	2.17	3.70[f]	6.30[e]
1–4	0.93	2.93	1.67	1.35	2.62[f]	3.65[f]
Semiannual						
1	2.68	5.27[f]	0.08	5.61[f]	1.99	10.10[e]
1–2	1.24	0.82	1.02	2.69	0.99	3.61[f]
1–3	0.55	0.29	1.17	1.02	0.43	2.67
Annual						
1	0.03	2.13	0.14	1.61	2.25	4.96[f]
1–2	0.35	97.19	4.17	1.31	0.18	2.64

Source: Worksheets (monthly data) underlying table 15-1.

a. F-values for the share of the influencing variable in explaining the variance not accounted for by autoregression of the dependent variable.

b. Number of lags of corresponding lengths – i.e., months, quarters, etc.

c. February 1968 – June 1975 for monthly data; 1968:2–1975:2 for quarterly data; 1968–1975 for annual data.

d. August 1975 – December 1982 for monthly data; 1968:4–1982:4 for quarterly data; 1975–1982 for annual data.

e. Significant at the 1 percent level.

f. Significant at the 5 percent level.

supported by the results for the subperiods, which fail to reveal any causal relationships before 1975 but clearly establish an almost purely unidirectional one, from *D* to *WO*, for the later years. As the observation intervals lengthen, however, influences running in the opposite direction become more pronounced—they predominate in the quarterly data and remain the sole influences in the semiannual and annual data.[16]

The presence of $D \rightarrow WO$ causality in the monthly data for the post-1975 period and its absence in the earlier period support the claim made earlier in this chapter, that inflation shortened the lag with which the COLA insufficiency was compensated for. This shortening of the lag was made possible because, for what were originally "tax-engineering" reasons, a considerable share of labor remuneration in Israel takes the form of payments linked to specific allowances for travel, car, or telephone expenditures. Regarded as reimbursements (and therefore not formally covered by the COLA), these wage items are adjusted periodically according to increases in the relevant costs. Some of these adjustments are closely synchronized with COLA payments; others depart from them considerably in both timing and magnitude. In particular, travel allowances are adjusted to changes in the domestic price of fuel, and therefore to the foreign-exchange rate. Since the introduction of a crawling-peg exchange system almost concurrently with the 1975 COLA reform, and especially in the wake of the floating of the Israeli currency in October 1977, adjustments in fuel prices and in travel allowances were made roughly every month. The 1975 reforms were preceded by a reform in the personal income tax system that abolished all tax exemptions on allowances of the type described above. Thus, at the very time that the original reason for the existence of such allowances was removed, the combined effect of partial indexation and of continuous devaluations endowed them with a new role as short-term COLA substitutes.

The linkage of wage components other than the COLA to some price or another does not protect real wages from long-term erosion by inflation. By common practice, adjustments in these components follow government decisions to remunerate public-sector employees. Unlike the COLA linkage, the linkage of these wage components is not bound by contract, and though made with fairly regular periodicity, the exact timing of adjustments may vary. Moreover, not only are some such allowances adjusted at much longer intervals than the COLA, but even the most frequently adjusted ones are subject to some policy discretion, as the specific prices to which they are geared (such as the price of fuel) are, to a great extent, controlled by the government. By its very nature, the resultant degree of imperfection in the substitutability of other linkage mechanisms for the COLA varies somewhat haphazardly from month to month. Nevertheless, when accumulated over a longer period, the various measures contributing to it may be manipulated to allow for the systematic erosion of wage increases yielded in the short run by these same (as well as by other) mechanisms. Such manipulation may explain why, although no systematic *WO* → *D* pattern is observable in tests based on monthly data, it does emerge in observations of longer intervals.

But the main means of neutralizing part of the non-COLA wage increases—that is, the mechanism underlying the influence running from *WO* to *D* observed in the semiannual and annual data—seems to have been the *timing* of government-induced price hikes. Prices that are controlled by or rates that are unilaterally fixed by the government (such as indirect taxes, electricity charges, and municipal rates) have accounted for 20 percent of the CPI in recent years (Bank of Israel, *Annual Report 1981,* table III.1). In addition, the high import component in production makes the price level in Israel highly sensitive to the foreign-exchange rate.[17] When a subsidy cut, rate or tax hike, or exchange depreciation is timed to occur close to the end or just at the beginning of a COLA adjustment interval, the payment of most or all of the compensating allowance is postponed until the next adjustment date—that is, by nearly the full length of the adjustment interval. The resultant opportunity to erode real wages, always freely exploited by the government, though of marginal consequence at low rates of inflation, became quite significant in the late 1970s and early 1980s. Thus, while the advent of high inflation rates caused part of the COLA role to be taken over by other, shorter-lagged mechanisms, it also allowed the government more scope in frustrating this role in the longer run, through the combined effect of partial indexation, discretionary wielding of other substitute mechanisms, and discretionary timing of changes in directly controlled prices.[18]

To estimate the magnitude of the resultant erosion, I used the regression equations used earlier for the Granger causality tests to express *D* in terms of the current and lagged values of *WO* only. Table 15-4 presents the corresponding coefficients derived from regressions run on one-year-lagged annual data.[19] These coefficients show that nearly one-third of the real wage increases yielded by mechanisms other than the COLA are eroded within the same year, another 40 percent within the subsequent one, and so on, until only about one-fifth are retained in the long run.[20]

Why did the Histadrut reconcile itself for a long time to an imperfect indexation mechanism, under which real wage gains became largely illusory within a year or two? The answer seems to lie in the scope thus provided for trade-union activity. A comparison of the figures in columns 3 and 5 of Table 15-1 reveals that even when real wages fell, the regular labor-market mechanisms yielded real gains of 10–15 percent, and that in other years these gains were at least twice as high as the ultimate overall increase in real wages. In other words, the margin thus left to traditional wage bargaining was much greater than it would have been under perfect indexation (or, for that matter, in the absence of inflation). The Histadrut on several occasions openly stated its preference for this state of affairs; this

TABLE 15-4. Proportion of real wage increases eroded over time[a]

Time lag	Annual	Cumulated
Concurrent	–0.319	–0.319
1 year	–0.398	–0.717
2 years	–0.055	–0.772
3 years	–0.008	–0.780

Source: Regressions based on worksheets (monthly data) underlying table 15-1.

a. Derived from regression equations of WO and WO_{-1} and D on D_{-1}, for annual observations.

Regressing D directly on both current and 1-year lagged annual values of WO yields similar results:

$$D = -\underset{3.39}{0.373WO} - \underset{3.79}{0.432WO_{-1}}$$

$$R^2 = 0.740$$
$$\text{D.W.} = 1.94$$

Both the constant term and the coefficients on longer lags are statistically insignificant.

preference is also evident from its rejection, in early 1983, of a government proposal to restore the formal indexation rate to 100 percent in exchange for a moratorium on all other wage increases.

The maintenance of a broad bargaining margin did not serve merely to provide the trade unions (and possibly also employers) with some practically futile but politically useful leverage. Assuming rank-and-file resistance to reductions in wage tariffs, changes in relative wages can hardly be effected without a rise in the overall wage level. Had the operation of all wage mechanisms other than the COLA been restricted to the magnitudes of column 3 in Table 15-1, the scope for changes in relative wages among industries and skill groups would have been greatly reduced—possibly to below the level necessitated by the changes that actually occurred in the structure of employment (see Chapter 5). Furthermore, it should be noted that despite both current and subsequent erosion, the operation of the non-COLA mechanisms did yield some tangible residuals, the lagged reactions of D to WO summing up to less than unity.

Wage Indexation and Economic Stability

The theoretical literature on wage indexation emphasizes its destabilizing effects on output when inflation originates in real rather than monetary shocks (see, for example, Gray 1976; Fischer, 1977). This chapter has shown that Israel's COLA system was flexible enough to reduce the risk of real output destabilization: when warranted by general economic conditions, part or all of the COLA due was forgone, either voluntarily, as in 1966 and 1971, or by default, through a reduction in the *effective* indexation rate as a result of accelerated inflation or government manipulation. Indeed, the findings here provide some support for the argument that this effective rate itself should be regarded as endogenous to the inflationary process (and to the indexation arrangements existing in other markets; see N. Liviatan, 1983). The COLA, as such, did not produce the overshooting of the real wage. On the contrary, it seems to have provided a convenient mechanism for reducing the overshooting produced by the other labor-market mechanisms.

In the short run, changes in wage components other than the COLA—most conspicuously allowances linked effectively to either the CPI or the rate of exchange—have systematically compensated for the insufficiency of wage indexation proper. This insufficiency did not prevent real wages from rising quite rapidly in the last decade, but it was large enough to permit long-term containment of all other wage increases to roughly one-fifth of their original real magnitudes.

The conventional wisdom on the role of wage indexation in the inflationary process is that it transmits price increases into cost pushes. The findings here show that, insofar as wages did create or relay inflationary pressures, they did not do so through the COLA system. Indeed, it is doubtful whether wage increases of any kind constituted the main cost-push mechanism. In late 1977 the liberalization of the foreign-exchange system provided a previously unavailable daily register of the decline in the purchasing power of money, in the form of the "representative" dollar rate. Introduced first in quotations of real estate prices, this rate has progressively been adopted as the main basis for price adjustments, often of daily frequency, in the private sector of the economy. The resultant cost-push mechanism is certainly more rapid than could be generated by a quarterly or even a monthly linkage of wages to the CPI.[21]

Paradoxically, the exploitation of the indexation system as a tool of wage policy may have had a destabilizing effect on the economy. Government policies designed to contain or reduce real wages seem to have been intended to reduce private consumption rather than to lower labor costs; hence the reliance on price and rate increases and exchange rate hikes, in contrast to direct taxation or social-contract type income policies. This policy, however, appears to have backfired, for such hikes inevitably affect all economic agents. Trying to recoup themselves, they create new cost-push effects of the sort observed here to have operated in the short run in the labor market, but with a much shorter time lag. With the initial achievements of its policies thus melting away, the government may again resort to the same steps as before. This persistent attempt to erode incomes through government-induced inflation may well be a major factor in the persistence of Israeli inflation (see Kleiman, 1977c, and Chapter 16 in this volume).

16

Accelerating Inflation and Balance-of-Payments Crises, 1973 – 1984

Nissan Liviatan and Sylvia Piterman

The inflationary process in Israel over the past decade (1973–1984) has been a puzzle to economists. The increase in the government's budget deficit, traditionally considered to be the main cause of inflation, may explain part of the rise in inflation in 1974 but does not seem to explain its sharp acceleration in the second half of the decade. In fact this chapter presents evidence for an opposite tendency, namely, that the recent acceleration of inflation has been associated with a *reduction* in the real budget deficit.

Another indicator of the fiscal approach is the government's revenue from printing money. The data show that this component of the deficit did not increase with the acceleration of inflation. There is also some doubt as to whether the revenue from inflation was offset by *losses* of revenue as a result of inflation.

Since the theory of "revenue-motivated inflation" does not seem to work, we must look for other mechanisms. Monetary accommodation is certainly a necessary condition for inflation, but we have to identify the force driving it.

This chapter shows that there is a clear empirical relation between inflation and balance-of-payments (BOP) crises. It also describes the mechanism by which the BOP crises are translated into inflation. Some of the ideas used in our model are drawn from other studies (Bruno and Sussman, 1979, 1980; Piterman, 1981; Ablin, 1982; Shiffer, 1982; Litvin, Meridor, and Spivak, 1982, 1983, 1984; Plessner, 1983; Bruno, 1984; N. Liviatan, 1984; Sokoler, 1984). Here we integrate these ideas with some new ones into a more comprehensive scheme whose main features are described as follows.

In ordinary times the government stabilizes the level of inflation by managing the exchange rate, determining changes in government-controlled prices, and setting monetary targets. When a BOP crisis develops (for reasons discussed later), the government temporarily suspends its stabilizing policies and resorts to drastic devaluations and similar increases in controlled prices. In our view, these price shocks perform an important role in alleviating the immediate pressure on the BOP and on the Central Bank's reserves (for example, a sharp nominal devaluation creates a temporary real devaluation). In so doing, they give the government some time to implement various restrictive measures. The translation of the initial cost push into a rise in the general price level is facilitated by widespread indexation schemes in the labor and capital markets. The transformation of the price-level shock into a new level of inflation is caused by an interaction of lags in the adjustment process and by a general feeling that the BOP problem is being given priority over stabilization of the inflation level. It is clear that a process of this kind cannot occur without monetary accommodation to inflationary expectations.

This is the essence of the process that has been operating in the Israeli economy since 1973. The process was different in earlier years (when Israel adhered more closely to a fixed exchange rate system), and it may be different in the future.

The causes of BOP crises were various. The 1974 crisis was largely a fiscal one, combined with a deterioration in the terms of trade; the 1979 crisis was strongly influenced by monetary factors; and the 1983 crisis was associated with the exchange rate policy. The final section of this chapter draws some conclusions from these experiences and discusses useful future policies to combat inflation.

Inflation and the Government Budget

The most commonly cited cause of inflation is the government's budget deficit. According to this explanation, the government prints money to finance the deficit, and as long as the demand for money is less than unit elastic, a larger real deficit will result in a higher inflation rate. This approach can be applied to an open economy if the exchange rate is flexible in the long run, and in the Israeli economy this has certainly been the case since 1975, when a crawling peg was introduced, followed in 1977 by a flexible rate system. However, even in the earlier period the effective exchange rate was adjusted continuously, and the formal exchange rate was adjusted in "jumps" every few years. Consequently, from a longer-term perspective, it was sufficiently flexible.

Table 16-1 analyzes the development of the government deficit in 1963–1983, with the data averaged over five- or ten-year periods to obtain some long-term trends. In the first period, 1963–1972, inflation averaged 6–7 percent annually. In the second, 1973–1977, inflation shot up to a new plateau of around 40 percent following the Yom Kippur War and the first world energy crisis. In the third period, 1978–1983, inflation rose to a still higher plateau of about 130 percent annually. At the end of this period inflation again leaped to a new plateau of 400 percent a year.

In this analysis we use a twofold classification. The first classification distinguishes between domestic deficit and total deficit, with the latter including the government's foreign deficit. Total deficit means, essentially, domestic deficit *less* the part financed by foreign aid. Ideally, we would like to measure the permanent level of foreign aid, but this is an elusive item. In practice, we use two alternative definitions of foreign aid—one based on unilateral transfers and one that includes, in addition, net long-term foreign borrowing. In 1973–1983 Israel received foreign aid to finance its domestic deficit; this aid amounted to about 2 percent of GNP according to the first definition, and to about 5 percent according to the second. The permanence of these measures of foreign aid is not quite clear. It is even possible that in the long run only the domestic deficit is relevant. We therefore found it useful to present all three measures.

The second classification concerns the nature of the domestic deficit. The concept of deficit that includes direct public investment seems to exaggerate the impact of the deficit on inflation, since part of the investment is in principle similar to investment in ordinary firms run by the government. We therefore present alternative measures of the deficit—with and without public investment (which normally amounts to 5–6 percent of GNP).

Another consideration is specific to the Israeli economy and relates to the fact that government borrowing from the public was index linked whereas government lending to the private sector (mainly to firms) was not. As long as inflation remained low (in 1963–1983), unlinked loans contained only a small subsidy through low interest rates. However, as inflation jumped unexpectedly to a new plateau in 1974, nominal interest rates exhibited considerable institutional rigidity, so that the government's receipts from the repayment of these loans eroded substantially in real terms. This result became known as the "inflationary subsidy embodied in government loans," or simply the "credit subsidy."

The significant aspect of the credit subsidy from the government-deficit point of view is that it was not financed by increases in other taxes but mainly by increases in the net government debt. As a result the credit subsidy raised the government deficit dramatically, by 10 percent of GNP in 1973–1977. Since 1974 the government has made an effort to reduce the stock of nonlinked loans, and in 1979 it introduced indexation for all new loans. However, the unexpected jump in inflation to a new plateau in 1979 offset the tendency to reduce the credit subsidy, and it remained a high 7 percent or so of GNP. Only in 1984 did the credit subsidy fall to a negligible proportion.

Including the credit subsidy in the deficit is questionable on two counts. First, as suggested by the Ricardian Equivalence Proposition (see Barro, 1974), the subsidy may have been offset by expectations of future taxes that were related to increased bond finance. Second, the subsidy is largely endogenous to the inflation process. For these reasons we present alternative definitions of the deficit—with and without the credit subsidy.

TABLE 16-1. Alternative definitions of government deficit, as percentage of GNP and related data, 1963–1983

	1963–72	1973–77	1978–83
Extended[a] domestic deficit (d)	4.1	22.1	13.2
d *plus* government foreign deficit (d^*)	7.0	22.2	11.4
d^* *minus* long-term government foreign borrowing	2.7	16.4	8.7
Ordinary[b] domestic deficit (d')	3.3	12.0	6.2
d' *plus* government foreign deficit (d'^*)	5.8	10.1	4.4
d'^* *minus* long-term government foreign borrowing	1.4	6.3	1.7
d' *minus* government investment ($\bar{d}$)	−4.6	3.6	0.5
$\bar{d}$ *plus* government foreign deficit ($\bar{d}^*$)	−1.7	1.7	−1.3
$\bar{d}^*$ *minus* long-term government foreign borrowing	−6.1	−2.1	−4.0
Inflation	7.4	32.8	107.5
Government domestic consumption and investment	27.6	34.6	31.9
Government domestic consumption	20.1	26.1	26.2
Taxes[c]	24.3	22.6	25.7
Government foreign deficit	2.9	−2.1	−1.8
Government foreign deficit *minus* long-term government foreign borrowing[d]	−1.4	−5.7	−4.5

Sources: Liviatan and Piterman (1984a); Bank of Israel, *Annual Report, 1982* (table II-1, p.16; table V-A11, p.80; table VII-2 pp.128-129.

Note: Our deficit series differ in certain respects from those used in the Bank of Israel *Annual Report*. The main difference is that our series try to exclude the element of nominal interest which should not be there. As a result, our d^* series is smaller than the corresponding Bank of Israel series by 3 percent of GNP on average in 1973–1983. On the other hand, the difference between the d series is small (about 1 percent of GNP on average).

a. Including credit subsidy.

b. Excluding credit subsidy.

c. Net of real interest payments on net domestic debt.

d. Translated into Israeli currency by the annual average of the dollar exchange rate (see Bank of Israel, Foreign Exchange Department, 1984).

Table 16-1 shows that according to all the alternative definitions the government deficit increased in 1973–1977 relative to 1963–1972. The increase is largest when the deficit includes the credit subsidy. As was pointed out, however, this may not be a very meaningful comparison. The other estimates of the total deficit indicate that it rose by about 4–5 percentage points of GNP in 1973–1977. The result is in line with the fiscal theory of inflation, which predicts a positive relation between the deficit and inflation. The other periods, however, show the opposite pattern: according to *all* the definitions, the government deficit declined in 1978–1983 while inflation increased steeply. These developments, which are in contrast with the traditional approach, suggest that the increase in inflation in 1978–1983 cannot be attributed to the government's need for budget finance.

It is also instructive to compare the third period (1978–1983) with the first (1963–1972): when the credit subsidy is excluded, the change in the size of the deficit is small. According to these definitions, the size of the deficit when inflation reached an annual level of 130 percent is similar to the size of the deficit in the noninflationary period. In this connection it is interesting to note that the credit subsidy practically vanished in 1984 through the erosion of nonindexed loan

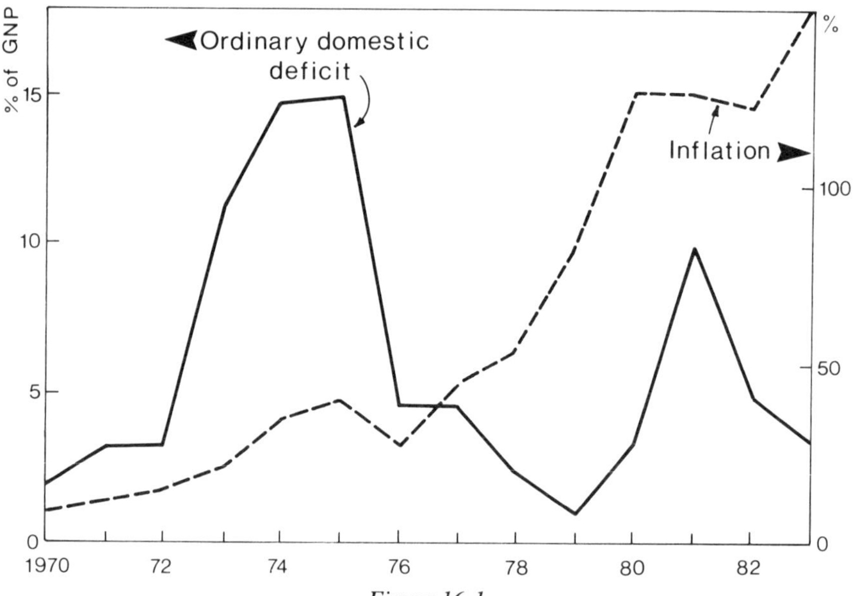

Figure 16-1
The government's domestic deficit (as a percentage of GNP) and inflation, 1970–1983. (Liviatan and Piterman, 1984a.)

balances and the shift to indexed loans. The other budget components were not significantly affected by this change. Consequently, the government budget deficit of 1984 or 1985 may turn out to be similar in size to that of the noninflationary period while inflation continues to run at an annual rate of 400 percent.

Note that the lack of relationship between the government deficit and recent inflation also holds for the components of the deficit. Specifically, the increase in the rate of inflation in 1979–1983 was associated with a reduction in the real level of public spending and with an increase in taxation.

So far we have focused on the deficit's long-term effect on inflation. Alternatively, one may adopt the standard Keynesian approach and inquire whether there is a short-term or cyclical relationship between changes in the government deficit and inflation. Figure 16-1 shows that such a relationship did indeed exist in 1974–1976, when the budget deficit first rose as a result of increases in domestic military spending, and then fell as a result of severe cuts in expenditure. However, in the other big inflation jumps there is no sign of a connection with an increased deficit. If anything, the deficit showed a tendency to decline in 1979 and 1983 (these phenomena are discussed later).

The Problem of the Government Debt

Since 1973 the government has accumulated considerable internal and external debts through continuous budget deficits. It is often argued that this debt exerts additional inflationary pressures, beyond those of the deficit itself. There is clearly no room for such an argument in the framework of long-term equilibrium, since the debt is endogenously determined by the deficit in conjunction with other financial parameters. We must therefore look into the shorter-term aspects of this problem.

One way in which the external debt may affect inflation is through the need to finance the increasing burden of this debt by inflationary methods. However, although the government's net foreign debt increased from 30 to 40 percent of GNP in 1973–1984, this was never considered to be a serious repayment burden. In fact throughout the decade the government continued to receive a positive net inflow of sizable medium- and long-term loans.

In the same period there was an impressive increase in the net *internal* debt—from about 50 percent of GNP in 1970 to 115 percent in 1982–83 (Auerbach, 1984). Several arguments hold that this increase is inflationary. According to one argument, when the debt-GNP ratio is very high, the economy reaches a "saturation level" with respect to this debt and has to resort to inflationary finance of the budget. Because the ratio of net internal debt to GNP has been fairly stable since 1978, it is hard to explain the big jumps in inflation in 1979 and 1983 on these grounds. We must point out, however, that the data for 1984, compared with those for the pre-1983 BOP crisis, show a marked reduction in the share of domestic deficit financed by internal debt and an increase in the share financed by the sale of foreign exchange to the public.

These developments were associated with a massive increase in the effective public debt as a result of the government's guarantees to support the value of bank shares held by the public. At the same time tax receipts were eroded considerably as a result of accelerated inflation and the crises in the banking system. It seems that these developments tended to undermine the credibility of the government's ability to service the internal debt.

If the foregoing evaluation is correct, it implies that in the future the government may face crises in its foreign-exchange reserves if it continues to maintain large deficits. These crises may lead to devaluations that will stimulate inflation. This may indicate a channel through which the internal debt, combined with a continued budget deficit, may affect inflation in the future.

Another argument concerns the ability of the large internal debt to help accommodate price increases. While this argument is true, it relates not so much to the size of the debt as to its liquidity. The latter is a result of the government's policy of stabilizing the real rate of return to its bonds. With a more flexible monetary system allowing bond rates to fluctuate, this problem would be much less serious. We must also point out that a considerable part of the debt does not contain an inflationary potential; this segment was accumulated in the mid-1970s as a means of financing the credit subsidy mentioned earlier, which reached 10 percent of GNP annually in those years, and can be viewed as being held in reserve against additional taxes. It should also be remembered that inflation led to increased demand for liquid government bonds as a substitute for money; this component, which amounts to some 10 percent of GNP, is absorbed in the asset portfolio without creating inflationary pressure.

Finally, a substantial portion of the debt was incurred as a means of financing public investment. Much of this investment generates the revenue required to repay the interest on the government bonds. Consequently, from a long-term perspective it is not inflationary. Other parts of public investment that do not yield direct revenues to the government may present difficulties in the financing of interest payments. These difficulties result from the cost of raising taxation (see Barro, 1979) when gross tax rates are as high as they are in the Israeli economy. Repayment of interest may present a problem for the future, but it can be dealt with by a tax reform designed to reduce gross tax rates along with transfer payments (noting that *net* taxes in Israel are not particularly high).

On the whole, then, it is difficult to find any clear relationship between the increased debt-GNP ratio over the past decade and the development of inflation.

Government Revenue from Inflation

According to the inflation-tax theory, increased inflation results from the government's desire to increase its revenues from inflation under conditions of a stable and less-than-unit-elastic demand function for money. The need for larger inflation-tax revenues may be the result of an increased deficit or of a reduction in the share of the deficit financed by bonds. The concept of the deficit held constant in the last case is the one gross of interest payments (see N. Liviatan, 1983).

Table 16-2 presents various estimates of the government's revenue from inflation as a percentage of GNP. The first line measures the real value of additions to the money base; the second measures the rate of depreciation of the base. Under steady-state conditions these measures are identical, but when inflation is on the increase we should expect the first estimate to be lower as a result of the reduction of real balances (as is the case in our data). The first line shows that inflation never increased government revenues from printing money. Although in the second period (1973–1977) the erosion of the money base increased (line 2), it was compensated for by a reduction in real balances. According to both definitions, revenues from inflation fell in the third period (1978–1983), when inflation accelerated.

The third line shows a measure of the net inflation tax (Sokoler, 1984) that subtracts from line 2 the interest paid on nonlinked bank reserves, reflecting the net erosion of the money base. This measure yields results similar to the traditional ones but shows that in 1982–1983 the yield from the inflation tax dropped to 1.7 percent of GNP.

The data presented so far show that, ex post, the government did not gain any revenue from increasing inflation. This result, however, is based on the assumption that the demand for money is stable. If the demand for money falls, the same real deficit will require a higher rate of inflation (provided the demand for money

TABLE 16-2. Government revenues from printing money and from inflation tax, 1968–1983 (as percentage of GNP)

	1968–1972	1973–1977	1978–1983	1982–1983
$\Delta H/Y$	2.7	2.4	1.8	2.1
πh	1.1	3.3	2.7	2.4
$(\pi - r)h$	0.8	3.0	2.3	1.7

Source: Sokoler (1984).

Note: H = monetary base; ΔH = annual addition to H; Y = nominal GNP; $h = H/Y$; π = rate of inflation. r = rate of interest on the monetary base.

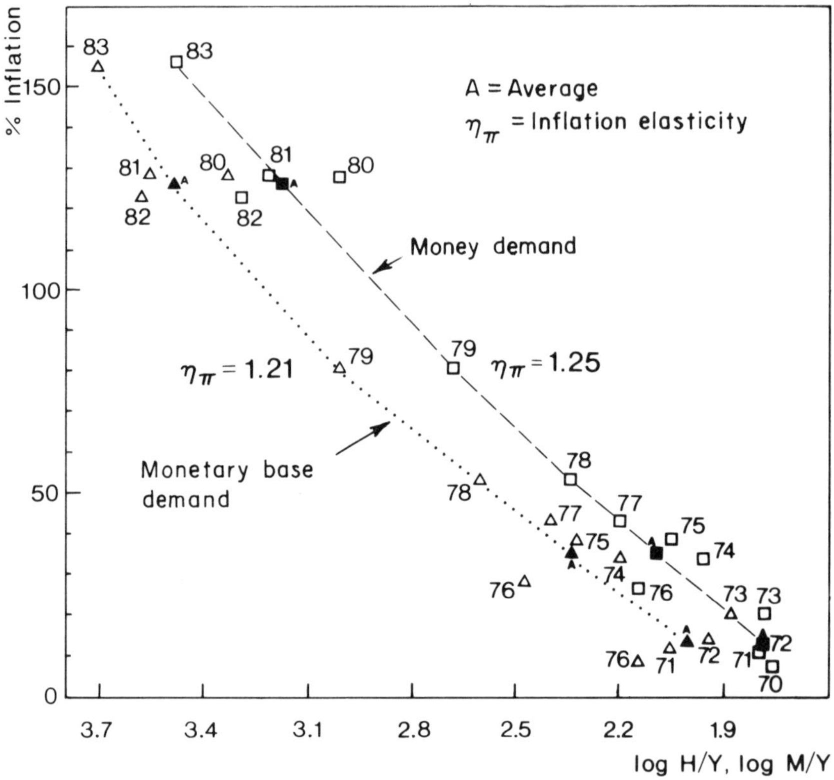

Figure 16-2
Empirical money demand curve and monetary base demand curve, 1970–1983. (Liviatan and Piterman, 1984a.)

is less than unit elastic). In fact it has been argued that the introduction of new money substitutes following the liberalization of November 1977 reduced the demand for nonindexed money (which is the only type of money relevant for inflation-tax purposes).

Figure 16-2 shows the empirical relation between the rate of inflation on an annual basis and the logarithm of real balances (relative to GNP). The upper curve relates to money (M_1), the lower one to the money base. Assuming the semilogarithmic representation is appropriate, we see no evidence suggesting that a structural shift occurred in the long-term relationship around 1978. In particular, the two years following the liberalization (1978 and 1979) are situated precisely on the line predicted by earlier years. (For an opposite view concerning the structural shift in the demand for money see Leiderman and Merom, 1983; Melnick, 1983.)

A possible explanation for the demand curve's lack of sensitivity to the introduction of short-term, dollar-linked deposits in 1977 is that this move did not constitute a significant change in the capital market, where near-moneys in the form of stabilized index-linked government bonds had already existed for a long time (see Bronfeld and Brenner, 1977; Ben-Bassat and Marom, 1980). According to these empirical demand curves, the economy entered the elastic range of the demand for money in 1979. If this is so, the government could not possibly have obtained any inflation-tax gains from stepping up inflation. Also, the relatively small magnitude of the government's revenue from inflation—2–3 percent of GNP—casts some doubt on the revenue motive of inflation, in view of its political and economic costs (see Kleiman, 1984).

Finally, it has been argued that *net* inflation tax in Israel has been negative (Kleiman, 1974; Sokoler, 1984). The reasoning is that credit subsidization rises automatically with inflation, and since this subsidy was much larger than the erosion of the money base, the result is a negative net tax. As mentioned earlier, however, the credit subsidy may have been financed by government bonds, which represent future taxes. Under this assumption, the credit subsidy had no effect on inflation. But if some of the additional bonds were expected to be redeemed by the printing of more money, then such expectations might have raised inflation in the current period.

Because the inflation tax has been fairly small and has not increased, there seems to be a good case for assuming that the credit subsidy was indeed largely offset by expected future taxes. However, if part of it was expected to be financed by inflationary methods, it could easily turn the net revenue from inflation into a negative figure. This has important implications for the role assigned to shifts in the demand for money within the framework of an inflationary tax model; for example, if the net inflation tax is zero, then no shifts of this kind can explain changes in long-term inflation.

It seems clear from the discussion above that the increase in inflation is not due primarily to the size of the government's budget deficit nor to the government's alleged inflation-tax motive. What, then, *are* the causes of inflation? To answer this question we must consider monetary accommodation in the Israeli economy in conjunction with external and internal shocks to the price system.

The Erosion of the Money Base and the Shift to Indexed Money

The most important features of Israel's financial asset structure in 1970–1983 were the shrinking money base and the shift to money substitutes ("indexed money"). Table 16-3 shows how money (M_1) shrank from 40 percent of liquid assets (M_4) in 1970 and to 10 percent in 1983. Relative to GNP, M_1 shrank from 17 percent in the mid-1960s to about 3 percent in 1983.

The shift away from money as a result of increased inflation led to the acquisi-

TABLE 16-3. Selected monetary aggregates as percentage of GNP and M_4 1966–1983 (annual averages)

	H/Y	M_1/Y	M_4/Y	M_1/M_4	M_2/M_4
1966	12	17	43	41	61
1970	12	17	45	38	60
1975	10	13	48	28	38
1980	4	5	36	12	16
1983	2	3	32	10	21

Sources: Liviatan and Piterman (1984a).

Note: H = monetary base; M_1 = currency *plus* demand deposits; $M_2 = M_1$ *plus* nonlinked time deposits and CDs; $M_4 = M_2$ *plus* foreign-currency linked deposits and index-linked negotiable bonds; Y = nominal GNP.

tion of liquid assets linked to the general price level or to the foreign exchange rate. These liquid assets (included in M_4 in Table 16-3) consist of negotiable government bonds and short-term bank deposits—the latter being linked to the exchange rate. The real market price of these bonds is stabilized by the Central Bank; thus they are a close substitute for money. The real market value of linked deposits is stabilized by their short-term nature and by the policy that restricts deviations of the real exchange rate from the purchasing power parity (PPP) rule. This arrangement enables the public to hold only minimal quantities of ordinary money.

Every inflationary economy has to solve the problem of finding substitutes for the shrinking money base. Some economies do this by using semilegal foreign currency. The Israeli system seems to have gone to the extreme of fully institutionalizing and encouraging government-supported money substitutes. One advantage of this system is that it saves some costs of using foreign currency as a money substitute. Another advantage is that it reduces some of the pressures on foreign currency reserves when there are expectations of a large devaluation, because the public has the option of investing in dollar-linked deposits. A third advantage is that this system encourages financial savings in an inflationary setting.

But this system suffers from some important shortcomings. The use of government-supported money substitutes reduces the demand for the money base. When the base is small, and when any additional need for base money can be satisfied by the sale of money substitutes at fixed terms (involving a small fee), the price level becomes "almost" indeterminate; that is, an arbitrary increase in the price level leaves the equilibrium in the commodities and assets markets virtually unchanged. Under such a system cost pushes tend to be translated fairly easily into increases in the general price level. However, the indeterminacy of the price level applies only to a conventional monetary system that operates through fixed bank reserve ratios and the like. In principle, the Central Bank can directly impose nominal credit ceilings, and thus possibly provide the system with a nominal anchor. But the effectiveness of this policy is reduced (though by no means eliminated) by the pegging of real rates of return on government bonds.

A common argument in monetary theory maintains that the introduction of money substitutes tends not only to shift the demand curve for money leftward but also to increase its *elasticity*. We assume that this is one of the implications of the Israeli monetary system. The implication is that, in general, the case for a revenue-motivated inflation is weak. Relying on this consideration and on the empirical evidence presented earlier, let us assume that inflation is *not* caused by revenue considerations. There is therefore no reason to suppose that the economy operates at a point where the demand for money is less than unit elastic. In view of the evidence presented here, let us suppose that demand for money is elastic. Then, an increase in inflation will involve a reduction in government revenues from inflation. It follows that under these conditions the government's real deficit in no way restricts the increase in inflation. In other words, an increase in long-term inflation can be accommodated by a *reduction* in the government's deficit.

The Inflation Steps

The fact that the Israeli economy has a considerable degree of built-in, automatic, as well as discretionary monetary accommodation does not explain what generates inflation. To discover the force driving this process we must first trace the general pattern of inflation. The inflationary process in Israel in 1974–1983 was typically characterized by occasional sharp jumps, or steps, followed by long intervals with no increase. The first step extended roughly from 1974 to 1978 (the 40 percent step); the second from 1979 to the first half of 1983 (the 130 percent step); and the last, which seems to be a distinct step in its own right, began in the last quarter of 1983 (the 400 percent step).

The behavior of inflation along the first step was more variable than along the others. The reason seems to be that stabilizing monetary policies were not used as extensively as in the second step. Owing to this variability it is somewhat questionable whether 1978 falls into the first or the second step. More detailed analysis of the data (Figure 16-3) shows, however, that the drastic change in the inflation rate occurred around the middle of 1979.

The second step is the classic one. It began with a dramatic price shock in the second half of 1979 and ended with another shock at the end of 1983. In between, inflation remained at a fairly constant level, with occasional reductions.

The last step is still very young. It began in October 1983 but shows considerable stability, like the preceding steps (Figure 16-3). No one can tell whether it will

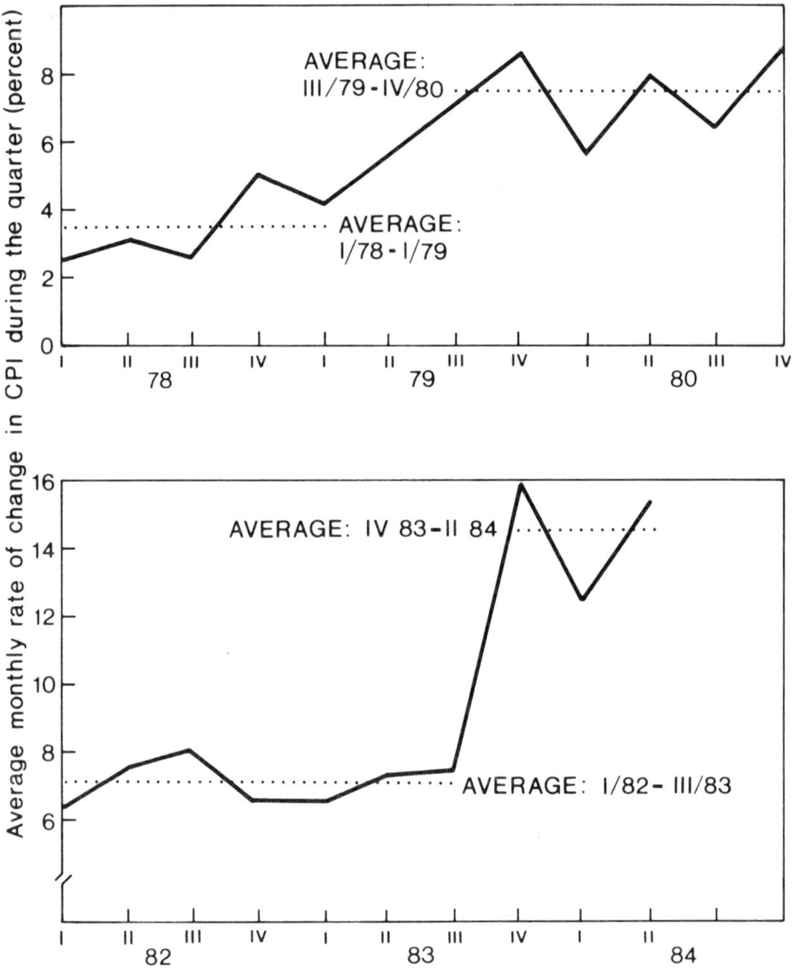

Figure 16-3
Average monthly rate of change in CPI, 1978:1 – 1982:2. (Liviatan and Piterman, 1984a.)

develop into a full-fledged step or whether it is merely a prelude to a new step. One possibility is that the steps will become shorter. It is also possible that inflation has reached the stage at which no new steps can be tolerated. At this time we cannot say much about either possibility.

Table 16-4 provides an alternative view of the inflation steps through changes in the velocity of circulation, which is assumed to be an indicator of inflationary expectations (Gottlieb and Piterman, 1984). These data indicate clear jumps in

TABLE 16-4. Velocity and inflation, 1970–1983

	Income velocity of money (M_1)[a]	Velocity of checking accounts
1970	8.2	21
1971	8.7	22
1972	8.5	24
1973	8.8	25
1974	10.7	28
1975	11.5	31
1976	12.8	35
1977	13.6	38
1978	16.6	45
1979	23.4	69
1980	31.0	104
1981	37.9	160
1982	42.5	201
1983	50.1	227

Source: Liviatan and Piterman (1984a).
a. Income = GNP *plus* civilian imports.

the public's attitude toward inflation in 1974–75 and in 1979–80, with relative stability (though with an upward trend) in between. The 1974–1978 step stands out more clearly in these series than in the series of actual rates of inflation.

Price Shocks and the Balance of Payments

Our purpose is to discover the causes for the jumps in the inflation rate and to investigate the mechanism by which inflation was stabilized along a given step. The most important empirical fact concerning recent inflationary developments in Israel is that all three inflationary jumps occurred in conjunction with BOP crises. Figure 16-4 shows the positive relation between peaks of current-account deficits in the private sector and increases in inflation. In fact every major BOP crisis led to a new inflation step.

The annual data used in Figure 16-4 conceal some interesting facts. It is often thought that the Yom Kippur War of October 1973 set off the BOP crisis and the acceleration of inflation. However, more detailed analysis shows that the import surplus had already increased by about 6 percent of GNP in the first nine months of 1973. During the same period the annual rate of inflation was close to 25 percent. From the viewpoint of the present analysis it is important to stress this

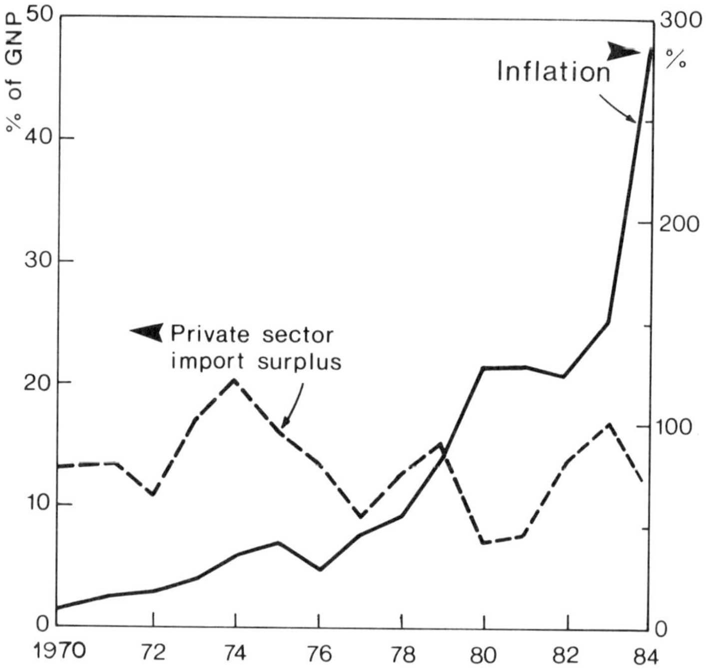

Figure 16-4
The private-sector import surplus (as a percentage of GNP) and inflation, 1970–1984. (Liviatan and Piterman, 1984a.)

association between inflation and BOP difficulties. Thus during 1972, before the BOP crisis developed, inflation ran at only 12 percent annually—or at about the same rate as in 1971 (which is not far from the 8 percent inflation in the first half of the 1960s).

In the 1979 step, inflation began to accelerate shortly (one quarter) before the deterioration in the private sector's balance of payments. It seems that the pressure of a miniboom in the domestic market caused an increase in inflation and later contributed to the BOP crisis; inflation was running at an annual rate of about 40 percent in the first three quarters of 1978, then jumped to 82 percent in the fourth quarter, and fell back to 66 percent in the quarter after that. These developments show that inflation could increase in the Israeli economy even in the absence of a BOP crisis. In our view, however, in the latter case inflation could be brought back to its original level by standard countercyclical measures (such as a restrictive credit policy or a reduction in government expenditures), whereas when the economy actually goes through a BOP crisis this is no longer possible.

The empirical one-to-one correspondence between BOP crises and sharp accelerations in inflation raises some important questions concerning the economic mechanism relating these phenomena and the government's role in the process. Figure 16-5 gives a clue to the answer: the big jumps in inflation are associated with drastic increases in the prices of imports and of government-controlled goods and services. Since the foreign exchange rate is "managed" by the government, we may infer that the sharp increase in government-controlled prices does in fact represent a policy of dealing with BOP crises.

The mere statistical fact that the series of import prices and of controlled prices show more pronounced reactions to BOP crises than the inflation series does not necessarily establish a causal relationship. The traumatic experience of October 1983 provides support for our conjecture that the price shock introduced by the government determined the course of events. Before that date, domestic inflation was stable; then government-controlled prices (including the exchange rate) shot up, in contrast to their gradual downward relative movement in the preceding period. Similarly, the crises of 1974 and 1979 each had a climax point in the fourth quarter of the year. Exactly as in October 1983, a "new government policy" was

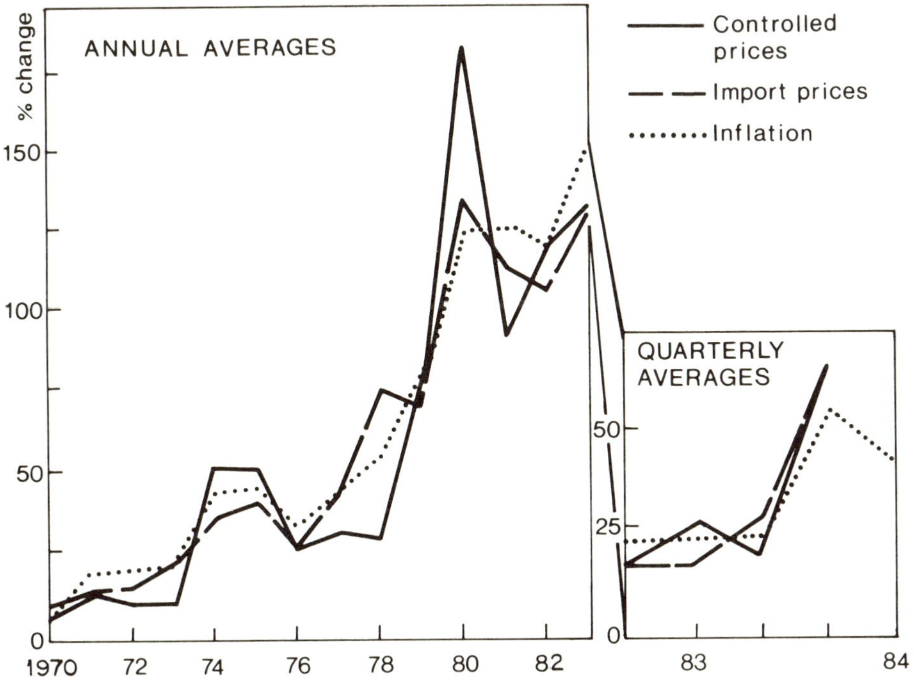

Figure 16-5

Percentage change in controlled prices, import prices, and inflation, annual averages 1971–1983 and quarterly averages 1983:1–1984:1. (Liviatan and Piterman, 1984a.)

announced, purporting to combat the BOP crisis. Each new policy included a drastic hike in controlled prices (and in two cases included a drastic devaluation). We therefore assume that essentially the same motivation underlay the government's price policy on all these occasions.

When the increase in government-controlled prices was not associated with BOP crises, they did not cause a jump in inflation. For example, the large devaluation of November 1977 (which was part of the liberalization scheme) raised inflation only temporarily. Similarly, the steep rise in controlled prices in the first half of 1982 did not trigger a new inflation step. In both cases the balance of payments was in relatively good shape.

Our view of the government's price-shock policy as a method of dealing with the BOP crisis raises two questions. First, what is the government's motivation for using this policy? Second, how are the shocks to the government-controlled prices (which are essentially onetime increases) transformed into long-term changes in inflation (that is, into the rate of change in prices)?

The government's motivation to carry out a drastic devaluation rests on two considerations. First, a drastic devaluation (with a surprise element in its exact timing) creates a temporary real devaluation despite the extensive indexation devices. This devaluation induces the postponement of imports of consumer durables and of firms' investment goods and thus alleviates pressure on the balance of payments until additional measures take effect.[1]

The second consideration concerns the assets markets. As the BOP crisis becomes evident, people form expectations of a depreciation that will reduce the foreign exchange reserves of the Central Bank (Kouri, 1976). One of the roles of a drastic devaluation is to appease speculators and to convince them that further devaluation is improbable.

Turning to other controlled prices, subsidized in varying degrees, we may point out the following considerations. First, the government wishes to use the reduction of subsidies as a means of reducing its real budget deficit and thus improve the balance of payments. Unlike other deficit-reduction measures, this measure can be implemented immediately, and this is a partial explanation of its drastic nature.

The second motivation for a drastic cut in subsidies is of a psychological nature and must be viewed within a broader framework of government policy in dealing with the BOP crisis. This policy involves slowing down economic activity and reducing real disposable income in the familiar Keynesian vein. Indeed, Figure 16-6 shows that the first two BOP crises were followed by reductions in real disposable income over considerable periods (and there are indications that this was true in 1984 as well, though modified by the announcement of elections). The drastic cuts in subsidies can be viewed as a signal to the public that "the party is over" and that people should be prepared for hard times ahead. The signal is

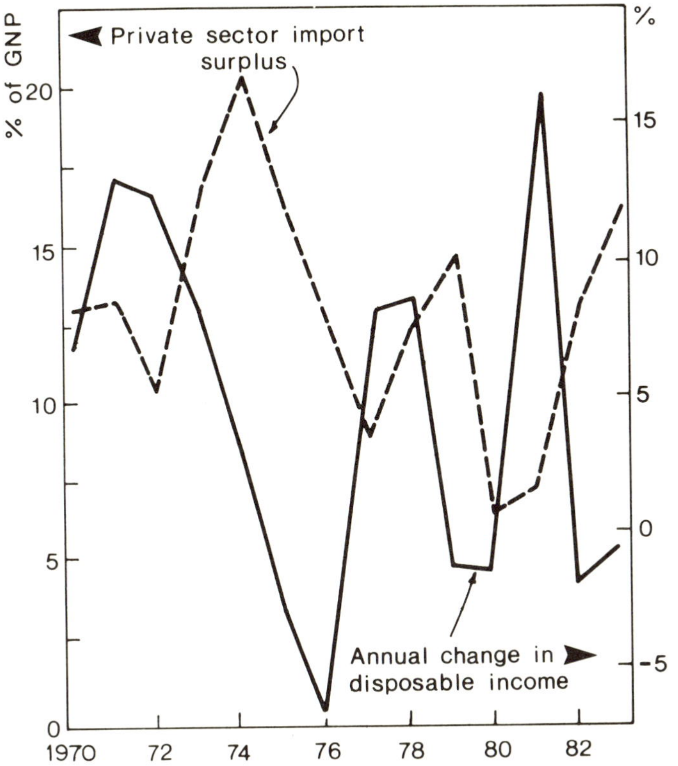

Figure 16-6
The private-sector import surplus and disposable income as a percentage of GNP, 1971–1982. (Liviatan and Piterman, 1984a.)

magnified by the fact that the sharp increases in both import prices and controlled prices cause a sharp (though temporary) erosion of real wages. (For a more detailed discussion of this issue see Liviatan and Piterman, 1984.)

The purpose of convincing the public, by means of a price shock, that a contractionary policy is under way is to induce a reduction in consumer spending, which usually means a reduction in imports. This psychological factor may be quantitatively more important in the short run than other, more conventional ones.

One may ask whether the government's price-shock policy is indeed a policy at all, in the sense that it is chosen from a set of alternatives. Is not the government's hand forced by the BOP crisis? The alternative policy seems to be the one of restrictive monetary and fiscal measures not associated with a direct cost push. These options are of course much more effective when used in early stages of the crisis. Such measures were in fact used in one way or another during the first two crises but became effective only after a considerable delay (unlike the price-shock policy). For example, after the 1974 crisis the government implemented a plan for the reduction of public spending that became fully effective only in 1976. Similarly, the restrictive monetary measures carried out after the 1979 crisis became fully effective only in 1980, when real interest rates on bank credit rose sharply. It seems that the price-shock technique has the advantage of swift implementation whose cost is an increase in inflationary tendencies (this, in an indirect way, is a short-term tradeoff between inflation and unemployment, since using the alternative policy may cause more unemployment in the short run).

Since the subsidies to domestic commodity prices in recent years have amounted to over 4 percent of GNP, this component cannot be excluded from any proposed budget cut. An alternative policy to a price shock may include a *gradual* reduction in the share of subsidies in controlled prices. However, the other components of the budget (especially expenditures) would have to bear the brunt of the cut in the early stages of implementation.

From Price Shock to Inflation Step

According to our theory, the first step in the acceleration of inflation is the deterioration of the economy's BOP situation. As the crisis intensifies, the government reacts by raising the prices it controls (for reasons outlined earlier). The automatic part of the monetary accommodation helps translate the initial shock of these prices into a shock to the general price level. We must now explain how the shock to the price level is transformed into a long-term increase in inflation.

One model addressing this problem focuses on the time lags in the adjustment process to nominal changes. An important source of these lags is wage contracts with partial indexation and with quarterly cost-of-living compensation clauses. Under these conditions, a price shock will generate a protracted adjustment process (Fischer, 1983). An important factor affecting the inertia of this process is the extent of monetary accommodation. If wages fully adjust to prices after some time lag as a result of the wage indexation model, then greater accommodation will increase the inertia of the original price shock. If money is fully adjusted to inflation with some lag, then any inflationary shock may become permanent.

One shortcoming of this model is that it treats all types of inflation shocks in the same way: a small shock to prices may lead to a permanent change in inflation just as a large shock will. The effect of an upward shift in inflation is symmetrical to that of a downward shift. This description does not characterize the Israeli economy.

It is reasonable to expect that during a relatively stable inflationary period, people form expectations about the "basic" level of inflation that corresponds to the relevant stage of the inflationary process. These expectations are reinforced by various government measures to build confidence in the stability of the current stage of inflation. These measures consist, first of all, of a managed exchange-rate policy that corresponds to recent inflationary history in Israel and abroad. This policy can be viewed as a lagged PPP rule. In addition, there is a policy of stabilizing government-controlled prices. Recently, these policy tools were even implemented in an attempt to *reduce* inflation: in September 1982 the government initiated a policy of slowing down the rate of devaluation and the rate of increase in controlled prices to 5 percent a month while inflation was running at 7–9 percent; this policy was abandoned in the third quarter of 1983, after it became evident that the basic inflation level remained unaffected.

Another means of stabilizing inflation is the use of nominal credit targets. Thus, after the inflation jump of 1979 the Central Bank initiated a policy of nominally raising commercial bank credit ceilings approximately in line with recent inflationary experience. This policy continued until the second half of 1982, when a more flexible system was introduced.

Other measures of this kind include the nominal component in government wage contracts and various other government contracts.

Owing to the existence of the stabilizing policies described, we may assume that the basic level of inflationary expectations changes only as a result of extraordinary developments. Only when these developments convince the public that the government can no longer control inflation at the existing basic level does the inflation enter a new stage. These extraordinary events can take various forms, such as excessive wage increases in the public sector. In practice, however, such shocks have occurred only in connection with BOP crises. One feature of the government's price-shock policy in dealing with the BOP crises is the public's growing conviction (usually conceded by the government) that the goal of stabilizing inflation must yield to the goal of improving the balance of payments.

We may now combine the two mechanisms outlined in this section. First, a price shock is extended to a lagged adjustment process accompanied by partial monetary adjustment. This adjustment may, for a while, appear to be a new step in the inflationary process, even if it is not. When these developments combine with a general feeling that the government has abandoned its inflation-stabilizing goal in favor of the BOP objective, the stage is set for an upward shift in the public's basic inflationary expectations. With a monetary system that fully accommodates persistent inflationary expectations, the actual level of inflation must soon follow suit.

This theory must be viewed in the specific economic context of the 1970s and 1980s. The model cannot be applied to the 1960s, when BOP problems, followed by a large devaluation in 1962, did not generate a long-term inflation. Yet it is worth noting that in the 1960s the economic system retained some features of a fixed-exchange economy that places severe limitations on monetary accommodation.

Our model assumes that the government uses the price-shock policy deliberately as a temporary measure to deal with the BOP crisis. Does the government take into consideration that this policy may have long-term consequences in the form of a new inflation step? Our impression is that this implication has not been realized until recently.

The Causes of the Inflation Steps

Given Israel's monetary regime, the cyclical BOP crises eventually lead to jumps in the basic rates of inflation. Thus we may identify the causes of inflation in Israel

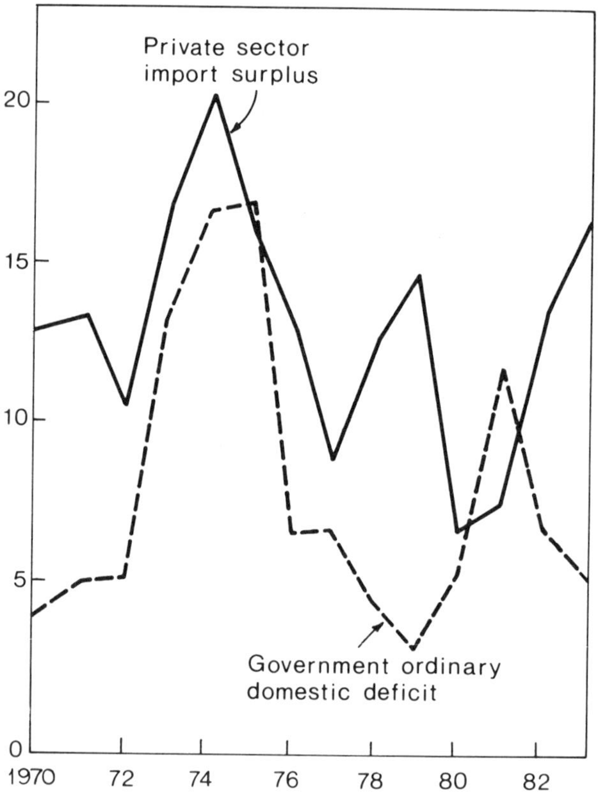

Figure 16-7
The private-sector import surplus and the government's domestic deficit, 1970–1982. (Liviatan and Piterman, 1984a.)

with the causes of the BOP crises. Reasonable as this approach may seem, it must be kept in proper perspective, since under a different monetary regime these crises would not have generated permanent increases in the rate of inflation.

In general, the BOP crises were caused by different factors. The 1974 crisis stemmed mainly from fiscal expansion and deteriorating terms of trade, while the 1979 crisis was strongly influenced by monetary factors. The third crisis is associated mainly with exchange-rate policy.

The Budget Deficit

We have already seen that the level of the government's budget deficit cannot explain the inflationary trend. However, since we have now shifted the emphasis to the cyclical aspect of BOP crises, we may inquire whether these are associated with *cyclical* increases in the budget deficit. Figure 16-7 shows the development of the private sector's import surplus along with the domestic deficit in the government's budget. The 1974 BOP crisis is associated with a sharp rise in the budget deficit, and the reduction in the budget deficit followed a reduction in the BOP deficit. However, this is the only case in which the two types of deficit are positively correlated. The other two crises developed when the budget deficit was decreasing. In fact one reason for this negative correlation (at least in 1979) is the policy of reducing the government deficit as a means of improving the balance of payments. Thus causality seems to run from the BOP crisis to the budget rather than vice versa. It seems, therefore, that the budget deficit cannot explain inflation in the past few years even in the roundabout way leading through the balance of payments.

Credit Expansion

Whereas the 1974 BOP crisis was associated to a considerable degree with fiscal expansion, the 1979 crisis was connected, among other things, with massive bank credit expansion in the two years before. In particular, the liberalization of credit regulations at the end of 1977 stimulated heavy borrowing from abroad and enabled an increase in domestic investment and in the level of economic activity, which contributed significantly to the 1979 crisis and consequently to the acceleration of inflation.

Import Prices

The first two BOP crises (1974 and 1979) were associated with sharp rises in import prices that contributed to the deterioration of the balance of payments. However, in view of the fact that export prices abroad also rose, it seems that the role of import prices has often been exaggerated. The terms of trade hit the balance of payments severely only in the 1974 crisis, when they worsened by 14 percent. In 1979 they worsened by only 5 percent, and in 1983 they improved by 1 percent.

Exchange Rate Policy

We have already noted that a managed exchange rate system was applied to stabilize inflation along a given step. However, the attempt to use the exchange rate more aggressively, as a means of reducing the basic level of inflation, was sustained for an interval of less than one year (starting in September 1982). This policy, known as "the 5 Percent Policy," attempted to "bend" the inflation of the general price level to that of government-controlled prices, and especially to the pace of exchange rate depreciation (which was set at 5 percent a month).

The main reason for the failure of this policy was the lack of credibility in its chances of succeeding. Since people considered this attempt as temporary, they tried to take advantage of the low exchange rate to acquire consumer durables and firms' investment goods. This move was facilitated by the fact that the real appreciation rendered borrowing abroad relatively cheap. Eventually the real appreciation of the domestic currency and the increase in the current-account deficit led to a reversal of this policy, and in October 1983 a full-fledged price shock went into effect. From our viewpoint, the 5 Percent Policy was inflationary, since it led directly to a BOP crisis.

The Role of Monetary Policy

In recent years some countries have used a restrictive monetary policy to reduce the level of inflation at the cost of increased unemployment. If this method were adopted in Israel, where inflation is high and institutionalized, the cost might have been higher. In any case the decision to reduce inflation drastically in such a way is one that far exceeds the powers of the Central Bank. Such a decision must involve the government as a whole, for the government must evaluate its readiness to take serious unemployment risks. Therefore, when we speak of monetary policy we mean less severe steps that may affect the unemployment rate only marginally. From the viewpoint of our model, there are some important areas in which monetary policy can restrain the acceleration of inflation. The role of monetary policy can be associated with the various phases of a typical inflation step.

We have already noted the role of monetary policy in stabilizing inflation along a given step. It seems that monetary policy has been quite effective in this respect, when applied to nominal credit targets in 1979–1982. The second role of monetary policy is associated with the phase of BOP deterioration. At this stage the public increases its purchases of foreign exchange in order to finance the growing import surplus and for speculative reasons (in expectation of a large devaluation). This trend causes a drain on commercial banks' nonlinked reserves and exerts pressure in the direction of credit contraction. If the Central Bank observes the classic "rules of the game" (see Dornbusch, 1980, chap. 7) it will not offset these tendencies. Consequently, the chances of reaching a BOP crisis diminish, even though the effectiveness of restrictive monetary policy is limited as a result of the stabilization of returns to government bonds.

An analysis of the financial data shows that every BOP crisis led to liquidity difficulties in the banking system as a result of the considerations mentioned above. However, in each case the Central Bank helped extricate the commercial banks by extending them loans under convenient terms. The data show that the banks' liquidity deficits (in real terms) increased at the beginning of each BOP crisis. The very fact that these deficits were made possible implies that the banks obtained an effective loan from the Central Bank on reasonable terms. The data also show that the actual reserve ratio of the commercial banks was reduced in each BOP crisis so as to enable them to overcome their liquidity difficulties. It is difficult to evaluate the extent of this monetary accommodation, but it certainly did not help prevent the aggravation of BOP difficulties.

In our model, monetary policy can also play an anti-inflationary role at the stage where the price shock is transformed into a new inflation step. At this stage, expectations are being formed regarding the new inflation plateau, and this process may be affected by the current severity of restrictive monetary policy. The October 1983 crisis provides an instructive example of the behavior of the Central Bank under these circumstances. In the first quarter after the price shock, the Central Bank restricted the nominal rate of expansion of commercial bank credit; however, at the beginning of 1984 it resumed almost full accommodation of bank credit to inflation.

Disinflationary Policies

In the following consideration of possible future anti-inflationary policy in Israel, it is important to remember that our model refers to a specific economic regime. One of the basic features of this regime is complete monetary accommodation to persistent inflationary expectations. In contrast to its response to BOP problems, the government has been unwilling to take a firm stand (and risk unemployment) to forestall increases in inflation.

This does not mean that nothing can be done to restrain inflation in the present economic regime. One simple lesson provided by our analysis is that acceleration of inflation can be avoided if the cyclical BOP crises are smooth. This task requires the implementation of a countercyclical policy aimed at the balance of payments, but without reliance on cost-push elements.

Although a reduction in the budget deficit may prevent acceleration of inflation, it cannot ensure a reduction in the basic level. For even if a reduction in the budget deficit does reduce the BOP deficit, there is no visible mechanism leading to a reduction in inflation. According to our approach, there seems to be nothing in the improvement of the balance of payments that can generate a process opposite to the one following a BOP crisis. At present, however, the limited objective of avoiding a further acceleration of inflation seems to be a significant one in view of the fact that the BOP crisis has not yet been overcome. A certain improvement in the BOP was recorded after the price shock of October 1983, but there seems to have been a reversal of this tendency following the announcement of new elections in July.

The danger of a new inflationary step can be averted only if the balance of payments is brought into line with its level in 1980–81. (The improvement will probably have to be even greater, given the additional external debt accumulated by Israel since then.) This effort calls for the standard types of contractionary monetary and fiscal policies, which must include a substantial countercyclical cut in government expenditures.

Currently there seems to be increasing concern about Israel's inflation rate, as well as greater readiness to adopt drastic anti-inflationary policies. We share the growing conviction that gradualist policies cannot be effective at this stage in the inflationary process. But according to our model, a drastic reduction of inflation requires some basic changes in the present monetary regime.

All the changes required in the monetary regime must proceed from a starting point of a "normal" state of the balance of payments. As long as a crisis prevails, there is always the danger of a new inflationary burst. The prerequisites to elimination of the current crisis are appropriate monetary and fiscal measures, although as we have already noted, these will not in themselves reduce the basic level of inflation.

The second step in any disinflationary policy should be a temporary wage-price freeze. This idea has recently been gaining a great deal of public support and is advocated by the major political parties despite the difficulties entailed in its implementation. Economists emphasize, of course, that the freeze should be accompanied by a similar policy in the monetary sector. One reason for such a freeze is the need to reduce the inflationary inertia inherent in the wage-indexation scheme. The main reason, however, is closely related to the fact that one cannot severely curtail the nominal expansion of monetary aggregates when inflation is running at an annual rate of 400 percent. Such a curtailment will cause a sharp real monetary contraction, which may lead to serious unemployment problems. The freeze is necessary in order to prevent this shock in the initial stages and to reduce the risk of unemployment in later stages. This consideration is extremely important, since the socially tolerable level of unemployment in Israel is much lower than in the United Kingdom or the United States.

It is advisable to implement the wage-price freeze only after the BOP objectives have been achieved. It is also important to remove distortions gradually in relative government-controlled prices before the freeze; these distortions are due to such factors as differential exchange rates and excessive subsidization, and they increase the potential of cost-push tendencies when the system is unfrozen.

An important advantage of this step-by-step procedure is that it ensures that real wages and the real exchange rate will be frozen at the correct levels. Simultaneous implementation of both stages always entails the risk of setting the relative price at values that are inconsistent with the planned budget cut. Some economists argue that the latter alternative is politically preferable, since it offers the immediate prize of arresting inflation. This may indeed be true, but if the mere announcement of this fiscal contraction is not credible, the freeze may bring harmful results.

If the first two stages are successfully implemented, the next task is to unfreeze the economy. At this point the issue of the monetary regime becomes all-important. Since the force driving Israel's inflation cannot be associated with the need to finance the budget, the reluctance to cut the supply of money must stem from the government's desire to avoid unemployment. It is well known that unemployment may result from inertia of inflationary expectations combined with a rigid monetary policy. As long as the public does not believe in the government's readiness to take a stand on the issue of monetary accommodation, disinflation has no real chance of success. When the government has adjusted its budget to solve the BOP problem and has implemented a wage-price freeze, its credibility for success in the disinflation policy will increase greatly, and this effect will in turn considerably reduce inflationary inertia and consequently the risk of unemployment. However, such risks will always remain, and the government must make it clear that it is ready to face them without giving up its monetary objectives. When the freeze ends, various individual prices and wages will be extremely out of line with their equilibrium level as a result of the original high level of inflation. When the system is unfrozen, these will constitute a sizable cost-push element that may easily generate a new inflationary spiral if monetary policy is accommodating. This is the moment of truth for the monetary system in the disinflation program.

Assuming the government is ready to stop monetary accommodation to cost pushes and to remaining inflationary expectations, we must consider the options available for implementation of this policy. We assume that the government's budget is balanced, in the sense that it does not rely on revenue from printing money. We also assume that the exchange rate follows a PPP rule. Under these conditions a restrictive policy concerning monetary aggregates will lead to an increase in real interest rates. To sustain this tendency, the government must severely curtail short-term capital flows (something that has not been done in Israel for some time).

The next problem is to select the targets for controlling the nominal expansion of the system. The usual procedure is to control the money base, but this is impossible in the current system of pegging real returns to government bonds. In this system, however, it is possible to fix the volume of total nominal bank credit and to use it as a nominal anchor. This strategy may not be enough, however; an additional measure might be to extend the nominal targets to the government budget as well.

To use the money base as a nominal anchor, it is necessary to remove the pegging of the real rate of return to government bonds. This strategy will increase demand for the money base and make it an effective nominal anchor provided the banking system maintains a rigid reserve ratio. We assume that there are severe restrictions on short-term capital flows in order to maintain control of the money base.

The widespread indexation coverage of bank credit and financial assets makes the control of these nominal targets extremely difficult. It would probably also be necessary to limit the indexation schemes as well as the linkage of export credit to the value of exports. Indexation plays a stabilizing role in the transition period, since it reduces the flight from money to commodities and to foreign exchange. It is therefore advisable to retain indexation on long-term financial instruments.

In addition to the transition period following the wage-price freeze, a complete disinflation scheme must consider later stages, which are beyond the scope of this chapter.

As an alternative to policies intended to strengthen the domestic money base, there has been a heated debate in Israel about a completely different solution, the well-known Dollarization Plan. In its extreme form it advocates the complete abandonment of domestic money and a switch to the U.S. dollar as legal tender in Israel (see N. Liviatan, 1984; Plessner, 1984).

Advocates of the plan point to its main advantage, namely, its ability to bring the three-digit inflation to an immediate halt and reduce it to approximately the U.S. level. They further argue that the credibility of dollar currency may make it possible to arrest the inflationary spiral with a relatively low increase in unemployment, and that the cost in terms of seigniorage payments to the United States is also relatively low (about 1 percent of GNP). Even some advocates concede, however, that a precondition for its implementation is the elimination of the current BOP crisis, which requires a substantial budget cut.

Opponents of the plan point to the loss of independence in the areas of exchange-rate and monetary policies and to the related increased reliance on unemployment as an adjustment mechanism. Of course, nationalist sentiment also opposes such a move.

The main obstacle to implementation of the Dollarization Plan, however, seems to be a financial one—the system's inability to cope with a run on the banks for dollars. The fact is that the amount of liquid assets that are now in the nature of short-term bank deposits, combined with the current flow of redemptions of government bonds, is far beyond the size of the actual and potential foreign currency reserves. To overcome these problems requires a basic change in the financial structure of the economy, and this objective cannot be achieved in the short run.

17

The Inflationary Process: Shocks and Accommodation

Michael Bruno and Stanley Fischer

Israel's annual inflation rate increased from 8 percent in 1965 to 300–400 percent in the first half of 1984. Up to 1977, the process of inflation in Israel does not appear to have been qualitatively different from that in the OECD countries (see Chapter 14). Indeed, even after jumping to 40–50 percent after the Yom Kippur War, inflation declined slowly to an annual rate of 25 percent by the first half of 1977. After the financial liberalization of late 1977, the economy appeared to move into a new era, with inflation firmly entrenched, and seemingly capable only of rising.

This chapter provides an overview and analysis of the inflationary process and tries to explain the increases in the inflation rate and the forces that keep it high and, on occasion, rising. There has been no shortage of explanations of inflation: it has been ascribed to indexation, to monetary policy, to the budget deficit, to the introduction of floating exchange rates, to "bubbles"—self-justifying expectations of inflation—to name only some of the most prominent. Several of these explanations provide necessary conditions for the continuation of the process, as we shall show below. Given successive governments' reluctance to force the inflation rate down through restrictive policy that might produce a major recession, serious economic questions remain about the forces driving inflation and the institutional adaptations that permit the economy to operate at a reasonable level of efficiency despite inflation. Our view is that institutional adaptations and accommodating monetary and fiscal policies have left the stabilizing forces in the economy very weak, and the inflation rate in a meta-stable equilibrium. Thus the inflation rate could decline as well as rise, but the expansionary thrust of fiscal and monetary policies during the period has made the adaptation of the inflationary process, including expectations formation, smoother upward and more rigid downward, even when cost-reducing factors were occasionally operative.

In developing our analytical framework below we assign roles to indexation, to financial structure, and to the exchange-rate system in determining the dynamics of the economy. We also focus on fiscal and monetary policies that have permitted the inflation to continue.

Analytical Framework

We use a standard aggregate supply-demand framework to analyze inflation. The particular Israeli emphasis comes in the description of the properties of assets and of wage indexation, in the policy choices that make the growth rate of money and the composition of the outstanding stock of government debt endogenous, and in the magnitudes of the government and current-account deficits that drive the accumulation of domestic government and foreign debts.

The position of the aggregate supply (AS) schedule depends on wages and associated payroll taxes, raw-material prices, the cost of capital, and technology; the position of the aggregate demand (AD) curve is determined by the value, liquidity, and composition of wealth, by the exchange rate and foreign variables —demand, prices, and interest rates—by fiscal policy variables, and by expectations of inflation and exchange-rate changes. Continuous shifts in the aggregate supply and demand curves trace the changing price level and output.

To analyze the dynamics of inflation, we write the aggregate supply and demand curves (which relate output to the nominal price level) as functions of their major driving variables. Thus,

$$Y_s = g(W/P, E/P, t, a), \tag{17.1}$$

where Y_s is the supply of output, W is the nominal wage (as a cost to the employer, and thus including payroll taxes), P is the price level, E is the nominal exchange rate that determines the domestic cost of imported raw materials, t is a variable representing the state of technology, and a represents missing supply variables, movements in which can be thought of as supply shocks (such as the world price of raw materials).

On the aggregate demand side we have

$$Y_d = f(H/P, V, G - T, E/P, Y^*, \pi^e, z). \tag{17.2}$$

We represent aggregate demand (Y_d) as a function of the real stock of high-powered money (H/P), real wealth (V), the government domestic demand surplus ($G - T$), the real exchange rate (E/P), foreign income (Y^*), the expected rate of inflation (π^e), and z, a demand shock variable representing demand factors. We shall subsequently consider the domestic budget deficit as a fraction (δ) of GNP. Because there is no agreed-upon measure of the liquidity of the stock of assets, we omit that determinant of aggregate demand from (17.2).

To understand the dynamics of the inflationary process, we need to analyze the determinants and dynamics of the variables specified in the aggregate supply and demand curves (17.1) and (17.2). On the aggregate supply side, wages are determined in biannual wage negotiations that fix a base wage level and indexation formulas for the adjustment of the wage to changes in the price level. Typically the indexation clauses have provided for partial (70–80 percent), semiannual and subsequently quarterly, compensation for price changes. The nonadjustment of wages for a period of three months at high rates of inflation makes for a marked within-quarter variation of wages; the less-than-complete compensation for inflation means that real wages at very high rates of inflation will fall rapidly over the life of a contract.[1] This account of the wage adjustment process makes it difficult to blame indexation as the main factor determining the behavior of wages, since even in the short run there are always discretionary elements in the wage-setting process.

The second argument in the supply function is the real exchange rate, representing the prices of imported raw materials.[2] A depreciation or devaluation (increase in E) will shift the AS schedule up, tending to increase prices and reduce output. If the Bank of Israel follows a purchasing power parity (PPP) rule, domestic price-level shocks are automatically transformed into inflationary exchange rate changes. We shall later discuss the behavior of the economy when the government was following a set of operating rules that include PPP for control of the exchange rate (from around 1975 onward).

Many of the most significant factors in the Israeli inflation enter in the first three arguments of the aggregate demand function (2), in the interaction of monetary and fiscal policies, and in the dynamics of asset supplies. Private-sector wealth consists of some nominal assets, largely currency and demand deposits; of various government liabilities indexed to either the price level or the foreign-exchange rate; of some foreign assets; and of consumer durables, housing, and private ownership of corporations. We simplify by concentrating on the stock of high-powered money (H), government bonds indexed to the price level (B_p), government bonds indexed to the exchange rate (B_f), and direct ownership of foreign exchange (F). Thus wealth is given by:

$$V = H/P + B_p + E \cdot B_f/P + E \cdot F/P. \tag{17.3}$$

In (17.3) B_f and F are the foreign-currency denominated values of holdings of foreign-currency linked bonds and foreign currency respectively. The dynamics of inflation in Israel are significantly affected by the fact that domestic bonds (B_p) are fixed in real value, and that the nominal value of much of the remainder of the government debt ($E \cdot B_f$) automatically increases when there is a devaluation. Thus the Israeli economy does not have the automatic inflation stabilizer in that an increase in the price level and/or the exchange rate reduces real private-sector wealth by reducing the real value of the outstanding stock of government debt, except for the possibility that the real value of the monetary base would fall. Indeed, if the government is pursuing a PPP exchange-rate policy, then any domestic inflationary shock automatically increases the nominal value of wealth virtually *pari passu.*

Examining the aggregate demand function (17.2), and assuming both that the government budget deficit is fixed in real terms[3] and that the exchange rate is determined by PPP, we see that the only potential element of nonhomogeneity or nonaccommodation to price rises on the demand side is H, the nominal stock of high-powered money. The monetary base, H, is a small nominal magnitude with which to control the price level (assuming a given real exchange rate and real wage), so that even if H were held strictly constant when the price level rose, it might be expected to exert at best a small and slow stabilizing influence.

Such stabilization would result from the rise in the rate of interest caused by the reduction in the real money base. But suppose the monetary authority is attempting to control the real rate of interest, as it has in Israel. Then the quantity of high-powered money becomes endogenous, and in response to an increase in the price level and consequent upward pressure on the interest rate, the stock of high-powered money is increased. Thus the stabilizing element that could have been provided by keeping H to a prescribed path is lost. There would accordingly be no forces on the demand side of the economy tending to resist rising prices. The price level then does not tend to return to its original level, or to any equilibrium level, unless some element of policy—be it monetary or fiscal—is directed to that end.

The above discussion implies that we could expect the aggregate demand (AD) schedule to be quite steep or virtually vertical. The very short-run AS curve, on the other hand, will be considerably flatter, because of imperfect wage indexation and as long as the economy is operating below capacity (which it did in the mid-1970s); the short run is defined here as the indexation period for wages. However, since wages have also been effectively indexed, though at a time lag (which has gradually become shorter). We could expect greater steepness in the AS curve in the move from the very short run (say, a quarter or less) to somewhat longer time spans (say, six months or more). The price level may thus become very sensitive to shocks. As we shall see, this problem has worsened as the inflationary process accelerated toward the end of the 1970s.

The steepness of the AD curve and relative flatness of the short-run AS curve would imply that in the short run, price-level changes would mainly be affected by cost factors (wages and input prices) and less by demand shifts, while demand shifts would feature large in short-run output changes (see Chapter 14).

Equating the supply (17.1) and the demand (17.2) relationships and looking at the implied equilibrium in rate-of-change form, we may write the rate of change of the price level ($\dot{P}/P = \pi$) as a linear function of the rates of change of the three key nominal magnitudes: the nominal wage ($\dot{w} = \dot{W}/W$), the exchange rate ($\dot{e} = \dot{E}/E$), and the money base ($\dot{m} = \dot{H}/H$), plus supply shift (μ_s) and demand shift (μ_d) factors. These are combined into one factor (μ), which can be expected to be dominated by the supply side. Thus,

$$\pi = \dot{p} = a_1\dot{w} + a_2\dot{e} + a_3\dot{m} + \mu, \tag{17.4}$$

where $p = \log P$, $m = \log H$, $w = \log W$, $e = \log E$, and a dot indicates the change in a variable.

The description of the price dynamics can be completed by a Phillips-type equation for wages as a function of prices and labor-market slack, and by adjustment rules for the exchange rate and the money base during periods for which these could not be considered to be exogenously determined.

Consider now the longer-run implications of such price dynamics when the above-nominal magnitudes are themselves each indexed to past inflation (π_{-1}) and/or to inflationary expectations (π^e). If the system is homogeneous we can summarize the inflationary process in the form

$$\pi_t = \alpha\pi_{t-1} + (1 - \alpha)\pi_t^e + \epsilon_t, \tag{17.5}$$

where ϵ_t is a summary statistic involving supply and demand shocks, μ, as well as shocks to w, e, and m.

Suppose that expectations are adaptive, with coefficient of adaptation β, so that

$$\pi_t^e = \beta\pi_{t-1} + (1 - \beta)\pi_{t-1}^e. \tag{17.6}$$

Solving (5) and (6) we obtain:

$$\pi_t - \pi_{t-1} = \epsilon_t - (1 - \alpha)(1 - \beta)\sum_{i=1}^{\infty} [\alpha(1 - \beta)]^{i-1}\epsilon_{t-i}. \tag{17.7}$$

Equation (17.7) shows that when $(1 - \alpha)(1 - \beta)$ becomes very small,[4] a positive shock $\epsilon_t > 0$ will be transmitted into an immediate jump in the *inflation rate* ($\Delta\pi_t = \pi_t - \pi_{t-1} > 0$) rather than just into a jump in the *price level.*[5] Thus, one puzzling feature of the Israeli inflation—the apparent tendency for a shock to the price level (such as a devaluation) to result in a permanent change in the inflation rate—can be explained as a result of accommodating macro policies.

But there is a second feature of the inflation that needs explanation: the inflation rate jumps up quite readily but does not fall in the same way. Suppose the indexation or the expectation-formation mechanisms are not symmetrical upward and downward. The coefficient of adaptation (β) is likely to depend on the state of the economy as perceived by individuals and firms. For example, when the general thrust of fiscal and monetary policy is highly expansionary and there is a temporary unexpected downward shift in inflation in period $t-1$ ($\pi_{t-1} - \pi^e_{t-1} < 0$), β may be very small (or zero) so that expectations are not revised downward—that is, in equation (17.6) we get $\pi^e_t \sim \pi^e_{t-1}$ even though $\pi_{t-1} < \pi^e_{t-1}$, while β would be large (or close to 1) when the unexpected shock is positive ($\pi_{t-1} > \pi^e_{t-1}$). The effect of such asymmetries is to make a sequence of positive and negative shocks of zero mean impart an upward thrust to the inflation rate.

If the inflation rate follows the random walk implied by (17.7) when $\alpha = 1$ or $\beta = 1$, then the inflation rate could, in the long run, be at any level. But if α is slightly less than one, that is, if there is any element of nonhomogeneity in the equation for the inflation rate, the system will tend—perhaps very slowly—to return to an equilibrium long-run inflation rate.[6]

In particular, fiscal policy considerations may determine the average growth rate of money, through the government budget constraint, even if monetary policy does not pursue explicit monetary growth targets. We can write the government budget constraint as

$$G - T = \delta Y = \dot{H}/P + \dot{B}. \tag{17.8}$$

We here suppress the difference between bonds indexed to the domestic price level and to the exchange rate, and omit direct government sales of foreign exchange, which will be added subsequently.

In steady state, the ratios $H/(P \cdot Y)$ and B/Y, where Y is real GNP, are constant. Accordingly, in steady state the growth rate of high-powered money $\dot{H}/H$ ($\dot{m}$) is equal to the inflation rate (π) plus the growth rate of output (g_y):

$$\dot{m} = \pi + g_y. \tag{17.9}$$

Similarly, the growth rate of bonds (g_b) is equal to the growth rate of output (g_y):

$$g_b = g_y. \tag{17.10}$$

Thus in steady state the government budget constraint becomes:

$$\delta = (\pi + g_y)(H/PY) + g_y(B/Y). \tag{17.11}$$

Now let h denote the ratio of the stock of real high-powered money to nominal GNP (H/PY), and b the ratio of bonds to GNP (B/Y). Then,

$$\pi = [\delta - g_y(h + b)]/h. \tag{17.12}$$

Equation (17.12) gives one approach to analyzing the determinants of the growth rate of the monetary base and thus, in steady state, of the inflation rate. The term following g_y in the denominator in (17.12) is the amount of the deficit that can be financed by the government through the sale of bonds and printing of money without increasing their respective ratios to GNP. The more rapid the growth rate of output, the greater the share of the deficit that can be financed in a noninflationary way. The larger the government deficit, δ, the higher the inflation rate in the steady state. And the larger the monetary base, the lower the inflation rate need be.

The government budget deficit obviously plays a major role in this steady-state analysis. There is no reason, though, to expect a close short-run connection between the inflation rate and the size of the government budget deficit; for when using the approach implied by (17.12), we used the quantity theory in equation (17.9) to link the inflation rate to the growth rate of money in the steady state. But in the short run there is at best a very loose connection between the growth rate of the stock of high-powered money and inflation.

We can now extend the government budget constraint (17.8) to include the government's foreign account and changes in the government's foreign debt ($\dot{FG}$). We get:

$$(\delta + \delta_f) \cdot Y = \dot{H}/P + \dot{B} + E \cdot \dot{FG}/P, \tag{17.8'}$$

where δ_f is the government's external deficit as a percentage of GNP. The external deficit (sometimes a surplus) is equal to the deficit on goods and services *minus* unilateral transfers.[7]

Equation (17.8′), the overall government budget constraint, shows that the government finances its total deficit in three ways: through the printing of high-powered money, through sales of bonds (indexed either to the price level or to the exchange rate), and through borrowing abroad. Sales of foreign exchange to domestic residents, one way of financing a domestic deficit, do not necessarily imply increases in the government's foreign indebtedness: if the government has an overall foreign surplus, then the sale of foreign exchange is merely the means by which the foreign surplus finances part of the domestic deficit. It should be noted that FG is the government's *net* foreign debt. Thus if the government runs down foreign exchange reserves to sell foreign currency to domestic residents it is, in terms of (17.8′), engaging in foreign borrowing.

The use of the government budget constraint (17.8) or (17.8′) does not necessarily imply that the government consciously decides on a particular growth rate of high-powered money as a means of financing its budget deficit. Rather, in the Israeli context it is much more likely that the government turns to printing money as its last resort in budget financing. First it decides what it needs to spend and how much it can raise through taxes (and foreign borrowing); then it sells as many bonds as it can at the existing interest rate and finances the rest by printing money (see also Fischer, 1984). According to this approach, relatively small changes in the deficit would be consistent in the long run with major changes in the growth rate of H, and thus of inflation. But the transitional costs of moving from a high-inflation to a low-inflation equilibrium could be sufficient to inhibit such a change. We believe this to be particularly important in the Israeli context.

The current stock of government debt is the result of past deficits, and the prospective size of the debt is a function of expected deficits. A large current debt may inhibit monetary policy by preventing aggressive use of interest rate variations for current stabilization purposes, lest increasing interest rates significantly increase the budget deficit or thwart the finance of future deficits because of fluctuations in bond prices. Prospective deficits influence aggregate demand and the terms at which the government can obtain both current and future financing.

The analytical framework presented in this section is reasonably conventional. The major departure from standard macroeconomic models lies in the structure of assets, for wage indexation is found in many countries. As we shall argue below, abnormal macroeconomic behavior in Israel must be attributed at least as much to specific policy choices that, for instance, produce large budget deficits and/or endogenize the rate of growth of money, as to peculiar structural characteristics of the economy.

Analysis of the Inflationary Economy

Since 1965 economic policy in Israel has been significantly affected by the experience of the 1965–1967 recession, when restrictive policies were implemented primarily to bring the current account deficit closer to balance, but also to counteract the then high (8 percent) rate of inflation. The resultant unemployment level of more than 10 percent brought both social demoralization and emigration, with the result that maintenance of low unemployment rates was considered a major policy goal during the crises of the 1970s. Despite the rising rate of inflation since 1970, there has been no strong political support for policies that would attempt to control inflation at the expense of temporary unemployment. Widespread indexation, particularly of asset returns, reduced the perceived and actual costs of any given rate of inflation and helped keep inflation from becoming the dominant economic policy issue.

The major features of the inflation process shown in Table 17-1 and Figure 17-1 are the generally rising trend of the inflation rate since 1965, and the apparent step nature of the changes. To understand the inflation process we have to understand reasons for both of these patterns.

TABLE 17-1. Inflation rate, growth rate, current-account deficit, and relative price changes, 1960:1-1984:1 (annual percentage rates, based on quarterly compounding)

Phase	Number of quarters (1)	CPI change (2)	GNP growth (3)	Current account deficit/ GDP[a] (4)	Real export price[b] (5)	Real import price[c] (6)	Real wage in mfg. (7)
1 Normal growth (1960:1–1965:1)	20	6.8	9.6[d]	19.9[d]	9.3[d]	2.7[d]	3.4
2 Recession (1965:1–1967:2)	9	6.1	–1.5	15.3	–1.1	–4.8	5.2
3 Recovery (1967:2–1970:1)	11	2.0	14.6	18.5	4.7	6.4	2.4
4 Boom (1970:1–1973:3)	14	14.4	9.1	22.0	2.2	2.9	2.2
5 War and oil shock (1973:3–1977:2)	15	36.0	2.6	30.9	–0.7	–0.4	2.9
6 Traverse (1977:2–1979:4)	10	71.0	3.0	23.5	5.3	4.8	1.0
7 Plateau (1979:4–1983:3)	15	123.3	1.6	19.6	–2.9	–3.5	7.5
8 Runaway inflation (1983:3–1984:1)	2	369.0	—	—	—	—	—

Sources: Quarterly national accounts, Central Bureau of Statistics.
a. Total deficit divided by GDP (this is a *level* ratio).
b. Rate of change of export prices, at effective exchange rate, deflated by CPI.
c. Rate of change of domestic import prices, at effective exchange rate, deflated by CPI.
d. Calculated from annual data.

Inflation Dynamics

On the demand side, expansive fiscal policy and accommodative monetary and exchange-rate policy have generally combined to maintain upward pressure on the price level and the rate of inflation, and as a result of the structure of the financial system and the policy choices made, the automatic forces that could stabilize inflation in response to supply shocks are very weak. Favorable shocks were usually exploited to help expand demand (in the last few years, consumption) and output, but unfavorable ones were not counteracted for any length of

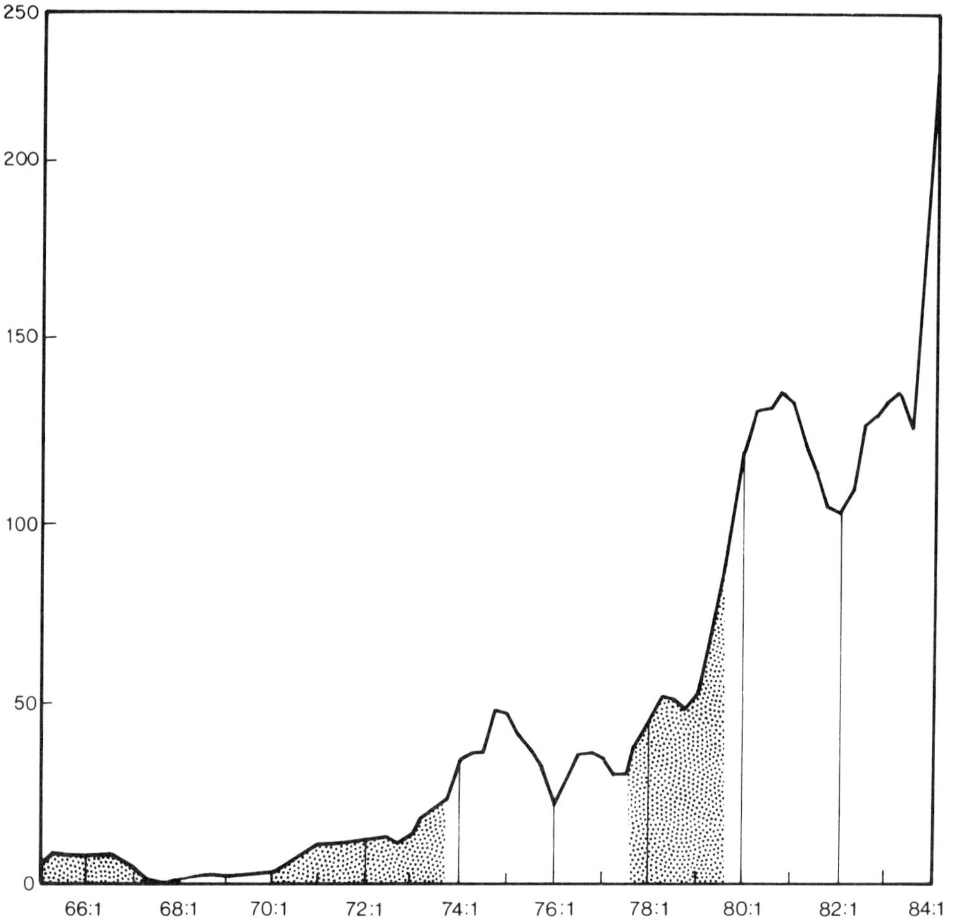

Figure 17-1
Annual rate of CPI inflation, each quarter over same quarter of previous year, 1966:1–1984:1 (percentages). (CBS data.)

time by restrictive discretionary policy. Temporary contractionary policies were undertaken (as in 1975–1977 and in 1980), usually accompanied by cost-increasing measures (devaluation, indirect taxes, and a cut in subsidies) that pushed up the AS curve, while the flatness of the AS curve implied that contraction showed up in output rather than in prices. A *short-run* account of inflationary dynamics will then be dominated by supply-side factors, which we discuss first. The important underlying role of the budget deficit and of the monetary system in accounting for shifts in long-run steady-state inflation will be discussed afterward.

The cost-side dynamics of inflation have featured in several accounts of the inflationary process in the 1960s and early 1970s, the best known being Artstein and Sussman's (1977) pair of annual wage and consumer-price equations for the period 1958–1975 (discussed briefly in Chapter 14 of this volume).[8] Prices are a function of wages and import prices plus a small, hardly significant, role for money; wages are a function of prices, unemployment, and the increased labor supply from the territories (a very important wage-moderating factor in the years 1968–1972).

It can be argued that with a high degree of correlation between the nominal magnitudes (prices, wages, exchange rates, and money) price equations of the typical kind are difficult to interpret, especially after 1975. However, we can partly sidestep this problem by running such an equation in real terms, namely, in the form of first differences with respect to past inflation. The following equation is obtained in terms of wholesale prices (to neutralize, to the extent possible, subsidies and demand elements) for the sixty-six quarters 1966:3–1982:4:

$$(17.13) \qquad \underset{}{\dot{p} - \dot{p}_{-1}} = \underset{(0.36)}{-0.26} + \underset{(0.09)}{0.35}(\dot{w} - \dot{p}_{-1}) + \underset{(0.05)}{0.28}(\dot{p}_n - \dot{p}_{-1})$$

$$\text{D.W.} = 2.01 \qquad \bar{R}^2 = 0.46$$

where p_n is import prices.[9]

An attempt to add monetary variables to this equation fails on the whole, except for an apparent five-quarter-lagged effect of real credit expansion on inflation in 1979:4–1982:4. We shall return to the important role of real import prices and real credit expansion in discussing the traverse to the higher inflation plateau.

We continue our discussion of cost-side adjustments in the inflationary process by recalling that wages (w) can in turn be related to lagged inflation, and that the exchange rate has followed an approximate PPP rule (plus occasional jumps) since the introduction of the crawling peg in 1975:3. Instead of using an equation such as (17.13), we can therefore run a regression of inflation acceleration ($\dot{p} - \dot{p}_{-1}$) on its own past lags plus the acceleration in exchange-rate adjustment ($\dot{e} - \dot{e}_{-1}$). Using four-quarter lags and running the regression over subperiods in 1965:1–1982:4, we find coefficients of 0.20–0.29 for ($\dot{e} - \dot{e}_{-1}$), similar to the ones found in the previous regression and also in Artstein and Sussman (1977); we also test and find that the inflation rate is homogeneous in terms of its own past lags.[10] What is more interesting is the finding, already recorded by Gottlieb and Piterman (1982), that the share of quarterly inflation "explained" by the inflation of the previous two quarters rises continuously over time. Table 17-2 presents the implied coefficients. These are evidence of both the considerable inertia (autore-

TABLE 17-2. Elasticity of inflation with respect to its own logs

	Number of observations	$\dot{p}_{-1}$	$\dot{p}_{-2}$	Sum of $\dot{p}_{-1}$ and $\dot{p}_{-2}$
1965:1–1971:1	25	0.37	0.19	0.56
1971:2–1975:2	17	0.32	–0.24	0.08
1975:3–1978:4	14	0.51	0.36	0.87
1979:1–1982:4	16	0.62	0.42	1.04
1975:3–1982:4	30	0.59	0.37	0.96

Source: Regressions, see text.

gressive nature) of the inflationary process and the shortening of the lag in the implicit indexation of all nominal magnitudes (including faster monetary accommodation).

Consider now the asymmetric response to upward and downward inflationary shocks. When we add the acceleration in prices of controlled (subsidized) products ($\Delta\dot{p}_k$) to the same regression together with the acceleration in exchange rates ($\Delta\dot{e}$), this time allowing for a different response to positive and negative shocks, we find the following coefficients (for the period 1975:3–1983:1)—

$\Delta\dot{e}^+$	$\Delta\dot{e}^-$	$\Delta\dot{p}_k^+$	$\Delta\dot{p}_k^-$
0.284	0.002	0.320	−0.003
(0.099)	(0.143)	(0.143)	(0.121)

As was noted earlier, expectations and price linkages are asymmetric when the general economic climate is expansionary. When the government is running a large and persistent deficit that shows no evidence of declining, cost reduction will be perceived as only temporary. Later we mention an application of this feature to the recent disinflation experience of 1981–82. At this point we turn to the role of fiscal and monetary variables.

Policy Variables

Table 17-3 shows the government budget deficit over successive subperiods for 1960–1983. It gives both the domestic budget deficit (column 4) as a measure of the contribution of the government to domestic demand, and the overall budget deficit (column 5), including the government's current-account (of the balance-of-payments) deficit; the overall deficit is an indication of both the rate of change

TABLE 17-3. Financing of the government budget as a percentage of GNP, 1960–1983

Period	Domestic expenditure[a] (1)	Net foreign expenditure[b] (2)	Taxes[c] (3)	Domestic deficit (1 – 3) (4)	Total deficit (4 + 2) (5)	Base money creation (6)	Domestic debt finance[d] (7)	Foreign debt finance (8)
1960–64	27.0	1.2	28.8	–1.8	–0.6	2.5	–3.3	0.3
1965–67	32.0	2.8	29.6	2.4	5.2	2.2	0	3.0
1968–73	41.0	6.6	34.4	6.6	13.2	3.2	5.4	4.6
1974–77	56.4	3.3	42.1	14.3	17.6	2.6	4.7	10.4
1978–80	60.7	2.0	45.5	15.2	17.2	2.0	7.3	6.9
1981–83	61.0	–0.3	46.5	14.4	14.1	2.1	7.2	4.9
1983[e]	59.0	–0.2	48.1	10.9	10.7	2.3	1.4	7.0

Sources: 1960–1980: Meridor (1983); 1981–1983: Bank of Israel, *Annual Report, 1983.*

Note: Definitions of columns 1, 4, 7 have been slightly altered between the two sources by an order of no more than 1–2 percent.

a. Includes goods and services, subsidies, transfers, and interest on the public debt.

b. Government expenditure abroad (mainly armaments) *plus* interest on debt *minus* unilateral transfers (mainly U.S. government).

c. Includes all direct and indirect taxes and transfers to government.

d. Includes indexed bonds and, after 1977, Bank of Israel PATAM accounts. Figures are net of repayments and of loans to the public sector: (8.9 percent in 1968–1973, 4.3 percent in 1974–1977, and very small afterwards.

e. Excludes 4 percent purchase by Bank of Israel of commercial bank shares (which could be added to columns 1, 4, 5 and 7).

of government debt—internal and external—and the amount of money printed. The domestic deficit climbed sharply as a percentage of GDP over successive periods from the start of the 1960s until shortly after the Yom Kippur War. It then remained more or less constant, before falling somewhat in 1982 and 1983. It is not only the trend in the domestic deficit that is noteworthy, but also its absolute size; the deficit is extremely large by international standards. With the growth rate of GDP very high until 1973, large deficits could be sustained without much growth in the debt-GDP ratio. But with the average deficit in excess of 15 percent of GDP since 1974, with money financing covering less than one-fifth of the deficit, and with GDP growing at only 3 percent, the debt-GDP ratio has risen sharply.

Table 17-4 presents indicators of monetary policy actions over the same period.

TABLE 17-4. Annual growth rate of monetary variables, 1960–1984 (percentages)[a]

Phase		CPI (π) (1)	Monetary base (H) (2)	Means of payment (M_1) (3)	Liquid assets (M_4) (4)	Bank credit[b] (5)	Real rate of return on indexed bonds (6)
1	Normal growth (1960:1–1965:1)	6.8	18.2	17.4	—	—	—
2	Recession (1965:1–1967:2)	6.1	10.6	16.4	—	—	—
3	Recovery (1967:2–1970:1)	2.0	4.7	9.1	—	—	—
4	Boom (1970:1–1973:3)	14.4	34.9	24.8	35.7	—	—
5	War and oil shock (1973:3–1977:2)	36.0	23.8	26.5	28.7	44.8	2.1[c]
6	Traverse (1977:2–1979:4)	71.0	25.8	37.0	75.1	102.9	2.3
7	Plateau (1979:4–1983:3)	123.3	103.2	97.1	126.6	106.1	2.5[d]

Source: Bank of Israel.

a. Columns 1 through 5 based on quarterly compounding.

b. Net of fuel credit.

c. Mean for 1975–1976.

d. Mean for 1980–1982 (in 1982 it was 1.9).

The increase in the growth rate of high-powered money from period to period stands out clearly, as does the increase in the growth rate of other nominal magnitudes. Much of this latter growth is automatic, however, as a result of the indexation of asset returns to either the price level or the exchange rate. The table also includes measures of the real interest rate on government bonds for the period 1975–1983. These have been impressively stable, a result both of the fixing of the real interest rate on new issues, and of the Bank of Israel's reluctance to allow prices of bonds to fluctuate in the secondary market.[11]

The government's policy, then, involves general fiscal and monetary expansion, stabilization of the real interest rate, and use of a PPP rule for the exchange rate during much of the period.

The Transition to Three-Digit Inflation

The major upward movement in the inflation rate after 1977 is associated with the massive devaluation that accompanied the foreign-exchange liberalization at the end of 1977. Over the two quarters from 1977:3 to 1978:1, the real dollar exchange rate rose 30 percent (less when measured against a basket of currencies, due to the dollar's appreciation). Because the devaluation was accompanied by reductions in tariffs and subsidies, the effective exchange rate fell less, thus mitigating the cost-push effects, but still leaving a large (20 percent) increase in the real cost of imported inputs. In addition, the value of dollar-linked assets rose considerably, creating demand-side inflationary pressures. By the middle of 1978 the one-time shock of the devaluation appeared to be over, with the inflation rate back to the 1977 level.

But in the second half of 1978 the inflation rate began to climb again, reaching the three-digit range at the end of 1979. What was the source of this rapid jump? There was some cost pressure from wages, which rose 6 percent in real terms in 1978, partly as a result of delayed indexation and partly as a result of wage negotiations, but no other major cost-push factor operated at the time: the second oil shock came only in 1979; the real exchange rate did not fall much further after the first quarter of 1978, and in fact rose in the fourth quarter of that year.

On the demand side, fiscal policy in 1978 was more expansionary than in 1977, with the domestic and total deficits well above the 1976–77 levels. The monetary base grew only 28 percent while prices rose 48 percent over the year. At the same time, however, the money stock (M_1) increased 45 percent while bank credit rose 80 percent. Studies of the demand for money (such as Leiderman and Marom, 1983; Melnick, 1983) typically find a significant shift in demand during 1978, away from assets denominated in local currency. Consistent with the econometric result is the fact that there was a concurrent major shift into PATAM (dollar-linked) accounts, and ways were discovered of using PATAM in current transactions (see Table 17-5).[12]

With a shift in demand away from Israeli-currency denominated assets increased rates of inflation were consistent with relatively low rates of money and particularly with money-base growth.

At the end of 1978 the Bank of Israel, acting independently of the Treasury, undertook a restrictive credit policy in an attempt to stabilize the growing balance-of-payments deficit and to control inflation. Ceilings were placed on the expansion of bank credit, but because free capital movements continued, imports of capital replaced domestic credit as a source of financing. The restrictive policy thus failed to reduce the growth of credit. The capital inflow problem was solved only in 1979, when capital imports were first prohibited and, when later permitted, were subject to heavy taxation.

TABLE 17-5. Government injection to money base and the rate of inflation, 1965–1983 (percentages)

	1965–1967	1968–1973	1974–1977	1978–1980	1981–1983
1. Financial asset ratio ($h + b$)	(0.5)[b]	0.6[c]	1.0	1.1	1.3
2. Percentage money base to GNP (h)	12.5	13.4	9.8	5.2	2.7
3. GNP growth (g_y)	3.2	10.3	2.6	3.5	1.6
4. Domestic government finance ratio (%)	−2.2	8.6	7.3	9.3	9.3
5. Growth factor (1 X 3)	1.6	6.2	2.6	3.9	2.1
6. Net injection (4 – 5)	0.6	2.4	4.7	5.4	7.2
7. Net injection/money base (6/2)	5	18	48	104	267
8. Inflation rate	5	11	40	97	141

Sources: Line 1: Yariv (1984); line 2: Bank of Israel; line 3: Central Bureau of Statistics; line 4: table 17.2 columns 6 and 7; line 8: Central Bureau of Statistics.

a. 1981–1983 data are subject to revision.

b. Assumed same as 1970.

c. Average for 1970–1973.

By that stage, however, the inflation rate was already well above its previous levels, and a prolonged period of restrictive policy would have been necessary to reduce it. The 1979 oil crisis imposed a greater supply shock on the economy than had the 1973 crisis (as Figure 17-2 shows, real import prices rose much more in the later period). At the same time, the government's domestic deficit rose. Monetary policy exerted some restraining influence by keeping the growth rate of bank credit low; once again low growth rates of the monetary base and the Israeli-currency denominated money supply were consistent with high rates of inflation because real demand for these assets fell. Despite the supply shock, demand policies allowed real GNP to rise by more than 5 percent in 1979; demand rose by more than 6.5 percent, and the current account deficit thus worsened.

Attempts to Arrest Inflation

With inflation firmly established at the three-digit level by the third quarter of 1979, and the government and current-account deficits increasing, a new finance minister was appointed at the end of 1979. Finance Minister Hurwitz assumed office determined to reduce the inflation rate and the current-account deficit the old-fashioned way, by cutting government demand and by restrictive monetary policy. The initial cuts in government spending took the form of reduced subsidies, which immediately raised the price level, so that the inflation rate for the last quarter of 1979 was 168 percent. Monetary policy was defined in terms of the expansion of credit for domestic purposes; export credits were freely granted.

The Hurwitz policy raised unemployment from less than 3 percent in 1979 to over 5 percent in 1980 (see Figure 17-3) and sharply reduced the current-account deficit by cutting imports. Despite growing unemployment, GNP increased in 1980, although domestic demand fell. The real exchange rate stayed virtually constant, so most of the improvement in the balance of payments was due to the fall in domestic income and the depletion of stocks. Monetary policy defined in terms of the nominal increase in bank credit was restrictive throughout the year, particularly in the first half, and the rate of investment fell.

Why did Hurwitz's policies reduce employment without reducing inflation until much later? In the first place, the initial measures to cut the budget deficit were themselves inflationary. In the second, it is typical in a recession for output to fall before inflation.

By the middle of the year, with the balance-of-payments deficit significantly reduced, political support for maintenance of contractionary policy was weakening, particularly in light of the approaching elections; and the finance minister's resignation at the end of the year marked the end of these policies. Since then, conventional contractionary policies have not been used in an attempt to reduce the inflation rate.

Figure 17-2
Index of real import prices and real wages, 1965:2–1983:4 (percentages).

At the beginning of 1981 Finance Minister Aridor introduced a new anti-inflationary policy, before the June elections. Its objective was to keep inflation rates down by working on the cost side and by keeping controlled prices from rising rapidly. Subsidies were accordingly increased, import tariffs slashed, and the exchange rate appreciated. Similar policies had been undertaken before other elections, though not with the same boldness. The policies had the desired effects, seen most clearly in an 80 percent (real) increase in consumer durable imports, and a fall in the inflation rate during the year (which may in part have been a delayed response to the earlier Hurwitz contractionary policy). The budget deficit increased sharply, and monetary policy was accommodating in that nominal magnitudes, with the exception of bank credit, rose more rapidly than prices. The balance-of-payments deficit also worsened.

The expansionary policies of 1981 began to take their toll in a rising inflation rate in the first three quarters of 1982. In October a new inflation stabilization policy was introduced, following the lines of the policy of early 1981. The hope was to move the economy to an inflation rate of 5 percent per month by keeping increases in the exchange rate and controlled prices to that level. These measures, together with their effects on expectations, were expected to move the economy to a new lower inflation equilibrium.

The policy succeeded in bringing the inflation rate down somewhat, but monetary policy was not supportive of the 5 percent inflation rate; all nominal magni-

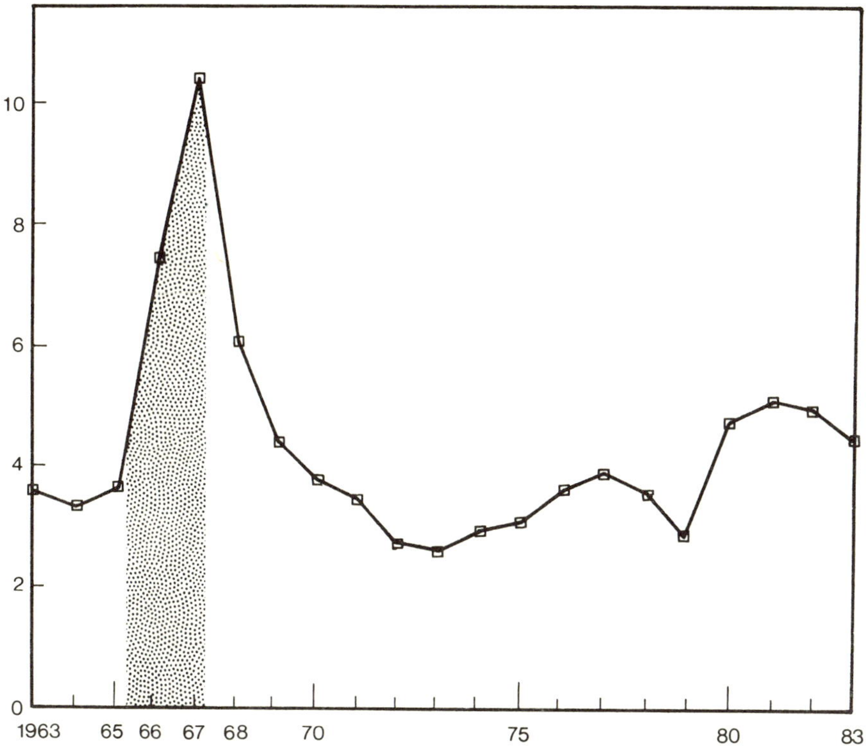

Figure 17-3
The unemployment rate, 1963–1983 (percentages). (CBS manpower surveys.)

tudes were expanding at well above 100 percent per year. This expansion may explain the asymmetry of response to downward adjustments in the exchange rate. Domestic prices were still rising at more than 100 percent per year, implying a rapid real exchange rate appreciation, together with an increasing current-account deficit. At the same time, the real wage was rising rapidly (see Figure 17-2).

The anti-inflationary policies were buying short-run success at the cost of a later inflationary outburst when the nominal and real exchange rates would have to be adjusted to deal with the current-account deficit. Real wages and income levels would likewise have to be reduced to levels more commensurate with domestic resources.

The Aridor policies failed as a result of the government's unwillingness to reduce aggregate demand sufficiently to justify the new 5 percent per month equilibrium. Even if, in principle, the economy did have another lower inflation equilibrium with the same policies,[13] fiscal and/or monetary policy should have been tightened early in the Aridor program, when it was clear that the real exchange rate was appreciating and that the policy could not be sustained.

When the long-delayed devaluation took place in October 1983, it again caused jumps in the price level and in the inflation rate. The price level increased by more than 50 percent from September to December 1983; the exchange rate increased by 68 percent over the same period. Cuts in subsidies contributed to the rise in prices. The real wage fell substantially over this period, once more showing the effects of the lags in the indexation system and the less than 100 percent indexation of wages to prices. The rate of inflation fell in the first quarter of 1984 to about 300 percent but remained well above the levels before the devaluation.

Any prospects for restrictive monetary and fiscal policy vanished with the announcement of elections for July 1984. The government once more increased subsidies and slowed the devaluation rate to less than the inflation rate. After a remarkably long period of quiet labor relations following the devaluation, labor negotiations in the second quarter of 1984 resulted in nominal wage increases that restored real wage levels to the pre–October 1983 levels. With monetary and fiscal policy expansionary, with the need for a postelection correction of the exchange rate becoming evident, and with widespread uncertainty about the type of policies to be followed after the elections, the inflation rate remained in the 300–400 percent range, and the black market exchange rate opened up a 25 percent premium over the official rate.

Shifts in the Inflation Rate: A Steady-State View

Although our approach to inflation dynamics may explain short-run shifts in inflation, it does not of itself provide an account of the components of the underlying long-run inflation rate. One summary way of looking at the latter is to apply the framework of equation (17.12) to the determinants of the monetary base and the implied steady-state inflation rate. For each subperiod we may calculate the difference between the ratio of domestic government finance (δ) and the part of the growth in net financial assets (money and debt) that individuals would be willing to hold given GNP growth and the average financial asset ratio, or $g_y(h + b)$. The ratio of the resulting net injection to the money base should be consistent with the underlying inflation rate.[14]

Table 17-5 shows the components of this calculation; line 7 presents the resulting index, line 8 the mean inflation rate, by subperiod. Since the money: base ratio is itself a function of the inflation rate, and the falling GNP growth rate may also be at least partly related to rising inflation, lines 7 and 8 should not be interpreted in pure one-way causality terms. Nonetheless, the results indicate that the shift in the underlying inflation rate from one phase to another could be related to three important successive developments: the rise in the deficit δ between the two wars (1968–1973), the decline in the growth rate after the 1973–74 crisis, and the probable drop in the demand for money after 1977. The index shows an implied money-base growth rate (267 percent) that is higher than actual inflation (141 percent) in 1981–1983. By the end of 1983, inflation did in fact catch up with this higher figure. Whereas the actual jump in inflation in October 1983 can be attributed to the dynamic effects of a delayed devaluation in a perfectly accommodated monetary system, this calculation at least shows that the more recent jump was not inconsistent with the underlying fiscal and monetary determinants.

Policy Issues

The Role of Indexation

Indexation is the factor most frequently cited as the chief cause of the Israeli inflation. Yet indexation has been widespread in the Israeli economy since the 1950s, and the inflation rate did not reach exaggerated levels until the 1970s. The standard view is correct in the sense that without indexation, the costs of inflation would have been so high that the inflation rate would not have reached its current levels. The government would have been forced to stabilize well before the three-digit range was reached. Beyond this valid point, we distinguish between two roles: indexation of wages and indexation of the values of financial assets. Because wage indexation is less than 100 percent, the pattern of typically increasing real wages seen in Figure 17-3 could not have been attained without discretionary wage fixing, especially in recent years. There is no reason to think that labor would have been more willing to take real wage cuts in the absence of indexation; nor is it likely, given the lags in indexation, that nominal wages would have adjusted significantly more slowly in the absence of indexation.

Indexation of financial asset returns does, however, significantly reduce the automatic stabilization of the economy. Price and exchange-rate shocks automatically affect the nominal value of large stocks of assets. The effect of a given devaluation on the balance of payments is thereby also reduced. More active accompanying fiscal policy could compensate for the loss of automatic stabilization, but variations in government spending and taxes are neither costless nor easily achieved.

The difficulties created for the stability of the system by the debt are a result not only of indexation but also of the size of the debt. If the debt were small, as it was in the 1950s and 1960s, the change in the nominal value of wealth resulting from a given shock to prices or the exchange rate would also be small, and the stabilizing power of the real balance effect would be proportionately greater. Moreover, the continued issuance of indexed rather than nominal debt can itself be viewed as an endogenous response to the need to finance large budget deficits: the public simply would not have been prepared to lend to the government on terms that gave the government the option to repudiate the debt through inflation.

So long as the debt and inflation continue to be large, there is no prospect for shifting to a different structure of assets, although steps could be taken to reduce the liquidity of the debt. A sharp cut in the government budget deficit sufficient to begin reducing the debt-GDP ratio would eventually both reduce the difficulties created by the indexation of the debt and make it possible to begin issuing different types of debt.

The Costs of Inflation

There has been very little research on the costs of inflation in Israel. The coincidence of the rise in the inflation rate after 1973 with the reduction in the growth rate is generally suspected to be more than that: we have already seen that a fall in the growth rate is likely to increase the inflation rate; less firmly established is the causal link from high inflation to low growth. It is not sufficient to point to the Israeli experience, for there has been a worldwide reduction in the growth rate of output, both in countries such as Japan, where the inflation rate fell from the 1960s on, and in countries such as Israel, where the inflation rate increased. Although we believe that the persistence of inflation is partly to blame for Israel's low growth, we are uncomfortably aware that the case has not been proved.

One source of the relationship between the growth rate of output and rising inflation may be the increasing diversion of resources to financial activities as inflation increases. Preliminary results by Kleiman (1984) suggest that increasing activity in the financial sector absorbed an extra 3–4 percent of GNP by 1982. The well-known measure of the costs of anticipated inflation as the area under the demand curve for high-powered money gives estimates of the cost of 160 percent inflation as being about 2–3 percent of GNP. This is an alternative estimate of the increased absorption of resources in making financial transactions.

These are useful lower-bound estimates of the costs of inflation, but the abundance of stories about problems such as the increasing inefficiency of the price system, the diversion of managers' time to financial instead of real output decisions, and the inefficiency and—with rising inflation—the progressive breakdown of the tax system suggests that the costs are much higher.

However, the indexation of assets in Israel means that one of the major costs of and concerns about (uncertain) inflation—the inability to protect the real value of savings—is not present, or at least is present only to the extent that there is uncertainty about the government's ability to meet its formal commitments. This difference accounts for the fact that less public concern is expressed about inflation in Israel than in other countries with much lower inflation rates.

Public Opinion about Inflation

The lack of overwhelming public pressure in Israel to end the inflation stems from two facts: there are pressing noneconomic issues before the electorate, and the costs of inflation are not perceived to be great.

The indexation system protects the public from what in other countries would be the major costs associated with high and uncertain inflation. Moreover, although the rise in inflation in Israel was accompanied by slower growth, it has in recent years also been accompanied by a rapidly rising standard of living. In 1980–1983, private consumption increased 28 percent (while GNP grew only 6 percent). Under these conditions the public may be excused for not seeing a pressing need to end inflation—particularly when it is well known that the adjustment process would require a transitory period of unemployment.

Stabilization Programs

The Israeli economy faces both real and nominal problems. The major real problem is that the balance-of-payments deficit is too large, leaving the economy sensitive both to political pressure from the U.S. government and to changes in opinion in the world capital markets; similarly, the budget deficit is too large, implying too rapid a growth of national debt and too great a diversion of the private sector's saving to government debt. The nominal problem is the need to reduce both the inflation rate and the sensitivity of the price level to shocks hitting the economy.

The first set of issues involves the question of whether to attempt to stabilize, and how rapidly. As the inflation rate has increased, more and more economists have expressed the view that reducing it to the low double-digit range is desirable, and that the only way to achieve this goal is a comprehensive stabilization program that attempts to make the adjustment rapidly rather than gradually. The desire to end inflation stems from the increasingly widespread perception that the economy and the financial system are out of control, tending over time to ever-higher inflation rates and to increasingly frequent balance-of-payments crises. The low growth–high inflation correlation has also influenced the argument.

The advocacy of a comprehensive and rapid solution is based on political-economic, and not purely economic, grounds. The failure of successive governments since 1977 to persist with restrictive policies for much more than six months at a time raises the fear that any government is unlikely to follow through with a gradualist program—such as a continuing series of budget cuts—designed to be maintained over several years. Hence the conclusion that the harsh medicine should be administered all at once.

All proposals for a stabilizing program begin with a cut in the budget deficit. The justifications for these cuts and their proposed sizes vary: for instance, Liviatan and Piterman argue in Chapter 16 that the budget deficit matters mainly because it affects the balance of payments, and that a cut in the order of 3–4 percent of GNP would be sufficient; others (ourselves included) argue that the large and growing debt so constrains monetary policy (because of the need to roll over the debt and prevent rising interest payments from making the budget deficit larger) and so increases the likelihood of future crises that a rapid move to a balanced budget is essential, so that the debt-GNP ratio can start falling.

It is also generally agreed that in the long run monetary policy should play a stronger role in the economy, with perhaps explicit adoption of monetary growth targets. Strict adherence to monetary targets in an extremely open economy is, however, unlikely, for exchange rate disturbances originating abroad will at times have to be offset by monetary policy.

The difficult issues of a stabilization program arise in discussion of the harshness of measures that should accompany the initial budget cuts, in the attempt to minimize the unemployment costs of the transition to a low inflation equilibrium. One approach that has received support is to attempt to move almost immediately to a zero- or low-inflation equilibrium by agreeing with the Histadrut to freeze nominal wages, by fixing the exchange rate, and by attempting to control prices. The difficulty with this approach is that the program would have to start with a real devaluation and changes in relative prices of goods; these moves would certainly make it difficult to control the absolute level of prices or could lead to damaging relative price distortions and greater unemployment. Another difficulty is that eventually readjustments of prices and the exchange rate will almost certainly be necessary, and that these readjustments could reignite inflation.

An alternative approach would first implement budget cuts and wait for unemployment to emerge before trying to reduce the inflation rate through a coordinated package of measures. This approach tries to solve the real problem first and the nominal one later. Its danger is that the large unemployment costs incurred at the beginning would lead to the abandonment of the second-stage, inflation-reduction, part of the program.

The issue of how to handle the large stock of indexed assets in the economy during this transition period (and to ensure the future stability of the economy) has also received attention. There have been many proposals to reduce the liquidity of the dollar-indexed PATAM accounts, though less detail on how to do this; in 1984 there was also some anxiety that a new government would in some way reduce the value of these assets as part of a stabilization program. A capital levy, which would reduce the value of the outstanding debt without unduly taxing those who had earlier purchased government debt was also on some agendas.

The last alternative to be discussed here is the proposal for dollarization, offered at the end of 1983 by Finance Minister Aridor in the wake of the failure of his previous policies. If the Israeli economy were indeed to move to complete use of the dollar, its long-run inflation rate would be that of the United States (except for minor deviations arising from changes in the prices of nontraded goods), and inflation would be ended quickly. There is no guarantee, however, that such a change would reduce the unemployment costs involved in the transition to a lower inflation rate.

From a purely economic viewpoint dollarization is undesirable because Israel would pay to the U.S. government the revenue that it would otherwise be obtaining for itself through the printing of money. In addition, it would be accepting the American exchange rate vis-a-vis other currencies: for instance, if Israel had been on the dollar in the last few years its currency would have appreciated substantially relative to European currencies. This would not have been a desirable development. There are of course also nationalist reasons not to dollarize. Adoption of a well-planned stabilization program would make it less likely that dollarization would ultimately become the only available solution for the economy.

References

Notes

Acknowledgments

Contributors

Index

References

Aaron, H. J. 1976. *Inflation and Income Tax.* Washington, D.C.: The Brookings Institution.

Ablin, R. 1979a. "Israel's Trade—Demand and Price: A Regression Analysis of the Short Run." *Bank of Israel Economic Review,* 45–46:23–59.

_____ 1979b. "A Lost Decade of Growth? Economic Policy since 1973." *Bank of Israel Economic Review,* 48–49:45–77.

_____ 1982. "Monetary Disorder and Early Economic Sorrow." *Economic Quarterly,* 30 (no. 113):164–170. Hebrew.

Abramov, Y. 1982. "The Grant Element in U.S. Loans to Israel." Seminar paper, The Hebrew University of Jerusalem. Hebrew.

Abramowitz, M. 1961. "The Nature and Significance of Kuznets Cycles." *Economic Development and Cultural Change,* 9 (April):225–248.

Achdut, L., and M. Carmi. 1981. *Twenty-five Years of the National Insurance Institute.* Jerusalem: National Insurance Institute. Hebrew.

Amir, S. 1981. "Changes in the Wage Function for Israel: Jewish Male Employees between 1968/69 and 1975/76." *Bank of Israel Economic Review,* 52:5–29.

_____ 1983. "Educational Structure and Wage Differentials of the Israeli Labor Force in the 1970s." Jerusalem: The Maurice Falk Institute for Economic Research in Israel, Discussion Paper 83.11.

_____ 1984. "Earning Differentials by Origin in Israel, 1957–1980." Jerusalem: Bank of Israel.

_____ 1985. "Educational Structure and Wage Differentials of the Israeli Labor Force." Ph.D. diss., The Hebrew University of Jerusalem.

Artstein, Y., and Z. Sussman. 1977. "Wage and Price Controls and the Effectiveness of Devaluations: The Israeli Experience." Jerusalem: Bank of Israel.

Atkinson, J. R., and J. E. Stiglitz. 1980. *Lectures on Public Economics.* New York and London: McGraw-Hill.

Auerbach, Z. 1984. "The Internal Debt—Opening Remarks." Jerusalem: Bank of Israel Research Department. Mimeograph. Hebrew.

Bachi, R. 1977. *The Population of Israel.* Jerusalem: Institute of Contemporary Jewry, The Hebrew University of Jerusalem, and Demographic Center, The Prime Minister's Office.

Bahral, U. 1965. *The Effect of Mass Immigration on Wages in Israel.* Jerusalem: The Maurice Falk Institute for Economic Research in Israel.

Baily, M. 1981. "Productivity and the Services of Capital and Labor." *Brookings Papers on Economic Activity,* 1:1–50.

Balassa, B., and T. Bertrand. 1970. "Growth Performance of Eastern European Economies and Comparable Western European Economies." *American Economic Review, Proceedings,* 60 (May):314–320.

Bank of Israel. Various years. *Annual Report.* Jerusalem.

Bank of Israel Research Department. Various issues. *Main Israeli Economic Data.* Jerusalem.

Barkai, H. 1980. "Defense Costs in Retrospect." Jerusalem: The Maurice Falk Institute for Economic Research in Israel, Research Paper 115. Hebrew.

——— 1984. "Israel's Energy Sector in the 1960s and 1970s." Jerusalem: The Maurice Falk Institute for Economic Research in Israel, Discussion Paper 84.03.

Bar-Nathan, M. 1983a. "Productivity and Factors of Production in the Construction Industry, 1960–1981." Jerusalem: Bank of Israel Research Department, Discussion Paper 83.08. Hebrew.

——— 1983b. "The Effect of the Increase in Raw Material Prices on Productivity and Profitability in Manufacturing, 1965–1980." *Bank of Israel Economic Review,* 57:53–78.

Barro, R. J. 1974. "Are Government Bonds Net Wealth?" *Journal of Political Economy,* 82:1095–1117.

——— 1979. "On the Determination of the Public Debt." *Journal of Political Economy,* 87:940–971.

Baruh, J. 1965. "Investment in Education and Human Capital in Israel." *Bank of Israel Bulletin,* 23:3–27.

——— 1966. "Changes in the Quality of Labor Input in Israel, 1950–61." *Bank of Israel Bulletin,* 25:32–43.

——— 1983. "Factor Proportions in Israel's Trade in Manufactures, 1965–1980." Jerusalem: Bank of Israel Research Department, Discussion Paper 83.11.

Becker, G. S. 1975. *Human Capital: A Theoretical and Empirical Analysis with Special Reference to Education.* 2d ed. New York: National Bureau of Economic Research.

——— 1981. *A Treatise on the Family.* Cambridge, Mass.: Harvard University Press.

Beham, M. 1968. *Monetary Aspects of the 1962 Devaluation.* Jerusalem: The Maurice Falk Institute for Economic Research in Israel.

Beham, M., and E. Kleiman. 1968. "The Cost of a Slowdown." *Banking Quarterly,* 29:31–42. Hebrew.

Ben-Bassat, A., and A. Marom. 1980. "Indicators for the Estimation of Liquidity of Financial Assets." Jerusalem: Bank of Israel Research Department.

Ben-Porath, Y. 1966. *The Arab Labor Force in Israel.* Jerusalem: The Maurice Falk Institute for Economic Research in Israel.

——— 1973a. "On East-West Differences in Occupational Structure in Israel." In *Israel: Social Structure and Change,* ed. M. Curtis and M. Chertoff. New Brunswick, N.J.: Transaction Books.

——— 1973b. "Economic Analysis of Fertility in Israel: Point and Counterpoint." *Journal of Political Economy,* 81:S202–S233.

——— 1973c. "Short-Term Fluctuations in Fertility and Economic Activity in Israel." *Demography,* 10 (May):185–204.

——— 1981. "Self-Employed and Wage-Earners in Israel: Findings from the Census of Population, 1972." Jerusalem: The Maurice Falk Institute for Economic Research in Israel, Discussion Paper 81.07.

——— 1983. "Ms. Jewish Mother Goes to Work—Trends in the Labor Force Participation of Women in Israel, 1955–1980." Jerusalem: The Maurice Falk Institute for Economic Research in Israel, Discussion Paper 83.10.

——— 1985. "Market, Government, and Israel's Muted Baby Boom." Jerusalem: The Maurice Falk Institute for Economic Research in Israel, Discussion Paper 85.06.

Ben-Porath, Y., and M. Bruno. 1977. "The Political Economy of a Tax Reform: Israel 1975." *Journal of Public Economics,* 7 (June):285–307.

Ben-Porath, Y., and R. Gronau. 1985. "Jewish Mother Goes to Work: Trends in the Labor Force Participation of Women in Israel, 1955–1980." *Journal of Labor Economics,* 3 (January):S310–S327.

Ben-Shahar, H. 1975. *Interest Rates and the Cost of Capital in Israel, 1952–62.* Basel: Kyklos Verlag.

Ben-Shahar, H., S. Bronfeld, and A. Cukierman. 1971. "The Capital Market in Israel." In *Israel and the Common Market,* ed. P. Uri. Jerusalem: Weidenfeld and Nicolson.

Berglas, E. 1970. "Security, Standard of Life, and Foreign Debt." *Economic Quarterly,* 17 (no. 67):191–202. Hebrew.

——— 1971. "Reform in Income Tax." *Economic Quarterly,* 18 (no. 71–72):232–239. Hebrew.

——— 1974. "Aspects of Guaranteed Income Plans." *Economic Quarterly,* 21 (no. 82):169–180. Hebrew.

——— 1980. "Evolvement of the Tax System during the Seventies and Future Implications." *Economic Quarterly,* 27 (no. 107):344–359. Hebrew.

——— 1983. "Defense and the Economy: The Israeli Experience." Jerusalem: The Maurice Falk Institute for Economic Research in Israel, Discussion Paper 83.01.

Berglas, E., et al. 1981. "The 'Threshold Fund': An Aid Program for Demobilized Soldiers." *Economic Quarterly,* 28 (no. 109):170–189. Hebrew.

British Petroleum. 1980. *Statistical Review of World Oil Industry.* London.

Break, G. F. 1984. "Avenue to Tax Reform: Peril and Possibilities." *National Tax Journal*, 37 (March):1–8.

Bregman, A. 1983. "The Slowdown of Industrial Productivity—Causes, Explanations, and Surprises." *Bank of Israel Economic Review*, 56:9–32. Hebrew.

Brezis, A., L. Leiderman, and R. Melnick. 1983. "The Interaction between Inflation and Monetary Aggregates in Israel." *Bank of Israel Economic Review*, 55:48–60.

Bronfeld, S., and R. Brenner. 1977. "Inflation and the Liquidity of Index-linked Bonds." *Bank of Israel Economic Review*, 44:1–28.

Bronfeld, S., and Y. Souari. 1980. "Taxes under Inflationary Conditions—Reflections on the Non-Implementation of the Gabbay Committee Recommendations." *Banking Quarterly*, 76:86–99. Hebrew.

Bruno M. 1962. *Interdependence, Resource Use, and Structural Change in Israel.* Jerusalem: Bank of Israel.

——— 1968. "Estimation of Factor Contribution to Growth under Structural Disequilibrium." *International Economic Review*, 9 (February):49–62.

——— 1982. "World Shocks, Comparative Macroeconomics, and the Productivity Puzzle." In *Slower Growth in the Western World*, ed. R. C. O. Matthews. London: Macmillan.

——— 1983. "Petrodollars and the Differential Growth Performance of Industrial and Middle Income Countries in the 1970s." New York: National Bureau of Economic Research, Working Paper 1056.

——— 1984. "Raw Materials, Profits, and the Productivity Slowdown." *Quarterly Journal of Economics*, 99:1–29.

Bruno, M., and J. Habib. 1976. "Taxes, Family Grants and Redistribution." *Journal of Public Economics*, 5 (January–February):57–69.

Bruno, M., and J. Sachs. 1981. "Supply versus Demand Approaches to the Problem of Stagflation." In *Macroeconomic Policies for Growth and Stability*, ed. H. Giersch. Kiel: Institut für Wirtschaft.

Bruno, M., and Z. Sussman. 1979. "Exchange Rate Flexibility, Inflation, and Structural Change: Israel under Alternative Regimes." *Journal of Development Economics*, 6:483–514.

——— 1980. "Floating vs. Crawling: Israel 1977–1979 by Hindsight." Jerusalem: The Maurice Falk Institute for Economic Research in Israel, Discussion Paper 80.3.

Bruton, H. 1967. "Productivity Growth in Latin America." *American Economic Review*, 57 (December):1099–1116.

Buch, V. 1982. "Capital Stock Series in Israel." Jerusalem: Bank of Israel Research Department. Hebrew.

——— 1984. "Capital Stock Series in Israel, 1960–1984: Updates." Jerusalem: Bank of Israel.

Burns, L. S., and L. Grebler. 1976. "Resource Allocation to Housing Investment: A Comparative International Study." *Economic Development and Cultural Change*, 25 (October):95–121.

Central Bureau of Statistics (CBS). Various years. *Income Surveys.* Jerusalem.

——— Various years. *Index of Industry and Crafts.* Jerusalem.

——— Various years. *Labor Force Surveys.* Jerusalem.

——— Various issues. *Monthly Bulletin of Statistics.* Jerusalem.

——— Various years. *National Expenditure on Education.* Jerusalem.

——— Various years. *National Expenditure on Health.* Jerusalem.

——— Various issues. *Special Publications Series.* Jerusalem.

——— Various years. *Statistical Abstract of Israel.* Jerusalem.

——— 1961. *Population and Housing Census.* Jerusalem.

——— 1968. *Family Expenditure Surveys.* Jerusalem: Special Publications Series, nos. 330, 368.

——— 1972. *Population and Housing Census.* Jerusalem.

——— 1975. *Family Expenditure Surveys.* Jerusalem: Special Publications Series, no. 378.

——— 1979a. *Family Expenditure Surveys.* Jerusalem: Special Publications Series, nos. 388, 563, 597.

——— 1979b. *The Level of Education of the Population in Israel.* Jerusalem: Special Publications Series, no. 604.

——— 1980. *Energy in Israel, 1970 to 1979.* Jerusalem: Special Publications Series, no. 660. Hebrew.

——— 1982. *Monthly Bulletin of Statistics* (Supplement). No. 4. Jerusalem.

——— 1983. "Energy in Israel." *Monthly Bulletin of Statistics* (Supplement). No. 5. Jerusalem.

Chenery, H. 1977. "Transitional Growth and World Industrialization." In *The International Allocation of Economic Activity,* ed. B. Ohlin, P. O. Hesselborn, and P. M. Wijkman. London: Macmillan.

——— 1979. *Structural Change and Development Policy.* London: Oxford University Press.

——— 1980. "Interactions between Industrialization and Exports." *American Economic Review, Proceedings,* 70 (May):281–287.

——— 1983. "Interaction between Theory and Observation in Development." *World Development,* 11:853–861.

Chenery, H., and M. Syrquin. 1975. *Patterns of Development, 1950–1970.* London: Oxford University Press.

——— 1980. "A Comparative Analysis of Industrial Growth." In *Economic Growth and Resources,* vol. 2, ed. R. C. O. Matthews. London: Macmillan.

Chenery, H., S. Robinson, and M. Syrquin. 1986. *Industrialization and Growth: A Comparative Study.* London: Oxford University Press.

Committee. 1966. Committee for the Examination of the COLA Arrangement. *Report.* Jerusalem. Hebrew.

Committee. 1971. Committee to Examine the Development of Income and the Social Gap. *Report.* Tel Aviv. Hebrew.

Committee. 1975a. Committee for the Examination of the COLA Arrangement. *Report.* Jerusalem. Hebrew.

Committee. 1975b. Committee for the Reform of the Personal Income Tax in Israel. *Report.* Jerusalem. Hebrew.

Committee. 1980. *Report of the Committee for Examining Taxation under Conditions of Inflation.* Jerusalem.

Controller of Banks. Various years. *Report.* Jerusalem: Bank of Israel.

Cornwall, J. 1977. *Modern Capitalism: Its Growth and Transformation.* New York: St. Martin's Press.

Davis, K., and C. Schoen. 1978. *Health and the War on Poverty: A Ten-Year Appraisal.* Washington, D.C.: Brookings Institution.

Dornbusch, R. 1980. *Open Economy Macroeconomics.* New York: Basic Books.

EEC. Various years. *Comptes Nationaux.* Luxembourg: Office Statistique des Communat Européennes.

Easterlin, R. A. 1961a. "Influences in European Overseas Emigration before World War I." *Economic Development and Cultural Change,* 9 (April):331–351b.

——— 1961b. "Israel's Development: Past Accomplishments and Future Problems." *Quarterly Journal of Economics,* 75:63–81.

——— 1968. *Population, Labor Force, and Long Swings in Economic Growth.* New York: National Bureau of Economic Research.

——— 1980. *Birth and Fortune: The Impact of Numbers on Personal Welfare.* New York: Basic Books.

Elkayam, D. 1982. "Excess Demand for Labour, Inflationary Expectations, and the Non-Substitution Hypothesis (1968–1980)." Jerusalem: Bank of Israel Research Department, Discussion Paper 82.87. Hebrew.

Enthoven, A. C. 1980. *Health Plan.* Menlo Park, Calif.: Addison-Wesley.

Feder, G. 1982. "On Exports and Economic Growth." *Journal of Development Economics,* 12:59–73.

Feldstein, M. 1981. *Hospital Costs of Health Insurance.* Cambridge, Mass.: Harvard University Press.

Finger, N. 1971. *The Impact of Government Subsidies on Industrial Management: The Israeli Experience.* New York: Praeger.

Fischer, S. 1977. "Wage Indexation and Macroeconomic Stability." *Journal of Monetary Economics,* Supplementary Series, 5:107–148.

——— 1983. "Indexation and Inflation." *Journal of Monetary Economics,* 12:519–541.

——— 1984. "The Economy of Israel." *Carnegie-Rochester Conference Series on Public Policy,* 20:7–52.

Fishelson, G., A. L. Hillman, and S. Hirsch. 1980. "Economic Integration of Israel in the EEC: The Factor Content of Israel's Trade in a Multilateral Setting." Tel Aviv: The David Horowitz Institution for the Research of Developing Countries, Paper 2/79.

Freeman, R. B. 1979. "The Effect of Demographic Factors on Age-Earning Profiles." *Journal of Human Resources,* 14:289–318.

——— 1982. "The Changing Economic Value of Higher Education in Developed Economies: A Report to the O.E.C.D." Cambridge, Mass.: Harvard Institute of Economic Research, Harvard University, Discussion Paper 874.

Friedlander, D. 1975. "Mass Immigration and Population Dynamics in Israel." *Demography,* 12 (November):581–99.

Fuchs, V. R. 1974. *Who Shall Live? Health Economics and Social Choice.* New York: Basic Books.

Gaathon, A. L. 1971. *Economic Productivity in Israel.* New York, Washington, and London: Praeger.

Gabbay, Y., Y. Haroeh, and B. Cukierman. 1976. "Average and Marginal Income Tax Rates." In *Issues in the Economy of Israel,* ed. N. Halevi and Y. Kop. Jerusalem: The Maurice Falk Institute for Economic Research in Israel. Hebrew.

Gottlieb, D. and S. Piterman. 1982. "Inflationary Expectations in Israel 1965–1980." Jerusalem: Bank of Israel Research Department, Discussion Paper 82.1. Hebrew.

Granger, C. W. J. 1969. "Investigating Causal Relations by Econometric Models and Cross-Spectral Methods." *Econometrica,* 37:424–438.

Gray, J. A. 1976. "Wage Indexation: A Macroeconomic Approach." *Journal of Monetary Economics,* 2:221–235.

Griliches, Z. 1970. "Notes on the Role of Education in Production Functions and Growth Accounting." In *Education Income and Human Capital,* ed. W. L. Hansen. New York: National Bureau of Economic Research.

Gronau, R. 1981. "Wives' Labor Force Participation, Wage Differentials, and Family Income Inequality: The Israeli Experience." Cambridge, Mass.: National Bureau of Economic Research, Working Paper 668.

Gross, E. 1983. "Wages in the Business and Public-Services Sectors in Israel." In *Studies in Economics 1981,* ed. Z. Sussman and M. Felber. Jerusalem: The Israel Economic Association. Hebrew.

Gross, E., and R. Meron. 1981. "The Effect of Possible Shortening of the Life Expectancy of Equipment on the Size of Capital Stock." Jerusalem: Bank of Israel Research Department, internal memorandum. Hebrew.

Gross, N. T. 1981. "A Note on the Periodization of the History of the Yishuv during the Mandatory Period." *Cathedra,* 18 (January):174–177. Hebrew.

Gross, N. T., and J. Metzer. 1977. "Public Finance in the Jewish Economy in Interwar Palestine." Jerusalem: The Maurice Falk Institute for Economic Research in Israel, Discussion Paper 77.06.

Gruenbaum (Gaathon), A. 1941. *National Income and Outlay in Palestine 1936.* Jerusalem: The Jewish Agency.

Habib, J. 1979. "An Integrated Approach to Taxes and Transfers." Jerusalem: The Maurice Falk Institute for Economic Research in Israel.

Halevi, N. 1969. "Economic Policy Discussion and Research in Israel." *American Economic Review,* 59:75–118.

——— 1971. "Exchange Control in Israel." In *Israel and the Common Market,* ed. P. Uri. Jerusalem: Weidenfeld and Nicolson.

——— 1972. "Effective Devaluation and Exports: Some Issues of Empirical Analysis, with Illustrations from Israel." *Economica,* 3:29–300.

——— 1979. "The Economic Development of the Yishuv in Palestine." Jerusalem:

The Maurice Falk Institute for Economic Research in Israel, Discussion Paper 79.14. Hebrew.

——— 1983a. "The Political Economy of Absorptive Capacity: Growth and Cycles in Jewish Palestine under the British." *Middle Eastern Studies,* 19:456–469.

——— 1983b. "The Structure and Development of Israel's Balance of Payments." Jerusalem: The Maurice Falk Institute for Economic Research in Israel, Discussion Paper 83.02.

Halevi, N., and R. Klinov-Malul. 1968. *The Economic Development of Israel.* Jerusalem: Bank of Israel and Praeger, Praeger Special Studies in International Economics and Development.

Halevi, N., and Y. Kop, eds. 1975. *Issues in the Economy of Israel.* Jerusalem: The Maurice Falk Institute for Economic Research in Israel.

Halevi, N., M. Teubal, and D. Tsiddon. 1983. "The Development of Israel's Industrial Exports, 1970–1980." Jerusalem: The Maurice Falk Institute for Economic Research in Israel (draft).

Hanoch, G. 1961. "Income Differentials in Israel." In The Maurice Falk Institute for Economic Research in Israel, *Fifth Report 1959 and 1960.* Jerusalem.

Hercowitz, Z. 1976. "The Stock of Education Capital in Israel and Its Distribution, 1961–1972." Jerusalem: The Maurice Falk Institute for Economic Research in Israel, Discussion Paper 76.09. Hebrew.

Hershkowitz, M. 1973. "The Hecksher-Ohlin Theory and the Factor Content of Israel's Foreign Trade, 1958 and 1965." Master's thesis, The Hebrew University of Jerusalem. Hebrew.

Hershkowitz, M., and Z. Sussman. 1971. "Growth, Induced Changes in Final Demand, Educational Requirements, and Wage Differentials." *Review of Economics and Statistics,* 53:169–175.

Horowitz, D. 1954. *The Economy of Israel.* Tel Aviv: Massada. Hebrew.

Hudson, E. A., and D. W. Jorgenson. 1978. "Energy Policy and U.S. Economic Growth." *American Economic Review,* 68:118–123.

International Bank for Reconstruction and Development (IBRD). Various years. *World Tables.* Baltimore.

International Labour Organization (ILO). Various years. *International Labor Statistics.* Geneva.

International Monetary Fund (IMF). Various years. *International Financial Statistics.* Washington, D.C.

Israel Electricity Corporation. Various years. *Annual Statistical Reports.* Jerusalem. Hebrew.

Jaffee, D., and E. Kleiman. 1977. "The Welfare Implications of Uneven Inflation." In *Inflation Theory and Anti-Inflation Policy,* ed. E. Landberg. London: Macmillan.

Jerome, H. 1926. *Migration and Business Cycles.* New York: National Bureau of Economic Research.

Jewish Agency. 1947. *Statistical Handbook of Jewish Palestine 1947.* Jerusalem.

Jorgenson, D. W. 1980. "The Answer Is Energy." Interview in *Challenge,* 23 (November–December):16–25.

Kaldor, N. 1966. *Causes of the Slow Rate of Economic Growth of the United Kingdom.* Cambridge: Cambridge University Press.

Kendrick, J. 1982. "International Comparisons of Recent Productivity Trends." In *Essays in Contemporary Economic Problems,* ed. W. Fellner. Washington: American Enterprise Institute.

Kleiman, E. 1974. "Inflation and the Redistribution of Public Wealth." *Economic Quarterly,* 21 (no. 83):238–257. Hebrew.

——— 1977a. "Index, Risk, and Relative Prices in Israel." Jerusalem: The Maurice Falk Institute for Economic Research in Israel, Discussion Paper 77.13.

——— 1977b. "Monetary Correction and Indexation: The Brazilian and Israeli Experience." *Explorations in Economic Research,* 4 (Winter):141–176.

——— 1977c. "Taxes and Inflation." *Israel Tax Quarterly,* 10 (December):87–96. Hebrew.

——— 1984. "Costs of Inflation." *Economic Quarterly,* 30 (no. 119):859–864. Hebrew.

Klinov, R. 1976. "Changes in Occupational Structure of the Labor Force, 1960–1974." In *Issues in the Economy of Israel,* ed. N. Halevi and Y. Kop. Jerusalem: The Maurice Falk Institute for Economic Research in Israel and the Israel Economic Association.

——— 1984. "The Industrial Structure of Product in Israel." Jerusalem: The Maurice Falk Institute for Economic Research in Israel, Discussion Paper 84.10.

Kochav, D., and Y. Lifshitz. 1973. "Defence Expenditures and Their Influence on the National Economy and the Industry." *Economic Quarterly,* 20 (no. 78–79):256–270. Hebrew.

Kondor, J. 1981. "Capital Utilization, Economies to Scale, and Productivity in the Business Sector (1964–1980)." *Economic Quarterly,* 29 (no. 110):235–242. Hebrew.

——— 1982. "Investment Function and the Loss to the Economy Due to Capital Subsidies." Tel Aviv: Sapir Development Center, Tel Aviv University, Discussion Paper 5-82.

Kop, Y. 1980. "Changes in the Age Structure and Their Application for the Demand for Public Services." Jerusalem: Brookdale Institution, Discussion Paper D-6480.

Kouri, P. J. K. 1976. "The Exchange Rate and the Balance of Payments in the Short Run and in the Long Run: A Monetary Approach." *Scandinavian Journal of Economics,* 78:280–304.

Kubo, Y., and S. Robinson. 1984. "Sources of Industrial Growth and Structural Change: A Comparative Analysis of Eight Economies." In UNIDO, *Proceedings of the Seventh International Conference on Input-Output Techniques.* New York: United Nations.

Kuznets, S. 1958. "Long Swings in the Growth of Population and in Related Economic Variables." *Proceedings of the American Philosophical Society,* 102:25–52.

——— 1960a. "Economic Structure and the Life of the Jews." In *The Jews,* ed. L. Finkelstein. 3d ed. Vol. 2. New York: Harper and Brothers.

——— 1960b. "Quantitative Aspects of the Economic Growth of Nations, Part V: Capital Formation Proportions." *Economic Development and Cultural Change,* 8 (July):1–96.

——— 1965. *Economic Growth and Structure: Selected Essays.* New York: W. W. Norton.

——— 1966. *Modern Economic Growth: Rate, Structure, and Spread.* New Haven: Yale University Press.

——— 1973a. "The Economic Development of Israel." *Economic Quarterly,* 20 (no. 78–79):189–209. Hebrew.

——— 1973b. *Population, Capital, and Growth.* New York: W. W. Norton.

Kuznets, S., and A. Rubin. 1954. "Immigration and the Foreign Born." New York: National Bureau of Economic Research, Occasional Paper 46.

Lamdany, R. 1982. "Emigration from Israel." Jerusalem: The Maurice Falk Institute for Economic Research in Israel, Discussion Paper 82.08.

Landsberger, M. 1963. "Changes in the Consumer Price Index of Different Income, Origin, and Family-Size Groups, 1954–62." *Bank of Israel Bulletin,* 19 (November):64–75. Hebrew.

Layard, P. R. G., and P. R. Fallon. 1975. "Capital-Skill Complementarity, Income Distribution, and Output Accounting." *Journal of Political Economy,* 2:279–301.

Leiderman, L., and A. Marom. 1983. "New Estimates of the Demand for Money in Israel." Jerusalem: Bank of Israel Research Department, Discussion Paper 83.9.

Levy, H. 1968. "Changes in Wage Differentials by Occupational Groups, 1957/58 to 1963/64." *Bank of Israel Bulletin,* 30 (May):50–78.

——— 1982. "Capital Structure, Inflation, and the Cost of Capital in Israeli Industry, 1964–1978." *Bank of Israel Economic Review,* 53:31–63.

Lifshitz, Y. 1975. "Defense Expenditure and the Allocation of Resources." In *Issues in the Economy of Israel,* ed. N. Halevi and Y. Kop. Jerusalem: The Maurice Falk Institute for Economic Research in Israel.

Litvin, U., and L. Meridor. 1982. "The Grant-Equivalent of Subsidized Investments in Israel." *Bank of Israel Economic Review,* 54:3–24. Hebrew.

Litvin, U., L. Meridor, and A. Spivak. 1982. "Inflation in Israel, 1971–1981, Provisional Report." Jerusalem: Bank of Israel Research Department. Hebrew.

——— 1983. "The Money Supply Process in Israel: A Case Study of the Real Bills Doctrine." Jerusalem: Bank of Israel Research Department.

——— 1984. "Inflation and the Process of Money Creation in Israel." Bank of Israel Research Department, Discussion Paper 84.4. Hebrew.

Liviatan, N. 1983. "Inflation and the Composition of Deficit Finance." In *Global Econometrics,* ed. F. G. Adams. Cambridge, Mass.: M.I.T. Press.

——— 1984. "Dollarization as a Monetary Reform." *Economic Quarterly,* 30 (no. 119):848–858. Hebrew.

Liviatan, N., and S. Piterman. 1984a. "Accelerating Inflation and Balance-of-Payments Crises: Israel 1973–1984." Jerusalem: Bank of Israel Research Department, Discussion Paper 84.06.

______ 1984b. "Accelerating Inflation and Balance-of-Payments Crises: Israel 1973–1984." Jerusalem: Bank of Israel Research Department, Discussion Paper 84.12. Hebrew.

Liviatan, O. 1981. "The Welfare of the Israeli Economy and World Price Increases." *Economic Quarterly,* 28 (no. 108):14–20. Hebrew.

Loftus, P. 1946. *National Income of Palestine, 1944.* Jerusalem: Government Printer.

Lubell, H., H. Weisbrod, and R. Kahana. 1958. *Israel's National Expenditure: 1950–1954.* Jerusalem: The Falk Project for Economic Research in Israel and Central Bureau of Statistics.

Lubitz, R. 1981. "Capital Formation and Savings in Major Industrial Countries." In Governors of the Federal Reserve System, *Public Policy and Capital Formation.* Washington, D.C.

Maddison, A. 1970. *Economic Progress and Policy in Developing Countries.* New York: W. W. Norton.

______ 1980a. "Economic Growth and Structural Change in the Advanced Countries." In *Western Economies in Transition,* ed. I. Leveson and J. W. Wheeler. Boulder, Colo.: Westview.

______ 1980b. "Phases of Capitalist Development." In *Economic Growth and Resources,* vol. 2, ed. R. C. O. Matthews. London: Macmillan.

Manzly, Y. 1970. "Measurement of Productivity and the Sources of Growth of Private Product in Israel, 1950–1967." *Bank of Israel Economic Review,* 35:39–56.

______ 1974. "Price Changes in the Consumption Basket of Various Income Groups in Israel." *Bank of Israel Bulletin,* 41 (April):35–55.

______ 1980. "Measurement of Productivity and the Sources of Economic Growth." Jerusalem: Bank of Israel Research Department. Mimeograph.

Marris, J. 1981. "International Comparisons of Real Product." Washington, D.C.: World Bank.

Massell, B. F. 1961. "A Disaggregated View of Technical Change." *Journal of Political Economy,* 59:547–557.

Matras, J., G. Noam, and Y. Bar-Haim. 1984. "Israeli Educated Men in the Transition to Adulthood: Patterns of Schooling, Military Service, and Employment." Jerusalem. Mimeograph.

Matthews, R., C. Feinstein, and C. Odling-Smee. 1982. *British Economic Growth.* Oxford: Oxford University Press.

Meade, J. E. 1978. *The Structure and Reform of Direct Taxation.* London: Allen & Unwin.

Medina, V. 1975. "The Criteria for Granting Cheap Industrial Development Credit." In *Issues in the Economy of Israel,* ed. N. Halevi and Y. Kop. Jerusalem: The Maurice Falk Institute for Economic Research in Israel.

Melnick, R. 1983. "Two Issues in the Demand for Money." Jerusalem: Bank of Israel Research Department, Discussion Paper 83.06. Hebrew.

Melnick, R., and M. Sokoler. 1984. "The Government's Revenue from Money Creation and the Inflationary Effects of a Decline in the Rate of Growth of GNP." *Journal of Monetary Economics,* 13:225–236.

Merhav, M. 1963. "Some Economic Consequences of a Large-Scale Renewal of Immigration." *Bank of Israel Bulletin,* 17 (January):3–38.

Meridor, L. Forthcoming. "The Government Budget and Its Relationship to Macro-Economic Developments in Israel, 1960–1983." Jerusalem: Bank of Israel. Hebrew.

Meron, R. 1982. "Economic Development in Judea, Samaria, and the Gaza District, 1970–1980." Jerusalem: Bank of Israel Research Department. Hebrew.

Metzer, J. 1982. "Fiscal Incidence and Resource Transfer between Jews and Arabs in Mandatory Palestine," *Research in Economic History,* 7:87–132.

——— 1983. "The Slowdown of Economic Growth in Israel: A Passing Phase or the End of the Big Spurt?" Jerusalem: The Maurice Falk Institute for Economic Research in Israel, Discussion Paper 83.03.

Michaely, M. 1971. *Israel's Foreign Exchange Rate System.* Jerusalem: The Maurice Falk Institute for Economic Research in Israel.

——— 1975. *Foreign Trade Regimes and Economic Development.* New York: National Bureau of Economic Research.

——— 1983. "The Floating Exchange Rate in Israel: 1977–1980." In *Exchange Rate and Trade Instability: Causes, Consequences and Remedies,* eds. D. Bigman and T. Taya. Cambridge, Mass.: Ballinger.

Mincer, J. 1978. "Family Migration Decisions." *Journal of Political Economy,* 86:749–773.

Ministry of Energy. 1981. *Israel's Energy Economy 1970–1980.* Jerusalem. Hebrew.

Ministry of Trade, Industry and Tourism. 1969. *Industry in Israel 1968–70.* Jerusalem.

——— 1980. *Industry in Israel 1979.* Jerusalem.

Morawetz, D. 1975. "Capital Utilization in Israeli Industry." Jerusalem: The Maurice Falk Institute for Economic Research in Israel, Discussion Paper 75.3.

——— 1977. *Twenty-five Years of Economic Development, 1950 to 1975.* Washington, D.C.: World Bank.

Nachmani, D. 1981. "The Distribution of Imports to Israel among Final Uses, 1971–1979." Jerusalem: Bank of Israel Research Department. Hebrew.

——— 1983. "Representation of the Trend in Monthly Time Series." Jerusalem: Bank of Israel Research Department. Hebrew.

Nahon, Y. 1985. "Patterns of Educational Expansion—The Ethnic Dimension." Jerusalem. Mimeograph. Hebrew.

Nathan, R., O. Gass, and D. Creamer. 1946. *Palestine: Problem and Promise: An Economic Study.* Washington, D.C.: Public Affairs Press.

Nerlove, M., A. Razin, and E. Sadka. 1984. "Income Redistribution Policies with Endogenous Fertility." *Journal of Public Economics,* 24 (July):221–230.

Nordhaus, W. D. 1977. *International Studies of Demand for Energy.* Amsterdam: North Holland.

——— 1980. "Oil and Economic Performance in Industrial Countries." *Brookings Papers on Economic Activity,* 2:343–347.

OECD. Various years. *National Income Accounts.* Paris.

——— 1976. *Public Expenditure on Education.* Paris.

——— 1977. *Public Expenditure on Health.* Paris.

——— 1979. *The Impact of the Newly Industrialising Countries on Production and Trade in Manufactures.* Paris.

——— 1984a. "Social Expenditure: Erosion or Evolution?" *OECD Observer,* 160 (January):1–6.

——— 1984b. *Expenditure on Health under Economic Constraints.* Paris.

——— 1984c. *Social Expenditure, 1960–1990: Its Growth and Control.* Paris.

Ofer, G. 1967. *The Service Industries in a Developing Economy: Israel as a Case Study.* New York: Praeger and the Bank of Israel.

——— 1976. "A Cross-Country Comparison of Industrial Structure." In *Issues in the Economy of Israel,* ed. N. Halevi and Y. Kop. Jerusalem: The Maurice Falk Institute for Economic Research in Israel and the Israel Economic Association. Hebrew.

Ohkawa, K. 1979. "Aggregate Growth and Product Allocation." In *Patterns of Japanese Economic Development, A Quantitative Appraisal,* ed. K. Ohkawa and M. Shinohara. New Haven: Yale University Press.

Ohkawa, K., and N. Takamatsu. 1983. "Capital Formation, Productivity, and Employment: Japan's Historical Experience and Its Possible Relevance to LDCs." Tokyo: International Development Center in Japan, Working Paper 26.

Olson, M. 1982. *The Rise and Decline of Nations.* New Haven and London: Yale University Press.

Pack, H. 1971. *Structural Change and Economic Policy in Israel.* New Haven: Yale University Press.

Patinkin, D. 1960, 1967. *The Israeli Economy: The First Decade.* Jerusalem: The Maurice Falk Institute for Economic Research in Israel.

Pechman, J. A., ed. 1980. *What Should Be Taxed: Income or Expenditure?* Washington, D.C.: The Brookings Institution.

Piterman, S. 1981. "Expectations of Devaluation, Capital Flows, Anti-Inflationary Policy, and Exchange Rate Policy." Jerusalem: Bank of Israel Research Department. Hebrew.

Plessner, Y. 1983. "The Theoretical and Empirical Foundation of Recent Israeli Economic Policy and Its Objectives." *Economic Quarterly,* 30 (no. 118):741–757. Hebrew.

——— 1984. "Dollarization—Monetary Stabilization Theory and Application." *Economic Quarterly,* 31 (no. 120):22–32. Hebrew.

Pomfret, R. W. T. 1976. *Trade Policies and Industrialization in a Small Open Economy: The Case of Israel.* Tubingen: J. C. B. Mohr (Paul Siebeck).

Sargent, T. J. 1979. *Macroeconomic Theory.* New York: Academic Press.

Shefer, E. 1983. "The Arms Race: Israel and the Confrontation Countries." In *Studies in Economics 1981,* ed. Z. Sussman and M. Felber. Jerusalem: The Israel Economic Association. Hebrew.

Shiffer, Z. F. 1982. "Money and Inflation in Israel: The Transition of an Economy." *Federal Reserve Bank of St. Louis Review,* 64 (August/September):28–40.

Sicron, M. 1957. *Immigration to Israel.* Jerusalem: The Falk Project for Economic Research in Israel and Central Bureau of Statistics.

Simon, J. L. 1977. *The Economics of Population Growth.* Princeton: Princeton University Press.

Sokoler, M. 1984. "The Inflation Tax on the Monetary Base, the Inflationary Subsidy Embodied in Government Loans, and Their Influence on the Inflationary Process in Israel." Bank of Israel Research Department, Discussion Paper 84.5. Hebrew.

State Comptroller. 1983. *Annual Report 1982.* Jerusalem: Government Printing Office. Hebrew.

Stein, J. B., and A. Lee. 1977. *Productivity Growth in Industrial Countries at the Sectoral Level, 1963–1974.* Santa Monica, Calif.: Rand Corporation Council on International Economic Policy.

Summers, R., I. Kravis, and A. Heston. 1980. "International Comparisons of Real Product and Its Composition: 1950–77." *Review of Income and Wealth,* Series 26:19–66.

Sussman, Z. 1982. "Is Growth Possible in Israel?" *Economic Quarterly,* 29 (no. 113):141–163. Hebrew.

Syrquin, M. 1984. "Economic Growth and Structural Change: Israel in an International Perspective." Jerusalem: The Maurice Falk Institute for Economic Research in Israel, Discussion Paper 84.08.

Szereszewski, R. 1968. *Essays on the Structure of the Jewish Economy in Palestine and Israel.* Jerusalem: The Maurice Falk Institute for Economic Research in Israel.

Tamari, M. 1980. *Corporate Finance under Conditions of Government Intervention: The Israeli Case, 1950–1972.* Jerusalem: Bank of Israel.

Temkin, A. 1983. "Inflation, Controlled Prices, and Subsidies in the Israel Economy: 1973–1980." Master's thesis, The Hebrew University of Jerusalem. Hebrew.

Toren, B. 1979. "The Industrial Subsidy for Location of Textile Mills in Development Towns in Israel." Ph.D. diss., The Hebrew University of Jerusalem. Hebrew.

Tsiddon, D. 1982. "Israel's Industrial Exports in the 1970s." Seminar paper, The Hebrew University of Jerusalem. Hebrew.

Unger, M., and B. Z. Zilberfarb. 1982. "Estimates of the Unrecorded Economy in Israel, 1954–77." Tel Aviv: Bar-Ilan University, Department of Economics, Discussion Paper DE-8203. Hebrew.

UNESCO. 1981. *Statistical Yearbook.* Geneva.

United Nations. 1950. *National and Per Capita Incomes, Seventy Countries, 1949.* New York: Statistical Papers, Series E, no. 1.

——— 1955. *Per Capita National Product of Fifty-five Countries, 1952–1954.* New York: Statistical Papers, Series E, no. 4.

——— Department of Economic and Social Affairs. 1979. *Trends and Characteristics of International Migration since 1950.* New York: Demographic Studies 64 (ST/ESA/Series A/64).

——— Department of Social Affairs. 1949. *Problems of Migration Statistics.* New York: Population Studies 5 (ST/SOA/Series A/S).

——— Economic and Social Council. 1976. "Social and Demographic Statistics, Migration Statistics." Draft Recommendations on Statistics of Intentional Mi-

gration. Report of the Secretary-General to Statistical Commission, 19th session. New Delhi (E/CN.3/483).
U.S. Department of State. 1950. *Point Four.* Publication 3719. Washington, D.C.
U.S. Department of the Treasury. 1977. *Blueprints for Basic Tax Reform.* Washington, D.C.
Wachter, M. L. 1976. "The Changing Cyclical Responsiveness of Wage Inflation." *Brookings Papers on Economic Activity,* 1:115–159.
Weinblatt, J. 1972. "The Influence of Effective Exchange Rates on Imports: 1950–67." In *Studies in Israel's Foreign Trade,* ed. N. Halevi and M. Michaely. Jerusalem: The Maurice Falk Institute for Economic Research in Israel. Hebrew.
_____ 1980. "The Determinants of Israel's Export Composition." Jerusalem: The Maurice Falk Institute for Economic Research in Israel, Discussion Paper 80.11.
Weisbrod, B. 1982. "An Economic Perspective on Medical Research." Madison: Center for Health, Economics, and Law, University of Wisconsin. Mimeograph.
Welch, F. 1970. "Education in Production." *Journal of Political Economy,* 78:35–59.
_____ 1979. "Effects of Cohort Size on Earnings: Baby-Boom Babies Financial Bust." *Journal of Political Economy,* 87:565–575.
Williamson, J. G. 1976. "The Sources of American Inequality, 1896–1948." *Review of Economics and Statistics,* 58 (November):387–397.
_____ 1980. "Immigrant-Inequality Trade-Offs in the Promised Land: Income Distribution and Absorptive Capacity prior to the Quotas." In *Conference on U.S. Immigration, Issues and Policies.* Chicago: University of Chicago.
Williamson, J. G., and L. J. De Bever. 1978. "Saving, Accumulation, and Modern Economic Growth: The Contemporary Relevance of Japanese History." *Journal of Japanese Studies,* 4:125–167.
Williamson, J. G., and P. Lindert. 1980. *American Inequality: A Macroeconomic History.* New York: Academic Press.
World Bank. n.d. *Memoranda.* Washington, D.C.
_____ Various years. *Atlas.* Washington, D.C.
_____ Various years. *World Development Report.* Washington, D.C.
_____ 1980. *World Tables.* 2d ed. Baltimore: Johns Hopkins University Press.
_____ 1983. *World Tables.* 3d ed. Baltimore: Johns Hopkins University Press.
_____ 1984. *World Tables.* 4th ed. Baltimore: Johns Hopkins University Press.
Yariv, D. 1984. "Estimation of the Public's Wealth and Its Development from 1970 to 1982." Jerusalem: Bank of Israel Research Department, Discussion Paper 84.10.
Yitzhaki, S. 1982. "A Tax Programming Model." *Journal of Public Economics,* 19 (October):107–20.
_____ 1983. "The Development of Taxation in the Third Decade of the State of Israel." Jerusalem: The Maurice Falk Institute for Economic Research in Israel, Discussion Paper 83.09. Hebrew.
Yoran, Y. 1984. "Inflation and Structural Change: The Case of Israel." *Economic Quarterly,* 31 (no. 122):217–245. Hebrew.
Zilberman, G. Forthcoming. "Econometric Model of Wealth in Israel, 1970–1981." Jerusalem: The Maurice Falk Institute for Economic Research in Israel. Hebrew.

Notes

Introduction

1. This section owes much to a prepublication version of Yoran (1984).

2. These figures are for the periods indicated and not for individual years; they are taken from Israel's Central Bureau of Statistics (CBS), *Statistical Abstract 1983,* pp. 160 and 391. See Chapter 14, Table 14-2, for rates of growth of the product wage in the business sector.

1. The Entwined Growth of Population and Product

1. The idea to incorporate the Mandate period in this analysis came from Moshe Syrquin, who performs his own long-term analysis in Chapter 2.

2. Documented in Amir (1985).

3. For a quantitative illustration of the effect of immigration on the economy see Merhav (1963).

4. The regression of the unemployment rate on lagged unemployment and the growth rate of population for 1924–1947 is the following:

$$U = -0.195 - \underset{(0.1)}{0.065}RP + \underset{(0.7)}{0.325}RP(t-1) + \underset{(3.7)}{0.568}U(t-1)$$

(0.1) (0.7) (3.7) (3.6)

$$(\overline{R}^2 = 0.57)$$

where U is the rate of unemployment and RP is the growth rate of the Jewish population.

2. Economic Growth and Structural Change

1. The extent to which the Jewish economy was a separate economy is discussed below and in the appendix to Syrquin (1984).

2. For example, Chenery and Syrquin (1975, 1980) and Chenery, Robinson, and Syrquin (1986). Basic English references on the economy of Jewish Palestine and of Israel (up to 1965) are Nathan, Gass, and Creamer (1946) and Halevi and Klinov-Malul (1968).

3. See Morawetz (1977) for comparisons for 1950–1977, and Chenery (1977) for the "transitional" grouping.

4. Additional estimates of relative income found in Syrquin (1984)—one based on official exchange rates for 1949 (United Nations, 1950) and Maddison's (1970, 1980b) estimates of real income in 1950—agree with the description here.

5. The rapid growth did not occur steadily, but in cycles of considerable magnitude. See Horowitz (1954) and Halevi (1979).

6. See Chapter 1 for tests of causality.

7. Ofer (1967, p. 4) quotes J. P. Loftus (1946, p. 24), Government Statistician in the 1940s: "for all important economic purposes, Palestine contains two different economies."

8. The periodization follows Maddison (1970, 1980b). Horowitz (1954) classifies 1920–1925 and 1932–1935 as prosperity years, 1926–1931 and 1936–1939 as depression years. This classification closely follows migration cycles, which Horowitz considers responsible for the fluctuations in economic activity. See also Chapter 1 in this volume.

9. For Jewish Palestine the capital elasticity was set at 0.5. Since the growth rates of capital and labor are similar, the productivity results are not sensitive to this assumption.

10. The figures for labor were not corrected for quality changes, but the results are probably not substantially affected by this omission. According to Halevi and Klinov-Malul (1968), labor quality declined slightly in the 1950s and rose slowly afterward. For the 1970s Metzer (Chapter 3 in this volume) concludes that the "overall quality of employed persons probably remained relatively constant."

11. Results from Balassa and Bertrand's 1970 study of seven centrally planned economies (CPEs), omitted because it covers only manufacturing, would place them in group *b*. The CPEs relied more on the expansion of factor inputs (in their case, capital) than on productivity growth.

12. The index is calculated from data in Gaathon (1971) and Metzer (Chapter 3 of this volume).

13. See note 2 above and Chenery (1979).

14. The patterns shown, from Chenery and Syrquin (1975), are derived from multiple regression estimates holding population size and the capital inflow ratio constant.

15. The trade figures are for all of Palestine and are thus overestimates. Szereszewski (1968) has a somewhat different distribution for 1936.

16. Because of the high level of capital inflow, the common practice in Israel is to present distributions such as those in Table 2-7 as shares of total resources (defined as GDP *plus* the import surplus). This approach eliminates or reduces many of the anomalies.

17. Chenery and Syrquin (1975) identified twenty-five countries as belonging in the 1960s to the small industry-oriented group (SM). Among these were Belgium, Greece, Jordan, Kenya, Panama, and Portugal. Table 2-9 compares the SM pattern with the average pattern for all countries.

18. The appendix to Syrquin (1984) contains a brief discussion of revealed comparative advantage and the factor content of trade.

19. Part of the increase in the share of services in output reflects an increase in the relative price of services.

20. Halevi and Klinov-Malul (1968, p. 6) mention a striking example: "One of the terms of reference given to Gaathon for the preparation of his Four Year Development Plan [in 1949] was that the share of the population in Agriculture should rise to 24 percent."

21. The derivation is presented in the appendix to Syrquin (1984).

22. Preliminary results appeared in Kubo and Robinson (1984) and Chenery (1980).

23. Maddison (1980a) reports a similar trend in the relative price of manufactures in advanced countries for 1950–1976.

24. See Cornwall (1977) and references there to studies of the importance of surplus labor in the growth of advanced countries since the 1950s.

25. A more extensive discussion of the non-Jewish labor force is found in the appendix to Syrquin (1984).

26. Dwight Perkins, commenting on an earlier draft of this chapter, made the interesting observation that when growth accelerated in Asian countries they had eliminated most entrenched interest groups of the feudal type and had achieved a national consensus on the need for growth.

3. The Slowdown of Economic Growth

1. The growth in unemployment to about 5 percent of the civilian labor force in 1980–1982 may indicate a weakening of the labor-hoarding tendency.

2. The correction was done by means of a divisia quality index using annual wage differentials by sex, schooling, and employment from the territories as weights.

3. The validity of the labor-quality corrections and their growth-accounting implications obviously depend on the soundness of the assumption that wage differentials and their pattern of change reflect quality differences. Since it is not at all clear that this assumption holds in the period considered, the quality corrections reported here should be viewed only as suggestive orders of magnitude.

4. The correlation between the annual rates of change of GDP in the business sector and of the Kondor-based utilization index in 1961–1981 (as constructed in Metzer, 1983, table A-5) is 0.846. The analogous correlation coefficients between GDP growth rates and the ratio of electricity consumption to stock of equipment are 0.573 for the ratios calculated on the basis of the ordinary stock of equipment in manufac-

turing and 0.713 for the life-span-corrected stock. The deficiency of Manzly's index lies primarily in its failure to reveal a decline in relative capital utilization during the recession of the mid-1960s.

5. For an extreme argument along these lines, claiming that most of Israel's declining growth of labor and capital in the 1970s was endogenous and reflected the adverse effect of the product growth slowdown on immigration and capital imports, see Ablin (1979b).

6. Hudson and Jorgenson (1978) and Jorgenson (1980) attribute the sudden slowdown of productivity in the industrialized countries to the energy price rise. This explanation rests on the substitution of labor for capital in the 1970s as result of the increase in energy prices, which raised the price of energy-complementary fixed capital relative to labor. According to Jorgenson, this substitution slowed productivity growth by causing the decline in the capital-labor ratio. But this line of reasoning does not fit the case of Israel, where the capital-labor ratio did not change after 1973 and the association between this ratio and productivity is quite weak.

7. Moreover, at least part of the returns to firms' financial activities are in the form of capital gains, which are not regarded as income derived from productive agents, and thus have a product- (and thus productivity-) reducing effect.

8. The exact numbers change somewhat when the growth-accounting calculation for manufacturing is based on an alternative data set derived from the CBS *Indexes of Industry and Crafts,* but the overall orders of magnitude and general outcome remain unchanged.

9. For the motives behind and consequences of similar demand-depressing policies associated with the mid-1960s slowdown see Beham and Kleiman (1968).

4. Investment Patterns

1. Halevi and Klinov-Malul (1968) attribute 40 to 65 percent of the growth in product per employed person to capital accumulation. Their estimate is based on (and shared by) Gaathon (1971). Metzer's more detailed growth accounting (Chapter 3) attributes a much smaller role to capital formation and a much larger one to residual, presumably "disembodied," total factor productivity. For an international survey of the controversy surrounding the role of capital in economic growth see Lubitz (1981).

2. A simple regression for 1960–1981, based on the acceleration principle, seems to fit the Israeli aggregate data quite well:

$$I = \text{Const} + \underset{(2.14)}{0.387\,Y} + \underset{(1.94)}{0.653\,Y_{-1}} - \underset{(-1.03)}{0.348\,Y_{-2}} + \underset{(1.05)}{0.253\,Y_{-3}} - \underset{(-5.32)}{0.173K}$$

$$R^2 = 0.965.$$

This regression presents a significant lagged response of investment. The residuals (which are still serially correlated, D.W. = 1.27) indicate that the 1966–1967 slowdown years are downward outliers, supporting the presumption that the downward dip in investment in those years was autonomous.

3. The data presented by Kuznets (1960b), Chenery and Syrquin (1975), and Syrquin (Chapter 2 of this volume) indicate that gross investment as a share of GDP increases mildly with per capita income, and a range of 20–24 percent can be seen as an average for countries comparable to Israel. Note that investment data are presented here relative to GNP, which was on average 1 percent lower than GDP until the early 1970s, and 3.5 percent lower than GDP in 1978–1982. As a proportion of GDP, therefore, investment fell more steeply than it did relative to GNP.

4. An alternative way of incorporating the import surplus and measuring the domestic investment effort is to consider investment's share of total domestic resources (GNP *plus* the import surplus). This index was, on average, 24 percent until 1975 and fell to about 19 percent in 1980–1982.

5. This statement ignores the possible gain on intramarginal investment. Nor is the grant component implicit in part of the foreign loans taken into account. On the other hand, as will be discussed later in the chapter, much of domestic investment has also been heavily subsidized.

6. Based on the long-term data presented by Kuznets (1960b) and an estimated 9–13 percent range for depreciation relative to GNP.

7. All of these indicators were computed in current prices. Given the decline in investment, the relative price of investment expenditure might have been expected to fall in the past decade. This, however, was not the case. The price of investment expenditure relative to the GNP deflator remained fairly level until 1972. With the investment boom of 1973–1974 it increased 9.7 percent. In 1975–1982 it increased further, even if not consistently, another 3.5 percent.

8. The accounting identity presented here is:

$$I + (G - T_{DOM}) = (Y - T_{DOM} - C) + M^{+}, \text{ or } I - S_{G,DOM} = S_{P,DOM} + M^{+},$$

where (in addition to the symbols from Table 4-1) T_{DOM} is domestic net receipts of the government, C and G are private and government consumption, and S refers to savings.

9. Direct foreign investment is included in the loans. It should be noted, however, that since 1967 (excluding 1972–1973) net direct investment has not exceeded 4 percent of domestic investment and since 1979 it has practically disappeared.

10. A similar intriguing question, in somewhat similar circumstances, has been posed for Japan. For attempted answers see Williamson and De Bever (1978) for the pre–World War II period, and Ohkawa (1979) for the postwar period.

11. Saving in Israel is estimated only as a residual of unconsumed income, with no corroboration through flow-of-funds accounting. There is, in particular, no systematic estimate of retained earnings, and thus no separation between personal and business savings.

12. The lag in the adjustment of current consumption was partly offset by a

significant increase in purchases of consumer durables, of which—rather arbitrarily—only dwellings are singled out as investment. The limited availability of mortgages implies that at the initial stage, as households build up funds, their aggregate purchase of residences would fall short of the savings released for the purpose.

13. The sources of gross capital stock data presented here are Gaathon (1971) for 1955, and Buch (1982) for 1960 on. Because of limitations on data, the share of transportation and communications in infrastructure capital stock includes only the construction component.

14. The rising implicit price of investment expenditure relative to GNP, referred to in note 7 above, is explainable by the relative price increase of construction and, in particular, of residential construction (see Figure 4-3). The price of residential construction relative to equipment investment, which was stable from 1954 to 1976, increased 50 percent in 1978–1982 (and 20 percent relative to GNP). This puzzling significant price increase may be partly explained as a delayed effect of the gap produced in the 1960s (see Figure 4-3) between the market price of dwellings and their construction cost. (The influx of Arab laborers into the construction industry after 1967 may explain the delay.) Another factor in the increase may be the general real wage increases in recent years (see the section on business-sector investment).

15. For an international comparison see Burns and Grebler (1976), who find from both cross-section and longitudinal analyses that the share of residential construction in GNP bears an inverted U-shape relation to per capita income.

16. This question is closely related to the one raised earlier concerning the increase in private savings. A comparison with Japan is revealing. The relative price of dwellings in Japan increased by over 80 percent in 1955–1970. The share of residential construction in GDP likewise increased from an average of about 2.5 percent in the 1950s to an average of 7.5 percent in the 1970s (*Japan Statistical Yearbook,* 1981, table 283 for price data; ibid., 1981 and 1968 for residential construction expenditure).

17. Net immigration correlates quite well with housing starts (see Bank of Israel, *Annual Report 1980,* p. 160), but the dominant causal relation since the mid-1950s might be from the state of the economy and correlated housing construction activity to immigration, rather than vice versa.

18. Data on the overall size of mortgages are based on annual reports by the Controller of Banks. Note that available statistics on the value of residential investment do not include the value of land; this value thus falls short of the market value of new housing.

19. CBS data, available only for 1970–1978, show that "directed" mortgages constituted on average 80 percent of total mortgages and were granted at average (unlinked) interest rates of between 6.6 percent (1970) and 13.2 percent (1978) (compared with average rates of 13.6 and 35.2 percent for nondirected mortgages, and annual inflation rates of 6 and 50 percent in the respective years). Berglas et al. (1981) estimate that in 1979, when partial linkage was introduced, the ex-ante perceived grant element in subsidized, directed mortgages was 48 percent.

20. According to the annual reports of the Bank of Israel, total gross investment

in the public sector, including nonprofit institutions and government enterprises, accounts for 55 percent of total nondwellings investment. If the average 35 percent share of dwelling investment initiated by government is included, then on average about 48 percent of gross fixed investment is conducted directly by the public sector.

21. Among the main features of the 1967 version of the law, an approved enterprise in the highest-priority development Zone A was entitled to a cash grant and to a long-term 6.5 percent unlinked loan, amounting (together) to up to 80 percent of its fixed investment; and to reduced taxes through accelerated depreciation, a lower corporate tax rate, and a five-year exemption from income taxes. Finger (1971) provided an extensive discussion of the various subsidy programs and their impact on entrepreneurial motivation. Medina (1975) examined the goals and allocation methods of the subsidized development loans, and Pack (1971, pp. 152–160) analyzed the extent to which the stated goals were in fact reflected in the differential investment levels in industrial subbranches.

22. This summary is based on Bank of Israel, *Annual Reports 1967* and *1973*, and on Ben-Shahar, Bronfeld, and Cukierman (1971).

23. Although firms ceased issuing bonds privately at market rates in the 1950s, as early as the mid-1960s the extensiveness of public credit made the average ratio of equity to total liabilities significantly lower in Israel than in the United States and the United Kingdom (though higher than in Japan) (Tamari, 1980, chap. 3). Since then the balance sheets of Israeli industrial firms have shown a steady further decrease in the equity ratio (Levy, 1982). In real terms, however, the equity ratio has been increasing since 1971, because rising inflation has eroded the debt.

24. The extent of credit subsidization poses major conceptual problems for national accounting. Litvin and Meridor (1982) argue convincingly that to maintain consistency with the basic principle of evaluating consumption by the prices to consumers, it is necessary to evaluate investment expenditure at the effective price faced by investors (since investment is presumably carried out to a margin where the discounted private value of future capital services equals that effective price). By this logic, we should reduce the national accounting estimate of investment by the value of the ex-ante grants. This change would also reduce the estimates of GNP and of the capital stock. (The existence of a corporate tax that creates a gap between the private and social values of capital services may, however, offset the effects of subsidization.)

25. As Litvin and Meridor (1982) note, it is conceivable that if subsidized loans were rationed, and investments were carried out to a level beyond the quantity constraints on loans, the ex-ante grants would be tantamount to (ex-ante) windfall capital gains, which do not alter factor costs or investment decisions. Other than (possibly) for housing loans in the big cities, business loans have apparently not been effectively rationed (see Kondor, 1982).

26. The argument is based on the idea that the premium of shift work (rather than a host of other reasons for excess capacity) is the main reason for underutilization. With more capital available and with the shiftwork wage unaltered, the profitability of opening a shift should increase.

27. The argument of how labor market distortions may reverse capital market distortions can be schematically presented by means of the static neoclassical framework. Let $K^D(\rho, w)$ be the aggregate demand for capital services, a negative function of the capital rental rate, ρ, and the wage rate, w (both expressed in output units). With a subsidized rental rate, ρ_d, the capital stock $K(\rho_d, w^*)$ would indeed be higher than in the "first best," $K^* = K(\rho^*, w^*)$, with undistorted ρ^*, w^*. However, an excessive labor cost, $w_d > w^*$, may even result in $K(\rho_d, w_d) < K^*$.

5. Changes in the Industrial Structure

1. Defined as 13+ and 0–12 years of schooling respectively. However, no such consistent measure exists for the period 1955–1964. Baruh (1966) used an index based on the cost of schooling. Herkowitz (1976) constructed a similar index. Both, however, assume perfect substitutability in production between different schooling levels, whereas I do not; hence their index is inappropriate for my purpose here. For 1955–1964 I use occupational categories in which L_{ED} consists of professional, technical, and administrative occupations.

2. The percentages of those with postsecondary schooling in the population age 25+ in the six peak countries are: United States (1979), 31.2; Canada (1976), 30.9; Israel (1980), 27.0; Sweden (1979), 15.4; Japan (1980), 14.3; United Kingdom (1976), 11.0 (UNESCO, *Statistical Yearbook 1981.*) Other countries lag considerably behind.

3. The respective intensities in 1971 were (Amir, 1983, tables 6, 7):

	Capital per worker (1970 000s of Israeli lira)	Workers with 13+ years of schooling/ total workers (percent)
Agriculture	6.0	4
"Other" manufacturing	3.4	5
"Education-intensive" manufacturing	2.9	16
Transportation	11.7	7
Construction	5.4	5
Trade	—	8
Financial and business services	1.2 (Financial and business services and Other services together)	35
Other services		9
Public and community services	2.9	40

4. Income elasticities for the various sectors (derived from CBS, *Special Publications Series,* nos. 602 and 656, and *Statistical Abstract 1978*) are: agriculture, 0.3; "other" manufacturing, 0.8; "education-intensive" manufacturing, 1.7; transportation, 1.6; construction, 1.7; financial and business services, 1.7; trade and personal

services, 2.0. For public services I assumed arbitrarily 2.0 but experimented later with 1.0. See also Klinov (1984), supplement S-III.

5. Details on the assumptions and procedures are described in Klinov (1984), supplement S-III.

6. Educational Structure and Wage Differentials of the Labor Force

1. Calculated as actual change (in percentage points) *minus* the change computed with the specified factors held constant.

2. The method of analysis and regression functions are presented in detail in Amir (1983), p. 11 and tables A-1 through A-4.

3. The tests of this hypothesis are formally based on a model of the labor market that includes supply and demand in relative terms. The model is presented in Amir (1983), pp. 16, 18–19.

4. Industrial structure will be analysed in terms of employment because of the low reliability of product data.

5. N_k = employed labor force ($k = 1971, 1979$), N_i^k = employed persons with i years of schooling ($i = 13+, 16$), and $N_i^k/N^k = b_i^k$, the education-i intensity of total employment. Similarly, $l_j^k = N_j^k/N_k$ is the proportion of employed persons in industry j ($j = 1, \ldots, n$), and b_{ij}^k is the proportion of employed persons with i years of schooling in the labor force of industry j.

Consider the identity

$$b_i^k \equiv \sum_j l_j^k b_{ij}^k,$$

and denote the percentage-point change between the two periods by $\Delta b_i = (b_i^{79} - b_i^{71})100$. This change can be decomposed into additive components of relative contributions to the change in the educational intensity of the labor force:

$$\Delta b_i = \underbrace{\sum_j l_j^{71} \Delta b_{ij}}_{A} + \underbrace{\sum_j \Delta l_j b_{ij}^{71}}_{B} + \underbrace{\sum_j \Delta l_j \Delta b_{ij}}_{C}$$

A represents the contribution of intraindustry educational change, *B* represents the contribution of the relative growth of education-intensive industries (interindustry change), and *C* is the interaction component (which can be broken down into intra- and interindustry components in proportion to *A* and *B*).

6. A breakdown for the 13+ years-of-schooling level showed similar results; see Amir (1983), table 6.

7. Annual average compared with the preceding year's average price level.

8. See Baruh (1983), who disaggregates manufacturing into forty-five industries and shows that in 1972–1980 the industrial composition of exports became relatively more education intensive (intraindustry changes held constant).

9. Litvin and Meridor (1982) estimate that the grant equivalent of investment loans reached over 50 percent of investment in 1977.

10. The estimates of these supply elasticities are based on the assumption that the supply preferences between sectors of educated men and women did not change during the 1970s; that is, the relative allocation between sectors would not have changed had the relative wage levels remained the same.

11. The estimates of elasticities of substitution between educated men and women employees are based on the assumption that during the 1970s technological changes in production and changes in other factors did not change the demand for educated women relative to that for educated men; that is, gender-based wage differentials would not have changed without the change that took place in their relative supply to the labor market. This is a rather strong assumption, especially in reference to the business sector, because changes in the product mix and in the supply of physical capital might have had different effects on the demand for men's and women's occupations. Elasticity estimates, especially those for the business sector, should therefore be treated with caution.

7. Diversity in Population and in the Labor Force

1. This section is based on Ben-Porath (1985).

2. I benefited here from an unpublished dissertation by Amir (1985).

3. The full distribution by years of schooling (not shown here) was weighted by earnings per hour of men in 1982. The earnings figures in Israeli shekels are: 0: 41.3; 1–4: 43.2; 5–8: 50.3; 9–12: 61.5; 13–15: 81.3; 16+: 94.9.

4. The discussion of women's participation is based on Ben-Porath and Gronau (1985).

8. Defense and the Economy

1. See, for example, Patinkin (1960) and Halevi and Klinov-Malul (1968). Papers dealing specifically with defense include Berglas (1970), Kochav and Lifshitz (1973), Lifshitz (1975), and Barkai (1980).

2. Countries such as Saudi Arabia and Libya may not be directly involved in the conflict but certainly play a role as a reservoir of military equipment for the others.

3. It should be remembered that loss of life and injury by enemy action or in the course of military service are not confined to times of open war.

4. For additional details see Berglas (1983).

5. In the latter case, GNP as well as defense expenditures may be understated, a fact that has a bearing on international comparisons of productivity.

6. Actual earnings at age 18–20 are not relevant, since persons of that age in the civilian labor force are by no means representative of those doing military service.

7. If the cost of reserve duty were defined as part of the defense budget, the army would have a strong incentive to reduce it.

8. There is a question of timing here. The present value of the cost can be imputed at the time of injury or, alternatively, at the time of actual payment. The loss in GNP and the timing of the tax burden are close to the period of payment.

9. Another imputed element not reflected in the estimates of unreported defense costs is the excess price imposed on the Israeli consumer of oil by the restrictions on the country's sources of supply, which arise from the fact that some of the major oil producers are among the countries confronting Israel. Nor are other effects of the economic boycott taken into account.

10. Local-currency expenditures include all payments in local currency and include the import component. Fuel consumption is part of local expenditures since it is locally refined.

11. This bias was maintained throughout the period by means of foreign-exchange controls, import duties and quotas, and export subsidies. Until the early 1970s defense imports were duty free; subsequently, defense imports paid a duty of 15 percent and, since its introduction in 1976, value-added tax. The flat-rate 15 percent duty was imposed on all imports in 1970–1977. Additional duty imposed on various commodities at different rates is not paid by the defense sector.

12. Military-aid loans are subject to terms reflecting the cost to the U.S. government (only slightly below the market rate), while loans given as part of economic aid pay a much lower rate of interest.

13. In 1975–1981 U.S. aid in the form of loans (excluding special loans following the Camp David accord) averaged $930 million annually, and debt retirement averaged $210 million. Although annual variations in borrowing and debt retirement were very small, interest payments rose from $86 million to $476 million. Interest payments will exceed net new borrowing by 1985, which is also about the time when debt retirement will start to rise (Bank of Israel, *Annual Report 1981,* p. 191, table VI-22 [Hebrew edition]).

14. These include supplementary education to soldiers who cannot read or write properly; provision of teachers to remote districts that lack civilian teachers; preparatory courses for soldiers planning to attend university; educational programs on Jewish culture and history, the geography of Israel, and Zionist values; and vocational training at the secondary level as well as many technical courses during army service.

15. In 1979–80 the Military Industry (a major producer of military equipment, fully owned by the state) exported over 60 percent of its total output; annual exports were (in millions of dollars): 101.4, 186.5, 206.2, 288.7 from 1977 through 1980 respectively (State Comptroller, *Annual Report 1982,* p. 723).

16. Statements to the effect that were it not for the defense industries there would be continuous mass unemployment and a much larger balance-of-payments deficit are based on the erroneous assumption that these industries have no economic alternative.

17. For the 1967 war I used the figures for 1963–1964 in order to avoid the effects of the recession of 1965–1966.

9. Public Spending on Civilian Services

1. The comparison of shares is made in current prices and includes changes in the relative price of various sectors. See the discussion on elasticities later in this chapter, and Chapter 6.

2. Growth due to the general level of inflation does not affect the shares and is subtracted uniformly from all magnitudes.

3. The rise in relative prices of services is a worldwide phenomenon, based largely on the increase in relative wages of service workers. In Israel such increases are sometimes registered even when relative wages are in fact declining. This phenomenon further underlines the unrealistic nature of the zero-productivity assumption.

4. This last observation is somewhat biased, since some officially recorded additional hours of instruction are used to compensate teachers for extra effort rather than for longer hours.

5. Current expenditure elasticity on a service is the ratio of the relative change in total burden (real growth plus change in the relative price of services) to the relative change in real GNP. Real elasticity is the ratio of the relative change in real growth of the service to the relative change in real GNP.

6. A small selection of American literature on the problems of health services is Fuchs (1974), Davis and Schoen (1978), Enthoven (1980), Feldstein (1981), and Weisbrod (1982).

10. The Development of the Transfer System and the Redistribution of Income

1. In a decile with more standard adults, a larger share of income is required for perfect equality.

2. The changes over time in efficiency will be a function of changes in the weight of each program, in their efficiency, and in the interaction between these changes.

3. The decline in the benefit rates per transfer recipient was even greater than in average benefit rates because coverage grew considerably over the decade.

4. Because most transfers were linked to the wage level, the decline was in relation to wages, whereas real transfer levels continued to increase.

11. Taxes and Transfers in an Inflationary Decade

1. The figures in Table 11-1 are from Meridor (forthcoming), the first study to organize the public-expenditure data in a manner that permits a comprehensive view of the budget finances. For the sake of consistency she was obliged to make several changes in the official data, resulting in minor differences between the figures in this table and those found in the official publications and further on in this chapter. For detailed definitions of the methods of calculation see Meridor (forthcoming).

2. The interest rate estimates are downward biased for several reasons, including

the absence of comprehensive records on fund-raising, the occasional lack of a clear distinction between principal and interest payments, and the practice of recording interest payments at the time of payment.

3. The constraint imposed by the size of the public debt can be defined as the maximum ability of the economy to bear interest payments. The relevant terms for such a discussion are, again, percentages of GNP. Denoting the debt and product in year i by d_i and y_i, respectively, with β as the annual growth rate of product, α as the increase in debt as percent of GNP, and $\delta = d/y$, yields:

$$d_2/y_2 = (d_1 + \alpha y_1)/(1 + \beta)y_1$$

and the growth rate of the public debt:

$$\delta_2/\delta_1 = (1 + \alpha/\delta_1)/(1 + \beta).$$

The figures for Israel in the beginning of the 1980s were: $\beta = 0.016, \alpha = 0.137, \delta = 1.5$; thus the annual growth rate of the debt as a percent of product was 7 percent. Earmarking 10 percent of GNP for interest payments is an extremely heavy burden on any taxation system; hence the need to prevent the GNP share of the debt from growing further. Such a policy implies $\alpha \leq \delta\beta$. As a long-term objective the debt should be smaller than product; therefore, it is necessary to maintain $\alpha < \beta$.

4. Tables 11-2 through 11-4 are based on national accounts concepts and data from CBS and the Bank of Israel. The figures in Table 11-1 are adjusted to budget concepts. There are three main differences: (1) Part of the taxes and foreign-trade support do not appear in Table 11-1, since Meridor (forthcoming) refers to them as a substitute for devaluation. (2) The definition of credit subsidization in Table 11-1 is adjusted to the budgetary outlays. (3) Net taxation in Table 11-1—but not in Table 11-2—includes compulsory loans and their repayment. Until 1975 compulsory loans were an important source of government finance; after the reform, their weight declined significantly (see Table 11-2). In several years after 1975 the repayment of such loans exceeded the income they brought in. The fact that compulsory loans are included in net taxation in Table 11-1, but not in Table 11-2, is the main reason for the drop in net taxation between 1975 and 1980, observed only in Table 11-1.

5. The gross taxation estimates in Israel are considerably downward biased owing to the existence of additional taxes that are not reflected in the tax statistics. This "taxation" is directly linked to the financing of the defense system via compulsory military service, reserve duty, and maintaining emergency stockpiles paid for by consumers. An estimate of these concealed taxes is presented in Chapter 8.

6. Many studies in this field have been conducted in the United States. They, too, point to the great importance of mutual interactive effects. For a survey and references to sources see Break (1984).

7. No official data are available on the subsidization of credit before the mid-1970s. Sokoler (1984) estimates the average subsidization rate in 1971–1975 as

similar to that in 1976–1980, whereas in the 1960s the rate was negligible. Subsidies, compulsory borrowing, and debt repayment in the pre-1975 period account for most of the difference in net taxes presented in Tables 11-1 and 11-2.

8. For the effect of compulsory loans on personal income tax, see Gabbay, Har-oeh, and Cukierman (1976). For the effect on total revenues, see Table 11-2.

9. When tax schedules are fully and continuously (monthly) linked to the consumer price index, changes in nominal income do not affect the tax burden. Since linkage was neither complete nor continuous, the increasing burden stems, among other things, from changes in nominal income as well.

10. The common argument that the tax burden increases as a result of a shift to a higher tax bracket is false. Even when there is no such shift, the tax burden will increase as long as the marginal rate is higher than the average rate. Consider a person who pays an average tax rate of 50 percent and a marginal rate of 60 percent; if his income doubles, then—since the marginal 60 percent is the maximum rate—it will apply to the entire increment to his income, and his average tax will go up to 55 percent although his tax bracket remains unchanged.

11. The employees' rate was 3.3 percent in 1970 and 4.6 percent in 1980. The NI tax is essentially a fixed percentage of earnings up to a prescribed ceiling, with very few exemptions. The changes during the 1970s were not only in the rates collected, but also in the tax ceiling, from 2.2 times an average employee's wage in 1970, to thrice that wage in 1980. But the acceleration of inflation and the delays in revising this ceiling (only twice a year since 1980) meant that, in effect, the 1980 ceiling was 2.1 times the average wage. This is an example of how inflation erodes NI collections. Since ceilings on NI benefits are updated more frequently than tax ceilings, inflation causes deficits in the NI accounts.

12. The definitions of receipts from wages differ between the two taxes, but the datum reflects the high weight of NI tax in total taxes levied on wage earners.

13. For more details on marginal tax rates for various income levels see Berglas (1980).

14. A more thorough analysis appears in Berglas (1974); Yitzhaki (1983); and Nerlove, Razin, and Sadka (1984).

15. Yitzhaki (1983) provides estimates of the efficiency of tax collection from wage earners and the self-employed.

16. VAT was also levied on defense imports; the latter, which accounted for 1.5 percent of product in 1975–1980, are not included in the present discussion.

17. Interest payments are given gross. However, the public sector also derives income from property not dealt with here. This income totaled approximately 3 percent of GNP in the second half of the 1970s. Because no rising trend is discernible for such income, it does not alter the present discussion.

18. With the acceleration of inflation to three-digit levels it was found that the existing linkage arrangements were not comprehensive enough. The linkage of government bonds to the previous month's index reduces the value of such bonds by 20 percent when the monthly index rises by 20 percent. The result was a substantial saving

in the real interest payments of the government, which is not taken into account in the data presented here. The public is, of course, aware of these losses, and the government will have to protect it from such losses in future savings schemes. On the other hand, these interest figures underestimate the cost of financing the public debt. To encourage savings, the government grants savers attractive tax benefits, discussed later in this chapter. The most glaring example of these benefits, called "complementary training funds," makes the employer's contribution tax exempt. This exemption alone is equivalent to an average real return of 45 percent to taxpayers in the 60 percent tax bracket. Provident funds enjoy similar benefits yielding a return of 15 percent. The benefit can increase even further if the NI component is taken into account. Thus accurate estimates of the real cost of the public debt are of crucial importance to any discussion of economic policy, and the sooner these are made, the better.

19. See Bank of Israel, *Annual Report 1983,* p. 103 (Hebrew version). There is some disagreement on how to define the correct base: should it be the first month after the tax reform or the first year in which it was in effect? However, alternative bases of calculation also result in considerable erosion.

20. Subsidized loans are granted, for example, to encourage investment. The degree of encouragement depends on the expected rate of inflation; when inflation exceeds expectations, unexpected profits accrue to investors and unexpected expenditures are incurred by the government.

21. See U.S. Treasury (1977), Meade (1978), and Pechman (1980). In certain respects Israel's income tax resembles a consumption tax, but the present analysis does not suffice to take a clear stand on the desirable tax base either on general principles or from the administrative viewpoint.

22. For formal proof of these theorems see Atkinson and Stiglitz (1980), p. 70.

23. It is important to distinguish between taxes on wages and taxes on wage earners. Employees, too, have considerable savings and enjoy the benefits of exemptions on their returns.

24. From the macroeconomic viewpoint, though not from the individual taxpayer's, the subsidization of the business sector offsets the taxes levied on it.

25. Savers who were astute enough to invest in several provident funds can enjoy the benefits of pension plans after quite a short period, even without increasing their total savings.

26. Other countries also extend considerable benefits to savings, but these benefits apparently are not as extensive as in Israel. In principle, it is accepted that when the payments into pension funds are tax exempt, the income derived from that source is taxable.

12. Perspectives on the Balance of Payments

1. Data for all tables and figures in this chapter are taken from the updated files of the CBS Balance of Payments Division. For definitions and methods see Halevi (1983b).

2. Whereas this ratio was not significantly different from the EEC average in the 1960s, it was at a much higher level from the mid-1970s.

3. For a detailed discussion of Israel's trade regime see Michaely (1975). A briefer discussion of exchange control until 1970 is in Halevi (1971).

4. In mid-1976 the crawling peg was to a basket of currencies rather than to the dollar, to take account of foreign fluctuations against the dollar.

5. For a discussion of this index and monthly data, see Michaely (1983).

6. All shares are computed from current price data.

7. Only two items are included in the balance of payments: payments to foreign carriers for freight and passengers, and costs incurred abroad by domestic carriers.

8. Computed from estimates by Nachmani (1981).

9. This method of estimating relative factor intensity was first used, for the 1972–1975 period, by Weinblatt (1980). It contrasts with the approach that compares factor intensity in exports with domestic production of import substitutes.

10. These estimates were prepared by Tsiddon (1982).

11. Air transportation, however, is more similar in geographic structure to foreign travel than to merchandise trade.

12. A discussion of these welfare gains and losses, together with estimates for Israel, appears in N. Liviatan (1983).

13. This is $X_{t-1}PX_{t-1}[(ITT_t/ITT_{t-1}) - 1][PM_t/PM_{t-1}]$, where X = quantity of exports; PX and PM = prices of exports and imports respectively; and ITT = the index of the terms of trade.

14. The loss is equal to $NT[1 - (PM_t/PM_{t-1})]$, where NT = net unilateral and long-term transfers.

15. The computation is: $2/3INT[(PM_t/PM_{72}) - 1] + 1/3INT[(PM_t/PM_{t-1}) - 1]$.

16. The terms-of-trade indexes, particularly for defense imports, are computed somewhat arbitrarily; therefore, these figures are more illustrative of relative than of exact sizes.

17. Loans given at less than market rates of interest have a grant element. Abramov (1982) has estimated this element to be from 5 to 15 percent of total net aid in recent years, and much higher in the early 1970s.

18. These were gross transfers. Israel agreed to transfer abroad part of these payments, totaling about $110 million.

19. Assets are grossly underestimated because they include only short-term assets held by official and financial institutions.

20. The Central Bureau of Statistics and the Bank of Israel differ as to how obligations should be measured. The latter's position is that bank obligations should be shown net of their assets abroad. The data in the table are shown gross.

21. Halevi (1969) presents a brief survey of the major contributions to this literature, mainly by Daniel Creamer, A. L. Gaathon, Abba Lerner, Michael Michaely, Don Patinkin, and David Pines.

22. Gross rather than net investment figures are used in line 6 because of doubts concerning the reliability of depreciation estimates in recent years (see Chapter 4).

13. The Energy Sector in the 1960s and 1970s

1. The prices used in calculating the energy price index are those paid by final consumers of electricity and oil distillates. The weights used are the fraction of a barrel of crude used to produce various oil products, including fuel oil used for electricity generation. Using physical data for weights has an obvious conceptual advantage, but since electricity generation is highly capital intensive, these weights understate the contribution of electricity prices to the index. More than 40 percent of crude was used for electricity generation. The relative energy price index is the energy price index deflated by the implicit GNP price index (see Table 13-1).

2. The single-equation models ignore the interaction of quantity and price variables and presume a unique dependence of the quantity consumed on prices and income. This issue and other technical features are extensively treated in Barkai (1984), pp. 5–6, nn. 7–8.

3. Ibid., p. 5, n. 7. Similar consumption functions were estimated for several oil distillates and for electricity (ibid., p. 6 and n. 8).

4. For more detailed data and references see ibid., pp. 8–10 and n. 11.

5. Ibid., p. 10 and n. 12.

6. Because this calculation implicitly assumes zero elasticity of demand for primary energy, and because prices fell between 1960 and 1970, this is the upper boundary of the welfare gain due to the drop in real prices. For periods in which prices were rising, the corresponding entries given in the following discussion represent the lower boundaries of welfare loss.

7. The conceptual basis and the technique of the welfare cost (or benefit) estimates are described in Barkai (1984), pp. 13–17 and tables 7–8, pp. 51–55.

8. Equity is, of course, a relevant consideration in this context. To consumer organizations in particular, equity would suggest that households should be shielded from the full brunt of the price revolutions. However, the direct passing on of costs to industrial consumers could not be rejected out of hand even on these grounds. In any case, they could have been of only minor consequence for setting the prices of oil distillates and of electricity to industrial and other business consumers, which were paying lower rates than households in the first place. Electricity generation accounted for about 45 percent of the total crude intake. Household consumption of electricity was only about 35 percent of the total electricity used; that is, households indirectly consumed about 15 percent of crude.

9. For the detailed argument and supporting data see Barkai (1984), pp. 17–27, table 7, and especially p. 51.

10. This is not to say that the subsidization of fuel was the only device used to subsidize electricity. Capital costs, which are a substantial fraction of this capital-intensive operation, were presumably not adequately covered in the late 1970s, the early 1980s in particular, and presumably, though to a smaller extent, in the 1960s.

11. According to an input-output matrix of the mid-1970s, the cost of fuel was about 60 percent of the unit cost of electricity generation and distribution. The cost of

capital services makes up most of the difference. Because the price ceilings imposed on electricity prices were part of the attempt to contain inflation, a fraction of the implicit real energy subsidy appears in the books of the (nationalized) Israel Electricity Corporation. My estimates of net government absorption from the energy sector, which are derived from the government revenue data, thus underestimate the true magnitudes, which grew substantially as inflation rates started soaring toward the end of the 1970s and particularly in the early 1980s. For a more detailed analysis and the data on taxes and absorption, see Barkai (1984), pp. 27–35 and table 6, p. 50.

12. The closing of the Suez Canal made the transshipment through Israel of oil destined for European markets a paying proposition in the short run. Expectations for long-term profits from this operation were based on the saving of Suez Canal dues and on the fact that many Mediterranean and some northern European ports could not be served by large tankers, and therefore needed transshipment in any case, which could be effected in Ashkelon, at the Mediterranean end of the pipeline.

13. Neither electricity nor fuel has been rationed since the early 1950s. Generating capacity tripled in the 1960s and quadrupled in the 1970s. The load coefficient at the end of the 1960s was high, which means that the system was under considerable strain during peaks in demand. The much lower rise in demand in the 1970s—demand doubled in this decade—and the more rapid expansion in capacity in the preceding decade allowed an ample margin even at peak demand, expressed in terms of lower load coefficients.

14. External Shocks and Domestic Response

1. For more details see Bruno (1983).

2. The mean output growth for Israel, 6.2 percent, is slightly above Metzer's estimate (see Chapter 3) of capacity growth after 1972 (5.5 percent), but well below his estimated rate for 1960–1972 (9.5). Thus, $y - \bar{y}$ shifts during the 1967–1972 upturn are excessive while the slowdown, especially after 1977, may be slightly overstated.

3. The relative vertical distance of the two curves in May 1977 was almost down to that of 1973. Part of this deceleration of inflation has to do with the slowdown of the creeping devaluation and a temporary increase in food subsidies (see Temkin, 1983).

4. A simple regression for 1964–1981 of the civilian deficit ratio on $y - \bar{y}$ (elasticity of 0.26) and the lagged terms of trade (elasticity of -0.18) gives $R^2 = 0.29$.

5. The growth in the civilian deficit ratio is already noticeable in the first three months of 1973 because of a sharp rise in imports.

6. This reduction was achieved despite a worldwide slump and a substantial worsening in the terms of trade.

7. That is, gross output (q), material inputs (n), and GDP (y) are assumed to be related in a two-stage production function: $q = q[y(k, l); n]$. For detailed analysis see Bruno and Sachs (1981).

8. An alternative would be to measure gross output (q) on the horizontal axis; this is the more relevant measure for a subsector such as manufacturing (discussed later).

9. These variables are defined in terms of their logarithms; therefore, the product of the exchange rate by the world price (which is the domestic price of the world good) is the sum of the logarithms ($p^* + e$) and the ratio of the two prices is the difference of the logarithms $[p - (p^* + e)]$.

10. When both S and D contract, π may obviously go either way.

11. It must also be assumed that the participation rate of women would have risen at the same rate that it actually did.

12. Defined as the nominal wage in the business sector deflated by GDP prices.

13. A complementary explanation rests on the repercussions on the business sector of an exogenous wage explosion in the strongly unionized and sheltered public sector. In 1976–1979 the real wage of public-sector employees grew at an annual average of 11 percent while the total economy's real wage growth was 7 percent. There is some evidence of a "reverse Scandinavian model" at work in those years (that is, the "sheltered" sector dictated the wage of the "exposed" sector, rather than the reverse).

14. These are mirror images of the horizontal shifts in Figures 14-1 and 14-2. The reservations expressed earlier concerning the implied uniform trend do not affect the subsequent regression results.

15. In 1979–1981 this variable shows an increase (real appreciation), as does 1981–1983 (excluded here).

16. There was a formal nominal devaluation of 17 percent in 1967, absorbed with only a slight price increase (see Figure 14-1).

17. The official rate was devalued from 4.20 Israeli pounds per dollar before 1974 to about 10.00 in three years. The real depreciation, shown in Figure 14-4, was of course much smaller—of the order of about 20 percent of the nominal depreciation.

18. This effective reduction in the labor supply to the business sector is shown in Figure 14-4 by a leftward shift in the vertical portion of S_2'. It is possible that the supply curve itself also continued to shift up during this period.

19. The demand variables used in the regressions are the residuals from a regression of each variable on its lagged value and thus avoid the uniform trend problem.

20. η_n is defined so as to be a positive number (that is, it is *minus* the normal price elasticity).

21. Capital letters denote actual variables (for example, imports, N), small letters their logarithms, and dotted variables their shifts over time (for example, $\dot{n}$ is the growth *rate* of N).

22. A temporary increase in private savings and a decline in investment (and in inventory movements) may suggest the explanation. Note that in model A, when both adjacent periods are taken together (1978–1982), the estimate fits in well.

23. Bank of Israel, *Annual Report 1982,* table 5a. In 1981 the number came down to -1.5 and in 1982 to -4.4. When unilateral transfers are left out the numbers are negative throughout.

24. In 1982–83 the real debt again rose much more rapidly.

25. To the extent that there was some indexation of money to inflation already in 1955–1974, equation (4) could be applied to work out the implied larger role of

devaluation on inflation. For example, if the elasticity of money with respect to prices is one-third, the indirect effect would be to augment the total role of the other factors in equation (4) by about 10 percent.

15. Indexation in the Labor Market

1. For the difference between ex-post and ex-ante indexation practices and for a survey of indexation in Israel until the mid-1970s, see Kleiman (1977b).

2. However, because of the lag in publishing the price index, the government can, by manipulating prices or exchange rates, reduce the effective real interest on its indexed obligations. For a discussion of these manipulations, see the fourth section of this chapter.

3. The COLA system has undergone many changes since its inception in 1941. This survey concentrates on its operation since the late 1960s. For a discussion of the effects of the COLA in the 1940s and 1950s, see Bahral (1965).

4. Wage drift is often considered as (and frequently is) a means of circumventing collective-bargaining agreements, especially when the wage increment resulting from the bargaining process is small. However, if the quality of work increases with experience, then, as the labor force ages, increases in actual wages should, up to a point, exceed the rise in wage tariffs agreed upon in collective contracts that presumably apply to work of a given quality.

5. In response to the acceleration of inflation in 1984, the COLA is now paid monthly, in the form of advances on a sliding scale dependent on the monthly rate of price increase.

6. For example, suppose the CPI, on the basis of January of a given year, was 110 in February and 120 in March and thereafter. Calculated on a quarterly basis, the ratio between the average price levels of the second and first quarters of that year would have been $120:110 = 1.091$, leading to a COLA of 9.1 percent payable from July onward. On the other hand, if prices in the last quarter of the preceding year had been stable, the periodic average calculation would have resulted in a COLA payment of only 10 percent at the end of the first quarter, compared with one of 20 percent under a point-to-point calculation.

7. With t denoting the individual's average income tax rate, π the inflation rate underlying the COLA payment, and both assumed to pertain to the same pretax income, the relative increase in disposable income is $\pi/(1 - t)$. Thus if $\pi = 10$ percent, COLA would have raised net income by 14.3 percent at $t = 0.3$, but only by 12.5 percent at $t = 0.2$. For individuals below the tax threshold, the increase would of course be limited to 10 percent. The ensuing rise in taxpayers' real disposable income, and especially its regressive effect, were probably unintentional. But up to a certain point on the income scale it operated to offset the effects of the ceiling on COLA payments.

8. This destabilizing effect of wage indexation when inflation is due to real shocks (in this case, a change in relative demand) has often been pointed out in the theoretical

literature on wage indexation. See, for example, Gray (1976) and Fischer (1977). On the other hand, with a uniform price rise at rate π, both curves would shift equiproportionately, their intersection at F leaving both the allocation of labor and the real wage unchanged—a result identical with that obtained by indexation.

9. An attempt by employers to protect real profits from the effect of a rise in import prices (or in indirect taxation) will lead to a similar outcome even in the absence of wage indexation.

10. The use of all CPI items as the price base for the COLA involved the reinstatement of imputed rent and the inclusion of fruit and vegetable prices (to reduce their seasonal effect, the parties to the COLA agreement had agreed to take the latter into account only once a year, in July). The inclusion of these elements was justified on grounds of simplicity and public confidence. The ceiling was retained partly because the Histadrut regarded it as a measure of achieving a more egalitarian wage distribution and ignored its effect on the distribution of income between capital and labor.

11. Although the average price level was 39 percent higher in 1975 than in 1974, price increases in 1975 amounted to only 23 percent, and prices were virtually stable from May to August of that year.

12. With the annual rate of inflation denoted by π and the rate of increase in the COLA by C, the effective rate of indexation is $R_e = C/\pi$; the real wage that would obtain in the absence of other adjustment mechanisms is

$$W_c = (1 + C)/(1 + \pi).$$

The erosion of W_c is defined as

$$D = 1 - W_c = (1 - R_e)\pi/(1 + \pi).$$

Given R_e, erosion will increase with π but at a decreasing rate.

13. As reported in Israel, nominal wages do not include employers' contributions to employees' social insurance or other charges levied from time to time on employers' wage bills. The present measure of real wages, calculated by deflating nominal wages by the CPI, thus represents the consumption wage, except that it does not take into account variations in personal income tax. The calculation of the real production wage is hampered not only by lack of data on nonwage labor costs but also by conceptual problems regarding the price index by which its nominal values should be deflated.

14. The results for the high-inflation period after the 1975 reform seem to represent a departure from an earlier norm. The cumulated contribution of the other mechanisms accounted for 35 percent of the end-of-year real wage in 1962–1967 (Committee, 1975a, table A-1), and for 40 percent in 1968–1973 (calculated from Table 15-1).

15. By this text, X is said to have a unidirectional influence on Y if lagged values of X explain a significant share of the variance in Y not accounted for by a regression on lagged values of itself, but not the other way round. For a standard reference see

Granger (1969). In interpreting the corresponding *F*-values, presented in Table 15-3, it should be borne in mind that as the COLA is paid on accumulated price increases, roughly two-thirds of its magnitude is already known a month before the actual COLA payment comes into effect.

16. This conclusion refers to the results obtained for 1968–1982 as a whole. Except for monthly data, tests conducted for each subperiod separately reveal no systematic results, probably because of the small number of degrees of freedom. Results similar to those described in the text were obtained for the residuals, from a time trend, of the quarterly and semiannual data.

17. This sensitivity was greatly increased by the floating of the Israeli pound (later the shekel) in October 1977, which provided a proxy for a daily index of changes in the purchasing power of money, in the form of the "representative" dollar exchange rate. See the final section of this chapter.

18. The results obtained here, of a long-term unidirectional influence from *WO* to *D*, stand in direct contrast to those of the Liviatan study for 1957–1981, and to the results obtained for 1968–1981 using his data. In all these studies the COLA erosion (or insufficiency) is measured by the complement to 1 of the "COLA real wage." The latter is defined here as the rate of change in the annual average of the monthly ratios of the COLA and CPI. Liviatan's study defines it as the rate of change in the ratio of the corresponding average annual indexes. Since the annual distributions of changes in the COLA and in the price level are by no means similar, this procedure fails to net out short-term variations in the two, and therefore also in *D* and in *WO*, which cancel each other out on an annual basis. Liviatan's annual observations thus reflect the short-term influences that have been shown earlier to run from *D* to *WO*. Some element of such variations is also retained in the data here, where wages, which in the case of permanent employees are paid once monthly, were deflated by the average price level for the whole month. Despite Israel's high current inflation rate there has been no demand so far for more frequent payments. This fact suggests that the adaptation of institutional arrangements to economic phenomena is rather slow.

19. See Sargent (1979). Calculations based on lags of up to two years yield somewhat higher estimates for current erosion and for one-year-lagged effects, but a lower one for the accumulated long-term erosion effect, with some offsetting variations among the interim coefficients.

20. As shown in note 12 above, the erosion of real wages is $D = (1 - R_e)\pi/(1 + \pi)$, where R_e denotes the effective indexation rate. With $D = 0.8(\Delta W/W)$, the value of the corresponding effective indexation rate can be expressed as a decreasing function of $\Delta W/W$ and an increasing function of π:

$$R_e = 1 - 0.8(\Delta W/W)(1 + \pi)/\pi.$$

Given an annual gross wage increase of 15 percent and an inflation rate of 100 percent, the steady-state erosion effect estimated here is equivalent to that of an effective indexation rate of 0.76.

21. The whole subject of the operation and effects of daily linkage to the exchange rate has not so far received the attention it seems to deserve. In particular, the existing state of the data does not allow a proper evaluation of the effect of such daily linkage on income distribution.

16. Accelerating Inflation and Balance-of-Payments Crises

1. This presentation needs to be qualified in two respects. Although the rate of devaluation was stepped up very rapidly in the second quarter of 1979 (119 percent devaluation against the dollar, compared with 36 percent in the preceding quarter and 22 percent in the preceding years, all in annual rates), it did not cause any immediate real increase in import prices. Moreover, the big devaluations made in the other crises coincided with dramatic increases in controlled prices. It is therefore impossible to isolate the impact of these devaluations on import demand.

17. The Inflationary Process

1. Special indexation adjustments to wages are paid more often than quarterly if the inflation rate exceeds a specified level. For more details on wage indexation see Chapter 15.

2. We do not explicitly discuss other factors affecting the rate of shift of the aggregate supply curve beyond noting that supply factors played a significant role in the slowdown of growth in Israel since the early 1970s (see Chapter 14). The growth slowdown in turn affected the inflation rate, as we discuss later.

3. In fact there have been two elements making for an *increase* in the real deficit with a rise in the price level. One was the unindexed debt of the private sector (which by 1984 had virtually been eroded by inflation); the other was the lag in the collection of taxes.

4. As the degree of inflation itself accelerates, the degree of persistence, α (that is, direct indexation of the nominal magnitudes), will tend to increase toward unity. Likewise, the coefficient of adaptation of expectations (β) rises toward unity.

5. If expectations are rational, we obtain

$$\pi_t = \pi_{t-1} + \epsilon_t + [(1-\alpha)/\alpha]_{t-1}\epsilon_t, \qquad (7')$$

where ${}_{t-1}\epsilon_t$ is the expectation, formed at $(t-1)$, of ϵ_t. In this case the key determinant of the behavior of the inflation rate is α.

6. Note the distinction between the questions whether the price level or the inflation rate returns to a steady-state level. Suppose the inflation rate is described by $\pi_t = \alpha + 0.95\pi_{t-1} + \epsilon_t$, where ϵ_t is white noise. Then the expected long-run rate of inflation is determinate and equal to $[\alpha/(1-0.95) = 20\alpha]$. But shocks to the *price level* are permanent. If the price level jumps by 10 percent today there is no expectation that subsequently the price level will tend to return to its original level or expected path.

7. Capital gains or losses on the outstanding debt have to be treated consistently in definitions of the service account and the external deficit.

8. For a quarterly regression of the same kind see Bruno and Sussman (1979). After 1977, regressions based on annual data would miss a considerable part of the dynamics. See also Zilberman (forthcoming).

9. The correlation coefficient (ρ) between $\dot{w} - \dot{p}_{-1}$ and $\dot{p}_n - \dot{p}_{-1}$ for the whole period 1966:3–1982:4 is 0.24, but this turns out to be dominated by high collinearity during the first oil crisis, 1973:4–1977:1 ($\rho = 0.571$), while the correlation is virtually nil in all other periods: 1966:3–1977:3 ($\rho = -0.025$), 1977:2–1982:4 ($\rho = 0.066$). We also tested the equation for the implied homogeneity assumption by adding $\dot{p}_{-1}$ to the righthand side. This gives a zero coefficient (−0.005 with standard error 0.037). It is also remarkably stable with respect to length of period or breakup into subperiods.

10. We do this by adding $\dot{p}_{-4}$ in the regression of $(\dot{p} - \dot{p}_{-1})$ on its own three lags [down to $(\dot{p}_{-3} - \dot{p}_{-4})$], testing for a zero coefficient on $\dot{p}_{-4}$, and then working out the implied coefficients for the lagged inflation rates. Here the CPI index was used for p.

11. In some periods, however, the Bank of Israel has allowed the interest rate on bank loans (as opposed to that on government bonds) to change.

12. On the eve of the monetary reform, PATAM (demand and time) deposits were equal to half the lira-denominated money supply; by the end of 1979 they had risen to three times the value. Evidence for a drop in the demand for money is discernible from the implied elasticity of change in the money-base ratio (h) in Table 17-5 with respect to the change in inflation (π). The change from 1965–1967 to 1974–1977 is $\pi\Delta h/(h\Delta\pi) = -0.64$; from 1974–1977 to 1978–1980, −0.82; and from 1978–1980 to 1981–1983, −1.09.

13. With the growth rate of high-powered money the only nominal anchor in the system, there may be another, lower, inflation equilibrium for the economy with unchanged fiscal policy variables, and the same amount of revenue being obtained from the printing of money.

14. For an empirical application of this framework to the analysis of the jumps in the inflation rate, see Melnick (1983) and Melnick and Sokoler (1984). A similar framework was first discussed by N. Liviatan (1983).

Acknowledgments

Introduction

I thank the Hoover Institution for its hospitality and support. I benefited from comments and suggestions by Moses Abramowitz, Kenneth Arrow, Aaron Director, Shmual Eisenstadt, Maggie Eisenstaedt, Stanley Fischer, Zvi Griliches, Nachum Gross, Nadav Halevi, Bronwyn Hall, Ruth Klinov, Simon Kuznets, R. C. O. Matthews, Joram Mayshar, Jacob Metzer, Gur Ofer, Amos Tversky, and Menachem Yaari. I thank Audrey Carlson for her help in preparing the manuscript.

2. Economic Growth and Structural Change

For comments on draft of this chapter I am grateful to Michael Bruno, Yoram Ben-Porath, Jacob Metzer, D. Perkins, and Simon Kuznets. Technical notes and some of the statistical data appear in the appendix to Syrquin (1984).

3. The Slowdown of Economic Growth

For helpful suggestions and comments on a draft I am grateful to Yoram Ben-Porath, Michael Bruno, Stanley Engerman, Zvi Griliches, Ephraim Kleiman, Ruth Klinov, Simon Kuznets, Moshe Syrquin, and participants in the joint Falk Institute and Hebrew University Economics Department seminar on the Israeli economy. I thank Moshe Bar-Nathan, Arie Bregman, and Yehuda Manzly of the Bank of Israel Research Department for their cooperation in providing me with data and unpublished research material. Last but not least, I thank Yaron Lotan for his devoted and able research assistance, and Maggie Eisenstaedt for her careful editing and skillful graphics.

4. Investment Patterns

I thank Victor Buch, Efraim Gross, Yaakov Lavie, and Rafi Melnick of the Bank of Israel for supplying data and other much-needed information. I am also grateful to Yoram Ben-Porath, Ezra Hadar, Nadav Halevi, Ephraim Kleiman, Simon Kuznets, and Moshe Syrquin for their helpful comments on drafts of this chapter.

5. Changes in the Industrial Structure

This study was partly financed by a grant from the Ford Foundation received through the Israel Foundations Trustees. I thank Jonathan Issacs and Danny Rosenman for their conscientious assistance and imaginative suggestions.

6. Educational Structure and Wage Differentials of the Labor Force

This chapter is based on Amir (1983), which analyzes additional aspects of the subject and presents further evidence. I am grateful for helpful comments and suggestions from Mary Jane Bauman, Yoram Ben-Porath, Susanne Freund, Zvi Griliches, Ruth Klinov, Sherwin Rosen, and the participants in seminars on drafts of this chapter, held at the Bank of Israel, the Maurice Falk Institute for Economic Research in Israel, and the University of Chicago. Yardena Slovik provided most helpful research assistance. Thanks are also due to Susan Tamari for her help.

8. Defense and the Economy

I wish to thank Nadav Halevi and Yoram Ben-Porath for helpful comments, and Susanne Freund for editorial assistance.

11. Taxes and Transfers in an Inflationary Decade

I wish to thank my colleague Ephraim Sadka for many helpful comments.

12. Perspectives on the Balance of Payments

The initial research for this chapter was partly financed by a grant from the Ford Foundation received through the Israel Foundations Trustees. The CBS Foreign Trade and Balance of Payments Divisions, and particularly Reuven Graf, provided invaluable assistance. I am indebted to Yarom Ariav, Eytan Levi, Yael Rothblum, and Danny Tsiddon for technical assistance. Yoram Ben-Porath, Michael Bruno, Irving Kravis, Simon Kuznets, Michael Michaely, and members of the CBS Balance of Payments Division made helpful comments on a larger draft version that became Falk Discussion Paper 83.02.

13. The Energy Sector in the 1960s and 1970s

I am deeply grateful to Ms. Daliah Steiner for her invaluable systematic work in collecting, processing, and analyzing the data. I am also indebted to Michael Bruno, E. Shefer, and Z. Weiss for helpful comments on various drafts.

14. External Shocks and Domestic Response

I am grateful to Carlos Bachrach for very able research assistance. I also want to thank Haim Barkai, Yoram Ben-Porath, Stanley Fischer, Mordecai Fraenkel, Nadav Halevi, and Jeffrey Sachs for helpful comments on a draft.

16. Accelerating Inflation and Balance-of-Payments Crises

We wish to express our gratitude to members of the Bank of Israel's Research Department for many useful discussions on topics concerning this chapter. We are also grateful to David Semana for research assistance. A more detailed version of this chapter was prepared in Hebrew (Liviatan and Piterman, 1984b) and is available in English from the Maurice Falk Institute for Economic Research, The Hebrew University of Jerusalem, Mount Scopus, 91905 Jerusalem, Israel.

17. The Inflationary Process

This chapter was written in the spring of 1984, while Stanley Fischer was Max Bogen Visiting Professor of Economics at the Hebrew University of Jerusalem. We are grateful to Carlos Bachrach for research assistance and to the National Science Foundation for financial support. We are indebted to Yoram Ben-Porath and Rafi Melnick for helpful comments on a draft.

Contributors

Shmuel Amir
Bank of Israel, Research Department
Haim Barkai
The Hebrew University of Jerusalem, Department of Economics
Yoram Ben-Porath
The Hebrew University of Jerusalem, Department of Economics
Eitan Berglas
University of Tel-Aviv, Department of Economics
Michael Bruno
The Hebrew University of Jerusalem, Department of Economics
Stanley Fischer
Massachusetts Institute of Technology, Department of Economics
Yehuda Geva
The National Insurance Institute
Jack Habib
The Brookdale Institute of Gerontology and Adult Human Development and The Hebrew University of Jerusalem, Department of Economics
Nadav Halevi
The Hebrew University of Jerusalem, Department of Economics
Ephraim Kleiman
The Hebrew University of Jerusalem, Department of Economics
Ruth Klinov
The Hebrew University of Jerusalem, Department of Economics
Nissan Liviatan
The Hebrew University of Jerusalem, Department of Economics
Joram Mayshar
The Hebrew University of Jerusalem, Department of Economics
Jacob Metzer
The Hebrew University of Jerusalem, Department of Economics
Gur Ofer
The Hebrew University of Jerusalem, Department of Economics
Sylvia Piterman
Bank of Israel, Research Department
Moshe Syrquin
Bar-Ilan University, Department of Economics

Index